The Age of Optimism

1870

A

Manners and Morals
Editor: Richard Friedenthal

Manners and Morals in

The Age of Optimism 1848–1914

by James Laver

HARPER & ROW, PUBLISHERS
NEW YORK AND EVANSTON

MANNERS AND MORALS IN THE AGE OF OPTIMISM: 1848–1914.
Copyright © 1966 by James Laver.

FIRST US EDITION
LIBRARY OF CONGRESS CATALOG CARD NUMBER: 66–20741

Contents

Illustrations

H.P.Robinson, *Fading Away*, c. 1858 (*Royal Photographic Society of Great Britain*)
The English Sunday, seen by a Frenchman, 1884
Samuel Butler, *Family Prayers*, 1864. St John's College, Cambridge
Mr and Mrs Gladstone at Dalmeny, 1880 (By courtesy of the Earl of Rosebery)
Queen Victoria at Biarritz (*Collection Sirot*)

MONDE AND DEMI-MONDE (*between pages 72 and 73*)

Alexandre Dumas *père* and Adah Isaacs Menken (*Collection Sirot*)
Photograph of the Comtesse de Castiglione (*Collection Braun*)
Title-page of the *Mémoires de Marguerite Bellanger*, 1900
Empress Eugénie by François Xavier Winterhalter (*A.C.Cooper*)
The Imperial Court at Fontainebleau in 1860 (*Collection Sirot*)
Jean Baptiste Carpeaux' *La Danse* defaced with ink (*Collection Sirot*)
Edmond Morin, An Actress's Dressing-Room, 1882
Edouard Manet, *Nana*. Kunsthalle, Hamburg
Félix Nadar in a (studio) balloon (*Collection Sirot*)
Victor Hugo on the Rocher des Proverits, St Helier, Jersey, 1853 (*Radio Times Hulton Picture Library*)
French riverside party, 1850 (*Collection Sirot*)

POVERTY AND PROSTITUTION (*between pages 104 and 105*)

Gustave Doré, *A Street in Whitechapel*. From Louis Enault's *London*, 1876
New ward for the casual poor at Marylebone Workhouse, 1867
Newcastle Slum, c. 1880 (*Radio Times Hulton Picture Library*)
Shanty town in the neighbourhood of Berlin, 1872 (*Deutsche Fotothek*)
London coffee-stall. From Henry Mayhew's *London Labour and the London Poor*, 1861–2
Félicien Rops, *Prostitution*, c. 1885
Kate Hamilton's Night House. From Henry Mayhew's *The Great World of London*, 1856
Conducting the night charges to the Marlborough Street Police Court, c. 1860
Ford Madox Brown, *The Last of England*, 1852–5. Tate Gallery, London
Female convicts at work, during the silent hour, in Brixton Prison, From Henry Mayhew's *The Great World of London*, 1856
Chasseur and his wife, c. 1850 (*Collection Sirot*)
French washerwomen, c. 1860 (*Collection Sirot*)

RELAXATIONS AND DISSIPATIONS (*between pages 152 and 153*)

Honoré Daumier, *Drama*, c. 1858. Bayerische Staatsgemäldesammlungen, Munich
A scene on Boulogne pier, c. 1862
Cremorne Gardens, 'The Chinese Platform', c. 1858
The Cyder Cellars, c. 1850 (*Radio Times Hulton Picture Library*)
Edgar Degas, *The Ballet of Robert Le Diable*, 1872. Metropolitan Museum of Art
Adolf Menzel, *The Théâtre Gymnase*, 1856. Staatliche Museen – Nationalgalerie – Berlin

Melodrama poster, Chanfran as 'Rube', c. 1872 (*The Bettman Archive*)
Hermann the Lion Tamer, c. 1860 (*Collection Sirot*)
The Siamese Twins (*Collection Sirot*)
Fiddling clowns, c. 1870 (*Collection Sirot*)
P. T. Barnum with General and Mrs Tom Thumb. Museum of the City of New York
Prince Alfred, Duke of Edinburgh, as Bacchus (*Radio Times Hulton Picture Library*)
German students, c. 1860 (*Collection Sirot*)
Skating in Vienna, 1887; photograph by Oscar van Zel (*Gernsheim Collection, University of Texas*)
Constantin Guys, *Children playing horse and carriage*. Metropolitan Museum of Art, Rogers Fund, 1937
A private dance, 1880 (*Collection Sirot*)

THE BACK OF THE PICTURE (*between pages 168 and 169*)

Street Arabs in Stepney, 1888; photograph by Paul Martin. Victoria and Albert Museum
Italian woman delousing children (*Collection Sirot*)
Salvation Army shelter, 1892
Brothel in the Upper Tenderloin District of San Francisco, c. 1885 (*Historical Picture Service*)
Brothel in the Rue des Moulins; photograph by Gauzi (*Edita S. A.*)
Copenhagen brothel, c. 1910. Copenhagen City Archives
Courtesan's bedroom c. 1900 (*Collection Sirot*)
Iron-founders at Varieux (*Collection Sirot*)
Necktie workshop in a New York tenement, 1890; photograph by Jacob A. Riis. Museum of the City of New York
'Bandit's Roost'; photograph by Jacob A. Riss. Museum of the City of New York
Night refuge, Paris, 1905 (*Collection Yvan Christ*)
Soup kitchen for the poor in Czechoslovakia (*Czechoslovak State Library*)

EMANCIPATED WOMAN (*between pages 184 and 185*)

Georges Sand, c. 1870 (*Collection Sirot*)
George Cruikshank, *The Bloomers in Hyde Park*, 1852
Ladies' Dress Reform Meeting, Boston, 1874 (*The Bettman Archive*)
Work girls in a factory in the Austrian Empire, 1897 (*Czechoslovak State Library*)
Telegraph girls. From *The Graphic*, 1871
Sea-battery, Normandy, 1893 (*Collection Yvan Christ*)
Isadora Duncan with her pupils (*Brown Brothers*)
Learning to Ride, c. 1890; photograph by Alice Austen. Historical Museum, Richmondtown
Alice Austen and two friends, 1891; photograph by Alice Austen. Historical Museum, Richmondtown
Suffragette sandwich-women, 1914 (*Radio Times Hulton Picture Library*)
Alumnae parade at Vassar College, 1903 (*Brown Brothers*)
Lady working a vacuum cleaner, c. 1910 (*Brown Brothers*)

Aija, 'Fille de Joie' (*Collection Sirot*)
Statue of Cléo de Mérode by J. A. J. Falguière, 1896 (*Collection Viollet*)
Liane de Pougy (*Collection Sirot*)
La Belle Otéro (*Collection Sirot*)
Death-bed of President Félix Faure (official version). From *L'Illustration*
Aubrey Beardsley, *The Fat Woman*. Tate Gallery, London

THEATRE AND MUSIC (*between pages 240 and 241*)

Camille Clifford, 'The Gibson Girl' (*Gernsheim Collection*)
Puccini's *Girl of the Golden West* at the Metropolitan Opera, New York, in 1913,
with Caruso, Amato and Destinn (*Brown Brothers*)
Cavalieri. Victoria and Albert Museum
Melba as Manon (*Falk*)
The Joachim Quartet, after a painting by Lajos Bruck. Bournemouth Public
Library
Everett Shinn, *London Hippodrome*, 1902. Art Institute of Chicago
Georges Seurat, Study for *Le Chahut*. Courtauld Institute Galleries, University
of London
Anna Held (*Brown Brothers*)
Design by Léon Bakst for Ida Rubinstein's costume in *St Sebastian*, a ballet
by D'Annunzio and Debussy for Diaghilev, 1911
Stanislavski's production of Chehov's *Uncle Vanya* at the Moscow Arts Theatre
in 1899 (*Garzanti Editore*, from *Storia del Teatro*)
Nijinsky (*Collection Sirot*)
Wassily Kandinsky, *The Singer*, 1902–3 (by courtesy of Mme Nina Kandinsky)

BEFORE THE WAR (*between pages 248 and 249*)

Edvard Munch, *Anxiety*, 1896. Museum of Modern Art
Fashions at an art exhibition in Paris, 1907 (*Mansell Collection*)
Caricature by Bruno Paul of Prussian tourists in Bavaria. From *Simplicissimus*,
1899
L'Impudique Albion, a caricature of Edward VII from *L'Assiette au Beurre*, 1903
The King and Queen of Rumania travelling by modern transport, 1901
(*Collection Sirot*)
Henley Regatta, 1914 (*Radio Times Hulton Picture Library*)
The race-course at Nice, *c.* 1911 (*Collection Sirot*)
Billings horseback dinner at Sherry's, Fifth Avenue, 1903; photograph by
Byron. Museum of the City of New York
George Wesley Bellows, *The Stag at Sharkey's*. Cleveland Museum of Art
Gino Severini, *Dynamic Hieroglyph of the Bal Tabarin*, 1912. Museum of Modern
Art
Archduke Franz Ferdinand and his family (*Bildarchiv der ö. N. B.*)
The blood-stained tunic of Franz Ferdinand after his assassination at Sarajevo
(*Bildarchiv der ö. N. B.*)

Rights reserved ADAGP and SPADEM.

Picture research by Mark Peploe.

1 The Year of Revolutions

The year 1848 has gone down to history as the Year of Revolutions. The accepted phrase for the whole decade is 'the Hungry Forties', and it goes far to explain the social and political explosions which took place all over Europe. The poor in England were, perhaps, worse off than those in countries like France where the peasant still maintained his independence, for the enclosures at the end of the eighteenth century had reduced the English rural workers to the level of landless labourers with no security of tenure and no means of augmenting their incomes.

A survivor into the present century recalled, in a letter to the editor of *The Hungry Forties* his own memories of the 'good old days':

They were anything but good times to my dear father and mother and us five children. His wages were but 9s. per week, with 2 pence per day that I got for frightening the crows off a farmer's wheat, making another 11d. per week to keep seven of us, and father had to pay 6 pounds per year out of that for his house to live in, so you may guess how we lived with the 4-lb loaf at $11\frac{1}{2}$d., tea from 5 to 8 shillings per lb, and with sugar at 9 pence per lb. Then meat – mutton, beef and poultry – I don't know how they were sold – we could only see those things. One ounce of tea and a pound of bacon a week, with a dish or two of swedes thrown in if we could get them, as the potatoes were a failure after the disease set in.[1]

The penalties for obtaining food by illicit means were savage. Mrs Cobden Unwin quotes another contemporary:

(in) 1844 men was brought to justice for sheep-stealing, sent to Van Dieman's Land for 14 years. If you took a pheasant by night, 14 years. Two men in this village had 14. . . . In 1844 it was not safe to go out after dark if you had any money on you. Burgaly (*sic*), highway robbery, fowl stealing because men were starving. Men would steal sheep to get sent away.

1 *The Hungry Forties, Descriptive Letters . . . from Contemporary Witnesses, with an Introduction by Mrs Cobden Unwin*. 1904.

The economic position of the whole country was far from satisfactory. England, in fact, had hardly yet recovered from the strain of the struggle with Napoleon, and, between 1815 and 1845, only the middle twenties could be reckoned as prosperous years. The railway loan did something to remedy unemployment and created some transient fortunes: for many small investors it was an unmitigated disaster. There was a cotton slump in the early forties and, of course, the Irish Famine which, by the influx of cheap labour into England did much to depress the level of wages.

Not only that. The new machines had driven down the prices of manufactured products, and, for a time, merely intensified the poverty of the workers. Conditions in factories were appalling, wages low and the hours of work incredibly long. In a worsted mill at Huddersfield, to take only one example, the hours of labour were from five in the morning until eight at night with one thirty minute break at noon, and this not only for adults but for children of seven, who received for fourteen and a half hours per day the sum of two-and-sixpence per *week*. In some mills children of five were employed, under conditions of harsh discipline, being mercilessly 'straffed' if they spoke to one another or fell asleep at the machine.

In coal-mines it was even worse. The employers:

took the child – boy or girl – at six years of age; they carried the little thing away from the light of Heaven into the black and gloomy pit; they placed it behind a door, and ordered it to pull this door to let the corves, or trucks, come through, and to keep it shut when they were not passing. The child was set at the door in the dark – at first they gave it a candle, which would burn for an hour or two and then go out. They kept the little creature there for twelve interminable hours. If the child cried, or went to sleep, or neglected to pull the door open, they beat that child. . . .

When a child grew strong enough, he or she – boy or girl – was promoted to the post of drawer, or thrutcher. The drawer, boy or girl alike, clad in a short pair of trousers and nothing else, had a belt tied round the waist and a chain attached by one end to the belt and the other to the corve or truck . . . the chain passing between the legs. . . . When the boys grew up they became hewers, but the women, if they stayed in the pit, remained drawers or thrutchers, continuing to the end of the day to push or drag the truck dressed in nothing but a pair of short trousers. . . . So many children were wanted, that in one colliery employing 400 hands there were 100 under twenty, and 56 under thirteen. In another, where there was an inundation, there were 44 children of whom 26 were drowned, of these 11 were girls and 15 boys; 9 were under ten years of age.[1]

It was the condition of the children that first excited the compassion of the humanitarians, and four years before Victoria came to the throne, Lord Ashley (later to be better known as Lord Shaftesbury) had succeeded

[1] Sir Walter Besant, in *The Graphic*, Jubilee Number, 1887.

in pushing through Parliament the first important Factory Act. This enacted that children under thirteen should not work more than forty-eight hours a week, and those under eighteen should not work more than sixty-eight hours a week! His further proposal to limit the daily hours of work to ten was rejected in 1844 but three years later he succeeded – and operatives in the manufacturing districts all over the country marched in processions to express their joy.

These Acts were only pushed through Parliament in the teeth of the most violent opposition, not so much from the landowning and *rentier* class as from the new manufacturers and the economists of the school of *laissez faire* who were convinced that nothing could be done to interfere with the iron laws of economics without ruining the country and making the workers even poorer than before. Unfortunately the same doctrine made it impossible, in spite of the efforts of well-meaning men, to cope with the terrible sufferings of the poor on the other side of the Irish Sea.

Factory Acts were not needed in Ireland for the good reason that there were no factories, or hardly any. It was an almost entirely rural economy and while the failure of the potato crops (or rather the succession of failures which took place in the forties) was to the English agricultural labourer a new burden; to the Irish peasant it was an unparalleled disaster. The Irish Famine lies outside our period, and the dreadful details must be sought elsewhere.[1] It is enough to note that the population of Ireland which was more than eight million at the beginning of Victoria's reign was reduced, by death and emigration, to little more than half, and that during the worst period, 15,000 Irish people were dying of famine daily.

It was in vain that attempts were made to turn the discontent in Ireland into political channels. A series of articles was published in the *Nation*, the organ of Irish nationalism. They issued from the pen of 'John Fenshaw Ellis', the *nom de plume* of a young lady named Jane Francesca Elgee (later to be known as 'Speranza', Lady Wilde, the mother of Oscar Wilde) and were nothing less than a call to arms:

We must be free! In the name of your trampled, insulted, degraded country; in the name of all heroic virtues, of all that makes life illustrious or death divine; in the name of your starved, your exiled, your dead; by your martyrs in prison cells and felon chains; in the name of God and man; by the listening earth and the watching Heaven, lift up your right hand and swear by your undying soul, by your hopes of immortality, never to lay down your arms, never to cease hostilities; till you regenerate and save this fallen land!

Oh! for a hundred thousand muskets glittering brightly in the light of heaven, and the monumental barricades stretching across each of our noble streets made desolate by England – circling round that doomed Castle, made desolate by

1 *e.g.* in Cecil Woodham-Smith, *The Great Hunger*, 1962.

England, where the foreign tyrant has held his council of treason and iniquity for seven hundred years. . . .

We appeal to the whole Irish Nation. . . . One bold, one decisive move. One instant to take breath, and then a rising; a rush, a charge from north, south, east, and west upon the English garrison, and *the land is ours !*[1]

But this inflammatory appeal fell on deaf ears. There was no spirit of resistance left in the country. Famine had done its work too well.

In England the spirit of revolt took the form of Chartism and there is no doubt that the Chartist Agitation was extremely alarming to the Government and to all timid, conservative souls. It is not that there was anything very revolutionary in the Charter itself with its demand for annual elections, one man one vote, the secret ballot and payment of Members of Parliament, but the language held by the orators at monster meetings all over the country went far beyond these reasonable proposals. Torchlight processions were organized and tens of thousands of artisans marched to the appointed place, and as Grummage, the old Chartist, tells us:

The very appearance of such a vast number of flaming torches only seemed more effectively to inflame the minds alike of speakers and bearers. O'Connor, Stephens and McDougall, were frequent attendants at the torch-light meetings and their language was almost unrestrained by any motives of prudence. Incitements to the use of arms formed the staple of the speeches of the two latter gentlemen . . . Stephens did not hesitate to declare that the ruling class were nothing better than a gang of murderers, whose blood was required to satisfy the demands of public justice.

Among other torch-light meetings held about this time, there was one that took place in the town of Hyde. . . . No less than fifty thousand persons walked in the procession, which was headed by a band of music, and a large number of banners were to be seen in the blazing light. One of these was Stephens' favourite device, 'For children and wife, we'll war to the knife!'

On another, the scriptural quotation, 'He that hath no sword, let him sell his garment and buy one'. A third bore the inscription . . . 'Universal suffrage or universal vengeance!' Another banner showed the words 'Remember the bloody deeds of Peterloo!' while a fifth bore the ominous inscription, 'Tyrants, believe and tremble!' There were a large number of caps of liberty carried upon poles, and, at intervals, the loud reports from pistols announced the fact that persons in the meeting were armed.

Chartism was the English working man's protest against his exclusion from the Reform Act of 1832. After all it was the proletarian unrest and the threat of revolution that had helped to force the Act through Parliament but the working men were not benefited by it: they did not even get the

1 *The Nation*, 29 July, 1848.

vote. A handful of Radical MPs, in conjunction with such typical members of the labouring classes as cotton spinners, weavers, tailors and black-smiths, drafted a new bill with 'six points': manhood suffrage, annual Parliaments, election by secret ballot, abolition of property qualifications for electing representatives, payment of members of Parliament, and equitably devised electoral districts (i.e. no more 'rotten boroughs'). It was Daniel O'Connell who baptized this programme with the name of the 'People's Charter'.

The programme was political in form but the driving force behind it was economic, in particular the price of bread. Engels, who came to England in the forties and was employed in his father's business in Manchester, saw this clearly. Chartism, he said,[1] was 'purely a working-man's cause', the 'struggle of the proletariat against the bourgeoisie'.

Mass meetings (called so for the first time) were held all over the country; torchlight parades (another novelty) took place in all the manu-facturing towns. Orators, sprung from the ranks of the people, employed a language calculated to inflame the crowds – 'Every brick in yonder factory is cemented with the blood of women and children' – and to alarm those in authority – 'If the rights of the poor are trampled under foot, then down with the throne, down with aristocracy, down with the bishops, down with the clergy, burn the churches, down with all rank, all title, and all dignity'.[2]

It is not surprising that there were riots, and that the government ordered soldiers to be present at the larger meetings. Sometimes this led to bloodshed. Several of the Chartist leaders were tried for sedition. Several million people signed the great petition to Parliament, which included the words: 'The Reform Act has effected a transfer of power from one domineering faction to another and left the people as helpless as before'. Yet the mere fact of presenting a petition to Parliament showed that the Chartists still hoped to implement their (after all, very mild) programme by constitutional means.

In the rest of Europe it was very different. Thrones were toppling everywhere in 1848. In March there was an insurrection in Berlin. The King of Prussia, Frederick William IV bowed, for the moment, to the storm, promised reforms and even allowed the Constitutional Assembly to draft a constitution.

In Bavaria, Lola Montez (now Countess Landsberg), the mistress of old King Ludwig I, had succeeded in doing what might have seemed impossible: to unite, in opposition to the monarchy, the Jesuits and the University students. She fled to Switzerland and in March the King followed her, having abdicated in favour of his son Maximilian II.

1 F. Engels, *Condition of the Working Classes in 1844*.
2 R. G. Grummage, *History of the Chartist Movement*, 1894.

In Vienna, the weak 'Dumpling' Emperor Ferdinand I gained a momentary popularity by yielding to popular demand and dismissing the all-powerful Metternich. There had been rumblings of the gathering storm for some years. In 1846 there were revolutionary outbreaks in Cracovia and Galatia. The harvests had been very bad and, between 1845 and 1847 the price of flour had risen nearly three hundred per cent. Bakeries had been plundered in the outskirts of the capital and in Vienna itself the butchers had rioted in protest against the establishment of municipal slaughter houses. Metternich warned the Emperor in January 1848 that: 'the wind of insurrection . . . is driving subversive parties to overthrow established and legitimate institutions, and because Austria is considered the essential representative of these, it has become the main target at which they aim.'

A group of intellectuals had addressed a petition to the Minister of the Interior against the rigid censorship of the Press. The censorship, which had a tight grip on the theatre also, had forbidden the staging of Schiller's *William Tell*. It had also forbidden any mention in the newspapers of Milan where there had been riots against the Austrian excise. The Austrian dominions in Italy were in ferment, as were all the Italian states, even the States of the Church. Pope Pius IX, who had begun with a reputation for liberalism, fled from Rome to Gaeta disguised as a simple priest.

It is however in France that the story of the Year of Revolutions can be seen most clearly, and if we seem to concentrate upon what took place in Paris, it is because it was the French who fired the train to the powder barrel. The situation was summed up by the extremely well-informed correspondent of *The Illustrated London News*:

Long ere the year began it was seen that the policy pursued by Louis Philippe and M. Guizot would produce revolution in France; that revolution in that country would give an impetus to the cause for which the Italians had both plotted secretly and agitated openly, for the last thirty years; that Germany would commence the long-meditated task of establishing free institutions; and that Europe generally would be roused into commotion, wherever there was a country that had not settled, after some fashion or other, the great question of the right of the middle classes to a share in their own Government. . . . The anticipated blow was struck in France; the anticipated consequences followed throughout Europe.[1]

The great question, be it noted, was 'the right of the *middle classes* to a share in their own government'. The French Revolution, although much of its driving force came from the discontent of the masses, had been essentially a bourgeois movement. Even the Terrorists were concerned with the abolition of political privilege, not with the redistribution of

1 *The Illustrated London News*, vol. 13, 1848, p. 417.

property. Whatever Robespierre was, he was not a socialist, still less a communist: indeed the very words had not yet been invented. It was left to a later generation and to isolated thinkers like Saint-Simon to question the economic basis of the existing system.

Count Henri de Saint-Simon brought out his *Nouveau Christianisme* in 1825 and the name is indicative of his approach. The movement inaugurated by him was a quasi-religious one, and his followers organized themselves in a 'Sacred College of the Apostles'. They were accused of advocating free love (and one of their chiefs, Enfantin, certainly did so), but the essence of the pamphlet which they issued in their defence in 1830 is contained in the phrase: 'We demand that land, capital and all the instruments of labour shall become common property'. This was enough to scare the bourgeoisie just rising into wealth and political power.

Another influential thinker was François Charles Fourier who tried to establish communities of people working according to communal principles. They all failed, including the thirty-four which had been founded in the United States. Robert Owen, the English philanthropist, also tried to establish communities in England and America. The one at New Harmony, Indiana, was the most ambitious, and in it Owen sank much of his fortune. None of these projects survived their founders. In 1835, however, he organized an 'Association of All Classes of All Nations' and it was at the meetings of this association that the word socialism first became current.

These three men may be said to represent the Utopian stage of socialist thinking. They were not political revolutionaries; they did not believe in violence; they wanted to establish socialism by persuasion and the force of example. Louis Blanc, on the other hand, who brought out his *Organisation du Travail* in 1839, thought that violent upheaval was inevitable in order to remedy the existing evils of society. The practical part of his programme was the setting up of 'National Workshops' in which the members would choose their own managers and dispose of their own profits.

Even more radical was Proudhon who wished to set up a kind of barter system based on the 'true-value' of the workman's labour. His pamphlet *What is Property?*, which appeared in 1840, presented the bourgeoisie with the startling paradox: 'Property is theft'. Both Louis Blanc and Proudhon were to become members of the French Provisional Government in 1848.

Meanwhile in Germany Feuerbach and Karl Marx were elaborating the ideology of revolt. The former would have nothing to do with the Christian idealism of the Utopians. He called religion 'the dream of the human mind', a phrase which is the obvious forerunner of 'religion is the opium of the people'. Karl Marx wrote the greater part of the *Communist Mani-*

festo which appeared only a few days before the revolution which unseated Louis Philippe and which closed with the defiant words: 'The communists disdain to conceal their views and aims. They openly declare that their ends can be obtained only by the forcible overthrow of all existing social conditions. Let the ruling class tremble at a communist revolution. The proletarians have nothing to lose but their chains, they have a world to win. Working-men of all countries, unite.'

In spite of these rumblings Louis Philippe remained calm, not to say complacent. A week before the Revolution broke out, he was visited by Jerome, ex-King of Westphalia, who expressed his disquietude. Louis Philippe smiled and said, '*Mon prince*, I fear nothing'; and added: 'I am necessary.'

Some of the most vivid pictures of what was happening in Paris we owe to the pen of Victor Hugo[1] who was himself involved in many of the events. He was a Deputy and, on 23 February, in a cab on his way to the Chamber, he saw an immense crowd of men in workmen's blouses and caps marching in the same direction; it was with some difficulty that he got through to the Assembly. A regiment of infantry was guarding the bridge, and squadrons of cavalry were charging about the Place de la Concorde.

At midnight the *tocsin* rang out all over Paris and barricades sprang up everywhere.[2] The government called out the *Garde nationale*, which did not respond. Next day Louis Philippe abdicated in favour of his son the Comte de Paris, with the Duchess of Orleans as Regent. The Duchess, with admirable courage, went to the Chamber holding by the hand her two young sons the Comte de Paris and the Duc de Chartres. She was acclaimed by the deputies; but, suddenly, the Chamber was invaded by a mob including many men of the *Garde nationale* with their arms and flags. The royal party was bustled away to safety, and Lamartine, who was immensely popular with nearly all factions, made a speech against any idea of a regency. A provisional government was constituted on the spot and set out immediately for the Hôtel de Ville.

It is interesting to note that, in the Chamber, the word 'Republic' had not yet been pronounced, but in the street it was very different. Bands of men and women were circulating everywhere shouting '*Vive la République*', and singing the Marseillaise. There was no mistaking the temper of the people, and the mob indeed had already sacked the Tuileries. Louis Philippe and his family were in flight. Lamartine harangued the crowd outside the Hôtel de Ville and was applauded. He refused however to

1 Victor Hugo, *Souvenirs Personnels, 1848–1851, réunis et présentés par Henri Guillemin.* 1952.

2 Victor Hugo estimated that more than 1,500 barricades were erected in the streets of Paris during the night of February 24.

abolish the Tricolour and to replace it by the Red Flag. On 27 February the Republic was ceremonially inaugurated in the Place de la Bastille, and a tree of Liberty was planted in the Champ de Mars. Paris rejoiced. For the moment, it seemed as if all parties were prepared to support the Provisional Government.

Among the revolutionaries there was an extraordinary degree of idealism, and they were far from being anti-Christian. A political prisoner under Louis Philippe could say quite sincerely to the visiting chaplain: 'I admire Jesus Christ. He was a republican like me.' And when the mob invaded the Tuileries after the flight of the King, they respected the royal chapel. One of them cried, lifting the crucifix: 'Behold Jesus, the Great Tribune'. All present took off their hats and following the crucifix, held high by a prefect of the École Polytechnique, the crowd moved forward to shouts of 'Vive Jésus! Vive le Christ!'

The clergy themselves were, with rare exception, favourable to the Republican movement, and the Archbishop of Paris, Mgr Affre, ordered special services of thanksgiving in all the churches of his diocese for the success of the Revolution of February. One of the articles of the projected Constitution was that a Tree of Liberty should be planted in every commune of France and the clergy attended the celebrations and sprinkled the trees with holy water. (It was only later, when the Trees of Liberty were nearly all dead, that the rumour got around that they had been sprinkled with *poisoned* holy water.) An impressive memorial service for those who had been killed in the Revolution was held at the Madeleine and attended by all the members of the Provisional Government. After the ceremony an immense procession moved along the boulevards: squadrons of cavalry, batteries of artillery, companies of infantry, bands, clergy, funeral cars and relatives of the victims. Among those who rode in the official carriages were Auguste Blanqui and Huber, shortly to play a somewhat different rôle in public affairs.

Blanqui was an impressive figure. Of his forty years he had spent nine in prison, four of them in solitary confinement. His hair had grown white in captivity, and he was proud of it. Pride, says Hugo, was the only joy he knew, and at the root of it was the hope of vengeance. He went about in rags, with a battered hat and boots with holes in them, drank only water, ate only bread and did not care where he slept. He had no vices; he never looked at a woman. He had no affections. When he was released from prison on the fall of Louis Philippe he went immediately to Paris. His old mother spent three days looking for him, without success. When told of this he said: 'It is not a question of my mother; it is a question of my club.' Once it was established he demanded the execution of Lamartine – and his own brother.

The word 'club' had an ominous ring. Forgetting perhaps the part which the 'clubs' had played in the first French Revolution, the Provisional Government decided to encourage their revival. On 19 April 1848, the walls of Paris were placarded with a notice which read: 'Citizens! The Republic lives on liberty and discussion; the clubs are for the Republic a need, for the citizens a right. . . . The Provisional Government gives its protection to the clubs.'

In response to this naive appeal small groups were formed in all the popular quarters and it was in them that were organized all the violent outbreaks that followed.

One of the most dangerous was the gathering in the Salle Valentino. To this flocked those who had been political prisoners under Louis Philippe: Sabrier, Huber, Barbès, Blanqui. Huber, who had been confined in the dungeons of Mont Saint-Michel, was too ill to stand but, seated in a chair, pale and furious, he burst forth into a torrent of invective:

Citizens, do you know what I have seen? I went to the Hôtel de Ville and saw them refuse admission to our brothers of the barricades. . . . The barefooted were turned away; only those with well-polished boots were admitted. The well-dressed people are the masters. They are reaching out their claws – claws in yellow gloves. . . . The old society is defending itself. Let us make a break and begin the assault!

This discourse was answered by cries of 'To arms! To the Hôtel de Ville. Down with the Provisional Government!'

There were shouts of 'Down with the rich', but some of those present thought this was going too far, and the meeting ended with the Republicans fighting among themselves. The march on the Hôtel de Ville was, for the moment, postponed.

There was an outbreak of republican newspapers, the titles of which give a sufficient indication of their tone: *Le Robespierre, Spartacus, Le Bonheur Publique, Le Bonnet Rouge: Journal des Sans-Culottes, La Montagne, Le Tribunal Révolutionnaire* and *La Guillotine.* There was even one entitled *La Christ Républicain.* George Sand collaborated in *La Vraie République.* Even Alexandre Dumas joined in the fray with a paper called *Le Mois* (unkind critics rebaptized it *Le Moi*). One revolutionary sheet advertised itself as 'edited by the *canaille*, sold by the *canaille*, bought by the *canaille*', a slogan which was not likely to recommend it to respectable citizens. There was, of course, a number of more moderate papers, and even some short-lived journals (a foretaste of things to come) with such titles as *Le Bonapartiste* and *Le Petit Caporal.*

The theatres – for the moment – were solidly republican. On 5 March a general assembly of actors took place at the Ambigu Theatre where it was decided to support the new régime. A procession was immediately formed and moved towards the Hôtel de Ville to announce its adhesion to the

Provisional Government. The theatres had been shut for only two days during the upheaval of February. Now they hastened to put on some hastily written republican plays, and some old favourites of the first Revolution such as *Horace*. A favourite piece was Ponsard's tragedy *Lucrèce*. The subject – the fall of the Tarquins and the proclamation of the Roman Republic – was well calculated to please the audience, and the principal part was taken by Rachel. The royal box was, strangely enough, occupied by an ordinary bourgeois family, but in the box opposite sat the principal members of the Provisional Government who joined in the applause whenever Brutus on stage uttered a republican sentiment. At the end of the play Rachel came back on the stage and sang the *Marseillaise*. A contemporary chronicler tells us that:

Her singing – or rather her acting – of this national hymn was on this occasion sublime. Her chant was as solemn and inspired as a sibylline priestess; and as she knelt and pressed the tricoloured flag to her heart the entire theatre broke out into a long, loud, and uncontrollable burst of transport. . . . It was said that M. Ledru Rollin imagined this scene; and that it was by his solicitations that Mlle Rachel – a still more ardent and enthusiastic republican than himself, if such were possible – undertook to rouse, by this hymn, the zeal and ardour of the more educated classes of French society. Her manner of rendering it was grand, but it was the grandeur of hatred and revenge, not of patriotism. She seemed to be not the genius of Liberty, but the sanguinary Nemesis; not the utterer of a hymn of liberty, but of an awful, abominable, and yet beautiful chant of vengeance and execration. It produced its effect, however. Its power and genius were unquestionable, and long haunted the memory of those who heard it.[1]

George Sand was one of those who rushed in to celebrate this honeymoon of all classes. With incredible speed she wrote a play which was actually put on at the Théâtre de la République (the new name for the Théâtre Français) on 9 April 1848. It was called *Le Roi Attend* and one of the characters was Molière who (rather, one would have thought, out of character) addressed the audience in the following terms:

I see the King, but he is no longer called Louis XIV, he is called the People, the Sovereign People. It is a word I did not know, a word as great as Eternity. This Sovereign is as great as all the Kings, because he is good, because he has no interest in deceit, because, instead of courtiers, he has only brothers!

It soon became plain, however, that some at least of those who had made the Revolution of February were far from content with its results. On Monday, 15 May, the National Assembly was in session, debating the attitude of the Provisional Government to the uprisings in Italy and

---

1 *The Illustrated London News*, 1848, p. 436.

Poland. Meanwhile a crowd had gathered in the Place de la Bastille, ostensibly to support the Polish cause, but those who were directing their movements had more immediate objects in view. A procession was formed heading for the National Assembly, but it seemed peaceful and friendly enough. General Courtois who was in command of the *Gardes nationaux* shook hands with the leaders of the column and his troops made no effort to halt the marching column which, by the time it reached the Place de la Concorde, numbered about 20,000. These crossed the bridge without opposition; the leaders forced their way into the Chamber and took over the proceedings. Louis Blanc installed himself at the very desk of the President; Raspail made a speech and was followed by Blanqui, Barbès, and Louis Blanc himself, vying with one another in revolutionary proposals. They called for the establishment of a Ministry of Progress and Labour, for a capital levy of a milliard of francs. Then Huber shouted from the tribune: 'In the name of the People, the National Assembly, which has refused to listen to its voice, is dissolved.' A single deputy whose name was Guichard managed to force his way through the threatening mob and call the *Garde Mobile* to the rescue. Barbès and his friends, driven out, marched to the Hôtel de Ville amid shouts of 'The National Assembly is dissolved! Long live the revolutionary government. Long live Barbès!' The troops followed, with cannon. They encountered no resistance, and Barbès was arrested with some sixty others. The Assembly continued its deliberations, its first act being to dismiss General Courtois, and to replace him by General Clément Thomas. The Revolution of May was written off as a failure.

The Revolution had thrown everything into confusion: business and industry were at a standstill. There was an alarming rise in the number of unemployed. To remedy this state of affairs the Provisional Government introduced a number of projects (national works, unemployment benefit and even a national health scheme) which have found a place in modern society but which, by reason of lack of organization, were premature in 1848. National Workshops were established, and attracted not only the workers of Paris but many from the provinces who began to swarm into the capital. But as the difference between pay for work and unemployment pay was only fivepence there was not much inducement to labour. The frightened bourgeois, out of whose pocket the payments were to come, was horrified to see, all over Paris, groups of men playing cards, smoking, reading the revolutionary papers and making speeches. There were among them, no doubt, many honest labourers who would have been glad to work but were not only discouraged but actively prevented from doing so by a turbulent minority.

The Champs-Elysées were occupied by a kind of permanent fair, full of acrobats, jugglers, fortune-tellers, vendors of patent medicines and the

1848

Barricade during the Revolution in Dresden, March 1848

Jean Louis Meissonier, *La Barricade*, Paris, 1848

Execution of a rebel in Rome, 1848

Opposite top: Burgher guard firing on a mob of workmen, near the hospital in Berlin, October 1848

Opposite centre: Prussian troops pursued by men of the town guard, Mainz, May 1848

Opposite bottom: Siege of Györ in Hungary during the uprising of July 1849

Right: Barricades at the Bridge Tower, Prague, June 1848

Franz Schams, *Students' Guard Room in the University*, Vienna, 1848

Funeral at the Church of the Madeleine, Paris, of the victims of the insurrection of June 1848

Bread riots in Berlin, April 1847

Emigrants waiting for the boat at Cork, 1850

Victoria the Guardian Angel!
Caricature of Queen Victoria
giving asylum to the dis-
placed monarchs of Europe
in 1848

Switzerland 1849: *Family Concert in Basle* by Sebastian Gutzwiller

like, but the public of out-of-works who frequented the alleys was very different from the elegances of a few months before. No longer did an endless file of carriages, tilburys and equestrians circulate from the Rond-Point to the Arc de Triomphe and beyond, into the avenues of the Bois. The occasional private carriage caused astonishment since all good citizens had now resigned themselves to travel by public omnibus. Disillusion with the Republic continued to grow, not least among the lower middle classes: the small shopkeepers and the like who saw their livelihood threatened. The honeymoon between them and the proletariat was over.

Meanwhile the extreme republicans continued to organize meetings and demonstrations, making normal business and the return of confidence impossible. Secretly they were gathering arms and ammunition; and in June they struck again. The Communists were to provide the spearhead of the assault but around them were grouped all varieties of those discontented with the turn affairs had taken. The plan of campaign was well conceived and ably carried out. The insurgents disposed of some forty thousand men; workmen, many of them unemployed for some time, old soldiers, ex-convicts and the riffraff of the Paris slums. In the Revolution which had overthrown Louis Philippe there were no doubt similar elements but they were joined in temporary alliance with students, young shopmen, clerks and the like. From the new movement these, alarmed by the doctrines preached by Barbès, Blanqui and the rest, were noticeably absent.

We may allow the Paris correspondent of *The Illustrated London News* to take up the story. The Communists and their followers:

knew that they had made one Revolution in February; they had been flattered and caressed for their pains: they attempted another in May, doubtless expecting a similar result. The attempt was premature, rash, and ill-conducted. The middle classes, no longer apathetic, were active. It failed, as a matter of course; and its leaders, Blanqui, Cabet, Raspail, Albert (*ouvrier*), and the other chiefs of the Red Republican or Communist factions, were transferred to the dungeon of Vincennes, to await punishment for the heavy crimes of treason against the National Representative and the safety of the Republic.

The breach continued to widen. The feud between the Communists and the anti-Communists in and out of the Government, in the National Assembly, and in the streets, was rendered more bitter and more desperate by the result of the 15th of May. The one party prepared for a more vigorous attack – the other for a still more obstinate defence. The Red Republicans determined to found a Republic of their own, upon the overthrow of that previously existing; and the Moderates, or. as they were derisively called, the 'Pale Republicans', determined, if once called to arms by the faction of Communism, to crush it for ever. The necessity for disbanding the immense army of workmen, amounting to more than 120,000 men – composed not merely of Parisian operatives but of idle and dissolute adventurers, galley slaves, and plunderers who had flocked into Paris from all parts of the country, and who were consuming the very vitals of the Republic, at a period of commercial and monetary pressure – brought the feud to a crisis. The sincere operatives, aided by the villainous plunderers – the whole of them well organized, commanded by resolute chiefs – designing men whose names are as yet concealed, prepared in secret for the final struggle. Discarding all the old cries of mere fractions of the people – thinking nothing of Buonapartism, Louis-Philippism, or Henri-Cinquism – they commenced operations on Thursday week [22 June 1848] in the name of the 'Red Republic – democratic and social'.

The offensive operations of the insurgents were planned and executed with consummate skill. Their strategy has excited the imagination of men whose trade is war. They were well supplied with arms and ammunition; and they were aided by an amount of zeal, daring and savage enthusiasm on the part of the lower orders of the population, male and female, which is perfectly marvellous. On their side the defenders of order manifested resolution, coolness, and perseverance; and the Garde Nationale, the troops of the line, and the Garde Mobile vied with each other in bravery and self-sacrifice. The last named body elicited the surprise as well as the gratitude of Paris. It is composed chiefly of lads under twenty years of age, mostly belonging to the working classes; and their zeal in defence of order was so great and so constant, and testified by so many acts of heroism, that, while it drew upon them the applause of the well-disposed inhabitants of the capital, it excited a feeling of intense hatred in the minds of the insurgents. The latter had evidently calculated upon their support; and their indignation was so much the greater, when they found that these 'children of the people', as they called them, had turned their arms against the workmen. Whenever any of this devoted band fell into the power of the insurgents, they were slaughtered remorselessly; and among the many fearful episodes of the struggle, it is related that the heads of many of them were cut off by women and stuck on poles at the head of a barricade which they had lost their lives in attempting to storm.[1]

The general public was revolted by these excesses. With great heroism the Archbishop of Paris, attended by another priest, went to the Place de la Bastille where one of the barricades had been erected and attempted to address the insurgents. He was shot in the loins from behind, and after lingering for twenty-four hours, expired of the wound. The bullet probably came from the window of a neighbouring house, and may have hit the Archbishop by accident. The insurgents denied all intention of killing him, but his death steeled the hearts of those who were determined to settle with the Red Republic once and for all.

Faced with 40,000 armed insurgents barricaded in the very heart of Paris, the National Assembly handed over all the executive powers of the Provisional Government to the Minister of War, General Cavaignac. Cavaignac was a very competent soldier, who had learned his trade in the

1 *The Illustrated London News*, 1 July, 1848.

hard school of the Sahara. He put down the rebellion with ruthless efficiency and the Republic – for a time – was saved.

For now another name had begun to occupy men's minds; Louis Napoleon Bonaparte was still in exile in London and it is one of the ironies of history (or is it?) that during the Chartist agitation in the early months of 1848 he was sworn in as a special constable and given a beat in Piccadilly between Park Lane and Dover Street. In May he wrote a letter to the French authorities, demanding the restoration of his rights as a French citizen and when this was granted he put himself forward as a parliamentary candidate. He was elected a Deputy for Paris and also (by the odd pluralism legal in France) for the Departments of the Seine, Corsica, the Yonne and the Charente-Inférieur. The Government, alarmed, issued orders for his arrest (but he couldn't be arrested for he was still safely in London) and shortly afterwards, with amazing inconsistency, ratified his election as a Deputy. Louis Napoleon played a careful hand, wrote a letter to the President expressing his regret for certain disturbances by his supporters in Paris – and resigned his seat. For the moment he had got what he wanted; he had impressed his name and his image on the minds of the French nation. Perhaps (who could tell?) it might, for the second time, call in a Bonaparte to save it from Republican excess.

There was little doubt that the people of Paris were growing heartily sick of the disorders which had plagued the city ever since the flight of Louis Philippe. If the tone of the theatres could be taken as an indication, the swing round was already complete. After the first explosion of republican enthusiasm they had been going through a bad time. The bourgeois was afraid to go and the people, in spite of some performances being free of charge, were finding their drama in the streets of Paris. The Constituent Assembly on 17 July, voted a subsidy of 680,000 francs in order to keep the theatres open, but this did not prevent the resentment of the actors and the dramatic authors from finding expression in plays ridiculing socialist ideas. As early as 28 October 1848 the Vaudeville put on a *Folie Socialiste en 3 actes* entitled *Property is Theft* – the famous slogan of Proudhon. The first act took place in the Garden of Eden and the Serpent was represented by an actor made up to look like Proudhon. When the Serpent announced the proclamation of the Republic the news was received with a *chant funèbre*. One could scarcely speak more clearly, and the President of the National Assembly, M. Marrast, proposed to intervene on the ground that the piece was an attack on the dignity of the National Assembly, of which Proudhon was a member. To his eternal credit, Proudhon had the sense to decline to have anything to do with the proposal, and *Property is Theft* continued to play to crowded houses.[1] It was arranged that Proudhon

---

1 Alfred Darimon, *A travers une Révolution*, 1884.

himself should attend a performance, in the decent obscurity of one of the boxes. He was shocked not by the political implications of the piece but by the extravagant décolletage of the leading lady – 'It's not drama,' he said, 'it's pornography.'

Drama or not, it showed plainly which way the wind was blowing. Ordinary people, who only wanted to get on with their own lives, were tired of socialist theories which had been the excuse for so much bloodshed. But, ungratefully, if understandably, they were equally tired of the military rigour of the man who had saved them: Cavaignac, in Guedalla's excellent phrase, had 'distributed punishments and multiplied his enemies with the strict impartiality of an honest man'.[1] Louis Napoleon, elected Deputy for the second time, was allowed to come to Paris and take his seat in the Chamber. He made little impression and seldom spoke. He felt compelled to do so, however, when the Chamber was debating the new Constitution and an amendment was proposed by which all members of royal and imperial families would be excluded from the Presidency. Louis Napoleon naturally opposed this, but he spoke badly, in a halting fashion. By a strange irony, this was what saved him. The Assembly, used to the eloquence of republican orators, felt that it had nothing to fear from 'this inarticulate young man with a foreign accent'. The amendment was defeated, and Louis Napoleon was able to offer himself as a candidate for the Presidency.

The Election took place on 10 December 1848 and when the votes were counted it was found that he had a majority of four million, out of a poll of seven million. Cavaignac and the other candidates were nowhere. A Napoleon was President of the French Republic. In France, as elsewhere, the Year of Revolutions had come to an end.

It was certainly one of the milestones of history. When it was over the left wing had been defeated all over Europe. The King of Prussia was back on his throne and tore up the Constitution he had been persuaded to guarantee in a moment of panic.

The Emperor of Austria, Ferdinand i, abdicated on 2 December 1848 and retired to the Palace of the Hradchin in Prague where he lingered for twenty-seven years. His brother, the Archduke Francis Charles, a weak and unpopular man, was persuaded to renounce his right to the succession in favour of his own son, the eighteen-year-old Francis Joseph who, in spite of all disasters, survived as Emperor until his death during the First World War.

Cobden's prophecy that, with the exception of England and Russia there was no throne in Europe worth ten years' purchase, turned out to be completely wrong.

1 Philip Guedalla, *The Second Empire*, 1922.

Not only the Socialists but the Nationalists were repressed, and against the rebellious Hungarians the new Austrian Emperor took a terrible revenge. Women, even those of the highest aristocracy, were seized, stripped naked and flogged in the streets of Budapest. Count Louis Batthyany, who had been one of the leaders of the revolt, avoided hanging by poisoning himself, but the Emperor ordered his lifeless body to be hung from the gallows erected for his execution. Even the Italian advance was stayed; for Radetsky, the Austrian commander, defeated the army which the Piedmontese had sent to aid the revolting provinces, and the republics which had been established in Florence, Rome and Venice, collapsed. King Charles Albert of Sardinia abdicated and was replaced by Victor Emmanuel II. The unification of Italy was postponed for a decade.

In France revolutionary movements were not to get another chance until his defeat at Sedan had swept Napoleon III from power and the Commune was established in Paris. That too was defeated and the militant spirit of the workers crushed. In England the Chartist Movement simply fizzled out like a damp squib. One of Cobden's anonymous correspondents wrote: 'The Chartist Demonstration is put down – clean smothered think the Whigs. Let them take care they are not mistaken.'[1] They were not mistaken. The Chartists *had* been 'clean smothered'.

'Old-time Chartists despaired,' says Herman Ausubel:

Many of them had sacrificed both income and career for their political principles. Yet, had they come all the way for this? In 1850 a Halifax Chartist reported despondently that since there was no Chartist society in his town, or in any of the nearby villages, it was impossible to raise funds for reform. Many active Chartists had emigrated and those who remained, he confessed bitterly but accurately, 'have become so thoroughly disgusted at the indifference and utter inattention of the multitude to their best interests that they too are resolved to make no more sacrifices in a public cause.' Chartists in other parts of the country had the same tale of working class apathy to report. The exhilarating days of immense meetings, indescribably enthusiastic receptions and deafening acclamations belonged to the remote Chartist past.

All over Europe the bourgeoisie breathed again; and in England they had particular reason to congratulate themselves. Both revolution and reaction had been defeated, and the government felt sufficiently sure of itself to give asylum to refugees of all political complexions; Louis Blanc and Louis Philippe, Guizot and Kossuth, Metternich and Mazzini.

Brighter times were at hand; after the 'Hungry Forties' came the expanding and prosperous fifties. The gold discoveries in California in 1848 were followed by similar strikes in Australia in 1850; and although Cobden and many economists prophesied that the result would be a

---

1 Quoted by Herman Ausubel, *In Hard Times.* 1960.

disastrous fall in the value of money, these forebodings were not realized. Although the gold holdings of the Bank of England rose from about eight millions at the beginning of our period to twenty-two millions in 1853, the Bank Rate remained at two per cent and the growth of trade was steadily stimulated. The harvests of 1853–4 were a failure, but there was a large increase in the demand for English goods, much of it from the gold-mining countries themselves. Within a single year the value of exports increased by twenty-five per cent, and there was a general rise in wages due to the scarcity of labour. The Great Exhibition of 1851 set the seal on the country's triumphant advance in manufacture and commerce. England had become the 'workshop of the world'. The Age of Optimism had begun.

Mid-Victorian England

If not the accession of the young Queen, then at least her marriage to Albert was universally felt to have begun a new epoch. The bourgeois public saw in the Royal pair the realization of their own ideal of married bliss: a household sullied by no breath of scandal, with a conscientious husband and a dutiful and adoring wife. It should be noted that it was the wife who adored and the husband who received this adoration. Strong willed though the Queen was herself and conscious of her position, she showed herself throughout her life strongly opposed to any idea that husband and wife should be equal partners. The husband was the head of the household to a degree which the modern world finds almost incredible. Even a woman like Caroline Norton, who in the early-Victorian period had struggled so heroically to keep her children and her own literary earnings from the clutches of the husband who had deserted her, could still say: 'I believe in the natural superiority of the man as I do in the existence of a God. The natural position of woman is inferiority to a man, that is a thing of God's appointing, not of man's devising.'

Perhaps there never was another period in history when it would be true to say that the wife was considered theoretically an angel and was practically a slave. She had no property of her own; anything she possessed before marriage became her husband's property absolutely; anything she earned after marriage, even if she were separated from her husband, was his; even her house-keeping money or the money in her purse when she went shopping was not legally her own. If a pickpocket stole her purse and was caught he was not accused of stealing *her* property but her husband's. Of course, in practice, human nature being what it is, many a strong-minded woman wore the breeches and controlled the purse strings, but this made no difference to her legal position.

The laureate of Patriarchalism undiluted was Coventry Patmore. After his marriage in 1847 to Emily Andrews he decided to become the poet of connubial bliss. He was then twenty-four, she was probably younger, and he found in her the ideal wife, according to his own very exacting notions of what the ideal wife should be. She accepted her role with (in her own words) 'instant submission to your slightest wish', and (in his words) 'did her duty to me, her children, her neighbours, and to God, with a lovely, unnoticeable evenness and completeness.' When friends came to call – and Patmore's friends included Ruskin, Browning and Carlyle – she effaced herself behind her needlework and never ventured to join in the conversation unless invited to do so. That she had some talent as a writer is shown by her book of children's verse entitled *Nursery Rhymes by Mrs Motherly*. Any more ambitious work, she felt, might be thought to compete with her husband's pretensions as a poet.

For Patmore was a poet, and he resolved to celebrate in verse what had hitherto been strangely neglected by all those authors whose theme had been love. What kind of love was it that had been the subject of so many outpourings; adulterous love for the most part, or the unhappy loves of Romeo and Juliet. Patmore resolved to write about the tranquil, happy love of married people.

The background, of course, was what we should now call 'the Establishment', the circumstances comfortable, the characters cultivated and well-behaved. In short the heroine was the daughter of a dean and the first instalment of what was to develop into almost an epic was concerned with her courtship. It was called *The Betrothal* and was published in 1854. In later instalments, published during the next six years, she is married, gives birth to children and dies young. The entire work was entitled *The Angel in the House* and it woke such an echo in Victorian hearts that it was an instant success.

In the poem the bereaved husband continues to burn incense to the memory of his dead wife; but the effect was a little spoilt by the fact that when the poet's real wife died in 1862, he waited a mere three years before marrying again. His new wife, Marianne Byles, was slightly older than he (he was forty-two), and we do not know if she was quite as submissive as the first. She was however a woman of great piety and she soon converted her husband to her own Roman Catholic faith.[1] What was more, she was wealthy and Patmore was able to retire from his post as an assistant librarian at the British Museum and devote himself entirely to poetry. But he never took up again the theme of connubial bliss.

It is easy to make fun of the humdrum jog-trot of some of the verses in

---

1 In *The Angel in the House* Patmore had written:
> Maid, choosing man, remember this:
> You take his nature with his name.
> Ask, too, what his religion is,
> For you will soon be of the same.

But it didn't work out that way.

The Angel in the House. The hero of the poem, Frederick, admits that his object is

> To win a woman for his wife.

and continues

> I never went to Ball I confer or Fête
> Or Show, but in pursuit express
> Of my predestinated mate . . .
> And, in the records of my breast,
> Red-lettered, eminently fair.
> Stood sixteen, who beyond the rest,
> By turns till then had been my care:
> At Berlin three, one at St. Cloud,
> At Chatteris, near Cambridge, one,
> At Ely four, in London two,
> Two at Bowness, in Paris none,[1]
> And, last and best, in Sarum three . . .

His eye has fallen upon the three daughters of the Dean and he finally decides upon Honoria. He goes away for a few days to think things over, and then

> Grown weary with a week's exile
> From those fair friends, I rode to see
> The church-restorings; lounged awhile,
> And met the Dean; was asked to tea . . .

The old gentleman likes him, invites him, after a decent interval, to dinner and leads him on:

> He hoped the business was not bad
> I came about: then the wine pass'd.
> A full glass prefaced my reply:
> I loved his daughter, Honor; he knew
> My estate and prospects; might I try
> To win her? To mine eyes tears flew.
> He thought 'twas that. I might. He gave
> His true consent, if I could get
> Her love. A dear, good Girl! she'd have
> Only three thousand pounds as yet;
> More bye and bye.

---

1 And quite right, too! The whole passage reads like a comic diminuendo of Don Juan's boast: *ma in Spagna mille et tre!* But of course Frederick had not actually made love to the ladies but had been 'faithful to his future wife'.

33

C

The only purpose in quoting these verses which seem to us so ludicrous is that they were eagerly welcomed by a considerable public which saw in them a touching realism. And lest we should seem to be unfair to Coventry Patmore, it is as well to admit that some of the verses in *The Angel in the House* do manage to express a noble idealism in felicitous terms:

> Ah, wasteful woman, she who may
> On her sweet self set her own price,
> Knowing he cannot choose but pay,
> How has she cheapen'd paradise;
> How given for nought her priceless gift,
> How spoil'd the bread and spill'd the wine,
> Which, spent with due, respective thrift,
> Had made brutes men, and men divine.

The whole Victorian attitude to sex was strangely remote from our own. Wives were supposed to submit themselves to the animal passions of men, not to take any pleasure in the act of union themselves. It was denounced as a monstrous slander on the purity of good women that this was even possible and the unfortunate fact is that in such a climate of opinion many a middle class married woman went through life and bore innumerable children without having her own sexual desires either provoked or satisfied. The contempt in which old maids were held hurried many a Victorian girl into marriage without any notion of what it entailed, and the shock of the wedding night must often have set up a life-long neurosis. This was probably responsible for much of the invalidism which is so marked a feature in the life of the Victorian woman, both in fiction and in fact. The only joy which a nice woman was expected to have was the joy of bearing and bringing up children.

As birth control had not yet been heard of, at least among middle class English families, these children tended to be very numerous. They were born in pain and in danger, and as there were few of the precautions against infection which are now taken for granted the infant mortality rate was still extremely high. It was taken for granted that quite a large proportion of all children born should die in infancy and this was accepted with grief but with resignation as the act of God.

In the working classes, of course, the rate of infant mortality was even higher than it was in the middle classes. Life was lived in appalling conditions of poverty and overcrowding and in the slums at least the gloomy prophecies of Malthus seemed only too obviously to have been fulfilled; but the remedy which he suggested for overpopulation was certainly not likely to be adopted by the bulk of mankind. He proposed quite calmly that the sex act should only be performed when it was desired to have a child, that is to say some half a dozen times in thirty years. That he should have made such a suggestion at all is a strange reflection on his own sexual needs.

The whole idea of birth control seems to have been unacceptable to the Victorian mind and its early advocates met with a storm of obloquy. It is true that as early as 1822 the 'radical tailor' Francis Place in his *Illustrations and Proofs of the Theory of Population* urged 'married persons to avail themselves of such precautionary means as would, without being injurious to health, or destructive of female delicacy, prevent conception'. Place went further: he printed and distributed handbills giving information on contraception, but he only knew of two methods by which this might be effected: *coitus interruptus* and the use by the female partner of a sponge. The first of these is undesirable for various medical and psychological reasons and the second often ineffective. It was not until the sixties that Dr R. T. Trawl gave more reliable information. It is perhaps unnecessary to say that such works were unknown to the majority of middle class families and never came into the hands of the working classes at all. The result was a 'population-explosion'.

That the population of the metropolis increased enormously in the decade following the Great Exhibition of 1851 is obvious enough to anyone who walks about the streets of London today and notes the prodigious number of houses built in the style of the fifties, with a portico and two pillars. But there was another reason for the multiplication of such houses: the sudden decision of the vast majority of the prosperous tradesmen and merchants of the City not to live any longer 'over the shop'.

They moved out to South Kensington, to Bayswater and to Notting Hill, and yet further afield. The ideal of the country gentleman still attracted the middle classes who long persisted in behaving as if they lived in the country. Every visiting foreigner noticed this English passion for the *idea* of the country. That acute observer Hippolyte Taine remarked that:

From London Bridge to Hampton Court there are eight miles, about three leagues of buildings. After those streets and quarters built all of a piece, in blocks, and to one design, like a hive, come innumerable houses built for their owners' enjoyment, cottages set in lawn and trees, and in every style, Gothic, Greek, Byzantine, Medieval, or Renaissance Italian or in a mixture of every variation on these styles. As a rule they are built in rows, or in groups of five, six, twenty, all identical and visibly built by the same contractor, like so many examples of the same vase or bronze. They turn out houses as we turn out Paris fancy-goods. What a multitude of easy, comfortable, wealthy households! The whole implies large profits from quick turnover, an opulent free-spending middle-class, very different from our own, financially straightened and looking twice at every penny spent. The most modest houses, built of brown brick, are pretty by reason of their cleanness; the window panes are polished like mirrors, there is almost always a small garden, green and full of flowers, and the façade will be covered by a creeper or a climbing plant.

R. J. Cruickshank amusingly sums up the mixed motives of those who took part in this diaspora:

Fashion, and snobbery, and the medical profession all pointed outwards. Did Mr Midas suffer from a cough and night sweats after a day in Lombard Street? Then Battersea, with its soft, relaxing river airs, its sheltered warmth, fostering half tropical shrubs and palms, was the place for him. Did Mr Croesus, the poor fellow, need placating? Were his nerves jangled by jobbers and speculators? Why then, the promised gusts of the heights of Muswell Hill were the very thing. Dr Tooting! Dr Hornsey! How many a master of the pepper and spice markets, how many a great captain of the jute or hemp trade, has owed his renewed vigour to your kind administrations. Acton! Through your revivifying airs, you are a stepping stone to the Alderman's Baronetcy. Gipsy Hill! – from your peak the corn-chandler's family first sighted the delectable prospect of the House of Lords. It was that very sage woman Mrs Caudle who made the discovery that, when people get on in trade, London air always disagrees with them. She laid down the celebrated law of medicine, which has since brought great profit to Harley Street, that 'delicate health comes with money'. When Mrs Caudle was plaguing her husband, the doll merchant, to leave the smoke of the city, she thought first of the silvan peace of Brixton 'So select!' said she. '*There* nobody visits nobody, unless they're somebody.'[1]

When they were first built, the houses of the fifties with their generous balconies, their noble pediments, and, of course, their pillars, the whole faced with newly painted stucco, must have presented an appearance attractive enough. They were by modern standards, large houses, but by all previous standards, they were, owing to the high cost of land, very narrow houses. They were houses on end. The rooms were arranged on top of one another. This was the vital fact. Great as has been the social divisions in the typical eighteenth century country house, masters and servants were, at least in the physical sense, on the same level. Now that society was confronted with a perpetual symbol of its hierarchical structure, the servants became quite literally, the 'lower classes'.

'High Life Below Stairs', chuckled the satirists, rejoicing in what seemed to them a daring paradox. 'Below stairs' were the kitchens, pantries, larders, and sitting-room for the servants – if any such were provided. On the ground floor (raised, usually, somewhat above the ground and reached by an imposing flight of steps) the domain of gentility commenced. The front room was the dining-room, the back room (there were only two) was a study or occasional room. The first floor was given over entirely to one fine apartment, sometimes divided by folding doors but generally treated as one. This was the drawing-room, the best room in the building, the sacred shrine of the Lady of the House, the gilded cage of her daughters

1 R. J. Cruikshank, *Charles Dickens and Early Victorian England*, 1949.

whose 'household duties' had now dwindled to a little dusting of the innumerable 'knick-knacks' that adorned the almost equally numerous 'wot-nots'. The names suggest that the resources of language had been exhausted by the profusion of trifles.

Above the drawing-room was the 'front bedroom', occupied by the master and mistress, and another bedroom. The one or two floors above were shared by servants and children. Pure undiluted gentility did not rise above the second floor. In the whole history of architecture there never was a more class-conscious house, than this astounding product of Victorian democracy.

In the period in which it was built and for half a century afterwards, the typical Victorian house served its purpose well enough. The 'servant problem' excited smiles in *Punch* and some complaints, no doubt, at ladies' tea parties, but it was not yet insoluble. Mr Gladstone was doing his best to abolish the terrible imposition of income tax at sevenpence in the pound. Rates were low and coal was plentiful. For the middle class at least the world was a comfortable world; there seemed no reason why it should not go on forever. People knew exactly where they were: in the basement or on the first floor.

Of course there were many social levels even in the world of 'above stairs'. Gulfs yawned between Belgravia and Earls Court. A lady of the sixties could decide it was socially unwise to visit anyone who lived 'north of the Park'. The great houses still persisted in Mayfair and St James's, but we are dealing with typical figures; and if the typical English figure in 1750 was the country gentleman, the typical figure in 1850 was the city merchant, with a house, bigger or smaller, nearer to Hyde Park Corner or more remote, as circumstances might dictate, but built to the same plan and harbouring the same kind of domestic set-up. This was the kind of 'home' that the poor dreamed of having and the prosperous were proud to contemplate as the reward of their labours. Home, with a dignified and fruitful wife, dutiful sons, obedient daughters, and domestics who, if individually tiresome, were, as a class, in plentiful supply.

This was the Shrine of Domesticity, dear to Victorian sentiment, and English men liked to think that in no other country in the world could be found its like. Poor misguided foreigners, in particular Frenchmen, might eat their meals in restaurants or even spend long hours at café tables on the boulevards, but the Englishman had his home from which, in theory at least, he never wished to be separated. Even when he went for a holiday to the sea-side he took his family with him and boasted (if he had comfortable lodgings) that he had found a 'home from home'. It must have been very agreeable for the Tired Business Man to know that, at the end of his cab or omnibus ride from the City, his slippers were awaiting him, embroidered by the hand of wife or daughter, and carefully warming before the fire. It must have been very pleasant to know that *there*, at least, he was king of the castle.

As Morton M. Hunt points out the new 'clinging vine' ideal for woman was essentially a middle-class phenomenon:

Along with modesty, virtue, sweetness, and similar qualities, she was supposed to be weak, fearful, and anxious to lean on, and be dominated by, a strong kind man. Having no tradition ∩f land inheritance, middle-class women had no marriage settlements and were wholly dependent on their husbands, any dowry being completely controlled by the husband, and divorce being all but impossible. Change and education, never much prized by the middle-class husband, went out of vogue, and 'Bluestocking' became a term of reproach. Industrialism itself directly fostered the clinging-vine concept; the making of clothes, food, and medicine, and the tending of children, were moving outside the home, depriving the middle-class wife of many of her functions, though leaving her cloistered.[1]

In a word the nineteenth-century bourgeois wife was less useful to her husband than wives had ever been before – less practically useful that is. Her function was to promote his egotism by her very dependency and also to serve as a status symbol, to prove to his neighbours that he could afford to give his wife a 'lady's life', and his daughters also. 'My daughter, I am glad to say, has no need to work.' In some such phrase must many a rising shop-keeper, who had just moved into South Kensington or Bayswater, have congratulated himself.

The Victorian Age saw an extraordinary development of a social phenomenon which has, no doubt, existed since the beginning of time, but which became so widespread in the middle of the nineteenth century that a word had to be found for it. That word was snobbery, and curiously enough, in the Early Victorian period it had not at all its present connotation. 'Snob' was the opposite of 'nob'. The 'nobs' were the aristocrats, the 'snobs' were simply cads. As late as the middle fifties *Punch* was making jokes about 'Snobs at the Seaside', i.e. young bounders who persisted in rowing too near to the ladies' bathing place.

It was Thackeray who gave the word 'snob' its modern meaning. His *Book of Snobs* is concerned with one particular kind of cad, the vulgarian who strives to force his way into a higher rank of Society than the one to which he is entitled by birth. And as almost everybody at that period was trying to do precisely that, the word narrowed its sense and became too useful to be discarded.

It is interesting to note that the anonymous author of *The Habits of Good Society*, published in 1855, does not make use of what seems to us the obvious word 'snobbery'. The word he uses is 'gentility' which would

1 Morton M. Hunt, *The Natural History of Love*, 1959.

seem an unjustified narrowing of the meaning. An alternative, used by other writers, was gentism, and we also find the word 'gent' used for one who is not quite, but would like to be thought, a gentleman. Our author declares that 'gentility' is to be found in all classes:

The Johnsons, retired haberdashers, cannot visit the Jacksons, retired linen-drapers, but have moved heaven and earth for an introduction to the Jamesons, who are not retired from anything. The Jamesons receive the Johnsons, but stiffly annihilate them at once by talking of 'our friends the Williamses', who have a cousin in Parliament, and the Williamses again are forever dragging the same cousin into their conversation that the Jamesons may be stupified. We go higher; the MP, although perhaps a Radical, will for ever be dogging the steps of the noble viscount opposite, and call the leader of his own party 'that fellow so-and-so'. The viscount is condescendingly gracious to the commoner, but deferential to the duke, and the duke himself will be as merry as Old King Cole if 'the blood' should happen to notice him more than usual Alas! poor worms, in what paltry shadows we can glory, and forget the end that lays us all in the common comfortless lap of mother earth!

Snobbery maintained a foothold even (if 'even' is the word) in the Established Church, whose extremes of wealth and poverty echoed those of secular society. Some of the bishops kept up the degree of state of a Cardinal de Rohan in the *Ancien Régime* in France. When the Bishop of Carlisle at the beginning of Victoria's reign (incidentally he was the nephew of the Duke of Northumberland) drove from his see to London he did so in a four-horse carriage with two postilions. The carriage of the Archbishop of Canterbury proceeded from Lambeth to the House of Lords accompanied by a troop of horse. Once a week he kept open house (open to all that is who presented themselves in Court dress) and his table was served by nearly fifty liveried servants. His income was in the region of £25,000 per annum.

At the other end of the scale were country clergymen whose income was about £200 a year, and that of their curates £50 a year. As these men were nearly always married and frequently produced large families, their state must often have approached destitution. Frequently, however, the country parson was the younger brother of the squire, and had some means of his own. If so he was 'received' by the County, joined in the hunt, occupied the second best house in the neighbourhood, and enjoyed the life of a country gentleman. 'Gentleman' was indeed the operative word. Augustus Hare tells a disquieting story of three young curates who presented them-selves at the 'big house'. One of them, who was related to the squire, was admitted by the front door. The other two, not being 'gentlemen' were sent round to the back and were given a meal in the servants' hall. In most country churches the service did not begin until the local lord or squire entered his pew, which was screened by curtains from the common herd and often had a coal fire in the corner. At Badminton, the country mansion of the Duke of Beaufort, the church was attached to the house and it was possible to walk into it from the library.

With snobbery went an ideal of 'respectability', which was in part a reaction against the licentiousness of the upper classes under the Regency. Its caricature was prudery and certainly prudery, which might be defined as a refusal to call things by their right names, was very prevalent in the Victorian middle classes. The most innocent words became charged with erotic significance. Even the good and sensible Thackeray hesitated to speak of ankles and for many people the word leg was utterly taboo.

The Victorians certainly had a complex about legs and it is curious to note that the agitation against open railway carriages (third class carriages were at first mere trucks) was not inspired by a dislike of discomfort but by the fear that the wind might derange the skirts of the female passengers and so reveal ankles or even calves, 'in such a manner that no woman possessing the slightest sense of decency would venture a second time into such travelling whirlwinds'.

Instead of legs people spoke of 'limbs', even when the legs in question belonged not to human beings but to articles of furniture; and the word bosom was substituted for breast even when it referred to the white meat of a chicken about to be carved. The Americans were reputed to go even further and to refer to a rump-steak as a 'seat-fixing'. Another dangerously exciting word was bed. People no longer went to bed; they 'retired to rest'.

The author of *The Habits of Good Society* was moved to protest against such absurdities and the state of mind which prompted them:

Honi soit qui mal y pense, and shame indeed to the man, still more to the woman, whose mind is so impure that the mere name of one common object immediately suggests another which decency excludes from conversation. . . . Or again, what more beautiful word than woman? woman, man's ruin first, and since then alternately his destroyer and saviour; woman who consoles, raises, cherishes us, refines us; and yet I must forget that you are a woman, and only call you a lady. . . . •If I speak of you as a woman, you leap up and tell me that you will not stay to be insulted.

Even men of genius were not exempt from the effects of the prevailing climate, and the strict propriety of leading novelists like Thackeray and Dickens seems to the modern mind to detract from their value as portrayers of real life. Thackeray prided himself that nothing he had written could 'bring a blush to the cheek of innocence'; and Dickens somehow managed, in *Oliver Twist*, to tell the harrowing story of Nancy, the wretched woman murdered by Bill Sykes, without ever mentioning the fact that she was a prostitute. The case of Dickens is certainly a curious one. He was a man who knew as much about 'low life' as any of his contemporaries. He loved

The Mid-Victorian Era

Queen Victoria and Prince Albert

Illustration from Soyer's *Modern Housewife* (1849): 'The Children who have cunningly reserved their infantine appetites for the grand national dish, the Blazing Plum Pudding.'

On the Road to Dinner, c. 1860. 'Going down to dinner' was a matter of rigid precedence; every young lady had to know the rules

William Holman Hunt, *The Awakening Conscience*, 1854. 'Every picture tells a story'

W. H. Egley, *In the Omnibus*, 1859

I. K. Brunel, the great engineer, standing in front of the chains of the Great Eastern Steamship, which he designed (1857)

Augustus Egg, *The Travelling Companions*, 1862. Two girls in a railway train near Menton on the Riviera

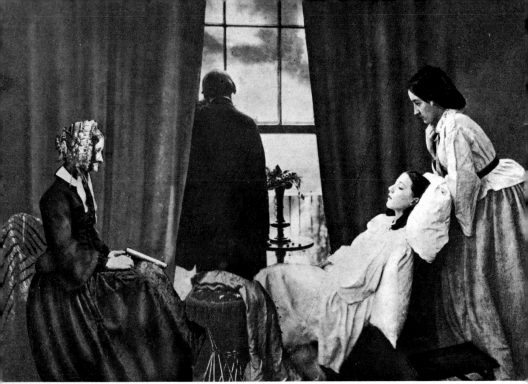

H. P. Robinson, *Fading Away*, c. 1858. Photographs were composed, like paintings, to tell a story

The English Sunday, seen by a Frenchman (1884)

Samuel Butler, *Family Prayers*. Butler wrote: 'In 1864, immediately upon my return from New Zealand, I began a picture called "Family Prayers" and which is certainly one of the very funniest things I have seen outside Italian votive pictures. I never finished it, but have kept it, and hope it will not be destroyed after my death.'

Mr and Mrs Gladstone at Dalmeny, 1880

Queen Victoria at Biarritz (the Queen is the figure on the bridge with a white parasol)

to walk about London by night and must have penetrated into some very unsavoury districts. His portraits of thieves and ragamuffins are penetrating and unforgettable. The one thing he leaves out is sex.

Yet he was a man to whom sex was extremely important, and those who revered him as a paragon of virtue (the modern 'Dickensians', the descendants of his first readers) must have received a rude shock when Thomas Wright of Olney first revealed that he too, like so many of his respectable contemporaries, kept a mistress.

The death of Dickens in 1870 had been followed by an orgy of panegyric in which he was hailed not only as 'the highest name in English literature since Shakespeare' but as 'the greatest moral reformer and benefactor of his time'. One American minister described him as 'holy as a surpliced priest'. There were protests against this canonization even in 1870, but 'in the end the canonizers had their way. The shrine was erected. The veil was drawn. Voices dropped to a reverent hush.'[1]

By 1936, the year in which Thomas Wright published his *Life of Charles Dickens*, the Dickens family had withdrawn all objection to the use of surviving letters and other documents, but the Dickensians refused to believe the story of Dickens's *affaire* with an actress even when it was confirmed by the testimony of Kate Perugini, Dickens's younger daughter in her conversations with Gladys Storey, who published them in her *Dickens and Daughter*.

Scholars are now in possession of the complete story, their findings based on thousands of letters in various public libraries in America. Scored out passages have been restored by the use of infra-red photography, the missing pieces of the puzzle had been put together and we now know that Dickens met Ellen Ternan in 1857, that a year later he made a public announcement, in his magazine *Household Works*, that he was separating from the mother of his ten children, that he set up the eighteen-year-old actress in her own establishment, that he communicated with her in code during his American tour in 1867 and 1868,[2] that he continued to be infatuated by her and that he left her £1,000 in his will. The point of retelling this story is not to diminish Dickens (it merely proves that he was a

---

1 Ada Nisbet, *Dickens and Ellen Ternan*, 1952.

2 This conclusion results from a fascinating piece of detection work by Ada Nisbet. In the Berg Collection in the New York Public Library is a series of memoranda sent by Dickens to his sub-editor, W. H. Wills. Under the heading 'Nelly', we read: 'On the day after my arrival out I will send you a short telegram at the office. Please copy its exact words, (as they will have a special meaning for her), and post them to her . . . by the very next post.' The telegram received by Wills read: 'Safe and well expect good letter full of hope'. While 'leafing through the pages of a very small pocket diary for the year 1867', Ada Nesbit came across the following note: 'Tel: all well, means *you come*; safe and well means *you don't come*'. Dickens had decided that it would be too risky to have his mistress with him during his American tour.

human being and not a plaster saint) but to emphasize the extraordinary 'conspiracy of silence' which Victorian – and post-Victorian – morality thought it necessary to maintain.

Of course, the Victorians would never have admitted to themselves or to anyone else that they suffered from an excess of prudery. What we would call prudery they called propriety, and Propriety, with a capital P, was certainly a most important god – or goddess – in the Victorian pantheon:

> Study first Propriety: for she is indeed the Pole-star
> Which shall guide the artless maiden through the mazes
>   of Vanity Fair;
> Nay, she is the golden chain which holdeth together
>   Society;
> The lamp by whose light young Psyche shall approach
>   unblamed her Eros.
> Verily Truth is as Eve, which was ashamed being naked;
> Therefore doth Propriety dress her with the fair foliage
>   of artifice . . .
> For verily, O my daughter, the world is a masquerade,
> And God made thee one thing, that thou mightest make
>   thyself another:
> A maiden's heart is as champagne, ever aspiring and
>   struggling upwards,
> And it needed that its notions be checked by the silvered
>   cork of Propriety:
> He that can afford the price, his be the precious treasure, ·
> Let him drink deeply of its sweetness, nor grumble if it
>   tastest of the cork.[1]

No understanding of English life in the second half of the nineteenth century is possible without some consideration of the part played in it by the so-called Public Schools. These were, of course (to the confusion of all non-English writers), private schools. They were called 'public' to distinguish them from the private tutoring which was largely the custom among the aristocracy in the eighteenth century. In origin the principal Public Schools were religious foundations, Eton having been established in the fifteenth century and Winchester even earlier. In addition to these were Harrow and Rugby, and they all maintained the closest relationship with the Established Church. They taught Latin and Greek and very little else, and, in the early nineteenth century, their discipline and general organization had been sadly relaxed.

It was Thomas Arnold who changed the system entirely. Becoming Headmaster of Rugby in 1827 he set himself to the task of reform with characteristic energy and determination. It is true that he did little or

1 Charles Stuart Calverley, *Verses and Translations*.

nothing to alter the curriculum, but he tightened up discipline, imposed a high moral tone and, for good or ill, introduced the system of government by the boys themselves: that is by the older boys, the prefects. These were empowered to inflict corporal punishment on the younger ones and also to use them as 'fags', to clean boots, make toast and generally act as servants to their sometimes kindly but often tyrannous masters. It is astonishing that such a system ever got itself accepted, but such was the force of Dr Arnold's personality that he not only imposed it on Rugby but on every other Public School in the country, of which there were now an increasing number such as Clifton, Haileybury and Marlborough, all comforming to the new pattern.

Dr Arnold himself was a strong advocate of corporal punishment, declaring absurd the notion that a boy was humiliated by being beaten. A French commentator expresses his astonishment 'that the boys seemed to share his opinions'.[1] The other points on which the formidable Head-master of Rugby insisted were regular attendance at the religious services in the school chapel and organized games. It was the first dawn of that ideal of 'Muscular Christianity' which had become almost a commonplace in the sixties and seventies.

O. F. Christie points out, very justly, 'that English society was reinforced by a great legion of moral and religious athletes, of a type which was quite inconceivable in the previous century. The Reverend Septimus Crisparkle (in *Edwin Drood*, 1869), with his cold baths and his boxing, is a character that could not have been encountered even by Mr Pickwick'.[2] But the new system did not only produce athletic parsons; it deeply affected also those who were destined for the Army, the Bar and the House of Commons.

In a generation a type had been created which was recognized all over the world as something distinctive. It became possible to pick out the 'public school man' almost at a glance. He was upright, reliable, clean-living, religious (or, at least, outwardly conformist). On the other hand, he was, in general, uninterested in intellectual pursuits and so afraid of emotion that he hesitated to show his feelings even to his family, and certainly not to the lower orders over whom he felt it both his destiny and his duty to rule.

Subconsciously, all this had a purpose; to provide an unending stream of colonial governors, district magistrates and the like in remote and un-healthy climates. It was as if the English character had stiffened itself, bracing its shoulders to support the new burden of Empire. No doubt the famous *flegme brittanique* was a national characteristic of long standing. But of how long standing? Certainly if a Victorian Englishman of the upper classes could have returned to the Age of Elizabeth he would have found a very different state of affairs. The Elizabethans behaved like a lot of

1 Jacques Chastenet, *La Vie Quotidienne en Angleterre*, 1941.
2 O. F. Christie, *The Transition from Aristocracy, 1832–1867*, 1927.

excitable Italians, and even as late as the Napoleonic Wars, the imperturbability of a Wellington was a noticeable exception. There is no doubt that the example of a man so much admired did something to mould the national character for the rest of the country, but the vital factor was the establishment of the Public Schools on the Arnold model.

All the products of the Public Schools did not become 'Muscular Christians', but nearly all conformed to the new ideal of gentlemen. It is necessary to stress the word 'new' for many who would have passed as gentlemen in the earlier years of the century would have been considered howling cads before Victoria's reign was over. The Prince Regent was called the First Gentleman of Europe, and he delivered himself of the opinion that a gentleman was a man who knew Greek, that is, had had a certain kind of education.

Some of the 'fine old English gentlemen' of the Regency and the years immediately following were gentlemen in the technical sense that they were untitled landed proprietors – esquires in fact, or 'squires'. They had forgotten whatever limited culture had been flogged into them at their Public Schools. They despised all intellectual pretensions and lived only for sport, mostly for hunting and shooting. It is no accident that this was the period of the sporting print and of the life reflected in the novels of Surtees.

A typical figure was the much admired Squire Mytton. He was a man of enormous hardihood and muscular strength with extensive estates in Shropshire. He swam his horse across the Severn, drove his coach and four at a breakneck pace through the night, drank at least six bottles of port a day. His idea of a good joke was to set a spring gun in the path his chaplain took on the way to service and then when it exploded to rush out and accuse the unfortunate man of shooting pheasants. For this, of course, was a very heinous crime. No one with less than £100 a year in freehold, or £150 a year in leasehold property was entitled to shoot game at all, and the poaching laws, administered by the country gentry themselves, were very severe. Spring guns and steel man-traps had not yet been made illegal.

Both Squire Mytton and Squire Osbaldeston, another of the same type, were great patrons of horse racing and neither was above a little sharp practice. Osbaldestone, as Wingfield-Stratford tells us:

is usually taken for the type of all that a sportsman and a gentleman ought to be, and yet even he was mixed up in at least one uncommonly fishy transaction on the turf. This involved him in a duel with Lord George Bentinck, from whom he had taken £200 by backing one of his own horses for a race in which, as he himself records, not without pride, he had secured a high handicap by previous deliberate pulling. For this manoeuvre Lord George had not unjustly taxed him with impudent robbery – and the Squire, who, having pocketed the money, promptly challenged Lord George, had some difficulty in getting anyone to act as his second. Indeed there is some reason to suspect that the seconds succeeded in averting what would have been sheer murder – for the Squire was a dead shot – by loading surreptitiously with blank.[1]

It is not a pretty picture.

One of the most picturesque figures of the period was George, Marquis of Aylesbury. He wore enormous hats, suits of loud colours and fancy waistcoats with guineas for buttons. He even drove a coster's donkey cart in Rotten Row, dressed in the traditional 'pearly' outfit and seemed to take a delight in outraging the conventions. In one sense he was a throw-back to those Regency dandies who had preferred the company of jockeys and stable boys to men of their own class, and his reputation as a racing man was not quite unclouded. He was, in fact, 'warned off the Turf'.

He married an actress, or rather a ballerina, in 1884, at a time when it was still unusual to do so, but his matrimonial affairs were as tangled as everything else in his life. He and Dolly Tester (whose real name was Dorothy Haseley) soon ceased to live together and although he settled upon her a trust fund of £100,000, it did not suffice to keep the broker's men out of her house. He himself died in 1904 deep in debt. He seems to have had a sense of humour, for one of his projects was to appear on the stage in America in a *pas de six* to be danced by bankrupt noblemen.

Long before the end of the century 'gentlemen' like this were an anachronism. The word gentleman had come to mean something quite different: it had come to mean the standard product of the Public Schools, and this is perhaps the most striking social phenomenon in the history of Victorian England.

1 Esmé Wingfield-Stratford, *The Making of a Gentleman*, 1938.

3 Monde and Demi-Monde

In France the Prince-President was not long in running into trouble with his Cabinet. One of his first acts was to nominate as Director of the National Museums, the Comte de Nieuwerkerke. This, says Victor Hugo, was acceptable enough, for Nieuwerkerke was a man of the world, a distinguished sculptor and *beau garçon*, but everybody knew that it was the last of these qualifications which had got him the job. He was, in fact, the lover of the Princesse Mathilde, Louis Napoleon's cousin, and it was she who had provided the funds for his electoral campaign, a sum, it was rumoured, of 200,000 francs. The Cabinet resisted, Louis Napoleon insisted, and Nieuwerkerke entered on his functions, which he carried out, it is admitted, admirably.

On 12 March 1849 the Prince President's allowances were doubled, to the great disgust of the Left, who saw in this move a restoration of the Civil List, as indeed it was. This was a necessity for him for he had other debts beside what he owed to the Princesse Mathilde. There was another woman who had provided him with funds for his great adventure, the lady known as 'Miss Howard'.

This was an assumed name. Her real name was Elizabeth Anne Haryett. She was born in 1824, the daughter, some say, of a Thames boatman, others of a bootmaker, but at all events of a man in humble circumstances. At fifteen she ran away with a horse-dealer, appeared briefly and without success on the stage, and then fell in with a major in the Life Guards who was extremely rich and set her up in a luxurious apartment in Oxford Street. Here she ran a gambling saloon frequented by the highest nobility.

It so happened that the major was a cousin by marriage of Lady Blessington and it is a sign of her slightly *déclassée* situation that he did not hesitate to bring his mistress to a party at Gore House. Here she met Louis Napoleon. Miss Howard was a beautiful young woman with a splendid figure and the profile of an antique cameo. The Imperial exile was much attracted and fell violently in love. She became his mistress, and the accommodating major not only put no obstacle in her way but allowed her to keep the ample fortune with which he had endowed her. She took a house (no. 9 Berkeley Street) and she and the Prince lived there for two years, until the fall of Louis Philippe and the establishment of the Republic made it possible for him to return to France.

Established as Prince-President he made no secret of his attachment to Miss Howard. Every afternoon at two o'clock he set off for the Bois de Boulogne in an open carriage drawn by two horses, followed by another carriage drawn by two horses. At the Rond-Point there waited two mounted servants with two other horses. Miss Howard also drove to the Rond-Point in an open two-horses carriage followed by two servants on horseback. The President and Miss Howard got out of their carriages, mounted their horses and trotted off into the Bois. They stopped at one of the refreshment pavilions to drink English grog, were picked up by their respective carriages and driven home, one to the Elysée, the other to a little private hotel in the Rue du Cirque which had the advantage of communicating with the President's Palace by a little door in the garden wall. Parisians saw nothing odd in this, although some of them wondered why no less than twelve horses should be needed for the simple pleasure of riding in the Bois with a mistress who actually lived, so to speak, next door.

In the provinces people were not always so indulgent. When the Prince-President was on an official visit to Tours he lodged at the *Préfecture* and Miss Howard at the house of a local bigwig who was on holiday. He happened to be a protestant and a puritan and on his return he enquired indignantly of the Minister of the Interior: 'Have we then returned to the epoch when the mistresses of kings paraded their infamy through all the towns of France?' He was an exception. The majority of Frenchmen, even if some of them hated Louis Napoleon, did not hate him for *that*.

Indeed Society as a whole welcomed the open relaxation of manners under the new régime. Since all danger from Red Revolution was now over, even sane socialism was discredited (and throughout 1849 the Paris theatres were filled with plays ridiculing socialist theories), since the *rentes* of the property-owning classes were now secure, people felt free to amuse themselves once more. The fashionable world took up where it had left off. When still no more than Prince-President, Louis Napoleon substituted for the rather stuffy receptions of Louis Philippe fêtes in the Orangerie of the Elysée Palace with Strauss and his orchestra to set the feet dancing. There could be seen such queens of elegance, as the Princesse Mathilde and Caroline Murat, the Marquise de Castelbajac, Madame de Polignac and the Countess Régnault de Saint-Jean d'Angely. There was an orgy of balls given by the Prince-President, the President of the Assembly, the Turkish Ambassador; balls in the aristocratic Faubourg Saint-Germain, balls in all the fashionable quarters, balls at the Hôtel de Ville.

Victor Hugo notes that titles of nobility, abolished by the republican constitution were already reappearing in social life. Even the invitations issued from the Elysée were worded: '*Le Président de la République prie Monsieur le comte – de venir passer la soirée*', etc.

Hugo gives a vivid description of a charity ball given in February 1849 in the Jardin d'Hiver which had been erected in the Champs Elysées:

It was an enormous iron cage, with two naves in the form of a cross, as big as four or five cathedrals, with an immense amount of glass. . . .[1] It was reached by a wooden gallery adorned with carpets and tapestries. When one entered the eye was dazzled by a flood of light, in which one could just make out all kinds of magnificent flowers and strange trees with the foliage and ferns of the tropics: banana-trees, palm-trees, cedars, large leaves and spines, strange branches twisted and mingled like those in a virgin forest. For the rest, nothing else there was virgin. The most beautiful women, the most beautiful cocottes of Paris whirled in that illumination like a swarm of insects in a ray of sunshine.

Some of the most spectacular entertainments were given by, or for actresses (the word 'actress' then, as now, covered a multitude of sins) and with these, says Octave Uzanne:

neither the aristocracy, nor the political world, nor the financial world, nor the official world could compete. It was a fury, a fever, a madness; there was nothing a fashionable man would stop at in order to be invited to these routs. Fine ladies, outraged by the attraction which the theatrical world exercised on part of their society, banded together to forbid their houses to those who had been present at an actress's ball. The association collected some of the grandest names in the Faubourg Saint-Germain, the Faubourg Saint-Honoré and the Chaussée d'Antin, but it was all without effect.[2]

The pioneer in organizing these *soirées d'actrices* was the celebrated Alice Ozy. It is true that she was not much of an actress, but she had a superb, slim body and did not in the least object to posing for artists 'in the altogether', nor to appearing as Eve in the Porte-Saint-Martin Theatre. The life of Alice Ozy is an example of the career open to a beautiful young woman without too many moral scruples. She was an embroideress in Belleville when she fell in love with a young actor and joined his troupe at the Variétés. By good fortune this particular company was invited to perform at the Tuileries before Louis Philippe and his family, and the Duc d'Aumale was so much attracted that he was soon to be seen waiting for her at the stage door. For Alice, however, even a King's son, fresh from his triumphs in Algeria, was overshadowed by a rich banker who set her up with house and carriage.

1 It was, in fact, an anticipation of the Crystal Palace to be erected in Hyde Park two years later.
2 O. Uzanne. *La Française du Siècle*, 1886.

She continued to act at the Variétés where, at that time, a play by Théophile Gautier was in rehearsal. He invited her to his house and was so much moved by the nude poses which she consented to take for him that he wrote a poem about her:

> *Un jour, au doux rêveur qui l'aime*
> *En train de montrer ses trésors,*
> *Elle voulut lire un poème,*
> *La poème de son beau corps . . .*

To know Gautier was to know all the interesting and talented men in Paris, including Victor Hugo who promised her a rôle in one of his plays. She became the mistress, however, not of Victor Hugo but of his son Charles. He was followed by Théodore Chassériau who painted her as a 'Sleeping Nymph'. Chassériau is still regarded as one of the great Romantic painters and he would have loomed even larger if he had not died in 1856 at the age of thirty-seven, *tué par trop d'amours*. Alice continued her glittering career, and admirers of the rank of the Duc de Morny and the Duke of Saxe-Weimar showered her with gifts. In one play she appeared on the stage as naked as the conventions of the time would allow, but on her head she wore a tiara worth (said the contemporary gossip writers) 200,000 francs.

Her example was followed by Madame Octave, of the Vaudeville, Mademoiselle Fuoco of the Opéra and the more celebrated *danseuse* Fanny Cerrito. Atala Bilboquet, the widow of an acrobat, gave a grand rout at mi-carême which almost had the result of changing many men's fashions, for she decreed that all her male guests should wear knee-breeches, and dandies, financiers, diplomats, artists and men of letters obeyed.

There was a veritable passion for the theatre at this period, to such an extent, that according to the witty chronicler, Auguste Villemot, theatrical values seemed to have invaded social life itself. 'Every salon,' he says, 'is a theatre, every screen a *coulisse*, every father-in-law a prompter. And then there are, in this social comedy, a thousand situations in which *l'amour* and *l'amour-propre* have their part to play.'

In private theatricals a whole series of delicious situations presented themselves, especially during the rehearsals. Hands could be pressed (if the stage directions so ordained), declarations of love could be made (in the words set down by the author of the play). And then, at the actual performance one could wear fantastic dresses, one could laugh (if one had good teeth) or smile (if they were only so-so). In fact, beauty, grace and coquetry had full play. The story is told of one amateur *comédienne* who had magnificent long hair which she was longing to display. She saw herself as Eve veiled only by her chevelure, and approached several dramatists with a

49

D

request for a suitable script. Finally she found a young and celebrated author who agreed to supply one but, unfortunately, he cast himself as the Serpent, a role which (as the malicious Villemot remarks), was already taken. The lady compromised by only playing parts in which she fainted. At such moments her hair became unfastened, quite naturally, and thus she was able to achieve the effect she desired.

The transition from Republic to Empire was effected with efficiency and dispatch and made no difference at all to the tempo of social life. During the night of 1 and 2 December 1851, those members of the National Assembly likely to prove difficult had been quietly arrested. Paris awoke to find the city placarded with a decree dissolving the Assembly and proclaiming martial law. Technically France was still a Republic, but the plebiscite held in the third week of December affirmed the conversion of the Second Republic into the Second Consulate, prelude to its conversion into the Second Empire.

The peculiar flavour of the Second Empire – its mental and moral climate – was due to a combination of material prosperity and the bankruptcy of idealism. Guizot, whom Louis Philippe flung to the wolves in a vain endeavour to save his throne, had been an austere and high-minded politician. Victor Cousin, the philosopher, had exalted in all sincerity 'the true, the beautiful and the good'. The Church, under the influence of men like Lammennais, had shown signs of moving towards a more liberal interpretation of its doctrines. The promoters of Utopian schemes, like Saint-Simon, were men of unshakeable faith in human nature. The most vehement of the Romanticists had been romantic in their attitude to life.

Now all this was changed. The world had suddenly become harder, more ruthless, more realistic. The power of money was beginning to be realized and even the old aristocracy began to dabble in stocks and shares. Some famous names were lent to the promotion of some very doubtful financial transactions. The rise of industry destroyed the old paternal relationship between employer and craftsman. All classes flung themselves into the pursuit of material gain; and while the bourgeoisie at least was outwardly pious, the Church itself seemed to have lost its idealism and to have ceased to ally itself with the best liberal thought. One has only to compare the tone of the powerful Catholic journalist Louis Veuillot with that of Catholic writers of the previous generation to sense the difference.

Napoleon III was not only an adventurer himself but was surrounded and supported by adventurers; and perhaps the most typical figure among them was the Emperor's illegitimate half-brother the Duc de Morny. His character and influence are admirably summed up by Albert Léon Guérard:

Cool, elegant, superior, a Don Juan who gambled on the stock market and held all political wires in his hand; a wit, an epicure, a leader of fashion, who affected to treat a matter of state in a careless, disdainful fashion and to concentrate his mind on a farce, a menu, or a cravat, he was one of the worst and one of the most fascinating men of the century. Sane, liberal, tactful, courteous when he chose, he made an admirable President of the Legislative Body; at the same time, cruel in cold blood, he was probably responsible for the worst features of the coup d'état; and thus got his country entangled in the senseless and ruinous Mexican war. Luckier than more deserving men, he died – in the heyday of the régime he had founded, served and dishonoured. His life was like his birth – splendid, but with a bar sinister.[1]

The character of the Emperor himself was full of ambiguities. He remained an enigma even to his intimates – if he can be said to have had any intimates, for there was always something mysteriously hidden behind those dull eyes and that impassible face. That he was *bon*, in the sense of being habitually kind to those with whom he came in contact, is universally admitted. He had a strong sense of family and those who saw him with the little Prince Imperial were touched by his paternal tenderness. But he had also a *soif de la femme* – a thirst for women – which could not be appeased.

That his marriage with Eugénie de Montijo was, at least to some extent, a love-match is obvious. Most of his advisers were convinced that he was making a great mistake in not finding a bride among the daughters of the royal houses of Europe. Certainly tentative advances had been made but without much success, and Lord Palmerston remarked, with his usual sagacity, that the Emperor was wise to have chosen as he did since 'he had no chance of a political alliance of any value, or of sufficient importance to counterbalance the annoyance of an ugly or epileptic wife whom he had never seen till she was presented to him as a bride'.

It is a curious commentary on the Emperor's entourage that quite a number of its most eminent members, knowing beforehand of his intention to marry Eugénie de Montijo, gambled on the Bourse. Marshall St Arnaud who had played for a rise, lost so heavily that (according to the Archives of the Prefecture of Police) he was on the verge of 'execution' and was only saved by the generosity of the Emperor. Achille Fould, the Minister of the Household, on the other hand, rightly anticipating that the announcement of the marriage would cause a disastrous fall in public securities, reaped a large fortune.

Yet, on the whole, the people of France were pleased. The new Empress was young and beautiful. What was more, she had elegance, a quality not often found in royal circles. She was probably the last ruler, or wife of a ruler, to exercise a real influence on fashion. From the day of her marriage at Notre Dame in January 1853, her dresses were copied as a matter of course. From Spain, her own country, she imported the bolero and the felt

1 A.L. Guérard, *French Civilization in the Nineteenth Century*, 1914.

hat, from Scotland, her mother's country, the plaid. And everything became very small: tiny veils, jointed umbrellas no bigger than saucers, little muffs, little handkerchiefs. Everything that is, except the crinoline which became ever bigger and bigger, and the chignon which needed to be augmented by a mass of false hair. But the very size of the chignons made hats extremely small. She was, in a very real sense, a dictator of fashion.

Ferdinand Bac with that tone of respectful irony so suitable for evoking the Second Empire, tells us that:

One day in 1860, when a trip to Savoy had been decided on, mysterious groups gathered in the Blue Salon. The Empress with a busy and mysterious air, went from one to the other. Something was in the air. Was it a conspiracy? And against whom? Differences arose, were combated, and resolved. One felt that something important was happening in secret. Several ladies had been seen to leave with an air of discontent. There were protestations and enthusiastic cries. . . .

Suddenly the Empress announced an important piece of news. A coup d'état? A revolution? Yes, indeed . . . and by women! Were they intending to return to the time of Lysistrata, to refuse obedience to the desires of men?

No! Something much more important had been accomplished, something much more grave for the future of women. They were launching the short skirt.[1]

It is true that it was not, by modern standards, a *very* short skirt – perhaps three inches above the ground. The 'noble faubourg' that is the old aristocracy which still regarded Eugénie as a parvenue, insisted on a crinoline which reached to the ground, but everyone else took up the new idea with enthusiasm, and the news went rapidly round: 'Monsieur Worth has given his consent'.

The name reminds us that a new power, a new dictator had arisen in the world of fashion, and it is astounding that the man who was able to carry out this coup d'état was an Englishman. Born in 1825 at the village of Bourne in Lincolnshire, he came to London as a youth and was employed for a time at Swan and Edgar's in Piccadilly Circus, at a salary of five shillings a week.

Before then he had been trained as a salesman at Allenby's – a small dress-goods house near Regent Street – and had been so successful that at thirteen he was made the firm's cashier. . . . Before his seventeenth birthday he set off for Paris with five pounds lent by his mother, a short reference from Mr Allenby and no knowledge whatever of the French language. . . . Within a year he joined the staff of Maison Gagelin the first house in Paris to sell ready-made coats and cashmere shawls to fashionable women . . . and it was not long before he suggested that the house should design dresses to suit the individual type and personality

1 F. Bac, *Napoléon III Inconnu*, 1932.

of each customer. Madame Gagelin was shocked to the core and Worth left her to set up a business of his own . . . at 7 Rue de la Paix. [1]

Here he rapidly attracted a fashionable clientèle, including Countess Walewska and Princess Metternich who brought him to the notice of the Empress. Soon he was employing eight hundred workers, had an annual turnover of twenty million francs, and was able to afford a fine chateau at Surennes, crammed with *objets d'art*. He was the first male couturier, and long remained unique, for it is interesting to note that the majority of *modistes* under the Second Empire were, in spite of his example, women – Madame Leroy, Madame Bonnard and Mesdemoiselles Laure, Alexandrine and Lucy Hoquet.

A contemporary account gives a vivid picture of his salon at the height of his glory:

At the time of the Imperial wedding it was Mme Palmyre who made the twenty *toilettes de soirée* and Mme Vignon the thirty-two *toilettes du jour* (inclusive of the wedding gowns) which figured in the Empress's *corbeille de mariage*. Later came the ascendancy of the Englishman Worth particularly in respect to evening gowns, and the rise of Laferrière as an artist in promenade and visiting *toilettes*. Mme Félicie long reigned supreme in the domain of mantles and coats while Virot and Lebeo triumphed in bonnets and hats. . . .

Worth, Laferrière, Virot, and others waited on the Empress, Princess Metternich, and a few other *grandes dames* but most of their customers went to them; there were afternoons when half the *élégantes* of Paris might be seen in the Rue de la Paix and adjoining thoroughfares. The stairs at Worths were likened to Jacob's ladder: an angel was to be met on every step. You fancied, too, that you were entering a hot house such was the pleasant warmth on quitting the cold street and such the wealth of camelias and other plants displayed both on the stairs and the landing, across which flitted one or another of the great costumiers' *jolies demoiselles*, invariably wearing a gown or chignon of the style that would be fashionable next day . . . on turning to the left you found a succession of salons with large oak tables, on which lay pieces of silk, satin, and other materials, with some of the finest artificial flowers that Paris could produce and an infinity of elegant *chiffons*. Handsome young men, cravatted *à la colin*, and wearing tightly buttoned frock-coats, stood here and there prepared to minister to the ladies' choice; but they did so in an easy nonchalant way . . . again, passing hither and thither, there were young girls whose gowns though black, represented the latest styles invented by the master, in such wise that by pointing to one or another of them a customer could at once indicate what kind of corsage or sash, or 'puff' she desired. The first-hand, elegant, but looking tired, was there also welcoming the customers with great dignity.

On some stands on the fourth floor you saw a few of the master's very latest creations, finished and ready for delivery, but shown to you just as a painter shows a picture in his studio before sending it to the salon or the Academy.

1 A.H.Beck, The House of Worth, *Leader Magazine*, 28 January 1950.

They stood there, those wonderful robes, three or four in a row, and admirably lighted – the wall behind them being, moreover, all 'looking glass', so that you at once perceived how the sash was arranged, how the tunic fell, and the train flowed. They were, too, often as intricate as five-set plays, they were elaborate, carefully studied compositions; and even as the value of the picture is not estimated according to the cost of the pigments that the artist may have employed, so the value of those gowns did not depend on the cost of the materials used in making them. The latter might not exceed 200 francs, but the amount of genius lavished on the design and the making might represent 2,000.

The fair clients gathered in ecstasy in front of these new creations, and while a little cry of admiration escaped from one of them, and a sigh or a purr of delight from another, something like a whirlwind of tulle and lace and *crêpe de Chine* would suddenly flit by and vanish into a room whence as the door opened there came a stream of pale light. That was the *salon de lumière*, where the windows were hermetically sealed and the walls were all huge mirrors. By the light of a dozen gas-jets with moveable shades, the lady who there tried on her new *toilette de bal* was seen as she would be seen the following night at the Tuileries. And now it was that the master made his appearance – a man rather below the average height, with a full, shiny face all pink and white, his fair hair parted in the middle, his whiskers closely cropped, his moustaches drooping and glittering like gold. He wore a perpetual smile, he seemed to bow without bending, perhaps because his short frocked-coat was so very tightly buttoned. As a rule it was only with customers that he spoke French – and then with a marked accent. His subordinates in the *salon de lumière* were usually English girls, Miss Mary, Miss Esther. And he always remained quite calm, he never made a fuss, never addressed an angry word to a subordinate. But his *coup d'oeil* was Napoleonic. He immediately detected a fault, and indicated in very few words what should be done to repair it. Not only did he fight against the crinoline succeeding in 1868 by reducing it to something like a *vertugadin*, but he also opposed the excessively *décolleté* bodice. 'I dress ladies,' he remarked one day to a journalist, 'Let the demi-monde go elsewhere!' Such was Mr Worth, the King of Fashion.

Eugénie, however, even clothed by Worth, soon ceased to satisfy the Emperor's amorous desires, and there were not lacking those who sought to turn these to their personal or political advantage. In the latter field the Italians were most active and their hopes were, as it turned out, well founded.

Virginie Oldoini came of an ancient noble family of Spezzia. Her father, the Marquese d'Oldoini, had been an attaché of the Piedmontese embassy in Spain. At fifteen Virginie was already a beautiful woman and was married off to the Conte Verasis de Castiglione. The young wife, who was the niece of Cavour, was soon separated from her husband and is thought to have become the mistress of the redoubtable King Vittorio Emmanuele. Cavour sent her to France, quite deliberately, just as Louis XIV had sent

'Madame Carwell' to the Court of Charles II. Her instructions were explicit: 'Succeed by any means you please, but succeed!'

Succeed she did, for when she appeared at the Tuileries in 1855 Napoleon III was soon at her feet, and that she became his mistress was scarcely a secret from anyone at court. One evening at Compiègne she excused herself from attending a performance at the chateau theatre saying that she had a migraine. The Emperor slipped out before the play was over, not un-noticed by the cold eye of his cousin, Princess Mathilde, who remarked that he had chosen the only moment when it was impossible for anyone to follow him. At Saint-Cloud during a picnic he rowed her in a small boat to a little island in the lake. They stayed there more than an hour and on their return received, as can be imagined, a very cold welcome from the Em-press, who immediately broke up the party.

Madame Van de Velde tells us that:

He disguised his *penchant* so little that it aroused the susceptibility of the Empress, who was habitually so coldly careless of her Consort's distractions. At a *bal costumé* at the Tuileries the Countess, insolently beautiful in a fanciful dress supposed to represent the Queen of Hearts, hung on the arm of the Emperor, who led her through the rooms. Her audacious drapery lifted over a perfect limb was caught high above the knee by a jewelled heart. The Emperor stopped before the Empress to allow his companion to make her obeisance, and annoyed by the coldness of Eugénie, remarked pointedly, 'Do you not admire the costume of the Countess?' 'Exceedingly', answered the Empress, whose Spanish blood asserted itself, for turning towards the proud beauty, she added, '*Vous mettez votre coeur bien bas, Madame.*' The Emperor bit his moustache and moved away. Others had heard, but Madame de Castiglione showed no signs of emotion or annoyance.[1]

The Emperor was far from being her only lover and she was not always above accepting a recompense for her favours. According to that malicious gossip Viel-Castel, the rich and cynical Lord Hertford, who lived in Paris, paid her a million francs for the privilege of sleeping with her for one night:

As a night which costs a million is an exceptional night, Hertford wished to experience with the Countess every kind of volupté. He was paying, and paying dearly, and reserved the right to have his own way. The Countess must have passed through every test of the most refined debauchery. Nothing was omitted. After such a night, she was in bed for three days, but now she appears to be completely recovered. She is more dazzling than ever.[2]

She was nonetheless a cold woman who loved nobody but herself – a narcissist in fact. She was proud of her small feet and kept a collection of

---

1 Madame Van de Velde, *Random Recollections of Court and Society*, 1888.
2 Comte H. de Viel-Castel, *Commérages*, 1930.

her shoes in a glass case. She was not without an influence on fashion, imposing her own taste for the peculiar deep violet known to dressmakers as 'quarter mourning' against the prevailing mode of rose-pinks, sky-blues and grass greens. There were those who followed her fashions rather than those launched by Eugénie.

Naturally the Empress hated her and, one evening in April 1857, when the Emperor was leaving the Castiglione's house at Passy in the private cab he used for his amorous adventures, three unknown men leapt at the horses' heads. The coachman, who had been selected for his reliability, succeeded in beating them off, and returned at full speed to the Tuileries. Shortly afterwards a bomb was found on the staircase at the Ermitage; no one now knows exactly what happened. An unknown man was shot by a Corsican police inspector. Perhaps the whole thing was a plant and, if so, the Empress was almost certainly behind it. For the danger to the life of the Emperor was made an excuse for the expulsion of the Contesse de Castiglione. The following night she was arrested and conducted to the Italian frontier, by order of the Minister of the Interior.

And then, a month later, to the astonishment of Paris, she appeared at a ball given by the Ministry of Marine in the suite of Princess Mathilde. The Empress was deeply offended and ceased to invite the Princess to the Tuileries.

Eugénie had other sources of anxiety beside her husband's liaison with the Contesse de Castiglione. The latter, in spite of her morals, was at least *grande dame*. Even more shocking to the pride of the Empress was Napoleon's *affaire* with the famous Marguerite Bellanger. In the Emperor's circle was a certain M. Mocquart, Chef de Cabinet, who had often proved himself useful by his discretion and his pliability. M. Mocquart owned a little house at Montretout, near Saint Cloud and this house had the advantage of a back door opening on the private park of the chateau. It was by taking advantage of this that an interview was arranged between the Emperor and the lady. Shortly afterwards Marguerite Bellanger, to the astonishment of her friends, disappeared entirely from her apartment in the Boulevard des Capucines. She reappeared at Biarritz some months later, once more in a house (this time, a seaside villa) belonging to M. Mocquart, who acted as a kind of guardian, or chaperon.

It was plain that she was the Emperor's mistress, and a year later, she let it be known that she was expecting his child. But the child was prematurely born and did not survive. And now begins an extraordinary mystification, the mystification one is tempted to call typical of everything in which Napoleon III had a hand.

When, during the Commune, the Palace of the Tuileries was pillaged by the mob, two letters were found, both in the handwriting of Marguerite Bellanger. One was addressed to the Emperor himself and one to a 'Monsieur' who seems to have been acting as some kind of intermediary. Both confess that Marguerite had been unfaithful to her Imperial lover. But, in reality, the situation was nothing like so simple. Ferdinand Bac, than whom no one knew more of the *dessous* of the period, tells us that:

Both these letters had been *dictated* to Mlle. The affair was quite complicated enough. The Emperor had made the daughter of a high dignitary pregnant and the doctor in the secret employment of the Emperor who had been looking after Mlle Bellanger suggested to the latter that she should say nothing of her own premature delivery but should pretend to be still pregnant for *reasons of State.* After some resistance Marguerite agreed to this fraudulent scheme and in due course the doctor brought to her the other woman's child. The true mother was, shortly afterwards, married in Notre Dame with the most brilliant ceremonial, to the sound of the great organ. . . . Everything was thus arranged for the best, but tattlers had reported to the Empress that her husband had a child by Mlle Bellanger. We do not know what reaction followed this discovery in the intimacy of the Tuileries; but it must have been sufficiently violent to call for the immediate intervention of M. Mocquart whose ingenuity was put to the proof. His audacious scheme, which may or may not have been approved by the Emperor, was to prove to the Empress, by means of the two letters, that the child's father was some other than the Emperor. . . . This fake avowal reassured the Empress. . . . She knew only too well what difficulties could be raised by an imperial bastard. . . .

Nonetheless the child, Auguste Bellanger, was provided for and given the Chateau de Mouchy which the Emperor himself bought for 700,000 francs. The gutter press got hold of the story but the outbreak of the Franco–Prussian War gave it something else to think about, and no more was heard of the matter. After 1871 Marguerite Bellanger, according to Madame Van de Velde, 'left France for Cassel, where she married an Englishman, a sailor, got tired of him, abandoned him, returned to France, bought a pretty little *hôtel* at St Cloud and lived there, unknown and uncared for, on the spoils of her one great *coup*, till her death.'

Napoleon III found his mistresses in every stratum of society: aristocrats, bourgeoises like Madame de Lamarre, cocottes of all grades, actresses and even a bare-back rider in the *Cirque Impérial*, Julie Mouton, who died as recently as 1910 in a state of complete destitution.

In most of his *affaires* the Emperor was reasonably discreet, but the same could not be said of another member of the Imperial family, Prince Napoleon. Universally known by the slightly contemptuous name of Plonplon, he, alone among the nephews of Napoleon I, resembled him in face and figure. He was violently jealous of Napoleon III, who for family reasons had to put up with his cousin's bad temper and indiscreet behaviour. He was lodged (officially) in the Palais Royal, but he had also a house, decorated in the Pompeian style, in the Avenue Montaigne. His wife, Princess Clotilde of Savoy, was pious and boring, and he had already had numerous mistresses including Rachel and Cora Pearl, when the famous journalist Émile de Girardin arranged a meeting with the as yet hardly known Anna Deslions. It is a commentary on the *moeurs* of the period that this interview took place at the house of another demi-mondaine, Esther Guimard. Anna Deslions was a frank vulgarian, and the other woman tried to impress upon her that it was necessary to mind her manners in the Prince's presence and to put up at least an appearance of resisting him. But, at the dinner party given by Esther Guimard, Anna and Plonplon were soon exchanging dirty jokes and laughing their heads off. Nonetheless Anna did 'resist' the Prince – until eleven o'clock that night.

He set her up in a magnificent establishment in the Rue Lord Byron, and the Goncourts, in a famous bravura passage in their *Journal*, have described her mode of life, and how she would receive her guests, who included some of the most celebrated men of the period, in a 'brocaded *robe de chambre* with slippers of the same colour embroidered in gold, a chemise of the finest linen garnished with Valenciennes lace . . . a petticoat garnished with lace worth three or four hundred francs, and *galant* accessories worth anything up to two thousand five hundred.' Her household was conducted with the utmost extravagance. She is supposed to have been the original of Zola's Nana and like Nana she was foolish enough not to put by anything (of the millions of francs that had passed through her hands) for a rainy day. Abandoned by Prince Napoleon she fell, after a succession of other rich lovers, into poverty and was only rescued from destitution by one of those she had ruined.

The *grandes cocottes* of the period might be divided into those who kept their gains and those who threw them away. Esther Guimard died miserably, Jeanne Desroches succumbed at twenty-five to galloping consumption, Pauline d'Angeville went mad, Caroline Letessier, in spite of having been the mistress of a whole series of Grand Dukes, finished in poverty. On the other hand, several of them married into the nobility of Europe. One became Princess Soltikoff, another (Rosalie Léon) became the wife of Prince Pierre de Wittgenstein, Jane de Tourbey died Comtesse de Loynes. It is a mistake to think that at this period there was a rigid dividing line between the monde and the demi-monde.

The term *demi-monde* was invented by Alexandre Dumas *fils*. His play of that name was produced at the Gymnase Theatre on 20 March 1855. It was an immediate success and the word passed into current use to designate that characteristic phenomenon of the Second Empire, the world of 'kept' women. Such women were not prostitutes in the accepted sense of the word. Their humbler sisters might be the inmates of brothels or ply for hire on the streets of Paris, seeking the chance encounter, the casual client. To belong to the demi-monde it was necessary to have an establishment properly furnished and staffed, and a carriage in which to drive in the Bois. Most demi-mondaines were faithful to one protector, or at least, to one at a time. Many of them had a salon, frequented by the most eminent men of the day. They were, perhaps, the nearest equivalent in history to the Aspasias of the Age of Pericles. They were not received into 'Society' and in theory at least, no respectable woman ever met them.

Of course something similar had existed in previous ages. In the eighteenth century, for example, it was taken for granted that an actress was a kept woman. But the extraordinary flowering of the demi-monde in the France of Napoleon III was due, in large measure, to the rigidity of the Civil Code introduced by Napoleon I. This gave all rights to the husband, and the 'woman taken in adultery' was, with rare exceptions, simply cast out. Like the unmarried girl who had 'committed a fault', a respectable life was henceforward almost impossible for her. She either sank into prostitution or, if she was a woman of spirit, found a rich protector, was set up, as the phrase went, *dans ses meubles*. In a word, she entered the demi-monde.

For some women this was a step down in the social scale but for many it was a step up. Ferdinand Bac, speaks of those who: *à force de tomber, se sont beaucoup élevés, et à force de s'élever se sont beaucoup couchés.'*

Some of them became famous and, indeed, occupied very much the same position in the public imagination that is occupied by film stars today. In the words of Alain Decaux:

several dozen women – out of many thousands – succeeded in raising themselves above the sad troupe. They were clever enough to climb one by one the steps which led to resplendent luxury. They dazzled Paris with their dresses, their jewels, their carriages and their receptions. The names of many of them were in the papers, and some of these names – and this would no doubt have surprised the women themselves – have not been forgotten. They are linked with our glittering image of the Second Empire. Indeed some of these women have found a place in History. . . . These women were *à la mode*. It was fashionable to pass for being their lover.[1]

In a previous generation the fashionable restaurants had been situated at the Palais Royal, but these had now fallen out of favour. There was a move to the boulevards, and we hear much of '*le grand seize*'. This meant Salon no. 16 of the Café Anglais with windows opening on the Boulevard des Italiens and on the Rue Marivaux. Here every evening assembled '*Les grands représentants de la haute noce*':[2] Gramont-Caderousse, the Prince of Orange, the young Duc de Rivoli, Prince Paul Demidoff, the Prince

1 A. Decaux, *Amours Second Empire*, 1958.
2 An untranslatable phrase. Perhaps the nearest we can get is: 'Those who represented the life of pleasure at its highest point'.

d'Aremberg, the Marquis of Modena and Prince Galitzine. Here these members of the *jeunesse dorée* supped joyously with the leading demi-mondaines and the actresses most in vogue. After supper baccarat was played, sometimes all night.

What struck contemporary moralists with horror was the shamelessness of the women of the demi-monde. They were to be seen everywhere: in the Bois where their equipages rivalled and even surpassed those of the Empress herself; in the theatres where they glittered with jewels in the most prominent boxes and where they were visited in the intervals by the most celebrated men of the day. They behaved as if they had nothing to hide; and some had not – in the quite literal sense.

Some of these *grandes horizontales* (the witty contemporary phrase for kept women) had no objection to being painted in the nude or even to appearing nude in public. We have already mentioned Alice Ozy. At the Jockey Club ball in 1864 Cora Pearl made her entrance clothed only in her long red hair. Marguerite Bellanger, the Emperor's mistress, appeared nude on the stage. 'My bosom,' she says proudly in her memoirs, 'was well rounded . . . my breasts were as firm as marble.' We should perhaps remind ourselves that 'nude', at this period, often meant clad in close-fitting white tights. But some did not hesitate to show themselves really nude before those men-about-town who were willing to pay for the privilege. It was a costly privilege and the famous Léonide Leblanc, who numbered among her lovers the Prince Napoleon, Gustave Courbet, Eugène de Talleyrand and the young Clemenceau, was popularly known as 'Mlle Maximum'. She was the *maîtresse-en-titre* of the Duc d'Aumale.

The rage for *tableaux vivants* reached even the Court. Artists of the calibre of Cabanel and Viollet-le-Duc did not hesitate to arrange at Compiègne biblical and mythological scenes nor did the *grandes dames de la Cour* hesitate to appear in them clad in white tights and very little else. There was an extraordinary desire, even among fine ladies, not to let their charms be lost to posterity. The Comtesse de Castiglione commissioned the well known painter Paul Baudry to depict her on a couch in the same attitude as the 'Naked Maja' of Goya. It is said that when she saw the finished picture she thought it more beautiful than she was herself and, in a rage, destroyed it. An unreasonable reaction! What would she have done if Baudry had shown her less beautiful than she was in reality?

Photography in its early days was almost *too* truthful, the cold eye of the camera disdaining those embellishments of the female form and feature that painting had so long taken for granted. Unfortunately for some of the beauties of the Second Empire the camera had already arrived and when we see a photograph of, for example, Cora Pearl we are hard put to it to explain how a woman with such a poor figure and such a commonplace face could ever have risen to such heights of notoriety. Henri d'Alméras attributes her success to 'clever and persistent publicity, invincible aplomb, the snobbery of men of the world and the immeasurable stupidity of the public'.[1]

Cora Pearl, an Englishwoman whose real name was Emma Crouch, had the added advantage of a knowledge of cosmetics. It is odd to hear that she found it necessary to import these from England. She bleached her hair, painted her eyelids blue, used face-powder and carmined her lips – in fact used all the means which have become commonplace in the twentieth century. In the middle of the nineteenth century they were found startling and provocative.

Photography had scarcely been invented before it began to be employed for nude poses. Already in 1837 the invention of Nicéphore Niepce, taken up by Daguerre, made it possible to dispense with lithography and other means of reproduction and to offer the public a picture taken from life. By the beginning of the 1840s there was a tremendous vogue for daguerro-types; studios sprang up everywhere and some of them specialized in imitating the painted nudes of the Salon. The daguerrotype had the disadvantage of being a single object (each one had to be made separately) but in 1841 Talbot invented the negative and by the beginning of our period it was possible to produce any number of 'prints' on sensitized paper. The way was open for an extensive commerce.

The most successful practitioners in the early days of the Second Empire were Pierre Petit and Disderi, and to their studios flocked actresses of the lighter stage, dancers from such *Bals publics* as the Mabille and the Closerie des Lilas. There was no lack of choice: 'nude, semi-nude, *déshabillé, décolleté* . . . academic nudes, draped or otherwise, suggestive nudes in white stockings and boots, open air nudes posed against a studio background. . . . Some of those who posed, married no doubt, wore a mask, or hid their faces with a fan. . . .'[2]

Later the photographers grew even more daring and, at the Paris Exhibition of 1867 it was possible to buy nude photographs of the Empress Eugénie and the Duchesse de Morny, the faces of these ladies having been skilfully joined by *collage* to the bodies of other women and then re-photographed. The author we have just quoted calls this '*un commerce bien parisien*'.

Perhaps it is not surprising that these activities did not pass without protest. In 1867 a sermon against nudity was preached from the pulpit of Notre Dame, and although the orator did try to distinguish between '*la nudité chaste*' and '*la nudité libertine, honteuse, provocante, audacieuse*' many in his congregation were convinced that all nudity was indecent. A certain M. Dubosc de Pesquidoux wrote to the press to complain of 'the shameful

1 H. d'Alméras, *La Vie Parisienne sous le Second Empire*, 1933.
2 Romi, *La Conquête du Nu*, 1957.

nudities which people the gardens and palaces of Paris'; and when Carpeaux's famous group *La Danse* was unveiled on the façade of the new, and not yet completed Opéra, there was a public outcry. A hostile crowd gathered and the journals were inundated with letters of protest. One *père de famille* declared that all his love of music would not induce him to bring his daughters to an opera house 'with the sign of a brothel outside'. The beautiful figures of what is now recognized as one of the masterpieces of French sculpture were splashed with ink. It was proposed to move the group inside, to the Foyer de la Danse and then it was the turn of the ballet girls themselves to protest. Since it was taken for granted that every *danseuse* was a kept woman (it was hardly possible for her to exist without somebody's 'protection') this was not without its irony. It is probable that *La Danse* was only saved from destruction by the outbreak of war. It is now one of the glories of Paris.

Of course some actresses and dancers were not only kept women but were possessed of great theatrical talent, even of genius. Rachel is an obvious example. Another was Hortense Schneider, whose success as a woman preceded her success as an artist. There was no lack of candidates for the honour of setting her up in her own establishment, and all the luxuries that went with it. The elegance of her carriage on the Bois and the splendid horses that drew it, were much admired, as well they might be, for they had been selected and paid for by the most eligible and knowledgeable man-about-town of his epoch, the Duc Ludovic de Gramont-Caderousse.

This young man was the most famous – and the most attractive – member of that *jeunesse dorée* which frequented Tortoni's and the *Maison d'Or*, the Jockey Club and the race-course, the Opera and the Variétés. He was the Beau Brummell of his time, but with infinitely more gaiety and wit. Also with infinitely more wealth, for he had in his stables twenty horses *pur sang*, and when he came to London as attaché at the French Embassy astounded the capital by the splendour of his establishment. It was in 1857 that his liaison with Hortense Schneider began and soon they were seen everywhere together. That he continued to be more than kind to such celebrated ladies as Julia Barucci and Anna Deslions did not trouble her in the least; she expected him to be equally complaisant. When he died of tuberculosis at the age of thirty-one he left her fifty thousand francs. She was the only woman mentioned in his will.

But although Hortense Schneider was willing to accept the homage of a man like Gramont-Caderousse, she was above all an artist. The theatre was never for her merely a means of launching herself into a life of *galanterie*. Disappointed for a time in her ambitions she was about to return to Bordeaux and, in 1864, had already given orders for her house in Paris to be closed and her furniture to be sold. One day she was dressing when there came a knock at the door. It was Offenbach. At first she refused to

admit him but he persisted and offered her the principal role in his new
operatta, *La Belle Hélène*. She accepted. What she made of it is part of
theatrical history. For the next six years, until the collapse of the Second
Empire, she went from triumph to triumph.

La Belle Hélène with Offenbach's music and a witty script by Meilhac
and Halévy was completely in tune with the spirit of the time. The gods of
Olympus spoke in the current idiom, like people of good society.

The essential character of that society was sceptical, lacking in respect. Respect
what? Virtue? Hardly a trace was left. Pleasure, egotism, high living went hand
in hand with speculation and the pursuit of wealth. Respect those who were
responsible for the country's destiny? But they were all adventurers. There was
nothing left to believe in. One made jokes, invented witticisms, went out to
supper. The most important thing was to laugh. Life itself was a joke. It was the
tone of the age and *La Belle Hélène* expressed it perfectly. . . . It offered to a
frivolous society a parody of itself.[1]

Hortense herself, say the authors of her life:

was no longer merely the spirit of operetta, but the incarnation of the epoch. She
was the incarnation of its luxury, its frivolity, its irreverence, its scepticism.
In a time when all ideals were laughed at, the little feet of Hortense trod under
foot the two things which, officially at least, were still respected: the Government
and the Army. . . . Without knowing it, she, who represented in herself the whole
fête impériale gave the first kick to the Empire.

All the sovereigns and princes who had come to Paris for the Exhibition
of 1867, crowded into her dressing-room; the Czar Alexander II, the
Grand Duke Constantine, the old King of Bavaria, the King of Portugal,
the King of the Belgians, the Prince of Wales. The King of Egypt became,
for a time, her lover. Another visitor to her lodge was a stout silent Prussian
whose name was – Bismarck. A strange confrontation of the woman who
was the very incarnation of the Second Empire and the man who was to
dig its grave.

Perhaps the most astonishing of all the *grandes cocottes* of the Second
Empire was la Païva. She was a Russian Jewess, married to a tailor in
Moscow, but she left husband and child to come to Paris (it would be
interesting to know how she raised the fare). There she became the mistress
of the composer Herz but he abandoned her in 1848 and went to America.
Thérèse Lachmann, for such was her name, then aged twenty-two, with a
rather coarse face but the figure of the Venus de Milo, was left penniless.
Ill and almost destitute she sent a note to Théophile Gautier and '*le bon
Théo*' went to see her in a poor hotel in a side-street off the Champs-
Elysées. He told the Goncourts that he had found her in bed in an almost

1 M.R. and T. Casevitz, *Hortense Schneider*, 1930.

empty room; but her eyes 'shone with a conquering flame', and she uttered the astonishing prophecy: 'One day, if I live, I shall have, a few yards from here, the most beautiful house in Paris.'

Perhaps it was Gautier who put her in touch with what was called, in the slang of the period, an 'ogress'. An 'ogress' was a woman who was willing to provide a promising recruit to the world of *galanterie* with dresses, jewellery, money and somewhere to live in return for a share of the hypothetical profits. Thus fitted out, and with a little bottle of chloroform in case of failure, she went to London and appeared in a box at Covent Garden. Alain Decaux describes her triumph: 'She had entered the theatre alone; she left it on the arm of Lord Stanley.'

Back in Paris, considerably enriched, she accepted a whole series of aristocratic lovers. The Portuguese Marquis de Païva, repulsed by her, was so much in love that he proposed marriage. She accepted, spent the wedding night in his arms and then said to him: 'Our bargain is complete. I have your title; you have had your night of love. I am a harlot and intend to remain a harlot. Go back to Portugal. I shall stay in Paris.' There was a judicial separation. Later Païva, ruined by gambling and women, blew his brains out. La Païva pursued her conquering career.

Her biggest prize was the Comte (later Prince) de Donnersmarck. This Silesian nobleman was extremely rich and la Païva played her usual game of refusing his advances until he had agreed to divide his fortune with her. Her share enabled her to buy a plot of land in the Champs Elysées and to build there at a cost of three million francs a house which became the wonder of Paris. The crimson damask on the walls of the salon was specially woven in Lyon and cost 800,000 francs. The staircase was carved in oynx and Paul Baudry painted the ceilings. The house still exists, in a Champs Elysées completely transformed by modern developments, next door to the Marignan cinema.

La Païva must have been an extremely intelligent woman for her salon attracted not only the aristocratic spendthrifts, but such men as Delacroix, Sainte-Beuve, Gautier, Taine, Flaubert and the brothers Goncourt. Only the Princesse Mathilde could boast a comparable constellation·of talent. And, not satisfied with this, la Païva played at politics. Gambetta was seen at her house and, incredible as it may seem, it was seriously proposed that Bismarck should meet him there. This, of course, was after the Franco–Prussian War.

By this time she had begun to be regarded with suspicion by the French authorities. Perhaps she had been a Prussian spy all along. It was noticed that when the victorious Prussians marched through Paris after the capitulation all the windows in the Champs Elysées had been closed, except hers. She decided to leave France and to settle at Neudeck where a palace was constructed for her by the still amorous Donnersmarck. She carried off the splendid necklace worn by Eugénie on state occasions. She had bought it after the fall of the Empire. There could be no more striking example of the triumph of the *grande cocotte*.

In England the *grande cocotte* never enjoyed quite so spectacular a reign; indeed many of the leading aspirants were compelled to cross the Channel to find full scope for their talents. Nonetheless, even in Puritan England it was impossible not to be aware of their existence and all men-about-town knew perfectly well how to get in touch with them.

One way in which a pretty girl could launch herself on a career of *galanterie* was to appear at one of the recognized *maisons de rendez-vous*, where all the proprieties were observed, but where all the women were on the look-out for rich admirers. Mayhew's account of the career of one such woman may perhaps be taken as typical.

A woman who called herself Lady— met her admirer at a house in Bolton Row that she was in the habit of frequenting. At first sight Lord— became enamoured and proposed *sur le champ*, after a little preliminary conversation, that she should live with him. The proposal with equal rapidity and eagerness was accepted, and without further deliberation his Lordship took a house for her in one of the terraces overlooking the Regent's Park, allowed her four thousand a year, and came as frequently as he could, to pass his time in her society. She immediately set up a carriage and stud, took a box at the opera on the pit tier and lived as she very well could, in excellent style. The munificence of her friend did not decrease by the lapse of time. She frequently received presents of jewellery from him and his marks of attention were constant as they were various. The continual contemplation of her charms instead of producing satiety added fuel to the fire, and he was never happy when out of her sight. This continued until one day he met a young man in her *loge* at the opera whom she introduced as her cousin. This incident aroused his suspicion, and he determined to watch her more closely. She was surrounded by spies and in reality did not possess one confidential attendant, for they were all bribed to betray her. For a time, more by accident than by precaution or care on her part, she succeeded in eluding their vigilance, but at last the catastrophe happened; she was surprised with her paramour in a position that placed doubt out of the question, and the next day his Lordship, with a few sarcastic remarks, gave her her *congé* and five hundred pounds.

Five hundred pounds in the middle fifties was no mean sum and, as Mayhew remarked, such women did not remain long, in the majority of cases, without finding another protector.

Another woman interviewed by Mayhew confessed that she had no objection to the life she was living and that she had all she wanted. The daughter of a shop keeper in Yarmouth she had been seduced at nineteen and set up in London. She had had four protectors in as many years and when Mayhew asked her what she thought would ultimately become of her

E

she answered: 'What an absurd question, I could marry tomorrow if I liked.'

During the London Season one of the main social occasions was the daily drive, or ride, in the Park. The nobility paraded in their coaches with bewigged and three-corner hatted coachmen and two liveried footmen behind. These footmen powdered their hair and wore a *tricorne* or a top hat. Fashionable ladies drove in the open Victoria, saucer shaped in order to give room for their spreading skirts. Some dashing young men drove a phaeton with a small page perched precariously on the back seat. The page wore a cockaded top hat and he was called a 'tiger' because of his waistcoat of black and yellow stripes. But there were many, both men and women, on horseback. Their friends and acquaintances walked on the wide gravel paths along Rotten Row or lounged against the railings which were only swept away during the Second World War. The whole affair was a pageant of the rich and well connected and, although similar to the parades in Paris and Vienna, earned the admiration of most foreigners for the elegance of the riders and the splendour of the equipages.

In the late fifties a new element entered into this parade of the *haut ton*. 'Into this glittering pageant,' says Cyril Pearl aptly enough, 'the fashionable whores of the sixties boldly insinuated themselves and very soon, by their dashing appearance, dominated it.'[1] And he digs out from the forgotten works of that lively journalist George Augustus Sala an ecstatic passage:

> The Amazons! The Lady Cavaliers! The Horse Women! Can any scene in the world equal Rotten Row at four in the afternoon and at the full tide of the season? Watch the sylphides as they fly or float past in their ravishing riding habits and intoxicatingly delightful hats; some with the orthodox cylindrical beaver, with the flowing veil; others with rogish little wide-awake, or partly cocked cavalier's hats and green plumes. And as the joyous cavalcade streams past . . . from time to time the naughty wind will flutter the skirt of a habit, and display a tiny, conquettish, brilliant little boot, with a military heel, and tightly strapped over it the Amazonian riding trousers. . . . You may chance to have with you a grim town Diogenes . . . who pointing with the finger of a hard buckskinned glove towards the *ecuyères* will say: 'Those are not all Countesses or Earl's daughters, my son. She on the bay yonder is Lais. Yonder goes Aspasia, with Jack Alcibiades on his black mare Tymon; see, they have stopped at the end of the ride to talk to Phryne in her brougham. Some of these dashing delightful creatures have covered themselves with shame, and their mothers with grief, and have brought their fathers grey hair with sorrow to the grave.'

What shocked old-fashioned people was that the aristocratic young men who rode in the Row or who lounged on the side-walk had no hesitation in greeting and speaking to these 'creatures'. They seemed indeed to be

1 C. Pearl, *The Girl with the Swansdown Seat*, 1955.

on the best of terms, as well they might be for the splendid horses and carriages and even the clothes on the fair lady's back had undoubtedly been paid for by one or other of their number. It was indeed a feather in the cap of a man-about-town to be known as the protector of one of these ladies. And the more money he was thought to spend upon her the higher his prestige rose, especially if the lady in question was a famous figure in the world of demi-monde.

Such women were known as 'pretty horse-breakers', from their skill in controlling the equine as well as the human beast, and the most notorious was the woman known as 'Skittles'. The best account of her impact on society is contained in a letter to *The Times* signed 'H' but actually written by a genial and gigantic man-about-town named James Matthew Higgins. Higgins calls her 'Anonyma' but everybody knew who she was. Those were the days when *The Times* gave ample space to its correspondents and Higgins's contribution is more like an article than a letter:

Sir – Early in the season of 1861 a young lady whom I must call Anonyma, for I have never been able to learn her name, made her appearance in Hyde Park. She was a charming creature, beautifully dressed, and she drove with great spirit two of the handsomest brown ponies eye ever beheld. Nobody in society had ever seen her before; nobody in society knew her name, or to whom she belonged, but there she was, prettier, better dressed, and sitting more gracefully in her carriage than any of the fine ladies who envied her her looks, her skill, or her equipage.

A good many young gentlemen seemed to be acquainted with her, but their recognition was generally limited to a respectful bow as she passed by, or to a few friendly words slyly interchanged on the step of her pony carriage when she drew up in some remote corner of the park. Anonyma seemed at first to be rather a shy damsel. She's somewhat bolder now. Last year she avoided crowds and effected unfrequented roads, where she could more freely exhibit her pony's marvellous action and talk to her male acquaintances with becoming privacy. When all the fashionable world was sauntering on foot, on horse back, and in carriages, along the Ladies' Mile by the side of the Serpentine Anonyma would take herself to the deserted thoroughfare leading from Apsley House to Kensington.

But as the fame of her beauty and her equipage spread, this privacy became impossible to her. The fashionable world eagerly migrated in search of her from the Ladies' Mile to Kensington Road. The highest ladies in the land enlisted themselves as her disciples. Driving became the rage. Three, four, five, six hundred guineas were given for a pair of ponies on the condition that they should be as handsome as Anonyma's, that they should show as much breeding as Anonyma's, that they should step as high as Anonyma's. If she wore a pork pie hat, they wore pork pie hats; if her paletot was made by Poole their paletots were made by Poole. If she reverted to more feminine attire, they reverted to it also. Where she drove they followed; and I must confess that, as yet, Anonyma has fairly distanced her fair competitors. They can none of them sit, dress, drive or look as well as she does; nor can they procure for money such ponies as Anonyma contrives to get – for love. But the result of all this pretty play poses a great public nuisance, and it's on that account, and not at all on account of my admiration for Anonyma and her stepping ponies that I now address you.

I have said that up to the beginning of last year the fashionable world chiefly affected the Ladies' Mile in the Park, and that the thoroughfare from Apsley House to Kensington was comparatively unfrequented save by Anonyma. But this year, when that road is more specially required to be kept open for the convenience of visitors to the exhibition, it is daily chocked with fashionable carriages – from five to seven – all on account of Anonyma. Chairs are placed along it on either side; the best *partis* that England knows, the toadies who cling to them, the snobs who copy them – all sit there watching for Anonyma. Expectation is raised to its highest pitch, a handsome woman drives rapidly by in a carriage drawn by thoroughbred ponies of surpassing shape and action, the driver is attired in the pork pie hat and the Poole paletot introduced by Anonyma, but alas! she causes no effect at all, for she is not Anonyma; she is only the Duchess of A—, the Marchioness of B—, the Countess of C—, or some other of Anonyma's eager imitators. The crowd disappointed reseat themselves and wait. At last their patience is rewarded. Anonyma and her ponies appear and they are satisfied. She threads her way dextrously, with an unconscious air, through the throng; commented upon by hundreds who admire and hundreds who envy her. She pulls up her ponies to speak to an acquaintance, and her carriage is instantly surrounded by a multitude; she turns and drives back again towards Apsley House, and then away into the unknown world, nobody knows whither. Meanwhile thousands returning from the exhibition are intolerably delayed by the crowd collected to gaze upon this pretty creature, and her pretty ponies, and the efforts of Sir Richard Nayne and his pleas to keep the thoroughfare open are utterly frustrated.

Could not you, sir, whose business it is to know everything and everybody, and who possibly, therefore, may know Anonyma herself, prevail on her to drive in some other portion of the Park as long as the exhibition lasts? If she will but consent to do this, the fashionable world will certainly follow her, and the road to the exhibition will be set free for the use of the public. I am, sir, your obedient servant, H.

It must have been entirely for his own amusement that Higgins took the trouble to write this letter to *The Times*, for one can hardly believe that he was really concerned with the question of traffic congestion in the Park. In any event the letter made the lady famous. Those who did not know already began eagerly to enquire who Anonyma might be. Letters were even received from abroad, as for example from Edward Holroyd in Melbourne, and his friend Sir William Hardman undertook to enlighten him:

Anonyma is 'Skittles', or according to the name on her card Miss Walters of equestrienne and pony driving celebrity. 'Anonyma' is the name given to her by *The Times*: 'Skittles' was bestowed upon her . . . as follows. The fair Walters was in liquor as was her habit, and being chaffed by sundry guardsmen of the baser sort she informed them in drunken but flowing period, not unmixed with bad language, that 'if they didn't hold their bloody row, she'd knock them down like a row of bloody skittles!' Thence forth was she known as 'Skittles'. A whore, sir, much sought after by fast young swells.

Certainly the repercussions of her fame were astonishing. Alfred Austin, the future Poet Laureate, published a pastiche of Pope, *The Season*, in which she figures.

> . . . spurning frown and foe,
> With slackened rein swift Skittles rules the Row,
> Though scowling Matrons stamping steeds restrain,
> She flaunts Propriety with flapping mane.

'Skittles' was 'kept' by Lord Hartington and so far from concealing the liaison he proclaimed it to the world by taking her to the Derby and being seen everywhere in her company. He set her up in a Mayfair mansion and gave her an allowance of £2,000 a year.

Even better provided for was Laura Bell, the daughter of a bailiff on the Irish estates of Lord Hertford. Leaving home, she spent a few months as a shopgirl in Belfast, then moved to London and got a job at Jay's Mourning Establishment in Regent Circus (as Oxford Circus was then called). Here she attracted the attention of the Nepalese Envoy, HRH Prince Jung Bahadur, and before she had finished had mulcted him of the prodigious sum of £250,000. Strange to relate, the Foreign Office, anxious to preserve British–Nepalese relations on an amicable basis, refunded this sum to the Prince.

An equally famous figure in this half-world was Agnes Willoughby. Her real name was Rogers and she claimed to be a clergyman's daughter – but that was almost common form. She was already well launched in the career of gallantry, was often seen in Rotten Row and was living in an elegant house in Blenheim Place, St John's Wood, with an income of two thousand a year provided by a man called Roberts, when at Ascot she was introduced to William Frederick Windham. R. W. Ketton-Cremer in his *Felbrigg, The Story of a House*, says, however: 'She lived in a handsome house in Piccadilly, which was maintained by a man named Roberts . . . although she had long been upon affectionate terms with Roberts, Agnes was at this time kept by another man, from whom she received a generous allowance.' Windham, known as 'Mad Windham' was an extraordinary character. He lived a dissipated life and was already well known to the brothel keepers of the Haymarket and its district. One of his oddities was to pretend to be a policeman and threaten to have harlots locked up. The police themselves seem to have regarded his activities with tolerant amusement. He was a friend of Roberts who was of the type of raffish man-about-town. He had a house in Piccadilly and kept his carriage but part of his income of five thousand a year was known to be derived from a string of brothels in Shepherd Street.

Windham was struck not only by the beauty of Agnes Willoughby (contemporary photographs show her to have been a good looking girl) but by her refinement; she was certainly very different from the prostitutes he had been accustomed to jostle in the West End. There can be little doubt that Agnes Willoughby was a designing wench and that both she and Roberts thought that they were on a good thing in enticing Windham into their toils. Windham was not only gullible, he was rich, at least potentially, although he had at the moment little ready cash as he had not yet come of age and the family estate was much encumbered. It is thought that Roberts, who was a timber merchant as well as a brothel keeper, had his eye on the woods at Felbrigg of which Windham would be able to dispose as soon as he came of age. Meanwhile Agnes secured a marriage settlement (for Windham was only too eager to marry her) of eight hundred pounds a year for life, to be increased to fifteen hundred when her husband should come into his settled estate. She also obtained from the young man jewellery to the value of fourteen thousand pounds, no doubt on credit.

Windham's family, especially his uncle, General Windham tried to intervene but their efforts were in vain and the marriage duly took place on the 30 August 1861. The honeymoon was spent in Paris and when it was over Windham took his bride to Felbrigg. He was still so besotted with her charm that as Mr Ketton-Cremer tells us:

According to the guard on the Norwich train, Agnes and Roberts placed a large dressing case in the middle of the carriage and covered it with cushions so as to form a bed. They pulled down the blinds, and Windham paid the guard to lock the door of the carriage. Then he spent the journey enjoyably between the guards van and the engine drivers cab. In this fashion the Squire of Felbrigg escorted his bride to his ancestral home.

General Windham now petitioned the Lords Justices for the holding of a commission *De Lunatico Inquirendo*, that is he tried to get his nephew certified as insane. Learned (and extremely expensive), counsel were briefed on both sides and Windham's eccentricities were gone into in the most extraordinary detail. One of the facts alleged was that he was in the habit of eating seventeen poached eggs for breakfast. This must have been the cheapest of his self-indulgences.

Not all the ladies who created a sensation by their beauty, or their horsemanship, or both, were *grandes cocottes* in the technical sense. In what category, for example, are we to place Adah Isaacs Menken? At a pinch she might be linked with Mrs Bloomer as a pioneer of Women's Rights, and certainly her appearance in England caused as much excitement.

One cannot say that the British were not given fair warning for when, after a spectacular career in America she decided to conquer Europe, her arrival in England in the summer of 1864 was preceded by a puff in an American newspaper: 'Miss Adah Isaacs Menken, who is leaving our shores, will astonish John Bull and Co. in the country where Good Queen Vic is at the head of affairs. The lovely Menken will doubtless be the cause of many duels among her masculine admirers in the British metropolis. . . .'

Her terms were too high for Drury Lane and she was at first turned down by Astley's, but one interview with the manager of the latter establishment was sufficient to make him change his mind in spite of the stiffness of her demands. A contemporary newspaper paragraph tells us that: 'The Management of the Theatre Royal, Astley's have had to guarantee Miss Menken one half of the nightly receipts during the run of *Mazeppa*, together with the cost of her grooms and equestrian directors; to place a stage box and well appointed dressing-room at her disposal; to engage a full company to support her; and to mount the piece with a perfection of detail worthy of the theatre and the artiste.'

The manager of Astley's was a certain Edward Tyrell Smith who had been in his time a publican, a policeman, an editor of a newspaper, the proprietor of a night house, an unsuccessful candidate for Parliament and finally a theatrical manager. He was one of the pioneers of theatrical publicity, a game at which the lady herself was no amateur. She made it her business to appear in public in as conspicuous a manner as possible and he saw to it that her doings were duly recorded in the press: 'Every fine afternoon she appears among the aristocracy in Hyde Park, either mounted on her famous black mare and escorted by a groom, or else driving in an open carriage, with a liveried coachman and footman complete. Her equipage is much admired by the fashionables.' Another reporter declares that: 'the public watch her day after day, driving up the Mall with her team of ponies. Duchesses, even if they are young and beautiful, pass unnoticed when La Belle Menken is in sight. Apparently impassive, and casting glances at no one, except the little "tiger" behind her, she sweeps along the Mall, the "observed of all observers".'

The astute Mr Smith was well aware that there was a certain piquancy in the show which she was proposing to put on for 'instead of the hero being impersonated in the customary fashion by an actor, he has secured a beautiful young woman from America, Miss Adah Isaacs Menken, to embody the role of *Mazeppa*. A skilful and daring equestrienne, she does all the perilous runs without a "double" and exhibits prodigious pluck and energy in the management of her mettlesone steed.'

It is an amusing example of the Victorian attitude that although the piece was 'adapted from Lord Byron's famous poem' it was to have no trace of 'the mass of obscenity and profaneness which his Lordship has bequeathed to posterity [and which] has now become a question between himself and his Creator'. The public was assured that the entertainment 'while holding the attention of all, would not bring a blush to the cheek of modesty'.

In spite of these protestations the posters with which London was plastered and which depicted the semi-nude figure of the daring equestrienne bound to the back of a galloping horse were denounced as a public scandal. This of course had the desired result and the opening night of 'Lord Byron's Celebrated Drama of *Mazeppa*, with a Grand Stud of Forty Horses, Two Hundred Soldiers, and a Superb Ballet' was a triumphant success.

The scantiness of the lady's costume was in the sixties considered startling. One of the newspapers described her appearance as that of 'Lady Godiva in a Shift'. The white tunic she wore was certainly rather short but she did wear white or pink tights underneath: it was the suggestion of nudity rather than nudity itself. The theatrical journal *The Orchestra* remarked:

Miss Adah Isaacs is less indelicate than her picture, though the enjoyment of her audience may not be increased by the circumstance. The reservation in favour of some little decency is due perhaps to the fear of the Lord Chamberlain, or to the conscience of Mr E. T. Smith . . . the applauding shouts that arise from an overcrowded house at every bold movement of the semi-nude actress prove that an insensitive public could stand a good deal more if it were offered them. That ladies attend the performance none can deny. We wonder if a lady – that is, a lady in the true acceptance – would go a second time ? . . . The attraction which draws full houses to Astley's lies undoubtedly in its impurity. People expect the voluptuous pictures scattered about London . . . to be realised by the American actress; and they go there for that purpose. . . . We ourselves should hesitate about taking a sister just now to Astley's. No, in the name of purity, let us have no more 'classical' importations from America or elsewhere.

The American Press in general did not subscribe to this Pecksniffian attitude; rather did it rejoice in the success of this Daughter of America:

The Menken waxeth fat in the land of Dukes and Duchesses; yes, she even basketh in the sunshine of Royalty. Astley's, where Menken and *Mazeppa* hold full sway, is still the great centre of attraction for sightseers, old and young, their Royal Nibs, and others of lesser degree. Among the celebrities who attended her performances up to the last advices were His Royal Highness the Duke of Cambridge, with the Duchess [sic] of Sefton; His Grace the Duke of Hamilton; and Lord and Lady Lincoln. The three latter visited the fair Mazeppa in her dressing-room after the first act. As the Duke of Cambridge always precedes the Prince of Wales in his Patronage of public amusements, it is expected that the

Monde and Demi-Monde

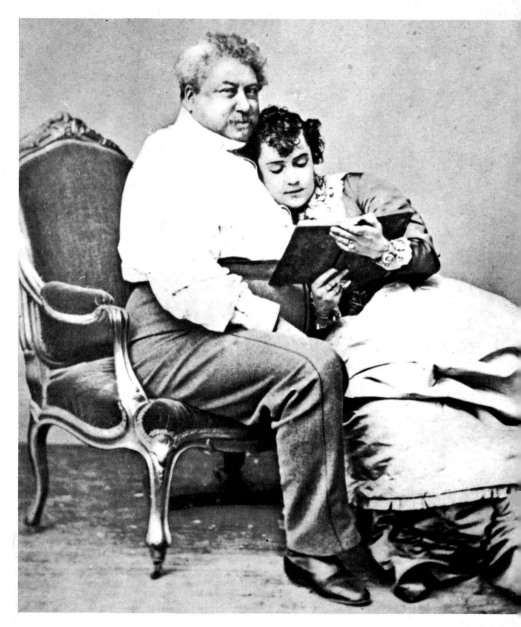

Alexandre Dumas *père* with Adah Isaacs Menken

Fancy portrait (photograph) of the
Comtesse de Castiglione, mistress
of Napoleon III

Title-page of the *Mémoires de
Marguerite Bellanger* (1900)

Empress Eugénie by François Xavier Winterhalter

Overleaf: The Imperial Court at Fontainebleau in 1860; the Emperor and
the Prince Imperial are in the small boat

Jean Baptiste Carpeaux'
La Danse, a sculpture group
outside the Paris *Opéra*,
defaced with ink (photo-
graph taken just after the
outrage)

Edmond Morin, *An
Actress's Dressing-Room*
(1882)

Edouard Manet, *Nana* (the heroine of Zola's novel)

Victor Hugo on the Rocher des Proverits, St Helier, Jersey (1853)

Left: The fashionable photographer Félix Nadar in a (studio) balloon

French riverside party, 1850

Prince and Princess will attend Astley's on their return to England, when Manager Smith will have the box fitted up with special grandeur to receive them. A copy of the Press notices of Miss Menken is to be printed on white satin and bound in purple velvet, and the Duke of Hamilton has promised to submit this to the Royalties.

All this bears the stamp of Smith's calculated publicity. It is unlikely that the Princess of Wales ever saw *Mazeppa*, but the Prince may quite easily have done so; in fact, given his temperament, he must have found the temptation hard to resist. We know that Dickens saw the performance (he failed to get in at the first attempt and was given a box by the lady herself) and visited her afterwards in her dressing-room.

These London triumphs were repeated in Paris where she appeared at the Gaieté in a piece entitled *Les Pirates De La Savane*. The distinguished theatrical critic Jules Clarétie doubted 'if anybody but Talma could have received a more rapturous ovation than the intrepid Miss Menken. Her courage will do much to make the piece a success, but her beauty will do more.' And her success was gained, as Horace Wyndham points out, in the face of stiff competition in the spring of 1867; Marie Rose was at the Opéra-Comique; a young beginner, Sarah Bernhardt, was at the Odéon; Hortense Schneider, in *La Belle Hélene*, was at the Variétés; and . . . Cora Pearl, in diamonds (and very little else) was exhibiting herself at the Bouffes-Parisiens. But all Paris flocked to see Adah Isaacs Menken and the hundredth performance was attended by Napoleon III and the Prince Imperial, the King of the Hellenes, Prince Oscar of Sweden, and the Duke of Edinburgh. The Empress Eugénie was not present. The occasion was duly recorded in the *Court Circular* but the Duke of Edinburgh's name was omitted, not, it is suggested, because the performance might be considered scandalous in itself, but because it took place on Sunday.

Adah Isaacs Menken however was not satisfied with these theatrical and social triumphs. Having written 'poems' she considered herself as a Woman of Letters and ardently desired to make the acquaintance of literary men. She had a particular admiration for Alexandre Dumas, and had even boasted before she went to Paris that he would be her lover. Her first sight of him in the *coulisses* of the Gaieté was a disappointment. 'Who is that fat fellow with the woolly hair?' she asked. Perhaps no one had told her that the great Dumas had negro blood. However she got in touch with him, bowled him over and in less than a fortnight had been installed by him in a luxurious apartment. There was even a rumour that 'Dumas is about to marry the young person at the Gaieté'.

In the shops which specialized in such wares large numbers of photographs were sold showing the ageing author and the young equestrienne in compromising poses and although most of these are admitted to have been fakes with the heads of Dumas and Adah Isaacs Menken superimposed on

73

the bodies of other people, genuine photographs of the two together did exist showing the couple in amorous embraces. Dumas became involved in a law suit to prevent their publication, and it is sufficient comment on their nature that Dumas in his evidence was compelled to distinguish between those with *caleçons* and those without.

In her romantic fashion Adah Isaacs Menken was in love with the quite elderly gentleman Dumas had now become. In a letter from Vienna (where she repeated her success in London and Paris) she sent a friend the autographed portrait of the great novelist with the words 'valued for his sake, as well as for the sake of the poor girl he honours with his love! Oh! How I wish you could know him! You could understand his great soul so well – the King of Romance, the Child of Gentleness and Love.'

She was however to be separated from Dumas for some time because her theatrical engagements took her once more to London in the summer of 1867. Here she repeated her triumphs and, in the Westminster Palace Hotel where she had a luxurious suite, she held what was in effect a literary salon. Here she received Charles Dickens, Charles Reade, Dante Gabriel Rossetti, Frederick Sandys and Algernon Charles Swinburne. Strangely enough it was upon Swinburne that she fastened her attention. Their relationship has some of the elements of farce as Swinburne was very far from having the temperament and physique of the large and potent Dumas. He was a very little man with a large disproportioned head surrounded by an aureole of red hair. Sir Edmund Gosse declares, in the article he wrote on Swinburne for the Dictionary of National Biography, that 'Swinburne now became intimate with Adah Isaacs Menken', but the word intimate has several meanings and doubts have been thrown on the little poet's capacity. It is said that Rossetti challenged the lady to sleep with Swinburne and she claimed to have done so. As is now well known Swinburne was a masochist, and masochists have always had a particular penchant for ladies who wear riding boots. It is quite easy to imagine Adah Isaacs Menken in the role of the *femme dompteuse*. She tried to interest him in her poetry and he is said to have replied: 'My darling, a woman with such beautiful legs as yours should not bother her head about poetry.' Like Dumas he consented to be photographed with her but there is no question here of *caleçons* or no *caleçons*. Swinburne is shown in a frock coat and the lady in a crinoline.

Her end was sad. She had sustained an internal injury during one of her performances which had resulted in an abscess in the region of the ribs. The doctors in Paris, to which city she had now returned, treated her for rheumatism. She died on 10 August 1868 and, gallant to the end, her last words were taken from a poem by Swinburne. They are repeated on her tomb in the cemetery of Montparnasse. Swinburne at least grieved for her, saying in a letter to his friend George Powell: 'It was a great shock to me, and a real grief. I was ill for some days. She was most lovable, as a friend as well as a mistress.'

Although she belonged to a very different world, an almost equally famous *equestrienne* was Lady Cardigan whose memoirs, when they finally appeared, revived memories of a life passed in defiance of convention. Born in 1824, she was the daughter of Spencer Horsey de Horsey (the names of real people are sometimes as appropriate as those invented by Dickens).

Her parents moved in the best circles, but when still a girl, she had caused comment by riding in the Park without a groom, for this was a gross violation of contemporary propriety. She was certainly very far from being the conventional Victorian miss. Indeed her attitude to life was one which the modern reader would think more appropriate to the cynical eighteenth century than to the middle of the nineteenth. Her account of a discovery she made about her own father throws such a flood of light on the state of affairs in good society that it is worth quoting in full:

One of my most amusing experiences about this time originated in my wish to see a rather *risqué* play at the Princess's Theatre.

'Papa,' said I one morning at breakfast, 'I wish you would take me to the Princess's Theatre; every one's talking about the play. Do let us go this evening.'

'Quite impossible,' answered Papa, with great decision. 'Quite impossible, Adeline – I am dining tonight with General Cavendish at the Club, a long-standing engagement, and,' he continued, in a tone of conscious virtue, 'even if I were disengaged, I should not think of taking my daughter to see such a play; nothing, my dear, is so degrading as a public display of lax morals, and it is the duty of every self-respecting person to discountenance such a performance. Let me hear no more about it,' and he opened *The Times* with an air of finality.

The evergreen fabrication of 'going to the Club', the most obvious and clumsy of lies invented by man to deceive woman, was as flourishing then as it is today. Perhaps it was more successful, as the telephone was not invented. I quite believed papa's statement, but I was deceived, as subsequent events showed.

I was very much annoyed. All the morning I brooded over papa's refusal, and then I suddenly made up my mind that I *would* go to the play in spite of him.

I rang for my maid. 'Parker,' I said, 'go at once to the Princess's Theatre and bespeak a box for me, and be ready to come with me tonight.'

'Alone, miss?' ventured Parker.

'Yes, alone, now don't waste a moment'; and no sooner had she set off than I wrote and despatched a letter to Lord Cardigan, who was a friend of papa, and asked him to come to my box at the Princess's that evening.

Parker and I arrived early and I settled down to enjoy myself. The overture commenced, and I was just about to inspect the audience when Lord Cardigan came into the box; he was rather agitated. 'Miss de Horsey,' he said, without any preliminaries, 'you must leave the theatre at once.'

'I'll do no such thing,' I said angrily. 'What on earth is the matter?'

'Well,' reluctantly answered Cardigan – 'Well, Miss de Horsey, your father and

General Cavendish are in the box opposite – with' (he looked at me apologetic-
ally) – 'with their mistresses! It will never do for you to be seen. Do, I implore
you, permit me to escort you home before the performance begins.'

I was seized with an uncontrollable desire to laugh. So this was the long-
standing engagement, *this* papa's parade of morality. I peeped out from the
curtains of the box – it was quite true; directly opposite to me there sat papa and
the General, with two very pretty women I did not remember seeing before.

'I *shall* see the play,' I said to Lord Cardigan, 'and you'll put me in a cab
before it is over; I shall be home before papa returns from – the Club,' and I
laughed again at the idea.[1]

In the event she was *not* home before her father for the driver of the
hackney-carriage was drunk and carried her to Islington. It was midnight
before she arrived back at her father's house at 8 Upper Grosvenor Street.
And the door was opened – by papa! However, Miss de Horsey was equal
to the occasion:

'Adeline,' said papa in an awful voice, 'explain yourself. Where have you been?
Is this an hour for a young lady to be out of doors? How dare you conduct
yourself in this manner?'

'I've been to the Princess's Theatre, papa,' I said demurely (he started); 'and
I saw you and General Cavendish there; I thought you were dining at the
Club . . . and I saw. . . .'

'Go to bed at once, Adeline,' interrupted papa, looking very sheepish, 'we'll
talk about your behaviour later.'

But he never mentioned the subject to me again!

Miss Horsey de Horsey seemed to take pleasure in flouting the conventions. Not content with riding in the Park without a groom she shortly
began to be seen in Rotten Row with Lord Cardigan, a married man. This
flirtation with the Hero of Balaclava completed the ruin of her reputation
and her subsequent marriage to him did little or nothing to clear it. When
the pair moved into the splendid Cardigan residence, Deene Park, the
'County' refused to call, and when, as Ralph Nevill tells us 'invitations were
issued for a great ball in the newly built hall, she and Lord Cardigan found
themselves alone with the band, for not a soul came! Only rather fast
bachelors from town came to the shooting parties at Deene, which was not
considered a respectable place for ladies to go to.'[2]

They missed quite a lot for the Cardigans lived on the grandest scale.
When the bridal pair arrived at Deene they were received by six hundred
tenants on horseback escorting the carriage from the station to the house;
and when the lady took her new husband to another of her estates, Kirk-
stall Abbey, she was received with a salute of fifteen guns and entertained

1 Countess of Cardigan and Lancastre, *My Recollections*, 1909.
2 R. Nevill, *The World of Fashion*, 1923.

three hundred of her Yorkshire tenantry to dinner. Even after her husband's death the social boycott continued, although to the end of her life, the imperturbable Lady Cardigan continued to hunt, to go to the races and to be seen at Cowes.

In her old age she had her revenge by publishing her memoirs which threw a lurid light on the behaviour of aristocratic Society in the Victorian era. Writing in 1909 she had no hesitation in giving the names of the men concerned and although she designates the ladies by means of an initial letter and a dash, it was by no means difficult to penetrate the transparent disguise. Everybody knew, for example, that 'Mrs D— W—' was Mrs Dudley Ward:

The modern woman, who has her own particular club, may be interested in hearing about a certain 'Parrot Club' which existed in the fifties. It had the smallest membership of any club, I should imagine, and its short history was in some ways an amazing one.

Three ladies – Mrs D— W—, Lady P— and Lady K—, had become rather tired of their husbands, and transferred their affections to three charming lovers, Lord Strathmore, Captain Vivian, and another gentleman whose name I forget.

As married lovers' meetings generally lead to the Divorce Court, one of the sextette hit upon the idea of renting a furnished house which would be a safe place for assignations. A house in Seymour Street, Portman Square, was therefore taken, and it was afterwards, for some unknown reason, called 'The Parrot Club'.

The arrangement answered splendidly for a time, as the ladies were all friends and their husbands never suspected them. Hence, each cheerfully believed that his wife's long absences from home were accounted for by shopping or theatre parties with one or other of her two friends.

The course of true love ran with great smoothness at Seymour Street until Lady K—, who liked variety, commenced to change her lovers with such alarming rapidity that the other two members were obliged to ask her to resign.

Captain Vivian and Lord Strathmore still enjoyed Mrs D— W—'s and Lady P—'s society, but unfortunately the unexpected happened which terminated the club's existence.

One morning Captain Vivian, who was smoking an after-breakfast cigar and possibly thinking of his next visit to the delightful 'Parrot Club', was told by his man that Mrs D— W—'s maid had called with a letter from her mistress.

'I'll see her at once,' said the Captain; the maid was shown in, and with a smile which betrayed intimate knowledge and infinite discretion, she handed him a delicate little note. Directly John Vivian broke the seal, and glanced at the contents, his face changed, and no wonder, for this is what he read:

'My dear Strathmore – Come to Seymour Street at 3, I'll be all alone.'

Now, as the name Vivian bears no resemblance to that of Strathmore, there was only one possible interpretation of the matter, and the furious lover turned to the trembling maid and said fiercely:

'Your mistress gave you *two* letters to deliver; this is Lord Strathmore's.

Where's mine?' In vain the girl protested that she had no other, but Vivian made her give up the note directed to him. He opened it and, alas for the duplicity of women, this is what it contained:

'Dear old Johnny – Don't come to Seymour Street today, because I am spending the day with my mother-in-law.'

'It is almost superfluous to add that the house in Seymour Street was soon 'To Let', and that a crestfallen lady's maid was looking for another situation.

Lady Cardigan tells another story even more revealing of aristocratic *mores*:

Constance de Burgh was one of my great friends, she was a very pretty, charming girl who married Lord Ward. . . . William Ward was a pleasant man, but he had extraordinary ideas of how to treat a wife . . . he had selected his wife partly on account of her beauty, and he treated her like some lovely slave he had bought. He had a strange, almost barbaric passion for precious stones, and he bought quantities of them and lavished them on his wife, who appeared at great entertainments literally ablaze with diamonds. What pleased Lord Ward more than anything was to make Constance put on all her jewels for his benefit when they were alone. He would admire her thus for hours, delighting in her lovely unclothed figure, and contrasting the sheen of her ropes of pearls with her delicate skin, as she sat on a black satin-covered couch. . . .

Plainly there was something of the sultan in Lord Ward's make-up but when he discovered his wife's adultery with Lord Dupplin he did not have her sewn into a sack and thrown into the Thames: he behaved as almost any mid-nineteenth century husband would have done: he turned her out of doors. The only extraordinary thing about his action was that he summoned all the servants – in the middle of the night – to witness it. The unhappy woman made her way on foot to her parents' house in Grosvenor Crescent, but they too shut the door in her face. She finally found a refuge with her singing master in Conduit Street and the next day left for Ostend. From there she went to that rendezvous of the déclassé, Bad-Ems where she shortly afterwards died in childbirth. There could be no plainer example of the 'double standard'. Men could do what they liked but for a Society woman there was only one rule: Thou shalt not be found out.

There must have been many a man of good connections whose wife was, in Tennyson's phrase, merely 'a little dearer than his dog, a little nobler than his horse' and who had many women in his life who were dearer only in the financial sense and nobler in no sense whatever. The man of pleasure, indeed, seems to have had only two passions: women and horses, and these two passions were often, as we have seen, strangely intertwined. Certainly women and horses provided the best and quickest means of getting rid of even substantial fortunes.

Betting in the last quarter of the nineteenth century was on a scale which today (even allowing for the fall in the value of money) would seem prodigious. According to J. B. Booth ('Costs' of *The Pink 'Un*) who ought to have known, the largest sum ever won on the Derby was the £100,000 which a certain Mr Naylor 'took out of the Ring in Macaroni's day'. A Mr Merry won £60,000 on Thormanby's Derby. In the course of his long career the famous Lord Chaplin won more money on the Derby than anyone else, but he wasn't always paid. When he won £20,000 from the Marquess of Hastings he allowed the debt to stand over for years, which was just as well as the total amount lost by the Marquess on his horse *Hermit* was the fantastic sum of £104,750.

Another heavy better of the period was the Duke of Hamilton, who succeeded to the title when his more famous father fell down the stairs of a Paris restaurant and broke his neck. He (the son) was an 'eccentric personality' to put it mildly. 'He dressed, frankly, like a howling cad, and the glaring colours of his costumes emphasized the crudeness of his bright red, curly hair. His nickname was "The Butcher" – due to his fondness for butcher blue shirts and ties. In addition, he wore conspicuous coral studs, a loud shawl-pattern vest, a brown billycock hat and coloured spats. When it is added that he stood almost six feet in height and was broad in proportion – later to become prodigiously fat – you may gather that he was a conspicuous personality.'[1]

He strolled up to the well-known French bookmaker Saffery at Auteuil where his horse Janoock was running and the following dialogue ensued:

'What price mine?'

'Seven to one, your Grace.'

'Seven thousand to one, Saffery – pounds, not francs.'

'Right, your Grace!'

'Twice, Saffery.'

'Right, your Grace!'

'Three times, Saffery.'

'I'll make it 6 to 1 this time, your Grace. Shall we make it £20,000 to £3,000?'

'Right, Saffery.'

The horse won and the bookmaker duly paid out £20,000. Even if the Duke had lost it it would not have troubled him. His income was supposed to be about £500 a day!

All the aristocratic gamblers were not so fortunate. It is estimated that at the Derby of 1867 more money was won and lost than on any other occasion before or since. Mr Henry Chaplin is reputed to have won £50,000 by the victory of his horse Hermit, and the Marquess of Hastings to have lost at least £100,000. This was a kind of poetic justice for, a few years before, Hastings had eloped with Chaplin's *fiancée* Lady Florence Paget; and Hastings a year after his prodigious loss on the Turf, died suddenly at the age of twenty-six.

1 J.B.Booth.

Abington Baird was another notorious plunger of the times. He was supposed to have got through three million pounds in his short and hectic career, most of it being spent on women and horses. He is said to have settled a hundred thousand pounds on a lady of the lighter stage and strange to say he borrowed this sum from the notorious moneylender Sam Lewis, at ten per cent interest, although he had at the time three or four times that amount in ready cash. He was frequently in trouble with the Stewards of the Jockey Club and as J. B. Booth remarks, 'It is difficult to imagine a gentleman rider and owner of Baird's eccentricities being tolerated for one moment on the turf at the present day, which is in many ways purer and more wholesome than that of the eighties and nineties.' He sometimes rode in such a state of intoxication that he could hardly stay on the horse's back. He also fancied himself as an amateur boxer and he was surrounded by a gang of pugilists who took care to let him beat them. Some of them thought up the ingenious story that he had actually killed a man by the force of his blow; he was so drunk at the time that he remembered nothing of it but parted with a large sum of money to hush the matter up. Another ingenious device was to involve him in imaginary quarrels. Once on a visit to America he threw a glass of champagne in a bartender's face. The man reached for his revolver whereupon two of the gang seized him and prevented him from firing. If he had fired Baird was told he would certainly have shot him dead. Both the bartender and the men who had 'saved' Baird's life received large sums and the victim never suspected that the whole affair had been arranged beforehand.

It is small wonder that such behaviour excited the disapprobation of the Victorian middle classes who regarded themselves as the guardians of the 'Nonconformist Conscience', and their anxiety was increased by the knowledge that the Prince of Wales was himself addicted to the vice of gambling. As a matter of fact his gambling was always on a moderate scale, but he frequented race meetings and was known to 'play cards for money' in private houses.

The Tranby Croft Affair was less remarkable in itself (a banal story of cheating at cards in high places) than for the violent reaction of public and press which followed. It is as an index of the moral climate of the day that it is still interesting to us. In the autumn of 1890, Mr Arthur Wilson's house, Tranby Croft, near Hull, was filled with a house party of guests gathered together for the St Leger and among these was the Prince of Wales. On the first evening of his arrival there was a game of baccarat, the counters, of values ranging up to ten pounds, being provided by the Prince. Much play was to be made of this afterwards although, as he then reasonably explained, the fact that the highest counter was worth no more than ten pounds was in itself a kind of peak on high play. During the course of the game the son of the house thought he saw one of the guests, Sir

William Gordon-Cumming cheating. He was doing this, under cover of his hand holding the cards, by increasing or decreasing his stake after the cards had been dealt by surreptitiously pushing counters backwards or forwards over the line which separated the money stake from the money held in reserve. Sir William Gordon-Cumming was a highly respected soldier, being Lieutenant-Colonel in the Scots Guards, but another guest, a subaltern in the same regiment also saw him cheating. That evening young Mr Wilson told his mother what had happened and the next morning he also told his brother-in-law Mr Lycett Green who told his wife. The next evening these five persons watched Sir William carefully. Again they saw him cheating.

The Prince was holding the bank and knew nothing whatever of what was going on. Those who had seen the cheating were in a very difficult position but they finally decided to consult the two most important guests in the house who were Lord Coventry and General Owen Williams, the latter a close personal friend of Sir William Gordon-Cumming. These two gentlemen decided that Sir William must be faced with the accusation against him and that the Prince should be told. Faced with his accusers Sir William denied that he had cheated at all, but in the Prince's eyes the evidence of the five witnesses told heavily against him, and in the end he agreed to sign a declaration to be witnessed by the Prince and others, that he would never play cards for money again as long as he lived. He agreed to make this declaration on the understanding that if he did so the matter would never be mentioned again by any of the persons concerned.

It is perhaps inevitable that a secret shared by so many should not be kept and shortly afterwards Sir William Gordon-Cumming received an anonymous letter which showed quite clearly that someone outside the circle of Tranby Croft was aware of what had happened. His reply was to bring an action for defamatory scandal against the five persons, including his hostess who had seen his cheating. He cited the Prince as a witness. This alone was enough to make the trial a sensation for no one could remember when a member of the Royal Family had ever been placed in such a situation before. As Sir William Gordon-Cumming's Counsel, the great Sir Edward Clarke argued that if the Prince of Wales and General Owen Williams had really believed in the cheating they would have reported the matter to the Military Authorities. They had not done so but when the Prince was asked by a jury whether he believed if Sir William had cheated he felt bound to say that he accepted the word of the five witnesses. It was indeed hard to believe that they had entered into a deliberate conspiracy against a man who was the guest of two of their number and the friend of all. A verdict was given against Sir William Gordon-Cumming and he retired into obscurity, a broken man.

F

It would be difficult to better the account given by E. F. Benson of the public reaction:

Not only in England but abroad the Press teamed with it. A German comic paper produced a cartoon showing the great door to Windsor Castle surmounted by the Prince of Wales's feathers and the motto 'Ich Deal'. French papers had columns of far more acid matter, and the Prince's private game of baccarat became the business of the whole world: you would have thought that baccarat was the sin that could never find remission. It was all very unpleasant, but what really mattered was the universal disgust of the English Press. The incident was made the occasion of the most virulent attacks on the Prince; Stead, in his *Review of Reviews* applied the test of the 'Prayer Gauge'. He calculated with ruthless arithmetic how many times in the various churches of the United Kingdom prayer had been offered during the last fifty years on behalf of the Prince of Wales since the day of his birth, and how many people had sincerely said 'Amen' and drew the conclusion that the baccarat scandal had been the only answer vouchsafed from on high to these millions of petitions. If the Prince himself had been detected cheating, he could not have been more savagely sentenced. In particular all papers of a serious or a literary turn, especially Church papers and Nonconformist papers, trumpeted their horror like great moral elephants piously running amok. They told their readers that the Prince carried gambling counters with his Royal device wherever he went, that he insisted that the party should join him in high play: that his host at Tranby Croft would never allow gambling in his house, but had been obliged to yield to the Prince's wishes. In a word he was made scape-goat for all that happened and all that was invented, and was denounced as the ring-leader in that odious vice of gambling which was undermining the morals of the country. He was exposed to an unparalleled tempest of abuse, and, owing to his position could not say a single word on his own behalf. . . . Doubtless in these attacks there was much genuine indignation that the heir of the throne should be mixed up in so un-savoury an affair, but it was obvious that in these attacks there was a great deal of insincere gusto. It was not every day that a leader writer in the *Camborne Chronicle* could lecture so exalted a personage, and he felt a smug Pharisaical satisfaction in joining loudly in the booing and thanking God that he had never played baccarat himself or even whist for money. But other more responsible journals felt the same and *The Times* published a leader at the end of the trial which in conclusion, expressed regret that the Prince, as well as Sir William Gordon-Cumming, had not signed a declaration that he, too, would never play cards again.

The Tranby Croft affair was indeed public property; but there were other events in the Prince's life known only – at least in all their ramifications – to a more restricted circle. The Prince was on friendly terms with Lord Aylesford and his wife and with Lord Blandford, eldest son of the Duke of Marlborough. He was much attracted by Lady Aylesford and carried on with her a flirtation which was in all probability, completely innocent. Unfortunately, he sent her a number of letters written (in the words of the Lord Chancellor, Lord Cairns) 'in a strain of undue familiarity and containing many foolish and somewhat stupid expressions'. Early in 1876 the Prince set off on a tour to India, taking Aylesford with him, and, on 20 February, the latter received a letter from his wife announcing that she had decided to elope with Blandford who had deserted his wife for her sake.

The Marlborough family was in an uproar; and Blandford's younger brother, Lord Randolph Churchill accused the Prince of Wales of having deliberately taken Aylesford with him to India in order to get him out of the way. Sir Philip Magnus in his recent life of King Edward VII[1] has shown that this was not true; it was Lady Aylesford herself who had urged her husband to go. Her own family now urged her to abandon all idea of an elopement, since the position of a divorced woman at that time was one of social ostracism. Under pressure she agreed and, surely very foolishly from every point of view, handed over to Blandford a packet of the Prince's letters. Blandford handed them to Lord Randolph Churchill who saw in them a means of compelling Aylesford to drop divorce proceedings against his wife.

With characteristic recklessness and indiscretion Randolph Churchill boasted to his friends that he 'held the Crown of England in his pocket'; and, with something more than indiscretion he actually showed the letters to the Princess of Wales. And, in the words of Sir Philip Magnus, 'he warned the Princess that the Prince would be subpoenaed to give evidence if Aylesford sued for a divorce; and that, if published, the Prince's letters to Lady Aylesford would ensure that His Royal Highness "would never sit upon the Throne of England".'

The Prince, outraged by this behaviour, challenged Lord Randolph Churchill to a duel, to be fought with pistols in France, and this foolish move enabled Churchill to send an insolent, but unanswerable reply that such a duel was impossible and unthinkable. Fortunately Aylesford, to save the Prince from scandal, abandoned his divorce proceedings, and Lord Randolph departed to America to escape the storm of obloquy which burst on his head. It is a mark of the Prince's extraordinarily forgiving nature that he afterwards forgave Lord Randolph Churchill and admitted him once more into the circle of his friends.

But what friends! Perhaps the old Queen had been right after all to warn him against 'the fast racing set', but it was too much to expect him to show his disapproval of them by 'not asking them to dinner, nor down to Sandringham – and, above all, not going to their houses'. One's sympathies are with the Prince. His mother excluded him from all public employment. What could he do but amuse himself as best he could?

---

1 Sir Philip Magnus. *King Edward VII*, 1964.

4 Poverty and Prostitution

All foreign visitors in the middle of the nineteenth century were impressed by the wealth of London and by its bustling commercial activity. Visiting the East End docks Hippolyte Taine notes:

These docks are prodigious, overwhelming; there are six of them, each a great port and each inhabited by a population of three-masted ships. Always ships, ships and more ships, lying side by side, showing the swelling lines of their prows, like handsome fishes, in their copper sheathing. One is from Australia and displaces 2,500 tons; others are of 3,000 or more, and they come from every corner of the world, for this is the whole world's meeting place. Most of them are magnificent; standing close under the hulls they are leviathans graceful and elegant as swans. A merchant, who had come to check the arrival of spices from Java and a trans-shipment of ice from Norway, told me that about 40,000 ships enter these docks every year and that as a rule there are between five and six thousand in the docks of the river at any given moment.[1]

Visitors were also conscious of the appalling poverty in districts around these same docks through which the wealth of the world flowed. Taine was particularly horrified by Shadwell:

By the depth of its poverty and misery, as by its extent, it is proportional to London's enormous size and wealth. I have seen the lowest quarters of Marseilles, Antwerp and Paris: they come nowhere near this. Squat houses, wretched streets of brick under red roofs crossing each other in all directions and leading dismally down to the river. Beggars, thieves and prostitutes, especially the latter, swarm in Shadwell Street. The grating music from dim cellars can be heard from the street; sometimes the violinist is a negro, and through open windows one sees unmade beds and women dancing. Three times in ten minutes I saw crowds collect round doorways, attracted by fights, especially by fights between women. One of them, her face covered with blood, tears in her eyes, drunk, was trying to fly at a man, while the mob watched and laughed, and as if the uproar were a

1 Hippolyte Taine. *Notes on England*. Tr. by Edward Hyams, 1957.

84

signal, the population of neighbouring 'lanes' came pouring into the street, children in rags, paupers, street women, as if a human sewer were suddenly clearing itself.

A few of the women show vestiges of former cleanliness, or wear a new dress; but most of them are in dirty, ill-assorted rags ... I noticed numerous black eyes, bandaged noses, cut cheeks. These women gesticulate with extraordinary vehemence, but their most horrible attribute is the voice – thin, shrill, cracked, like that of a sick owl.

From the moment you emerge from the tunnel, the whole place is alive with 'street-boys', bare-footed, filthy, turning cart-wheels for a penny. They swarm on the stairs down to the Thames, more stunted, more livid and more deformed, more repulsive than the street urchins of Paris; the climate, of course, is worse, and the gin murderous. Among them, leaning against the festering rails, or crouched inert on the steps, are men in the most astonishing rags: nobody who has not seen them can conceive what a frock coat or a pair of trousers can carry in layers of filth. They doze and day-dream, their faces earthy, livid, marbled with fine red lines. It was in this quarter that families were discovered whose only bed was a heap of soot; they had been sleeping on it for some months. For the human being reduced to these conditions there is only one refuge; drunkenness.

Here and there are rubbish dumps. Women work on them, sorting the rubbish for rags, bones, etc. One of them, old and wrinkled, had a short clay pipe in her mouth; they straightened up and stared at me from the midst of their muck-heap; dull, stupid, frightening faces, of female yahoos. Perhaps a pipe and a glass of gin is the last thought left in their idiot brains. Is it possible that anything but the instincts and appetites of a savage or a beast of burden can survive in them?

It was not only in the East End that Taine saw such sights; behind some of the grandest façades of West End houses there were pockets of poverty and hideous slums. It is true that some attempt had been made to eliminate them at the beginning of our period. New Oxford Street, which was opened for carriage traffic in March 1847, had been driven through the district known as 'the rookery of St Giles', long notorious as a veritable Alsatia of thieves, prostitutes and derelict humanity, but the immediate result was to crowd these people into an even narrower space. It was estimated that three thousand persons occupied ninety-five houses in a space of ground of little over an acre in Church Lane and Carrier Street. They were still there when Taine visited London:

I recall the lanes which open off Oxford Street, stifling alleys thick with human effluvia, troops of pale children crouching on filthy staircases; the street benches at London Bridge where all night whole families huddle close, heads hanging, shaking with cold; above all I recall Haymarket and the Strand at evening, where you cannot walk a hundred yards without knocking into twenty street-walkers; some of them ask you for a glass of gin; others say 'it's for my rent, Mister'. The impression is not one of debauchery but of abject, miserable poverty. One is sickened and wounded by this deplorable procession in those monumental streets. It seemed as if I was watching a march past of dead women. Here is a festering sore, the real sore on the body of English society.

Poverty was to be seen everywhere even at the Derby where Taine, after noting the astonishing procession of cabs and coaches, each with its baskets of pies and pastries, cold meats, melons, fruit and wine, especially champagne, notes the other side of the picture:

In the face of these preparations for a good blow-out the appearance of the numerous poor is a painful sight; they try to sell you a ha'penny doll, souvenirs of the Derby, persuade you to try your luck at the Aunt Sally shies, or to have your boots shined. Almost all of them look like wretched, beaten, mangey curs, waiting to be thrown a bone but without much hope. They have walked here during the night and count for their dinner on the vast *al fresco* banquet. Many of them have lain down to sleep anywhere on the ground, among the feet of the crowd, and sleep with their faces turned to the sky, and their mouths gaping. Their faces have an expression of dull stupefaction or painful sharpness. Most of them have bare feet, all are horribly dirty, and, what is worse, ridiculous: the reason for this is that they wear gentlemen's cast-off clothing, the women old, formerly stylish dresses and little hats once worn by young girls of family. This tatterdemalion attire, which has clad four or five bodies in succession, I always find painful to see. It is degrading; by wearing it a person admits and declares himself to be one of the off-scourings of society. In France a peasant, artisan or labourer is a man who is different but not inferior. His working blouse or overall is his own, as my suit is my own; it has been worn by nobody but himself. This readiness to wear rags is more than a mere singularity; it denotes a want of proper pride; the poor, in this country, resign themselves to being other people's doormats.

Perhaps it was the children who provided the most distressing picture of poverty. When we look through the pages of *Punch* for the middle years of the nineteenth century we constantly come across a little boy with bare feet and ragged clothes. Sometimes he is a crossing sweeper, making it possible for the trailing crinolines of the day to cross the road more or less unsullied, and expecting a penny or a ha'penny as a reward for his pains. Sometimes he chases cabs in the hope of receiving a similar sum for opening the door. Sometimes he turned cartwheels to amuse the passers-by.

This ragged little figure was the street arab, long since vanished from the thoroughfares of London but once a familiar sight. The street arabs (and as late as 1876 Dr Barnardo estimated that there were 30,000 of them in the metropolis) generally had no home. They literally lived on the streets and slept where they could in the corners of deserted buildings, under the arches of railways, or in the warehouses of the docks.

Those who lived near the docks were perhaps more fortunate than the others. They were known as mudlarks, and were boys – and sometimes girls – varying in age from eight to fourteen or fifteen. They were for the most part the children of coalwhippers who were employed to unload ships of coal. The fathers were in general robust men, for they otherwise could not have performed their job, and the children were much healthier than many other unfortunates in the great city, perhaps on account of the healthy life they led. But their clothes were in rags and they were always inexpressibly dirty. The legitimate part of their practice was simply to collect coal which had fallen overboard from the barges and was revealed in the mud of the river at low tide. But they often supplemented these gains by clambering unseen on to the barges and pushing the coal overboard. Sometimes they managed to steal onto a barge carrying scrap iron, the lighter pieces of which they were able to throw over the side to be collected later. Their scene of operations was, we are told, 'Shadwell and Wapping, along Bankside; above Waterloo Bridge, and from the Temple down to St Paul's Wharf. . . . As soon as the tide is out they make their appearance, and remain till it comes in.'

The work was not confined to young boys and girls, some of the mudlarks were

old women of the lowest grade, from fifty to sixty, who occasionally wade in the mud up to their knees. One of them may be seen beside the Thames Police-office, Wapping, picking up coals in the bed of the river, who appears to be about sixty-five years of age. She is a robust woman, dressed in an old cotton gown, with an old straw bonnet tied round with a handkerchief, and wanders about without shoes and stockings. This person has never been in custody. She may often be seen walking through the streets of the neighbourhood with a bag of coals on her head. The coals were sold to the poor families in the neighbourhood for a few pence.

The street arabs had to make a living as best they could and it is not surprising that they sometimes made it dishonestly. Dickens gives a convincing picture of what might happen to them when they fell into the hands of a man like Fagin, and they naturally figure largely in Mayhew's great work on the London poor. They were not regarded as a State responsibility unless both parents were proved dead or proved missing, in which case they were admitted to workhouses. No provision was made for their education for although a certain number of charity schools and Sunday schools existed they did not welcome hoards of unruly barefooted ragamuffins. The street arabs, therefore, grew up in a state of almost complete ignorance, unable even to read and write.

It was to cope with this situation that the Ragged School Movement was started. A beginning had been made in the early years of the century, and in 1844 the Ragged School Union was founded 'to give permanence, regularity and vigour to the existing ragged schools and promote the formation of new ones'. By 1861 the number of Ragged Schools controlled by the Union had risen to 176 and it was reckoned that some 25,000 children came under their care. The teaching was on a voluntary basis and such well known people as Quintin Hogg and General Gordon took part in it. They were, for the most part, fervent Evangelicals and their main purpose was to inculcate Christian doctrine by means of Bible study. But they soon found that no progress could be made until the children were at least taught to read and write. The organizers also found that they must embark on a programme of what we should call welfare. In a word, they had to feed the children as well as teach them. The problem was made more acute by the unemployment of the sixties when even adults had to be fed at public soup kitchens. The Destitute Children's Dinner Society, formed in 1867 and supported warmly by such figures as Lord Shaftesbury, drew enough public support to be able to provide meals of meat stew, vegetables and rice at a penny per head, or free if the penny was not forthcoming. Within a year the Society had thirty-seven dining-rooms and by the late eighties these had increased to sixty-four, serving some 17,000 dinners a week. It was later found necessary to provide sleeping accommodation for some of the children and various refuges were opened for this purpose in the abysmal slums of Seven Dials and Whitechapel. When from the background of our Welfare State we look back on the appalling conditions of the poor in England a century ago we should remember the heroic efforts of those who tried to remedy them.

The publication of Mayhew's great work stirred many consciences and in 1865 Frederick Greenwood, the first editor of the *Pall Mall Gazette*, commissioned his brother James to investigate the condition of the London poor. He began by passing a night in the casual ward of a workhouse. He was horrified by what he saw. About a year later during a winter of exceptional severity there was much destitution in the East End and three young men, inspired not so much by Mayhew as by Disraeli, resolved to investigate matters for themselves. Their names were Baldwyn Leighton, Sir Michael Hicks-Beach (afterwards Chancellor of the Exchequer) and Edward Denison, son of a former Bishop of Salisbury. Denison took a small house in Whitechapel in the very centre of the poverty-stricken district. Disraeli himself, then Prime Minister, was well aware of the youthful enthusiasm which inspired such actions and sent his private secretary to distribute alms. This was Montague Corry, afterwards Lord Rowton and the 'Rowton Houses' still in existence testify to his far-sighted zeal in effecting improvements.

Unfortunately not all those who became interested in the East End were moved by such lofty motives. 'Slumming' became for a time a fashionable craze and the ladies who drove down to the poorer quarters of London in their carriages and in all their finery probably excited more envy than gratitude and did more harm than good. This however should not blind us to the real work accomplished by men like Edward Denison and, later, Arnold Toynbee.

They were fighting the dominant philosophy of *laissez-faire*, for many good men were firmly convinced that charity defeated its own ends, and it was in answer to this doctrine that in the autumn of 1860 there appeared four essays in *The Cornhill Magazine*. They were signed John Ruskin and as he himself tells us 'they were reprobated in a violent manner, as far as I could hear, by most of the readers they met with.' The intelligent reading public was quite willing to listen to Ruskin on art, but here he was invading the territory of the economists and even venturing to throw doubts on the very existence of economic science. 'Among the delusions,' he said, 'which at different periods have possessed themselves of large masses of the human race, perhaps the most curious – certainly the least creditable – is the modern *soi-disant* science of political economy, based on the idea that an advantageous code of social action may be determined irrespectively of the influence of social affection.'[1]

The language may seem stilted, but the intention was plain. Ruskin was denying the fundamental assumption of the Manchester School, that there was such a thing as 'economic man', maintaining that 'the idea that directions for the gaining of wealth, irrespectively of the consideration of its moral sources . . . is perhaps the most insolently futile of all that ever beguiled men through their vices.' He demanded that wages should not be forced down to the lowest level, nor prices allowed to rise beyond reason in times of scarcity. In a word he demanded that society should take a hand in regulating the scramble of the so-called open market, that there should be heart as well as head in commercial relations. He even had the impudence (in the eyes of the exponents of *laissez-faire*) of suggesting that his proposals would in the end prove more profitable than any strict adherence to the supposed 'iron laws' of economics.

Ruskin ridiculed the classical economists' definition of the 'natural rate of wages' as 'that which will maintain the labourer', and asked, very pertinently: 'Maintain him! yes, but how? . . . first, to what length of life? Out of a given number of fed persons, how many are to be old – how many young? that is to say, will you arrange their maintenance so as to kill them early – say at thirty or thirty-five on the average, including deaths of weakly or ill-fed children? – or so as to enable them to live out a natural life?' And he declared boldly, in the teeth of all the exponents of the dismal science: that 'the final outcome and consummation of all wealth is in producing

1 John Ruskin, *Unto This Last*. Four Essays on the First Principles of Political Economy, 1899 Ed.

as many as possible full-breathed, bright-eyed, and happy-hearted human creatures,' and even ventured to ask 'whether, among natural manufactures, that of Souls of a good quality may not at last turn out a quite leadingly lucrative one'.

Perhaps the man who did most practical good was Dr Barnardo, at least so far as children were concerned. He had seen with his own eyes the destitute children sleeping on the streets in the East End of London and moved by the sight he rented a large house in Stepney to give them shelter. When his funds gave out he, with a few voluntary helpers, scrubbed the floors, whitewashed the walls and made the place habitable. He was determined not to get into debt and he had at first funds sufficient only for the housing of twenty-five boys. Having found homes for five of his orphans, the good doctor went forth with a lantern into the East End streets seeking five more 'wholly destitute lads, barefooted and ill-clad' to take their places. He had no difficulty in finding them and, as he was taking them back to the house another boy plucked at his sleeve and begged for admission. This was an eleven-year-old shoeblack named John Somers, but known among the other urchins as 'Carrots' on account of his red hair. Dr Barnardo reluctantly told him that he could not be admitted. A few days later a Billingsgate porter found him in an empty sugar barrel. He had died from exposure and starvation. Dr Barnardo resolved that such a tragedy would never happen again if he could prevent it and it was then that, setting aside his fear of running into financial difficulties, he put up outside his house the proud and heroic legend 'No Destitute Child Ever Refused Admission'.

The problem of dealing with the boys was as nothing compared with the problem of dealing with young girls in a similar state of poverty and even of destitution. For while the boys resorted to thieving, the girls resorted to prostitution.

It is probable that at no other time in English history, before or since, has prostitution been so rampant as it was in the mid-Victorian era. It was taken for granted that man, unlike woman, had sexual impulses which he could, perhaps with difficulty control but could never entirely extinguish. If his wife, frigid by definition, could not satisfy his needs, where was he to turn? Not, certainly, to the women of his own class, married or unmarried, except in very exceptional circumstances, but there were other women of other classes and they were in plentiful supply. Strange as it may seem, many respectable women were unaware of their existence or closed their eyes and their minds to it. They avoided those parts of London where prostitutes were to be seen yet, said the Director of Criminal Investigations in 1881:

From three o'clock in the afternoon, it is impossible for any respectable woman to walk from the top of Haymarket to Wellington Street Strand . . . from three or four o'clock in the afternoon, Villiers Street and Charing Cross Station and the Strand are crowded with prostitutes, who are openly soliciting prostitution in broad daylight. At half past twelve at night, a calculation was made a short time ago that there were five hundred prostitutes between Piccadilly Circus and the bottom of Waterloo Place.

Even as late as the nineties, it was almost impossible, Mrs Peel tells us, for a respectable woman to walk alone in Piccadilly, Regent Street or the Strand. 'At that time,' she says, 'I worked at the office of *Hearth and Home* in Fetter Lane, Fleet Street. Although I was quietly dressed, and I hope looked what I was, a respectable young woman, there was scarcely a day when I, while waiting for an omnibus, was not accosted. I perfected myself in the art of staring blankly through the ill-mannered persons who offered their undesired attentions.'[1]

There were two reasons for this boom in prostitution. It is an essentially urban phenomenon. In rural communities there may be much illicit intercourse, premarital experiment and even incest, but the women involved are rarely professionals. The enormous growth of towns in the nineteenth century created quite a new situation. The other, but related element involved has been neatly analysed by Irene Clephane:

Prostitution springs up in the first place wherever there is a shifting population of men separated from their homes – particularly in towns where sailors and soldiers and other chance passers congregate. Once established, of course, the resident male may take advantage of it; but it is not for him that it comes into being since he has less urgent need of it. The tremendous activity which went on during last century in the construction of canals, bridges and railways, and the building and improvement of roads, the best of which had hitherto been little better than cart tracks, kept a large body of rootless men earning good wages continuously moving about the country; and in their tracks followed venereal disease. Many a country district in England that, until the railway struck across it, was as innocent of venereal disease as were the South Sea Islands before white men took it there, is now, like those poisoned islands, rotten with it. Increased strength of the regular army, the vast increase in the number of men employed in the navy and in the merchant service who were deposited at intervals to roam in some fresh port with money in their pockets and no normal social ties to hold them, the immense army of commercial travellers which sprang up during the nineteenth century provided huge reserves of roving, female-hungry men in whose service was recruited a growing army of purchasable women, and the women were found readily enough among the slaves of the new industrial order.[2]

1 Mrs C.S. Peel, *Life's Enchanted Cup*, 1933.
2 Irene Clephane, *Towards Sex Freedom*, 1935.

This will not surprise us when we consider the appallingly low wages earned by women throughout the nineteenth century. The average working man's wage was low enough – rather under one pound a week – but most women earned only about half that sum. Even if we make every possible allowance for the fall in the value of money it is difficult to understand how any woman could maintain herself on ten shillings a week. Even this sum was not always forthcoming for the prosperity of many industries and factories was seasonal and for weeks on end the working girl had no money at all – except what she could earn by prostitution. In many industrial towns such women set up a temporary or sometimes even a permanent establishment with a man of their own class and in London this was the usual practice among, for example, costermongers. Most of the prostitutes to be found in London were not working girls in this sense; they were ex-domestic servants, barmaids, shop assistants. West-end milliners' shops in particular were recognized as recruiting grounds and in such institutions as the cigar divan the recruitment had already taken place. It was taken for granted that the girls who attended to the gentlemen in these establishments were purchasable and some of them even provided accommodation upstairs. Many of these girls no doubt, were not yet 'on the street' but they were already on the slippery slope that led there. Many of them at the beginning had been no more than foolish or had been seduced and abandoned by their first lover, sometimes the 'young master' of the house in which they were employed as domestic servants.

Ironically enough in view of the Victorian apotheosis of the home, an extraordinarily high proportion of prostitutes had started as domestic servants. In a calculation based on the 11,000 prostitutes who passed through the women's prison on Millbank during the eighties it is estimated that at least half came from this source. The conditions of domestic service were indeed such as to tempt many a young woman to try to escape from them. In the tall houses which now covered what had been the fields of Kensington and Bayswater the life of the domestic servant was unenviable. Underpaid, badly housed and overworked, she rose before light, laid fires, carried tubs of hot water up innumerable stairs, was hardly allowed any time off and was usually forbidden to have 'followers'. Few such girls deliberately adopted a life of prostitution; perhaps they were seduced by some visitor to the house who was generous enough to set them up, sometimes in conditions of considerable luxury in a little house in St John's Wood, already notorious as a district in which the man-about-town kept the 'little woman'.

It was just such an establishment that Holman Hunt had in mind when he painted his famous picture *The Awakening Conscience* exhibited in the Royal Academy of 1854. It created the greatest interest, as well it might. Archdeacon Farrar said that it represented 'the showily furnished room of a suburban house into which a man of wealth and rank has beguiled his victim'. All the critics commented on the high gloss of the furniture, 'hard, varnishy and new, unconsecrated by the domesticity of long use'; and Ruskin, in a letter to *The Times*, asked the rhetorical question: 'That furniture so carefully painted, even to the last vein of the rose-wood – is there nothing to be learnt from that terrible lustre of it, from its fatal newness; nothing there that had the old thoughts of home upon it, or what is ever to become a part of home?' For the 'story' without which no Victorian painting was complete we cannot improve on the Archdeacon:

The seducer has a sort of evil handsomeness, and is full of eager vivacity . . . his right arm is lightly thrown around the girl's waist and he has begun the song:

> Oft in the stilly night
> When slumber's chain has bound me,
> Fond memory brings the light
> Of other days around me.

But the words have touched, have startled the slumbering conscience of the sinning woman. She has turned from him with open lips and dilated eyes, and an expression of anguish and horror is passing convulsively across her features, as she recalls the parents and the pure home which she has abandoned for this evil and callous wretch.

The girl shown in Holman Hunt's picture was, after all, fortunate enough as compared with the vast majority of her erring sisters. Among the statements which Henry Mayhew took from a whole variety of poor people is one from a prostitute, the more horrifying from the fact that according to her own account she was barely twelve years old when she took to prostitution. She was only sixteen when she gave the following account of her life:

I am an orphan. When I was ten I was sent to service as maid of all work in a small tradesman's family. It was a hard place, and my mistress used me very cruelly, beating me often. When I had been in the place three weeks, my mother died; my father having died twelve years before. I stood my mistress's ill treatment for about six months. She beat me with sticks as well as with her hand. I was black and blue and at last I ran away. I got to Mrs —, a low lodging house. I didn't know before that there was such a place. I heard of it from some girls at the Glass House (baths and washhouses), where I went for shelter. I went with them to have a half-penny worth of coffee and they took me to the lodging house. I then had three shillings, and stayed about a month, and did nothing wrong, living on the three shillings and what I pawned my clothes for, as I got some pretty good things away with me. In the lodging house I saw nothing but what was bad, and heard nothing but what was bad. I was laughed at, and was told to swear. They said, 'Look at her for a d— modest fool' – sometimes worse than that, until by degrees I got to be as bad as they were. During this time I used to see boys and girls from ten and twelve years old sleeping together. I understood nothing wrong. I had never heard of such places before I ran away. I could neither read nor write. My mother was a good woman, and I wish I had had her to run away to. I saw things between almost children that I can't describe to you – very often I saw them, and that shocked me. At the month's end, when I was beat out, I met with a young man of fifteen – I myself was going on to twelve years old – and he persuaded me to take up with him. I stayed with him three months in the same lodging house, living with him as his wife, though we were mere children, and being true to him. At the three months end he was taken up for picking pockets, and got six months. I was sorry, for he was kind to me; though I was made ill through him; so I broke some windows in St Paul's Churchyard to get into prison to get cured. I had a month in the Compter and came out well. I was scolded very much in the Compter on account of the state I was in, being so young. I had 2s. 6d. given to me when I came out, and was forced to go into the streets for a living. I continued walking the streets for three years, sometimes making a good deal of money, sometimes none, feasting one day and starving the next. The beggar girls could persuade me to do anything they liked with my money. I was never happy all the time, but I could get no character and could not get out of the life. I lodged all this time at a lodging house at Kent Street. They were all thieves and bad girls. I have known between three and four dozen boys and girls sleep in one room. The beds were horrid filthy and full of vermin. There was very wicked carryings on . . . I can't go into all the particulars but whatever could take place in words or acts between boys and girls did take place, and in the midst of others. I am sorry to say that I took part in these bad ways myself, but I wasn't so bad as some of the others. There was only a candle burning all night, but in summer it was light a great part of the night. Some boys and girls slept without any clothes, and would dance about the room that way. I have seen them, and wicked as I was, felt ashamed. I have seen two dozen capering about the room that way; some mere children, the boys generally the youngest. There were no men or women present. There were often fights. But nobody ever interfered. This is carried on just the same as ever to this day and is the same every night. I have heard young girls shout out to one another how often they have been obliged to go to the hospital or the infirmary or the work-house. There was a great deal of boasting about what the boys and girls had stolen during the day. I have known boys and girls change their partners 'Just for a night'. At three years' end I stole a piece of beef from a butcher. I did it to get into prison. . . .

Many a girl, nearly all of them, goes out into the street from this penny and two-penny house, to get money for their favourite boys by prostitution. If the girl cannot get money she must steal something or will be beaten by her 'chap' when she comes home. I have seen them beaten, often kicked and beaten till they were blind from bloodshot, and their teeth knocked out from kicks from boots as the girls lay on the ground. The boys in their turn are out thieving all day, and the lodging house keeper will buy any stolen provisions from them and sell them to the lodgers. I never saw the police in the house.[1]

1 Henry Mayhew, *London Labour and the London Poor*, 4 vols. 1851–62.

Of course, not all prostitutes were at this low level of destitution. Indeed they were of all grades; and that curious raffish figure who called himself Baron Nicholson, and who probably knew more about the low life of London than anyone else before or since, noted in his scandal sheet *The Town* the snobbery which existed in the world of prostitution. The 'second class of courtesans', he informs us:

> are looked down upon by the first-rate women who ride about in the carriages of noble protectors. Then the theatre-women think themselves degraded by comparison with those who do the excessively swellish on the *pavé*. The dashing Cyprian who treads the aristocratic pavement of Regent Street by day scorns an alliance with those who do the same thing at night, and the well dressed street harlot looks with pitiable contempt upon the ragged, low-life characters.

Regent Street was for long the favourite rendezvous of the 'dashing Cyprian'. Well dressed prostitutes particularly frequented the arches of Nash's colonnade, to such an extent indeed that the Regent Street shop-keepers protested and with such effect that the colonnade was demolished in the early years of the new Queen's reign. The demolition of the colonnade gave pain to lovers of architecture and certainly brought no relief to the promoters of morality for, as George Augustus Sala noted in 1859, 'Perambulating Regent Street at all hours of the day and night, as I do now frequently, I see no diminution in the number of moustached, or rouged, or naughty faces, whose prototypes were familiar to me years agone, in the brilliant Quadrant.'

By this time the real centre of prostitution in London had shifted from the Covent Garden area where it had flourished in the earlier years of the century to the West End. Throughout the nineteenth century, and indeed until the Acts inspired by the Wolfenden Report swept the girls off the streets, the accepted parade ground was a rough quadrilateral enclosed by Regent Street, Piccadilly, Bond Street, and Grosvenor Street. Jermyn Street was also included and in Victorian times there were usually groups of girls outside the chaste portals of the Athenaeum. A favourite place of resort was the Burlington Arcade. This had the advantage of being under cover and much frequented at the close of the afternoon by men about town. Mayhew goes so far as to say that 'All the men in London walk there before dinner' and it is recorded that even the City clerks, or at least those young ones among them who wished to ape their 'betters', were in the habit of rushing from their offices to lounge for a few moments in these fashionable purlieus before going back to their homes in the suburbs.

A somewhat lower class of prostitute was to be found when night had fallen at the top of the Haymarket and in the little streets around. Many of these contained a number of small disreputable eating houses in the windows of which Albert Smith, writing in *Household Words* in 1857, noted

'The stale drooping lobsters, the gaping oysters, the mummified cold fowl with the trapping of flabby parsley, and the pale fly-spotted cigars'. These establishments were not exactly brothels but they often provided bedroom accommodation for prostitutes and their clients. There was nothing secret about the traffic. The pavements were crowded with garishly dressed women, and respectable visitors who might by chance have wandered into the area were warned by writers of the period to walk in the middle of the road if they wished to avoid being jostled, solicited or having their pockets picked. 'Prostitutes,' said *The Saturday Review*:

have seized upon the West End like an army of occupation. . . . The principal streets are in their hands. The pavement of the Haymarket they rule with a sway no prudent passenger will care to challenge after the sun has fallen. Portland Place is occupied by a French detachment of voluble habits, and by no means backward manners; and in Regent Street they have come to a compromise with respectability, mixing freely on both sides, but claiming one . . . as exclusively their own. . . . Men are generally safe till after dark; but female intruders . . . are liable to insult, or at least unflattering observation, at any hour of the day.

Much ink has been spilt in an endeavour to discover the exact statistics of prostitution in England in the middle of the nineteenth century. *The Lancet* in 1857 estimated that there were 80,000 prostitutes in the county of London and that out of every sixty houses in the metropolis, one at least was a brothel. Mayhew offered what seems a much more reasonable estimate of 7,000 prostitutes. Burgo Partridge[1] points out that if *The Lancet*'s figure was correct and if the girls averaged fifteen customers a week it would mean that they weekly received a number of men larger than the entire male population of London at the time, which is plainly absurd. *The Saturday Review* refused to accept 'Such loose and extemporaneous statistics'. However, there were certainly a great number of prostitutes about not only in London but in other great cities. Liverpool was said to have 2,000 women in the dock area brothels; Glasgow had 1,800; Manchester 1,500 and even the comparatively small town of Paisley 250. We are on firmer ground with the police reports which show that in the 1850s an average of more than 4,000 prostitutes were taken into custody for disorderly behaviour. This must plainly have been a minute proportion of the whole and most of the women concerned must have belonged to the lowest level of prostitution.

There were also a number of what Mayhew calls 'Introducing Houses'. Here the women did not reside but merely used the house as a place of resort in the daytime. He mentions a French woman who was in the habit of frequenting a notorious house in James's Street, Haymarket, who said that she came to town four or five times in the week. The husband knew

1 B. Partridge, *A History of Orgies*, 1958.

all about it for he came to fetch her home every evening about ten o'clock. Mayhew tells us how the matter was accomplished at

an introducing house of notoriety and good report in its way, somewhere in the neighbourhood of St George's Road, Pimlico. A well known professional man, a wealthy merchant, an MP, or a rich landed proprietor, calls upon the lady of the house and orders some champagne and enters into conversation about indifferent matters, until he is able delicately to broach the object he has in view. He explains that he wishes to meet with a quiet lady whose secrecy he can rely upon, and whom he can trust in every possible way. He would like her, we will imagine, to be vivacious, witty, and gay.

The lady of the house listens complacently and replies that she knows someone who exactly answers the description the amorous MP has given, and says that she will send a message to her at once if he wishes, but he must take his chance of her being at home; if she is out, an appointment will be made for the next day. In the meantime a messenger is despatched to the lady in question, who in all probability does not reside at any great distance; perhaps in Stanley Street, or Winchester Street, which streets everybody knows are contiguous to St George's Road, and inhabited by beauty that ridicules decorum and laughs at the virtuous restrictions that are highly conducive to a state of single blessedness and a condition of old-maidism. Some more champagne is ordered and consumed, every bottle of which costs the consumer 15s., making a profit to the vendor of at least seventy per cent. When the lady arrives the introduction takes place, and the matter is finally arranged as far as the introducer is concerned. The woman so introduced generally gives half the money she obtains from the man to the keeper of the house of introduction.

It is interesting to note the change of manners. Mayhew is quite frank in giving the name of the street if not the number of some of the most notorious resorts of his day. Nowadays he might run the risk of prosecution for publishing a kind of 'Ladies Directory'; for with that meticulous accuracy to which we have so often been indebted he even lists the favourite *noms-de-guerre* of the fashionable prostitutes at this period. These include Zulma, Calliope, Irma, Zélie, Amanda, Pamela, Natalie, Sidonia, Olympia, Flora, Thalia, Armande, Godiva, Malvina, Virginia, Palmira, Aspasia, Lucrece, Clara, Angelina, Flavia, Celina, Emily, Anais, Delphin and (the surprisingly simple) Fanny. A somewhat lower class chose to be known by such names (mostly French) as La Blonde, Belle-Cuisse, Faux Cul and Poil-ras. The last is very curious. Did the lady in question specialize in Muhammedan clients?

The houses where they were to be met with he had obviously investigated thoroughly and was even able to note their rise and fall. Writing in the early sixties he says:

It is curious to notice how the places of meeting and appointment have sprung up and increased within the last few years. Not many years ago Kate Hamilton,

97

if I am not misinformed, was knocking about town [meaning that she was on the streets herself]. Lizzi Davis's has only been open a year or two. Barns's very recently established, and the Oxford and Cambridge last season. The Café Riche three years ago used to be called Bignell's Café, Sams's is, I believe, the oldest of the night houses about the Haymarket. The Café Royal, or Kate's, is the largest and the most frequented, but it is not now so select as it used formerly to be. Mott's, or the Portland Rooms, used to be the most fashionable dancing place in London and is now in very good repute. Formerly only men in evening dress were admitted; now this distinction is abolished, and everyone indiscriminately admitted. This is beginning to have its effects, and in all likelihood, Mott's will in a short time lose its prestige. It is always so of places of this description. Some peculiarity about the house, or some clever and notorious woman presiding over its destinies, makes it famous; when these vanish or subside, then the place goes down gradually, and some other rival establishment takes its place.

Kate Hamilton was certainly a clever as well as a notorious woman. Her home was in Princes Street, Leicester Square, and was indeed a very superior establishment. No woman was admitted who did not reach the desired degree of elegance and sohpistication and no man unless having passed the two commissionaires at the gate and been peered at through a peep-hole, he seemed likely to have the money to spend and the willingness to spend it. Passing through a long narrow passage the visitor found himself in a large and brightly lit room in which sat enthroned on a dais the redoubtable *patronne*. She was extremely fat and ugly and in a loud harsh voice gave orders to the ladies in waiting who clustered around her throne. We usually think that cocktails came in with the 1920s and it is surprising to find that they were already being served at Kate Hamilton's in the 1850s, also that they had strange exotic names like Corpse Reviver which in itself is more relevant of Mrs Merrick than of Kate Hamilton. But the favourite drink was Champagne, of which enormous quantities were drunk to promote good humour and for the good of the house.

Men of the highest fashion were to be seen at Kate Hamilton's and even on occasion foreign royalty. The Ambassador of the King of Siam visited the establishment in 1857 and the Shah of Persia is known to have been there during his first visit to London in 1872. This event was celebrated in a Christmas poem *The Siliad* which appeared in *Beeton's Christmas Annual* for 1873. Kate Hamilton herself was already dead but the author, perhaps in remembrance of a former visit, still greets her thus:

> Oh buxom woman, handsome in thy day,
> Whose gay career the police courts cannot stay.

and he goes on to describe the royal visitor:

> What face is that, as dusky as the night,
> That jewelled form, those cruel, wicked eyes,

> That sparkle savagely at this surprise.
>> It is the Shah! a voice cries in the gloom . . .
> It *was* the Shah; the valued potentate,
>> Who's studying the secrets of our state,
> Which three fat actresses with might and main,
>> Had been in turn endeavouring to explain.

The place was certainly sumptuously furnished:

> The ceiling glass, tall mirrors lined the walls,
>> Beneath the footsteps on piled velvet falls,
> Three satin covered couches . . . one sky blue,
>> And one coal black, and one rich crimson hue.
> The pictures all one sentiment express;
>> 'Tis female loveliness unmarred by dress.

It was customary to take supper at Kate's and it was possible to call for such delicacies as oysters, lobsters and devilled kidneys. In the private rooms, coffee at the end of the meal was served by half naked girls:

> Hebes, this time in lowly disarray,
>> Bring odorous Mocha on a silver tray,
> And staying now and then to toy and pet,
>> With deftness roll the fragrant cigarette.
> The weeds they light we Nicotina call,
>> And dreamy ecstasy comes down on all;
> With what haps next, not ours it is to deal,
>> For clouds of smoke ascend and all conceal.

The Shah must have felt himself almost as well catered for as in his own harem.

After Kate Hamilton's death the establishment was carried on by William Barton who was soon in trouble with the police. The inspector claimed that he had found ninety men and ninety-five women on the premises. He also mentioned *en passant* that there were eight other houses of the same kind in the neighbourhood but hardly perhaps of the same class. Proceedings at some of them were not as orderly as at Kate Hamilton's for George Augustus Sala once got involved in a fight in a house in Panton Street and had to be taken to Charing Cross Hospital.

Another famous place of entertainment in mid-Victorian days was the Coal Hole Tavern which its proprietor Baron Nicholson advertised as being 'Opposite Exeter Hall'. As Exeter Hall was the headquarters of Evangelical Nonconformity there was a certain piquancy in this juxtaposition. While hymns were being sung and sermons preached in the abode of piety, on the opposite side of the street Baron Nicholson conducted a series of mock trials notable for their obscenity. It was one of the sights of London to go to see the Baron presiding like a real Lord of Appeal over the quasi legal proceedings. Baron Nicholson had originally presided over his mock assizes at the Garrick's Head, Bow Street, in the early forties, but later moved to more commodious premises: first at the Town Hotel opposite Covent Garden Theatre and later to the Coal Hole Tavern. Many eminent men attended the sessions and some at least found them amusing, but Greville who paid it one visit recalls in his diary that he thought it disgusting. What perhaps displeased him most was that the cases tried by the Baron were parodies, with the names only slightly changed, of actual cases before the Courts. He seems to have been particularly shocked by the fact that the witnesses were sworn not upon the Bible but upon *The Town*. *The Town* was another of Baron Nicholson's enterprises. It was a scandal sheet and like all such publications was not above a little blackmail on the side. Yet a writer of the standard of Blanchard Jerrald wrote for it and he seems to have got on very well with the Baron whom he describes as a kind of Falstaff. A piquant fact unearthed by Cyril Pearl was that Baron Nicholson was at the same time editing a religious magazine called *The Crown*, and in this, which is described as a 'High-priced and high-church' organ, he violently attacked his own writings in *The Town*. There is really something rather appealing in such unblushing effrontery. The 'Mimic Court of Law' was held at half-past nine and was followed by *Poses Plastiques*. These consisted of tableaux vivants the chief attraction of which was the women who posed in pink tights. Surviving photographs show them to be short-legged and buxom in the taste of the time. The Baron himself referred to them as 'Slightly-veiled daughters of Venus'.

Writers are seldom immune from the general tendency of mankind to look back with a certain nostalgia on days that are gone, when life was more fun than it seems to be at present, and this means, in general, the days when they themselves were young. Already in 1865 we find an anonymous author lamenting that:

Fast London or London by Night, has been greatly shorn of its glories of late years. There are many men who will tell strange stories of the Finish in Bridges Street, Covent Garden, of the Shades, of Mother H's, of Sally Sutherland's in St Alban's Place, the most exclusive of all night houses; of the Cider Cellars which died with poor old Baron Nicholson of facetious memory; of the Coal Hole, once a renowned resort of the bloods and Corinthians of the old time. Of Kate Hamilton's – dear old Kate, rotund and jovial – all gone – gone through the ivory gate. Dave Pelasco . . . Lizzie Davis, The Count, Sam, Bessie Harvey and others have migrated to other localities like Swallows at the approach of winter.

The writer in question does not specify which other 'localities' he had in mind, which is perhaps just as well as many of the people he mentions were by that time dead. *London by Night* from which the above words were taken, was written by an unknown author whose literary status is sufficiently indicated by the titles of some of his other works, chosen at random from a lengthy list – '*Left her Home, Incognita, The Women of Paris, Annie, or the Life of a Ladies Maid*, and best of all, *The Soiled Dove*.'

London by Night professes to tell the story of a woman's fall, tracing her career through increasing depths of degradation to her final suicide; but its real *raison d'être* is to be a kind of guide book to contemporary 'haunts of pleasure'. The author knew his London, or that part of it that he had chosen to describe, and his descriptions of Rosherville, of the Argyll Rooms, of the Holborn Casino, of Cremorne Gardens, are fascinating to amateurs of their modern equivalent.

The story itself is most amusing for the actors in the drama are so frankly puppets and the final tragedy so obviously perfunctory, that only the most unsophisticated reader is likely to be horrified by the crimes and orgies which fill the book, or moved by the inevitable quotation from *The Bridge of Sighs* which adorns but does not redeem the final page.

As a sidelight on mid-nineteenth century manners the work has real archaeological interest. Fragments of forgotten slang remain imbedded in the dialogue, making it sometimes almost unintelligible. To understand a phrase like 'Gammon buttered is his aversion but gammon unbuttered', must remain the reward of consummate scholarship. Such an admonition as 'Don't you flurry your superfluous fat, my juvenile Juggins', has all the fragile charm of an outmoded vulgarity. 'Who's the muslin?' breathes a poetry of its own, which the multiplicity of modern dress fabrics makes it impossible to recapture. Some of our phrases are older than we think. 'Hello old *beans*', says one of the characters, making a most curious use of the plural.

The heroine is very beautiful, she has an 'elaborate skin', and 'her commotion is faultless'. She is a respectable barmaid, but alas! 'A life of indigient (*sic*) virtue is not attractive to women', and she allows herself to be seduced by a gentleman who, presumably obeying the custom of the day, orders for 'his inamorata' a light repast of 'port-wine and filberts'. They go together to Rosherville and mix with a crowd of 'meritorious creatures whirling in the maze of the giddy waltz or walking through the figures of a staid quadrille'.

After the violent death of her first lover she moves for a while in exalted, if slightly disreputable, circles. The Marquess of Corinth meets her at the Argyll Rooms and is most assiduous in his attentions. Even then, places of amusement shut too early for the pleasure seekers who haunted them. 'There are no rounds to go now since the one o'clock act. . . . Kate's is closed and so is Mott's'. One of the ladies present, however, has an enviable knowledge of the night clubs of the period, and replies, 'I know one or two places where you can get some supper.' 'What are they?'
'Coney's, Rose Young's, and Clark's.'

The party goes to Rose Young's, 'a door with a grating in it at the top of the Haymarket'; and here the heroine finds a drunken man singing 'Champagne Charlie is my name', a ditty still preserved in the repertoire of an occasional reveller. The female characters of *London by Night* scorn any baser tipple – except gin. It is the heroine's passion for expensive liquor which ruins the poor clerk who falls in love with her at the Holborn Casino, a place of amusement which, the author reminds us, was originally a swimming bath.

Conscientiously the various pleasure resorts of the Metropolis are worked into the story. The Crystal Palace attracts by its fire-works, and Highbury Barn by its country air. To go to this latter place, which lingered as almost the last of London's pleasure gardens until 1871, a young man of 1865 thinks it necessary to put on a shooting suit and a pair of dog skin gloves. Cremorne survived Highbury Barn by about six years and the Eagle Tavern and gardens lasted until the early eighties. But of all the places mentioned by our anonymous author, Scott's alone survives until the present day. Perhaps the interior furnishings were different: 'They went in a cab to Scott's and taking possession of a box, ordered oysters unlimited.'

So the butterflies fluttered their rounds, the men in the inevitable 'stove pipe', the women in crinolines: but not the staid crinolines of former times, for 1865 was a naughty year, when the skirts of ladies suddenly left the ground and soared upward to a height of at least three inches, and by this extraordinary abandonment of their function displayed to the astonished eyes of spectators a multitude of adorable ankles – clad in elastic-sided *boots*.

Meanwhile our author traces the downward career of his heroine with grandiloquence and evident relish, but she remains as hard and inhuman as ever. The hot, scalding tears may stream through the fingers of each of her lovers in turn 'like a miniature cataract', but the object of their adoration or the occasion of their despair remains unmoved. It seems likely at one point in the story that vice will go unpunished and outraged virtue un-vindicated, but fortunately the author remembers in time his duty to the cause of public morality and by a series of arbitrary expedients – such as the death on the very eve of their marriage of the man who has asked her to be his wife – the wicked woman is brought to her knees. Abandoned by fortune, and no longer attractive enough to ensnare the Marquess of Corinth and his like she has to resort to Mme Sylphido, who, the author tells us 'belonged to the class of women, not numerous in London, but who you are always to meet with in Portland Place, Regent Street and Waterloo Place'.

The last act is played at 'Paddy's Goose' in the Ratcliffe Highway, a sad fall from the Argyll Rooms. Here, in this public house, haunted by rough sailors, the unfortunate girl whose progress we have traced through two hundred lurid pages, steals the bulging pocket-book of the recently returned emigrant and then drowns herself in the river in a fit of despair. With appropriate moral reflections the author brings his book to a close.

Girls who were tired of a life of toil found no difficulty in setting up in business as prostitutes. The general public failed to notice that behind almost every gaily dressed young woman walking in the Strand there walked at a decent distance an old hag, dressed in dingy clothes. She was, in fact, a spy hired never to let the young woman out of her sight. The young woman controlled by this system was known as a 'dress lodger'. She repaired to the headquarters of the organization in the afternoon and exchanged her own poor wardrobe for one much more striking and expensive. The proprietor lent her these things on trust, but he did not trust her very much. She might simply fail to return, she might waste her time in public houses, or she might take her clients to other houses of ill fame. If she pawned the clothes she had on she could not be sued for a debt contracted for immoral purposes.

If all prostitutes had inevitably ended in the gutter or the river as the sentimental novelists and playwrights liked to make out prostitution itself might have been easier to eradicate. Investigators who had really studied the problem held a different opinion and Mayhew, with his usual common-sense, remarked:

It is a vulgar error and a popular delusion, that the life of a prostitute is as revolting to herself as it appears to the moralist sternly lamenting over the condition of the fallen; but, on the contrary, investigation and sedulous scrutiny lead us to a very different conclusion. Authors gifted with vivid imaginations love to portray the misery that is brought upon an innocent and confiding girl by the perfidy and desertion of her seducer. The pulpit too frequently echoes to clerical denounciations and evangelical horror until those unacquainted with the actual facts tremble at the fate of those whose terrible lot they are taught rather to shudder at than commiserate. Women who in youth have lost their virtue often contrive to retain their reputation; and even when this is not the case, frequently amalgamate imperceptibly with the purer portion of the population and become excellent members of the community.

Prostitution in the mid-nineteenth century was as widespread and blatant in America as it was in England and France. Perhaps even more so; for America had the additional problems of a large immigrant population from countries where Puritanism had hardly been heard of, and of an expanding frontier where settled family life was almost impossible. The towns which sprang up during the gold-rush of 1849 were peopled by virile and lawless men who had often left their womenfolk behind them, and the saloons where they spent their quickly-gained money were often brothels as well. Even in the long-established cities further east prostitution was a paying proposition and the disorderly houses of New York and Chicago rivalled those of London and Paris.

The novelist George Lippard paints a picture of conditions in Philadelphia[1] which, in spite of his flamboyant style, is almost certainly based on actual observation, and the same could be said of his description of the night life of New York.[2] From J. D. McCabe, Jr[3] (says Eric John Dingwall[4] who has admirably summarized these forgotten writers) 'we learn that there were in 1880 some 600 brothels and ninety assignation houses in New York, together with 487 panel houses (i.e. those used in the prostitution plus robbery racket).' The famous abortionist of the period was a certain Madame Restell who ran what is described as a 'palace' at the corner of Fifth Avenue and 52nd Street, conveniently placed for the brothels and dance halls in the vicinity. She had many competitors in her profitable profession.

Chicago, in the last quarter of the nineteenth century, rivalled New York in the number and splendour of its brothels. That run by the 'fabulous' Everleigh sisters is thus described by Dingwall:

Golden silk curtains discreetly concealed the windows; thick carpets and expensive rugs covered the floors and even the spittoons were said to be of solid gold. On the first floor were a number of private parlors decorated in the taste of various nations, and in each room perfume was at regular intervals thrown up into the air by a series of ingeniously contrived fountains. Minna Everleigh, covered with jewels, welcomed each client, who was then introduced to the girls who were in evening dress and were so trained that their manners were perfect and their behaviour decorous. Business was strictly controlled, the girls receiving half of whatever they earned, and the charges for their services plus food and drink were enormous. Although the overheads were very heavy, it is probable that the net profits were something like four hundred dollars a day, each guest being expected to pay at least fifty dollars a visit.

In all countries where prostitution was rampant (perhaps it would be simpler to say 'in all countries') one of its most repugnant aspects was what came to be called the 'White Slave Traffic'. As Mayhew insisted, many under-paid and over-worked servant girls and seamstresses were not at all reluctant to adopt what seemed to them an easier and more attractive life. But even he was constrained to admit that many young girls were forced into prostitution against their will. He declares that in London in the middle of the nineteenth century, 'there were at least four hundred individuals who made a living by "trepanning" females from eleven to

1 George Lippard, *The Quaker City*, 1844.
2 George Lippard, *New York: its Upper Ten and Lower Million*, 1853.
3 J. D. McCabe, Jr, *The Secrets of the Great City*, 1868 *and New York by Sunlight and Gaslight*, 1882.
4 E. J. Dingwall, *The American Woman*, 1956.

Poverty and Prostitution

Gustave Doré, *A Street in Whitechapel* from Louis Énault's *London* (1876)

New ward for the
casual poor at
Marylebone Work-
house, 1867

Newcastle slum,
c. 1880

Shanty town in the
neighbourhood of Berlin,
1872

London coffee-stall,
from Henry Mayhew's
*London Labour and the
London Poor* (1861-2)

Félicien Rops, *Prostitution* (*c.* 1885)

Top: Kate Hamilton's Night House (1856)

Bottom: Conducting the night charges to the Marlborough Street Police Court, *c.* 1860

Ford Madox Brown, *The Last of England* (1852–5), the sadness of emigration

Female convicts at work, during the silent hour, in Brixton Prison (1856)

Chasseur and his wife,
c. 1850

French washerwomen, *c.* 1860

fifteen years of age for the purposes of prostitution'. They were decoyed under some pretext into a house where they were stripped of their respectable clothes and attired in all the gaudy finery of the prostitute. If they resisted they were beaten and probably raped. They were then launched on their career. Some of them became diseased within a few weeks and were then either sent to one of the hospitals under a fictitious name or merely turned into the street. It was reckoned that an average of between three and four thousand children between the ages of eleven and sixteen were admitted annually to the three largest hospitals suffering from venereal disease.

Even enlightened persons had a strangely ambivalent attitude to this scourge. Josephine Butler herself considered it 'a mischief to meddle' with it and said: 'It is a law of nature that children should suffer for the sins of their parents, and I do not think we can venture by legislative measures to interfere with that law.' A certain Dr Solly, one of the Council of the College of Surgeons went further and declared that 'far from considering syphilis as an evil, he regarded it, on the contrary, as a blessing. . . . Could the disease be exterminated which he hoped it could not, fornication would ride rampant through the land.'

It is small wonder that respectable people began to be alarmed by the state of affairs revealed in such works as William Aston's *Prostitution considered in its Moral, Social and Sanitary Aspects* which came out in 1857, and by the descriptions of Henry Mayhew in his *London Labour and the London Poor*. A body with the formidable name of the London Female Penitentiary Society had been formed early in the nineteenth century. In the 1850s the High Church Sisterhoods started a number of houses of refuge, for 'the immediate reception of such fallen women, as, desirous of forsaking their sin, knock at the door for admission'. Here the girls were expected to 'undergo a long course of discipline and training, and thus be prepared, by God's help, to return to the world'. But the world to which the girls returned was the world of domestic service to escape from which they had originally become prostitutes.

Curiously enough the Evangelicals who are usually supposed to have been more rigidly puritan than their High Church confrères took a somewhat more humane view of the problem. Instead of large penitentiary establishments they sought to found a number of homes on a smaller and more attractive scale. Aided by Charles Dickens, Baroness Burdett-Coutts founded one such home at Shepherd's Bush. It stood in a pleasant country lane and each inmate was allowed to have her little flower garden. The good work which Charles Dickens did in this connection has only recently begun to be appreciated, but others had the same idea and between 1853 and 1860 three large Evangelical Societies were formed: The Rescue Society, The London Female Preventive and Reformatory Institute, and the Homes of Hope. Lord Shaftesbury became the first President of the Rescue Society. These Evangelical Organizations did not wait for the prostitutes to 'knock at the door for admission' but sent their agents out into the streets to talk to the girls, give them tracts, and try and persuade them to enter one of the homes. Gladstone in his early days took part in this work. It is recorded that he used to walk about the streets of London at night armed with a stout cudgel to protect himself against any pimp or prostitute's bully who might seek to interfere with his activities. He continued to do this until after he had become Prime Minister, at some cost to his reputation, for there was an unworthy suspicion (shared unfortunately by the Queen herself) that his care for prostitutes was not wholly disinterested. It says much for his moral courage that he sometimes even took them back to his own house where they were cared for with all kindness by Mrs Gladstone.

One of the most extraordinary developments at this period was the founding in 1860 of the Midnight Movement. This took the novel form of having a number of cards printed with the words 'Madam, will you favour a few friends with your company at the above address. Refreshment is provided.' The address was the St James' Restaurant, Piccadilly, and here on 8 February 1860, some 260 prostitutes (half of those who had been invited) duly assembled. They found the largest room in the restaurant fitted out with small tables on which were the promised (non-alcoholic) refreshments. A contemporary print shows us the astonishing spectacle of a room full of women in all the finery of bonnets and crinolines listening with the utmost decorum to a sermon by the Reverend Baptist Noel in which he urged them with considerable eloquence to give up their way of life. Sixteen women responded and were sent to various homes.

Nearly twenty similar meetings were held in the same year in London and the Movement spread to such large provincial cities as Glasgow, Manchester, Nottingham, Liverpool, and Cardiff.

The Midnight Movement did not pass without criticism from those who thought that the subject of prostitution was too scabrous to be mentioned at all, but Miss Kathleen Heasman is surely justified in claiming that 'This was the first real break through in the so called conspiracy of silence which shrouded such subjects at Victorian times.'[1] Another step forward which was not really taken until the 1880s was to provide accommodation for the unmarried woman and her child. In general unmarried mothers had been compelled to go to the workhouse infirmary and their children were separated from them and either placed in orphanages or 'farmed out'. This meant that they were given into the care of baby farmers whose activities soon became notorious. They had no interest in the welfare of the

1 Kathleen Heasman, *Evangelicals in Action*, 1962.

children and many an unfortunate must have perished of neglect or even been done to death when the maintenance money was no longer forthcoming.

In spite of all their efforts many welfare workers began to realize that they were only touching the fringe of the problem. Prostitution was still rampant in all great cities and particularly in London, for while Victorian morality condemned the prostitute herself it took a very lenient view of the men who were her clients. The 'double standard' existed, indeed, in its most acute form and some earnest men and women, misguided or not, sought to remedy this state of affairs by promoting Leagues of Purity. The Social Purity Alliance was founded in 1874 and a little later the White Cross Army and the Gospel Purity Association which was under the leadership of a Salvationist. The men in the Association pledged themselves to purity and the girls who were formed into 'Snowdrop Bands' promised to offer no enticement to men. It is doubtful if such well-meaning efforts had much effect for most men continued to take their pleasure where they found it (that is, outside the sanctity of the home) and, after all, the 'enticement of men' is the whole purpose of fashion. If the Purity Leaders had had their way, English women would presumably have been as heavily veiled as those in Mohammedan countries. Paradoxically enough, the Purity Movement's best effect was to bring the whole question to public notice.

Much has been written about the conspiracy of silence in Victorian times and it is certainly true that one might read a whole library of novels of the period without discovering that there was anything called prostitution at all, but it is very different with the national newspapers. Mr Cyril Pearl whose book *The Girl with the Swansdown Seat* is such a valuable contribution to social history, was one of the first to go systematically through the files of *The Times* to find references to what was going on under the surface of respectability. That august journal opened its columns in 1858 to a whole series of letters from prostitutes, and one of these complained that the well meaning people who were endeavouring to abolish prostitution concentrated too much upon the lower part of the scale. 'Why,' she asks 'begin with the most abject and unprotected? . . . Why should the virtuous indignation of the present day be all expended on . . . the poor creature without a friend, while her more fortunate sister, whom I will call harlot, stares impudently out from her luxurious brougham?' *The Times* published another letter from this woman, but what is even more remarkable is that it consented to print a reply running to more than 3,500 words (more an essay than a letter) from a prostitute who maintained that she was not in the least ashamed of her profession. The child of drunken parents who both worked in a brick field she had been early impressed by certain visitors who came to her neighbourhood.

Some young lady who had quitted paternal restraints, or perhaps, been started off, none knew whither or how, to seek her fortune, would re-appear among us with a perfusion of ribands, fine clothes and lots of cash. . . . Treating indiscriminately was the order of the day on such occasions, without any more definite information of the means by which the dazzling transformation had been effected than could be conveyed by knowing winks and the words 'luck' and 'friends'. Then she would disappear and leave us in our dirt, penury, and obscurity. . . .

In the commencement of my fifteenth year, one of our be-ribboned visitors took me off, and introduced me to the great world, and thus commenced my career as what you better classes call a prostitute. I cannot say that I felt any other shame than the bashfulness of a noviciate introduced to strange society. Remarkable for good looks, and no less so for a good temper, I gained money, dressed gaily, and soon agreeably astonished my parents and own neighbours by making a descent on them. Passing over the vicissitudes of my career, alternating between reckless gaiety and extreme destitution, I improved myself greatly, and at the age of eighteen was living partly under the protection of one who thought he discovered that I had talent, and some good qualities, as well as beauty, who treated me more kindly and considerately than I had ever before been treated. . . . Under the protection of this gentleman, and encouraged by him, I commenced the work of my education; that portion of education that is comprised in some knowledge of my own language and the ordinary accomplishments of my sex; moral science, as I believe it is called, has always been an enigma to me, and is so to this day. . . .

Now what if I am a prostitute, what business has society to abuse me? Have I received any favours at the hand of society? If I am a hideous cancer in society, are not the causes of the disease to be sought in the rottenness of the carcass? Am I not its legitimate child, no bastard, sir? Why does my unnatural parent repudiate me? . . . I have neither stolen (at least not since I was a child) nor murdered, nor defrauded. I earn my money and pay my way, and try to do good with it according to my ideas of good. I do not get drunk, fight, nor create an uproar in the streets or out of them. I do not offend the public by open indecencies, I go to the Opera; I go to Almack's; I go to the theatre, I go to quiet, well-conducted casinos. . . . My milliner, my silk-mercer, my bootmakers, know, all of them, where I am and where I live, and they solicit my patronage as earnestly and as cringingly as if I were Madam, the Lady of the Rt. Rev. Patron of the Society for the Suppression of Vice. We come from the dregs of society, as our so-called betters call it. What business has society to have dregs – such dregs as we? You railers of the Society for the Suppression of Vice, you the pious, the moral, the respectable, as you call yourselves, who stand on your smooth and pleasant side of the great gulf you have dug and keep between yourself and the dregs, why don't you bridge it over or fill it up . . . why stand you there mouthing with a sleek face about morality? What is morality?

The letter is so well written and so free from mistakes (unless perhaps the use of the word noviciate instead of novice) that one wonders if the woman really wrote it herself. If she did the kind gentleman who kept her certainly educated her to some purpose. All the letters were well written, so much so that *The Saturday Review* asked sarcastically if 'the life of the prostitute is the best educational discipline in England'. But *The Times* stoutly maintained that 'we are not endeavouring to palm off a cunningly executed literary imposture'.

In spite of this public airing of the problem the vast majority shut its eyes resolutely to the facts, and it needed the heroism of such women as Josephine Butler to stir the public conscience, not only to prostitution in England but to what became known as the White Slave Traffic. During her campaign for the repeal of the Contagious Diseases Acts, Josephine Butler had found evidence of a regular traffic in young girls. In the early eighties a select committee of the House of Lords was considering the 'Law' relating to the 'Protection of Young Girls' and found to its dismay that the Law offered them no protection at all. A brothel keeper in The Hague was assured by his agent in London that there was no danger in his coming to England to select recruits as the English Law was powerless against him.

There can be little doubt that the white slave traffic was in full swing in Victorian London. It was a two-way traffic. In the reports submitted by a Mr Dalbert, agent for the 'Society for the Protection of Women and Children' to the London Magistrates, it was asserted that:

Women are imported from Belgium, and placed in houses of ill fame, where they are compelled to support their keepers in luxury and idleness by the proceeds of their dishonour. One house in particular was mentioned in Marylebone; the state of the law respecting brothels is so peculiar that the greatest difficulty is experienced in extricating these unfortunate creatures from their dreadful position . . . as this traffic is clandestine and conducted with the greatest caution, it is impossible to form any correct idea of its extent. There are numbers of foreign women about, but it is possible that many of them have come over here of their own free will, and not upon false pretences or compulsion. One meets with French, Spanish, Italian, Belgian and other women. The complaint made before the Metropolitan Magistrates a short while since was in favour of Belgian women. But the traffic is not confined to them alone. It would appear that the unfortunate creatures are deluded by all sorts of promises and cajolery, and when they arrive in this country are, in point of fact, imprisoned in certain houses of ill fame, whose keepers derive considerable emoluments from their durance. They are made to fetter themselves in some way or other to the trepanner, and they, in their simplemindedness, consider their deed binding, and look upon themselves, until the delusion is dispelled, as thoroughly in the power of their keepers.

English women are also taken to foreign parts by designing speculators. The English are known to congregate at Boulogne, at Havre, and Dieppe, at Ostend and other places. It is considered lucrative by the keepers of bawdy-houses at these towns to maintain an efficient supply of these English women for their resident countrymen; and though the supply is inadequate to the demand great numbers of girls are decoyed every year and placed in the 'maisons de passe' or 'maisons de joie' as they are sometimes called, where they are made to prostitute themselves.

A young Englishwoman who had in the end escaped from the clutches of the white slavers told her story to Mayhew:

When I was sixteen years old, my father, who kept a public house in Blooms-bury, got into difficulties and became bankrupt. I had no mother, and my relations, such as they were, insisted upon my keeping myself in some way or other . . . service suggested itself to me and my friends, and we set about finding a situation that I could fill. They told me I was pretty, and as I had not been accustomed to do anything laborious, they thought I would make a very good lady's maid. I advertised in a morning paper, and received three answers to my advertisement. The first I went to did not answer my expectations, and the second was moderately good; but I resolved to go to the third and see the nature of it before I came to my conclusion. Consequently I left the second open, and went to the third. It was addressed from a house in Bulstrode Street, near Welbeck Street. I was ushered into the house, and found a foreign lady waiting to receive me. She said she was going back to France, and wished for an English girl to accompany her, as she infinitely preferred English to French women. She offered me a high salary, and told me my duties would be light; in fact by comparing her statement of what I would have to do with that of the others I had visited, I found that it was more to my advantage to live with her than with them, so after a little consultation with myself I determined to accept her offer.

The foolish girl was then induced to sign a document which she did without reading it for fear of offending her new employer. The account continued:

We left St Katherine's Docks in the steamer for Boulogne, and instead of going to an hotel, as I expected, we proceeded to a private house in the Rue M— C— near the Rue de l'Ecu. I have further to tell you that three other young women accompanied us. One was a housemaid, one was a nursery governess, and the other one was a cook. I was introduced to them as people I would have to associate with when we arrived at Madame's house. In fact they were represented to be part of the establishment; and they, poor things, fully believed they were, being as much deluded as myself. The house that Madame brought us to was roomy and commodious, and, as I afterwards discovered, well, if not elegantly, furnished. We were shown into very good bedrooms, much better than I expected would be allotted to servants; and when I mentioned this to Madame, and thanked her for her kindness and consideration, she replied with a smile: 'Did I not tell you how well you would be treated? We do these things better in France than they do in England.'

Mayhew takes up the story:

I need not expatiate on what subsequently ensued. It is easy to imagine the horrors that the poor girl had to undergo. With some difficulty she was conquered and had to submit to her fate. She did not know a word of the language, and was ignorant of the only method she could adopt to ensure redress. But this she happily discovered in a somewhat singular manner. When her way of living had become intolerable to her, she determined to throw herself on the generosity of a young Englishman who was in the habit of frequenting the house she lived in, and who seemed to possess some sort of affection for her. She confessed her miserable position to him and implored him to protect her or to point out a means of safety, he at once replied, 'The best thing you can do is to go to the British Consul and lay your case before him. He will in all probability send you back to your own country.' It required little persuasion on her part to induce her friend to co-operate with her. The main thing to be managed was to escape from the house. This was next to impossible, as they were so carefully watched. But they were allowed occasionally, if they did not show any signs of discontent, to go out for a walk in the town. The ramparts were generally selected by this girl as her promenade, and when this privilege of walking out was allowed her, she was strictly enjoined not to neglect any opportunity that might offer itself. She arranged to meet her young friend there, and gave him notice of the day on which she would be able to go out . . . the plot succeeded, the Consul was appealed to and granted the girl a passport to return to England, also offering to supply her with money to pay her passage home. This necessity was obviated by the kindness of her young English friend, who generously gave her several pounds, and advised her to return at once to her friends.

The end of the story is unfortunately not so happy. 'Arrived in England she found her friends reluctant to believe the tale she told them, and found herself thrown on her own resources. Without a character, and with a mind very much disturbed, she found it difficult to do anything respectable, and at last had recourse to prostitution.' Perhaps she would have been better after all if she had stayed in the brothel abroad.

The Press was, in general, reluctant to report such matters for fear of offending its readers, but Josephine Butler and her friends determined to give them as much publicity as possible. Brussels was a centre of the traffic and the Brussels police had made some attempt to regulate it by requiring a birth certificate for every girl imported. It was proved, however, that nothing was easier than to obtain a genuine birth certificate from Somerset House relating to some other girl and so this police precaution availed nothing. A Bill to regulate this state of affairs had already passed the House of Lords but seemed unlikely to pass the Commons. Mrs Butler felt that if only the facts of child and young woman prostitutes were known there would be such a public outcry as would compel the Government to act.

For the opening of her Press campaign she selected the influential *Pall Mall Gazette*. She could not have made a better choice. It was in 1881 that a young journalist from Darlington joined the staff of the paper. His name was William Thomas Stead, and John Morley, the editor, was soon finding him 'invaluable; abounding in journalistic resource, eager in convictions, infinitely bold, candid [and] laborious in sure-footed mastery of all the facts'.[1] In 1884, W. T. Stead succeeded Morley as editor.

The Criminal Law Amendment Bill had been before Parliament since 1881. As the law stood the 'age of consent' was held to be thirteen years, and the sworn evidence of a child corrupted by a man was not accepted in the courts. Mrs Butler feared that the impending collapse of the Gladstone Government would jeopardize the Bill in the House of Commons.

Stead determined that it *should* be passed, and to this end he decided (after consulting the Archbishop of Canterbury, the Bishop of London and Cardinal Manning) to force the hands of the authorities by himself 'procuring for immoral purposes a girl of thirteen'. Before doing so, however, he resolved to investigate the whole question. He got together a band of 'special commissioners', with himself as the chief, and for a month these men, with some voluntary helpers, 'were in private communication with everybody, moral and immoral, who was supposed to be able to throw any light on the subject'.

Henry Labouchère, the editor of *Truth*, was certainly not afraid of a fight, but he was much more of a man of the world than Stead and he wrote warning him 'not to believe all he was told when drinking champagne with questionable characters'. It would have been well if such good advice had been accepted. Well-meaning people who try to investigate vice are sometimes the victims of leg-pullers, or of those determined to make the information they claim to be able to supply as sensational as possible. We may be sure that W. T. Stead's personal acquaintance with the seamy side of life was very slight. He gathered most of his facts in a Bohemian café in Leicester Square and the 'questionable characters' who supplied them (for a drink or a sovereign) were no doubt perfectly aware of the identity of the well-known journalist of striking appearance who was trying to pump them. Stead had persuaded himself that they took him for a man-about-town in search of adventure. He had dressed the part to the point of putting on patent-leather boots; this, he explained to a friend, 'made them think I was a nobleman'.

Stead was on surer ground in consulting General Booth, founder of the Salvation Army. The General passed him on to his son, Bramwell Booth, who introduced Stead to Rebecca Jarrett, an ex-procuress who had been 'converted' and was now a zealous Salvation Army Sister. Rebecca Jarrett naturally suspected the purity of Stead's motives, but Mrs Butler having convinced her that it was all in a good cause, she promised to revert for once to her former profession.

1 Lord Morley, *Recollections*, 1917.

She therefore called, in the Marylebone slum where she lived, on an old friend of hers, Mrs Broughton, with the trumped-up story[1] that she wanted a young servant girl. Now Mrs Broughton had a neighbour, Mrs Armstrong, the wife of a chimney-sweeper, and Mrs Armstrong had a daughter of thirteen called Eliza. After some persuasion, she parted with the girl. Stead afterwards declared that he had paid £5, but Mrs Armstrong denied this.

And now Stead's behaviour became extremely odd. He found a room in the house of 'an accommodating landlady', had the girl brought there and in order to make sure that 'a little harlot had not been palmed off' on him, she was physically examined by (of all people!) a French procuress named Louise Mourez. The *virgo intacta*, as she proved to be, was then carried off to a brothel in Poland Street, drugged, undressed, and put to bed. A little later Stead entered in the character of a client of the brothel.

Of course he did not seduce the child. Instead he had her removed to a nursing home where she was once more examined, this time by a doctor, and certified to be still a virgin. Not content with that, Stead had her taken to Paris – presumably to prove that it was possible – and kept her there for a time. Years later, Stead confessed that he was still 'amazed at the audacity with which I carried the thing through'. What amazes *us* is his obtuseness; his complete indifference to the feelings of the thirteen-year-old daughter of the chimney sweep. He had proved – or thought he had proved – his point and that was all he wanted, or thought of.

The campaign against the 'Maiden Tribute of Modern Babylon' could now be launched, and on Saturday, 4 July 1885, the front page of the *Pall Mall Gazette* contained an announcement warning 'All those who are squeamish and all those who are prudish, and all those who prefer to live in a fool's paradise of imaginary innocence and purity, selfishly oblivious of the horrible realities which torment those whose lives are passed in the London Inferno' not to read the paper on the following Monday, Tuesday, Wednesday and Thursday. Naturally enough, the circulation of the *Pall Mall Gazette* went up by leaps and bounds and the printers could hardly cope with the demand for copies. To the modern reader Stead's articles seem to be written in a somewhat flamboyant and sentimental vein, over-stressing the value of virginity as such:

This very night in London, and every night, year in and year out, not seven maidens only, but many times seven, selected almost as much by chance as those who in the Athenian market-place drew lots as to which should be flung into the Cretan labyrinth, will be offered up as the Maiden Tribute of Modern

---

1 It is certainly disconcerting to find that a Salvation Army woman was so ready to accept the doctrine that the end justifies the means.

H

Babylon.[1] Maidens they were when this morning dawned, but tonight their ruin will be accomplished, and tomorrow they will find themselves within the portals of London brotheldom. Within that labyrinth wander, like lost souls, the vast host of London prostitutes, whose numbers no man can compute, but who are probably not much below 50,000 strong. . . . Yet, so far from this great city being convulsed with woe, London cares for none of these things. . . . Nevertheless, I have not yet lost faith in the heart and conscience of the English folk, the sturdy innate chivalry and right thinking of our common people; and although I am no vain dreamer of Utopias peopled solely by Sir Galahads and vestal virgins,[2] I am not without hope that there may be some check placed upon this vast tribute of maidens, unwitting or unwilling, which is nightly levied in London by the vices of the rich upon the necessities of the poor. . . .

This was heady stuff and the sub-headings of Stead's articles: 'The Violation of Virgins', 'Confessions of a Brothel-Keeper', 'Strapping Girls Down' and 'Procuration in the West-end', were certainly not calculated to calm the public excitement. The *Pall Mall Gazette* ran out of paper and had to borrow from the *Globe*. Special trains with fresh supplies were rushed from the mills. The newsboys fought for copies and the editorial offices in Northumberland Street had to be protected by the police. Stead's articles had, in his own words, 'an effect unparalleled in the history of journalism'.

And now arises an awkward question to which no satisfactory answer has, even yet, been found. When a newspaper 'exposes' a vice-racket in such sensational terms to what public is it really appealing? To the handful of high-minded men and women who are genuinely concerned with raising moral standards or to the prurience of *l'homme moyen sensuel*? If a journal, in the process of denouncing vice, vastly increases its circulation, is it not itself sharing in the profits of vice? W. T. Stead was not the first to perceive that the highest moral tone could be combined with 'a systematic dallying with seductive images'.[3] To one of his contemporaries (and rivals) he was 'this shameless creature . . . openly dealing with the worst abominations in the plainest and foulest language. Nothing like it has ever been seen in any public print.' Another indignant editor prophesied that the *Pall Mall Gazette* would be 'kicked out of all virtuous homes'.

It was certainly kicked out of the Athenaeum; Marlborough House cancelled its subscription and Messrs W. H. Smith declined to sell the paper from their bookstalls. A German translation of the articles was suppressed in Vienna; the French Press gloated at this exposure of *l'hypocrisie anglaise*. Most of the English daily papers were hostile, but

1 Stead seems to have been a little mixed in his mythology, and it is certainly hard to blame ancient Babylon for what is alleged to have happened in Crete.

2 In More's Utopia at any rate there are no Sir Galahads and no vestal virgins.

3 Who *was* the first? Samuel Richardson, perhaps.

support for Stead came from some of the religious weeklies which were so much more influential than they are now. The *Christian Leader* declared Stead's campaign to be 'the most heroic service to humanity that has ever been rendered by a public journal in the entire history of the newspaper Press of the world. Only a motive of the purest and most exalted character could have inspired the determination of the conductors of the *Pall Mall Gazette* to make the revelations which during the past week have reverberated through every nook and corner of the Empire.' The *Methodist Times* and the *Christian* took much the same line.

Among public figures of the day the list of Stead's supporters is certainly impressive. It would be difficult to find in any age a group of people of more unquestioned integrity than Cardinal Manning, Dr Clifford, Mrs Bramwell Booth, Mrs Josephine Butler, Lord Shaftesbury and George Bernard Shaw. But many people, including some Members of Parliament called for a criminal prosecution of 'the author and publisher of these obscene articles in a paper called the *Pall Mall Gazette*'. Stead himself went to see the Home Secretary and offered him the alternatives of telling the House 'that the *Pall Mall Gazette* had covered itself with everlasting glory by this courageous attempt to extirpate a horrible evil' or of saying that 'it has committed an abominable outrage on public morals, and that you have instructed the law officers to prosecute me'. The Home Secretary declined to adopt either course of action. Instead he hurried through Parliament the Criminal Law Amendment Bill, which duly became law.

Stead was surely justified in claiming that 'it was one of the greatest achievements which any journalist single-handed had ever accomplished in the coercion of an unwilling legislature and a reluctant Ministry'. But by a singular irony he found that he had himself transgressed the new Act by failing to obtain the consent of the father of the girl he had purchased and by omitting to get a receipt from her mother for the money that had passed. The mother now contended, moreover, that she had not parted with her daughter for immoral purposes but in order that she should go into service. Stead's enemies decided to have him prosecuted. He was arrested and stood in the dock with three others who had helped him in his researches: Rebecca Jarrett, a journalist named Jacques, and Bramwell Booth. The trial lasted for twelve days and the judge took the line that the articles which had appeared in the *Pall Mall Gazette* were 'so filthy and disgusting that one cannot help fearing that they may have suggested to the innocent minds of women and children the existence of vice and wickedness which had never occurred to their minds before'. This, with all respect to the Bench, was completely beside the point. Stead was being prosecuted for a technical breach of the new law. Of this he and Rebecca Jarrett were found guilty, he being condemned to three months imprisonment and Rebecca Jarrett to six months. For the rest of his life W. T. Stead wore prison clothes on the anniversary of his prison sentence. His efforts and those of others probably did something to make the White Slavers' business more hazardous, but the main problem, the problem of prostitution itself, the Victorians did not succeed in solving. It would be pleasant to think that their descendants a hundred years later have succeeded any better.

Hymn Books and Chasubles

The strong religious element in Victorian culture was rightly stressed by such foreign observers as Elie Halévy,[1] and, says Christopher Dawson:

It is only from this angle that it is possible to comprehend that combination of moral idealism, social conformity and intellectual nonconformity that makes the Victorian Age so puzzling to the modern mind. The beliefs of early Victorian England may seem to us a strange compound of mutually inconsistent orthodoxies – the bleak rationalism of the Utilitarians and the narrow pietism of the Evangelicals, but they were like flint and steel to one another, and from their contact there sprang the spirit of moral idealism and the passion for reform which burn like fire beneath the hard surface of the age of iron and steam.[2]

It would indeed be difficult to over-estimate the part played in the Victorian Era by religion in its broadest sense. Or should we say in its narrowest sense? The new proletariat might be heathen and the aristocracy might remain to some extent aloof. The smaller country gentry – the squirearchy – were certainly touched by the spirit of religion, or at least conformity. Their old rumbustious, hard-drinking and wenching traditions were increasingly frowned upon even among themselves. It was estimated that in the representative county of Staffordshire, while in 1810 only two country families had family prayers, fifty years later there were only two that did not. This triumph of bourgeois morals was partly due to the example of the Court. It was at last possible, after the scandals of the Regency, to hold up the Royal Family as an example to all. This may have made the Court dull, but it probably saved the Monarchy. The middle classes had no wish to get rid of a Queen who incorporated in her life so many of their own ideals.

It would hardly be an exaggeration to call religion the dominant interest of vast numbers of the middle classes. It affected their thinking, it dictated

1 E. Halévy, *History of the English People in the Nineteenth Century.*
2 C. Dawson *in Ideas and Beliefs of the Victorians*, 1949.

their conduct, or at least it dictated their ethical ideals, however far short of them may have been their practice. The social climate of the time demanded that the respectable citizen should be religious, or should appear so, and the rising man in any profession soon found that his rise was (sometimes fatally) impeded if he did not go to church on Sunday.

What had happened was not a change of heart so much as a change of people. A new class had risen to power and this class – the middle class – had always been religious. The Puritan middle classes, defeated in their bid for power in the seventeenth century, had had to accept for more than a hundred years the rule of men who were tired of ecclesiastical controversy and determined to have no more wars of religion. Erastian bishops who were only too willing to treat the Church of England as a department of state had been appointed in large numbers as part of government policy. They were not in the least likely to be guilty of enthusiasm; and it is interesting to note that the word 'enthusiasm' was a term of abuse even to John Wesley.

It is true that there were 'High Churchmen' of the old school, but their High Churchmanship had nothing to do with what we should mean by the term today. It did not flirt with Rome or copy its ceremonies; it was not 'ritualistic'; it did not seek to reinterpret the Book of Common Prayer. Its slant was political rather than religious, Tory rather than Whig. Catholics in the eighteenth century were few and, excluded as they were, not only from all government office but from Oxford and Cambridge, made very little noise in the world. Nonconformists were equally excluded, but under the surface their influence persisted, largely through the dissenting academies which although few in number, were for the most part admirably conducted.

The religious revival inaugurated by Wesley and Whitfield had made its chief impact on the working classes, the early industrial workers and small tradespeople. It has been claimed, with some exaggeration, that the Wesleyan movement saved England from anything like a French Revolution. Certainly, it had some profound social effects. For the practice of a religion as austere and law-abiding as Methodism often led to growing prosperity and a rise in the social scale. By the time of the accession of Queen Victoria the descendants of Wesley's converts had become middle-middle class.

The principal Nonconformist bodies in the nineteenth century were the Methodists (divided into two main wings: those who followed Whitfield in accepting the doctrine of predestination and those who followed Wesley in rejecting it), the Baptists whose ministers were probably the most effective preachers of their time, the Congregationalists who had inherited the Puritan tradition of the seventeenth century, the Unitarians who rejected the divinity of Christ and appealed largely to intellectuals, and the Quakers who, from humble beginnings, had now risen to respectability and wealth.

All these bodies (with the exception of the Unitarians) based their doctrine on the infallibility of the Bible not only in its original tongues but in the English Authorized Version. The 'Plan of Salvation', according to them was that man had fallen from Grace in the Garden of Eden and could only be saved from Hell by the sacrifice of Calvary, freely believed in. It was necessary to be 'convicted of sin' by a process of 'conversion' preferably sudden, and 'salvation' was thus assured. It goes without saying that those who believed in predestination (i.e. the Presbyterians in England and Scotland, the Calvinistic Methodists and Lady Huntingdon's Connexion) believed that only those would be saved who were predestined to salvation by God. The rest of mankind, however nobly it might struggle to be good, was doomed to eternal torment. Compared with this monstrous doctrine, the hell-fire preaching of the rest of the Evangelicals seems positively mild and merciful. But we must not forget that for the vast majority of religious people in the nineteenth century the fear of hell was an ever-present reality, and while it may have kept a few from committing the sins they were inclined to, must have darkened many lives.

It is undeniable that many of the Evangelical leaders were public-spirited and high-minded men. They were the spear-head of the anti-slavery movement and in the forefront of the fight for the Factory Acts. Nevertheless they sought to impose (and in fact did impose) upon the people of England a gloomy fanaticism unparalleled since the seventeenth century Rule of the Saints. They frowned upon all amusements however innocent; they converted the Day of Rest into a day of pious exercises for themselves and a day of frustration and boredom for everyone else.

This Puritanism was not so much theological as moral. The problems of 'sanctification by grace', 'imputed righteousness' and predestination which had convulsed the seventeenth century were no longer debated with the same fervour. The emphasis now was on conduct and even religion was tinctured with utilitarianism. Although the old formulae continued to be used, the real driving force was no longer that a good life on earth ensured admission to heaven, but that a good life on earth led inevitably to prosperity on earth. To some extent, of course, this was true. A man who eats sparingly, drinks moderately, works hard and does not gamble is more likely to build up a successful business than a man of less sober habits. 'Honesty is the best policy' might seem a somewhat cynical gloss on moral rectitude; but was not this also true? It was only necessary to look at the Quakers. Their principles forbade them to make a profit of more than five per cent on a business transaction. When this became known everybody wanted to do business with them, with the result that the Quakers grew rich and, by the middle of the nineteenth century, some of their leading men were very rich indeed. Social historians like Tawney have pointed out the intimate connection between Puritan morals and the rise of capitalism. To the average Victorian bourgeois there was plain evidence that God approved of both.

But if material prosperity was the reward and the sign of goodness, it necessarily followed that poverty was the result of sin; indeed, was itself a sin. If the poor were poor it was because they were shiftless or immoral, or both. Nevertheless there *were* poor people who seemed to be struggling towards better things. These were known, by a revealing phrase, as the 'Deserving Poor', and a good deal of charity was exercised on their behalf. The undeserving poor deserved – and got – nothing.

We live in an entirely different moral climate and opinion has swung to such an opposite extreme that many well-meaning persons seem unwilling to admit any individual responsibility at all. Everything is blamed on 'Society', and we are apt to look upon Victorian morality as hypocritical. No doubt in much of it there was an element of calculation, conscious or unconscious. The 'Sabbath' (which now meant Sunday) must be left holy, not only because of Biblical injunction but because workers worked harder on six days of the week if they rested (like God himself) on the seventh. But let no man imagine that the prescribed day of rest was a day when the workers were free to amuse themselves. Sabbatarianism was pushed to such an extreme that even a walk was thought reprehensible. No amusement, no games of any kind were to be indulged in, and even young children were forbidden to play on the Lord's Day. Children were taught to sing:

> We must not play on Sunday,
> But we may play on Monday,
> On Tuesday and on Wednesday,
> On Thursday, Friday, Saturday
> Till Sunday comes again.
> We must not laugh on Sunday,
> But we may laugh on Monday, etc.

As Sir James Stephen remarked 'We may laugh (on Monday) at such extravagances, but they are only too likely to put children against religion for life.'

Even laughing on Monday was frowned upon in some pious households. A Mrs William Fison, in a book for children published in 1850, has the following exhortation:

Shrink not, my beloved young friends, from the attempt to conquer the habitual levity in which you have, perchance, till now indulged. Ask for strength from On High, and you will assuredly receive it; carry this, with all your other temptations, to the Throne of Grace, and you will receive the help you need.[1]

1 Mrs W. Fison, *Hints for the Earnest Student*, 1850.

It is a wonder that children had any 'levity' left in the conditions under which so many of them were brought up. Some of the means adopted in pious households to make children good smack more of the Marquis de Sade than of anything to be found in Scripture. Augustus Hare tells us of the discipline to which he was subjected in his early years:

I was not six years old before my mother – under the influence of the Maurices – began to follow out a code of penance with regard to me which was worthy of the ascetics of the desert. Hitherto I had never been allowed anything but roast mutton and rice pudding for dinner. Now all was changed. The most delicious puddings were talked of – *dilated* on – until I became, not greedy, but exceedingly curious about them. At length *le grand moment* arrived. They were put on the table before me and then, just as I was about to eat some of them, they were snatched away, and I was told to get up and carry them off to some poor person in the village.[1]

This was not the worst. Little Augustus had been savagely whipped for even suggesting that some local children might be allowed to play with him on his birthday. Deprived of child-companionship he bestowed his affections on a favourite cat called Selina. Seeing this his Aunt Esther, who was a sister of the much revered Frederick Bertram Maurice, decided that the child was endangering his salvation by bestowing upon a 'creature' the love which was due to God alone. She therefore insisted that the cat should be given to her and the wretched little boy was compelled by his mother to agree. 'I took Selina in a basket to the Rectory. For some days it almost comforted me for going to the Rectory, because then I possibly saw my idolized Selina. But soon there came a day when Selina was missing: Aunt Esther had ordered her to be . . . hung!'

It was a frequent practice to hang in nurseries a small picture (sometimes in the form of a porcelain plate) on which was depicted a large and menacing eye, surrounded by the legend: 'Thou God seest me.' The child knew that it could never escape from supervision even when no adult was present, and it had already been taught enough about the nature of God to make the all-seeing eye a perpetual terror. One of the most popular *children's* books of the period was *The Fairchild Family*.[2] Mr Fairchild is depicted as a good, kind father, and he has been explaining to his children God's 'Plan of Salvation':

'Papa,' said Lucy, 'I fear, from what you say, that there are very few real Christians in the world, and that a very great part of the human race will be finally lost.'

1 Augustus J. C. Hare, *The Years with Mother*. Being an abridgement of the first three volumes of *The Story of my Life*. Edited with notes and Introduction by Malcolm Burnes, 1952.
2 Mary Martha Sherwood, *The Fairchild Family*, 1847.

Mr Fairchild then reads a few passages from the Bible and goes on:

'From these verses we may learn, my dear children, that all people who are not brought to believe in God the Father, God the Son, and God the Holy Ghost, the Blessed and Holy Trinity, as they are shown to us in the Bible, remain in their sins, and are in a state of condemnation. . . .'

'Oh! papa, papa!' said the children, 'pray for us, that we may not be wicked and go to hell.'

'I would have you remember, my dear children,' said Mr Fairchild, 'that there is no such thing as being saved, except by the Lord Jesus Christ, through his death; nothing you can do yourselves can save you. Even if you could, from this time forward, live without sin, yet you are condemned already for your past sins. Neither can you keep even one of God's commandments without the help of the Holy Spirit.'

'Papa,' said Lucy, 'we will pray to the Holy Spirit to help us, and then we shall get better.'

Certainly the religion of the middle classes in Victorian England was of the crudest redemptionist type. Whether they were 'Anglican' or 'Nonconformists', and the Evangelical School had adherents in both camps, they could all have sung (and did sing) with conviction the revolting words of the hymn written (alas!) by William Cowper:

> There is a fountain filled with blood
> Drawn from Immanuel's veins;
> And sinner's, plunged beneath that flood,
> Lose all their guilty stains.

Evangelical places of worship were, in the main, gloomy and uninviting. Most of the Nonconformist chapels were frankly hideous and the churches of the Establishment (especially if the incumbent was 'Low') were not much better. The services were dreary in the extreme. Sir Walter Besant, looking back from the year of the Queen's Jubilee to his own childhood, remarks:

The musical part of the service was . . . taken slow – incredibly slow; no one now would believe, who is not old enough to remember, how slow it was. The voluntary at the beginning was a slow rumble; the Psalms were read by the clergyman and the clerk alternately, the Gloria alone being sung. . . . Two hymns were sung; they were always of the kind which expressed either the despair of the sinner or the doubtful joy of the believer. I say doubtful because he was constantly being warned not to be too confident, not to mistake a vague hope for the assurance of election, and because, with the rest of the congregation, he was always being told how few in number were those elect, and how extremely unlikely that there could be many of those few in one flock. . . . There were many kinds of preachers – the eloquent, the high and dry, the low and threatening, the forcible-feeble, the florid, the prosy, the scholarly – but they all seemed to preach the same doctrine of hopelessness, the same Gospel of Despair, the same Father of all Cruelty, the same Son who could help only a few. . . . Wretched, miserable creed! To think that unto this was brought the Divine Message of the Son of Man! And to think of the despairing deathbeds of the careless, the life-long terror of the most religious, and the agony of the survivors over the death of one 'cut off in his sins'.[1]

It is difficult for us to be fair to the Evangelicals of the Victorian Age, but there is another side to the picture and Canon Charles Smyth is surely justified when he says that:

the real strength of Evangelicalism lay not in the pulpit or [on] the platform, but in the home. To those who believe that the typical Evangelical sermon was about hell-fire, that the typical Evangelical layman is fairly represented by the father of Sir Edmund Gosse, and that the typical Victorian parent was Mr Barrett of Wimpole Street, this may sound surprising. But, to judge from memoirs and biographies, the Evangelical families of England were conspicuously happy families.[2]

Part of the stock-in-trade of Evangelical preachers consisted of the denunciation of 'the Scarlet Woman', the 'Whore of Babylon', by which opprobrious terms was signified the Church of Rome. It is difficult for us to recapture the sense of fear and hatred which the Papacy inspired in the minds of the majority of Englishmen in the middle years of the nineteenth century. They detested it on moral, political and religious grounds. English tourists to the Continent, if they ventured inside a Catholic church 'for the sake of the architecture', were shocked by its meretricious gaudiness and full of pity, mingled with disgust, for the unhappy 'victims of superstition' kneeling at its altars.

The 'Papal Aggression' of 1851, by which Pope Pius IX re-established the Catholic hierarchy in England, provoked a fury of indignation. One has only to turn the pages of *Punch* to realize the almost universal hostility. Cardinal Wiseman, the first Archbishop of Westminster, was subjected to a storm of abuse, even if it took the form of humorous punning on the names of the two principal persons involved:

> Pius and Wiseman think in flames to fry us.
> O impious Wiseman, and unwise man Pius.

The fear and indignation were sharpened by the knowledge that there were people in England who had been busy for some years undermining the Citadel of Protestantism from within. These were the members of the so-called 'Oxford Movement'. When Victoria came to the throne the first shot in the campaign had already been fired, for it was in 1833 that John

1 Sir W. Besant, 'Fifty Years Ago', *The Graphic Jubilee Number*, 1887.
2 In *Ideas and Beliefs of the Victorians*, 1949.

Keble had preached his famous sermon on 'Natural Apostasy', inspired by what must seem to most people Parliament's very reasonable proposal to abolish, or rather to merge, a number of redundant Irish bishoprics. The even more famous *Tracts for the Times*, most of which were written by John Henry Newman, appeared at intervals between 1833 and 1841. What Newman proposed was, in effect, an exaltation of the clerical office. It was an 'appeal to the clergy that they should vest their claim upon their commission derived through the bishops from the Apostles. . . . But this stress on the historical ministry necessarily led to a respectful attitude towards Rome, through which that ministry had reached England.'[1] The 'Thirty Nine Articles' had been, as Newman clearly saw, a deliberate attempt to include in the Anglican fold as wide a variety of religious belief as possible, and therefore, if it was permissable to interpret them in a 'Protestant' sense it was equally permissible to interpret them in a 'Catholic' sense. This subtlety, so foreign to the English mind, caused Newman to be accused of mental chicanery and suspected of being a crypto-Catholic.

In one of its aspects the Oxford Movement was part of the general movement of Romanticism. One has only to look at the architecture of the time to note the appetite for anything Gothic. If only, the architects and even the interior decorators seem to be saying, we could have lived in the Middle Ages! Then we could have enjoyed at first hand the splendour of the cathedrals, the glories of stained glass, the magnificence of ecclesiastical vestments, the sweet chanting of monks, statues and altar lights.

The Anglican Church still had its gothic buildings (slightly disfigured, it is true, by Protestant additions) but it had lost everything else. It is not to deny the sincerity of the Ritualists, as they were called, to admit that they were at best partly moved by aesthetic considerations. And Newman and those who followed him had the logic to realize that if you begin by regretting the Reformation you end by joining the Church of Rome.

The suspicions of the Evangelicals were not entirely unwarranted, for although two of the leaders of the Oxford Movement, Pusey and Keble, remained in the Anglican commission, Newman, in 1845, 'went over' to Rome and was followed by many others. Those who remained adopted more and more of the apparatus of 'Ritualism', much to the dismay of the average Englishman, as can be seen, once more, very plainly in the pages of *Punch*:

> Though crosses and candles we play with at home,
> To go the whole gander, there's no place like Rome;
> We've statues and relics to hallow us there,
> Which, save in museums, you'll not find elsewhere.
> Rome, Rome, sweet, sweet Rome!
> For all us Tractarians there's no place like Rome!

1 E. W. Watson, *The Church of England*, 1914.

Ritualism, in spite of the Queen's known disapproval of all 'Puseyites and Romanisers', became for a time a fashionable craze. Incense was burned in the drawing-rooms of Belgravia and bedrooms were decorated with candles and holy pictures. Sad to say, some fine old vestments, purchased from antique dealers, were cut up for cushions and drapes. Fashionable ladies thronged to St Barnabas's, Pimlico, the leading Tractarian church, to revel in ritual and to gaze upon the handsome Rector, the Rev. Mr Bennett, 'doing everything quite beautifully'. Some of them began to go to confession and even to invite clergymen (no longer parsons but 'priests') into their homes for tête-a-tête conversations. The reaction of the ordinary English husband is indicated by a cartoon in *Punch* in 1858 showing John Bull preparing to horsewhip a High Church cleric who is hearing confession in a drawing-room.

Attempts were made to put down Ritualism by law and under the Public Worship Regulation Act of 1874 a number of priests went to prison. In general, however, the law was allowed to remain a dead letter, although it is interesting to note that as late as 1903 no less than a hundred Members of Parliament urged that effective action should be taken against Ritualism.

Although the Victorian age was an age of religious faith, with crowded churches and chapels, much church building, fervent preaching, and missionary activity, 'beneath the surface of respectable religious conformity there was a turmoil of doubt and uncertainty. Nearly all the representatives of Victorian thought, nearly all the intellectuals, had to struggle with the problem of unbelief.'[1]

Some of the finest minds began to be shocked by the sheer immorality of the Christian scheme of salvation as depicted by the extreme exponents of both Catholic and Evangelical orthodoxy. The whole idea of a substitutionary atonement coupled with the threat of eternal torment to those who rejected it, seemed to them unethical. The notion of an angry God who could be propitiated by blood sacrifices (even if, in the end, He decided to provide the sacrifice Himself) was seen to be a primitive superstition which, incidentally, had been outgrown by both the Hindus and the Greeks five centuries before our era. Many whose moral character was above suspicion, like John Stuart Mill, Matthew Arnold, Leslie Stephen and George Eliot, were increasingly unable to believe in such a deity.

All this however (since high-minded ethical persons are always in a minority) might have made little stir in the world of orthodoxy had it not found itself threatened from another quarter – that of scientific discovery. What had long been known as 'German criticism', that is, the application to the Bible of textual scholarship, had begun, rather tardily, to make headway in England. The authenticity of some of the books of the Bible

1 A.R. Vidler, *The Church in an Age of Revolution*, 1961.

was questioned; but this too was largely a matter for the learned. What made most noise was what might be called the biological attack on the literal interpretation of Scripture, although many of the protagonists were undoubtedly unaware of the furore they were about to cause.

Belief in the Bible as an infallible record had survived the attacks of geologists like Sir Charles Lyell and Dean Buckland who had indicated that existing books and fossils showed that the earth was much older than the accepted period of about 6,000 years (4,000 years from the Creation to the birth of Christ and nineteen centuries after it). Philip Gosse, a respectable scientist and the father of Sir Edmund Gosse, had provided the answer: God had deliberately put the fossils into the rocks in order to tempt man's faith. Such an extraordinary notion of the behaviour of Deity seemed preferable to an acceptance of the extended time-scale proposed by the geologists.

Peace reigned once more, but towards the end of 1859 Charles Darwin brought out his *Origin of Species*, and to the general public it came as a thunderclap out of a clear sky. Darwin had written in a deliberately un-provocative manner; he had not related the doctrine of Natural Selection to human beings, but had merely expressed the hope that by its means, 'light will be thrown on the origin of man and his history'. Nonetheless· orthodox theologians saw the dangerous implications clearly enough and girded themselves for battle.

In 1860 there was a meeting of the British Association at Oxford. Darwin himself was not present, but his disciple Thomas Huxley was, and so was Samuel Wilberforce, Bishop of Oxford, who was not only renowned as an orator and a wit but was supposed to be a scientist by reason of having taken a degree in mathematics. An onlooker records that 'in a light, scoffing tone, florid and fluent, he assured us that there was nothing in the idea of evolution; rock-pigeons were what rock-pigeons had always been. Then turning to his antagonist with smiling insolence, he begged to know was it through his grandfather or his grandmother that he claimed his descent from a monkey.'

The 'antagonist' was, of course, Huxley who proceeded to demolish the bishop to such good effect that he received an ovation. It was plain that Darwinism was not to be so easily disposed of. The public excitement grew steadily, the usual reaction being a mixture of indignation and amusement. Jokes about men and monkeys began to appear in *Punch* in 1861. It was perhaps unfortunate that Darwin himself had a somewhat simian cast of countenance and the caricaturists seized the opportunity with both hands. One of *Punch*'s versifiers asked:

> Am I satyr or man?
> Pray tell me who can,
> And settle my place in the scale,

A man in ape's shape,
An anthropoid ape,
Or monkey deprived of its tail?

On a more serious level some of the best minds of the day were gravely disturbed by the doctrine of Evolution. As Alec Vidler puts it:

The whole scheme of Christian belief, which was based on the supposition that man had all at once been created with a fully formed capacity for communion with God, a capacity that the human race had lost through the disobedience of the first human pair, was thrown into disarray. The work of Christ had been to redress this primordial catastrophe. If that had not happened, then the doctrine of redemption and atonement stood in jeopardy too.

Even more disturbing was the idea of the 'Survival of the Fittest', and Tennyson expressed in noble language the anguished doubts which must have troubled many thoughtful minds:[1]

Are God and Nature then at strife,
That Nature lends such evil dreams?
So careful of the type she seems,
So careless of the single life; . . .

'So careful of the type?' but no.
From scarped cliff and quarried stone
She cries, 'A thousand types are gone;
I care for nothing, all shall go.

'Thou makest thine appeal to me;
I bring to life, I bring to death;
The spirit does but mean the breath;
I know no more.' And he, shall he,

Man, her last work, who seem'd so fair,
Such splendid purpose in his eyes,
Who roll'd the psalm to wintry skies,
Who built him fanes of fruitless prayer,

Who trusted God was love indeed
And love Creation's final law –
Tho' Nature, red in tooth and claw
With ravine, shriek'd against his creed –

Who loved, who suffer'd countless ills,
Who battled for the True, the Just,
Be blown about the desert dust
Or seal'd within the iron hills? . . .

1 *In Memoriam*, LV2, LVI 1–5, LV 3–4.

> I falter where I firmly trod,
> And falling with my weight of cares
> Upon the world's great altar-stairs
> That slope thro' darkness up to God,
>
> I stretch lame hands of faith, and grope,
> And gather dust and chaff, and call
> To what I feel is Lord of all,
> And faintly trust the larger hope.

Darwin's theories came as a great shock to the Victorian mind, but they did not (in spite of Tennyson's anguished cry) destroy its fundamental optimism. Darwin himself disclaimed all pessimistic conclusions, and in the final words of *The Origin of Species* states quite clearly his own conviction that:

as all living forms of life are the lineal descendants of those which lived long before the Silurian epoch, we may feel certain that the ordinary succession by generation has never been broken and that no cataclysm has desolated the whole world. Hence, we may look with some confidence to a secure future of unappreciable length. And as natural selection works solely for the good of each being, all corporate and mental environment will tend to progress towards perfection.

Such words of course gave great offence to those who still believed in Noah's Flood and the Second Coming of Christ; and the time was certainly a very disturbing one to the pious. Darwin and Huxley might be dismissed as atheists (which they were not) and Tennyson as a poet with a morbid mind (he was much criticized for the 'morbidity' of *In Memorium* in which the lines we have quoted appeared). But what if theologians and even the bishops themselves entered into the fray and not always, like Wilberforce, on the 'right' side? The very same year, 1860, which witnessed the beginning of the Darwinian controversy, saw the publication of a volume entitled *Essays and Reviews*. This was the work of seven contributors under the general editorship of Benjamin Jowett, the famous Master of Balliol, and they included Frederick Temple, then Headmaster of Rugby, C. W. Goodwin, Mark Pattison and others. The whole volume was a plea to be allowed 'to say what we think freely within the limits of the Church of England'. Perhaps the essay which gave most offence was C. W. Goodwin's on 'The Mosaic Cosmogony' in which he declared that the story of Creation as recorded in Genesis should be regarded as a Hebrew myth.

Essays and Reviews was violently attacked by Wilberforce (again!) and by many of the Anglican clergy, and the Bishops decided to take action. Two of the authors were accused and condemned by the Court of Arches for denying the inspiration of Sacrifice and the doctrine of eternal punishment. But the Judicial Committee of the Privy Council reversed this judgment and in the witty word of the Lord Chancellor, 'dismissed hell with costs, and took away from orthodox members of the Church of England their last hope of eternal damnation'. But when Gladstone nominated Temple to a bishopric there was a tremendous outcry. Nonetheless he became Bishop of Exeter and, in due course, Archbishop of Canterbury.

It was plain to the pious portion of the general public (and it was then a much larger body than it would be today) that the Bishops themselves were not to be trusted, and this opinion was fortified by the pronouncements of Bishop Colenso of Natal.

Bishop Colenso had a somewhat literal mind and he was troubled by the difficulties of the feeding arrangements in the Ark afloat upon the waters of the Flood. He came, regretfully, to the conclusion that 'the story told in the Book of Genesis is utterly incredible which involves the necessity of Noah taking in a supply of animals, or of animal food, for the special use of the carnivorous beasts and birds, and of Noah and his family taking round two or three times a day food and water to such a multitude of animals, supplying them daily with fresh litter (how stored and kept?) and removing the old, with other considerations of the same kind.' He also wondered how the Ark could have 'rested' for more than seventy days on the top of Mount Ararat, which is 17,000 feet high, without every living creature inside it being frozen to death.

These reasonable questions evoked a storm of vituperation. Pamphlets and books poured from the press. Colenso was accused of having betrayed the Christian religion and of not being quite right in the head. One author, after demolishing in one terrific broadside, Colenso, Darwin, Huxley and everyone else who dared to question the literal interpretation of Scripture, ended triumphantly with the words: 'Revelation neither invokes human science to confirm its truth, nor does it challenge human science to disturb them. It does not stoop to notice science at all; and in thus not deigning to regard it silently declines its feeble support – and as silently defies its puny opposition.'[1]

Many pious Victorians were doubtless comforted by these brave words, and the Evangelical wing of the Church of England and almost the entire Nonconformist body (with the exception of the Unitarians) continued to ignore both Darwinism and the Higher Criticism, and to preach 'Fundamentalist' Christianity in its crudest form. The last quarter of the nineteenth century indeed, saw a series of religious 'Revivals' in which the old blood-and-fire doctrines were preached with immense earnestness and to large congregations. Nonetheless it was becoming increasingly plain that Revivals even when promoted with all the apparatus of American publicity, were subject to the 'law of diminishing returns'.

1 J.R. Young, *Modern Scepticism*, 1865.

K

At a more intellectual level the rearguard action of Christian apologetics took on an air almost of desperation as the nineteenth century drew to its close. There were those known as the 'Reconcilers' who strove to make peace between Science and Genesis by allowing 'days' to mean long periods of time and by admitting that 'creation might be construed as a gradual process'. Gladstone was the last formidable exponent of this line of thought, but in his contest with Huxley in the pages of the *Nineteenth Century Review* the victory plainly rested with Huxley.

There were some who (while remaining Christians) abandoned the literal truth of Scripture altogether, maintaining that it was intended to teach spiritual truth only. This was dangerous ground, for many felt that if there never was a Garden of Eden and if the Fall of Man was no more than 'the possibility of a primeval deviation',[1] then the whole doctrine of the Redemption was in peril, and with it Christianity itself. With much justification it was said[2] that:

in England it was geology and the theory of evolution that changed us from a Christian to a pagan nation. . . . The art and literature and morality of Europe were based on the Bible, understood in the old simple way. The later Victorians, isolated in vast deserts of space and time, with God seemingly removed to the dim status of a remote Architect of the Universe, could no longer feel themselves one with those who dwelt contentedly in the little universe of past centuries. . . . And so Victorians moved out of man's ancestral home, with its temples, palaces, cottages and cathedrals, golden with age, tenderly formed by the hands of the makers, into the fine new city of science – so convenient, so hygienic, so reasonably planned – but devoid of human tenderness and ancient beauty. The loss has never been repaired and man today is still a displaced person in a land that he has yet to make his home.

Few of the Victorians, however, were at all conscious of the 'Waste Land' which their descendants were to inhabit. Even when they had lost their religious faith their moral fervour remained. The Agnostics themselves have been called 'a new Nonconformist sect', and the lives of most of the leaders were irreproachable, as if to point the lesson that it was possible for men to be good without any formal religion at all.

The religious Nonconformists regarded themselves as the guardians of public morality and in the last quarter of the nineteenth century they attained a position of political power which they never had before. The Nonconformist Conscience, as it was called, became effective in the eighties in a campaign to purify public life by driving out of it those whose conduct transgressed the strict laws of morality. How Melbourne or Palmerston would have laughed at such a notion, but politicians were soon to discover that their misdemeanours were now no laughing matter.

1 These are the words of Teilhard de Chardin, S.J.

2 By T. Sherwood Taylor in *Ideas and Beliefs of the Victorians*, London 1949. Dr Sherwood Taylor was Director of the Science Museum and a Catholic.

That Parnell was the lover of Mrs O'Shea must have been known to a wide circle which almost certainly included her husband and probably Gladstone himself. When the scandal broke the Reverend Hugh Price Hughes held a public meeting in St James's Hall where he thundered from the platform: 'What is morally wrong can never be politically right.' Gladstone (in spite of his own High Church proclivities) relied for much of his majority on the Nonconformist vote and Liberal agents all over the country warned him that the Party could only be saved by throwing Parnell overboard. So Parnell, the last person, perhaps, with whom a satisfactory system of Home Rule for Ireland could have been negotiated, passed out of public life, a broken man, and the stage was set for all the horrors of 'the Troubles'.

Similar hind-sight must regret the termination of the political career of Sir Charles Dilke, accused, like Parnell, of adultery with a married woman. Men of the world were convinced that Dilke's best course would have been to brazen it out. Instead he persisted in claiming to be the 'injured party' and even in spite of his known agnosticism took to going to church in an endeavour to win over the respectable to his cause. He was no doubt a brilliant man with a wide knowledge of Foreign Affairs and, had he continued in office, might have done much to prevent the outbreak of the First World War. But History is full of such 'ifs', and it is perhaps doubtful if Queen Victoria, after the scandal, would ever have accepted him as a Minister.

In any case the Nonconformists rejoiced at his downfall. *The Methodist Times* boasted that 'Sir Charles Dilke defied the Nonconformist Conscience and is a political outcast today. Parnell despised the Nonconformist Conscience and he destroyed himself and his party. Lord Rosebery ignored the Nonconformist Conscience for a racehorse and the world sees the result.'[1]

Adultery and horse-racing were, it would seem, equally repugnant to the Nonconformist Conscience, and many decent people must have been alarmed by Hugh Price Hughes' clarion call 'to abolish slavery, drunkenness, lust, gambling, ignorance, pauperism, mammonism and war'. Perhaps it would be simpler to abolish human nature and have done with it.

The Nonconformist Conscience persisted into the twentieth century, but in another form. It lost its evangelicalism but retained its moral fervour and played no small part not only in the development of the Labour Party but in creating the climate of public opinion in which social reform could flourish. The Welfare State is, in one sense, its creation, although the pioneers of the movement would probably look with pained surprise upon an affluent society which prefers the Bingo hall to the Nonconformist chapel and a pop singer to the most eloquent preacher in the world.

1 *The Methodist Times*, October 1896.

6 The Inner Man

The Englishman in the early years of the nineteenth century had a healthy contempt for everything foreign, particularly for foreign food. He despised French 'kickshaws' and 'made dishes', and a satirist like James Gilray could make savage fun of Germans eating salad and sauerkraut. By the middle of the century however the more sophisticated, especially those who had had the opportunity of travelling abroad, began to realize that there was at least one Continental country where dining was an art. 'They order these things better in France.'

The author of a book entitled *Host and Guest*[1] feels compelled to admit that while England in the mid-nineteenth century leads the world in many fields, she falls sadly behind in gastronomy:

Men dine to satisfy hunger in England, and to sustain and strengthen themselves for those avocations, professional, parliamentary, and commercial, into which they throw more eager energy, more properly-directed vigour, force and intensity than any other nation under the sun, not even excepting the Americans. It may be a humiliating confession, but in England no learned treatises have been written on the art of dining or dinner-giving . . . we can compare, combine and search out causes in morals, science, and legislation, but we have given no heed to the canons or combinations of cookery. We have given birth to a Bacon, a Locke, a Shakespeare, a Watt; but we are without a Vatel, a Béchamel . . . or a Carême. We have perfected railroads, steamboats, and canals, but we cannot make a *suprême de volaille* in perfection, nor arrange *des petits choux en profiteroles* . . . we have beaten the nations of the earth in fabrics of linen, woollen, and cotton; but we are ignorant of epigrams of lamb, and know nothing of *salpicons à la Venétienne*. We have invented the safety-lamp, the stocking-frame, and the spinning-jenny; but we hopelessly try our hands at *filets de lapereaux en turban*, and ignominiously fail in *salmis* of partridge *à la bourguignone*. . . . We have given liberty to the slave, and preached the pure word of the gospel to the nations subjected to our dominion and sway; but we still eat butter badly melted with

1 A. V. Kirwan, *Host and Guest*. A Book about Dinners, Wines and Desserts, 1864.

our roast veal, and we have not yet invented three hundred and sixty-four ways to dress eggs.

Our author admits that:

within the last thirty years great improvements have been introduced into the domestic cookery of the highest nobility, and within the last twenty years, owing to frequent intercommunication, such has been the rapid progress that one may fancy oneself dining in the Rue de Bourbon, the Rue de Grenelle, or the Rue St Florentin, instead of Grosvenor or Belgrave Square or Park Lane; but still, while anything is imperfect something remains to be done, and in the continuation of peace, we may look forward with hopefulness, not alone to an extended commerce, but to an improved cookery. . . . If we descend in England beyond the upper ten thousand, though the fried and roast are generally excellent, the attendance good, and the display of glass, crystal and plate much greater and better kept, than in any other country and capital in the world, yet the cookery is not to be compared to the finer *cuisine bourgeoise* of Paris . . . the gentry and higher middle classes in Paris enjoy an exquisite and not expensive cuisine bourgeoise, but English or foreigners are rarely met at their dinners . . . Englishmen, notwithstanding the extensive intercourse they have had with the Continent, still like to sit an hour or so over their wine, after the ladies have departed, whereas in Paris ladies and gentlemen leave the *salle à manger*, or dinner table, together, and retire to another room to coffee and conversation. The coffee and liqueurs dispatched, the dinner circle is dissolved by host and guests either proceeding to the theatres, or to some *cercle* and a *réunion*, where other friends are met . . . the parties sit down to their repast at six or seven, and separate at half past eight or half past nine, when it is not too late to go to the Italian or French opera, or even to the Theatre du Palais Royal, the Vaudeville or the Variétés. . . . It is a pity we do not adopt something of this system among all classes in England.

The dinner hour in England was getting later and later by a curious and apparently inevitable progression. In the course of three centuries it had been pushed forward by no less than ten hours. Henry VIII dined at ten o'clock in the morning, the Elizabethans at noon. By the middle of the eighteenth century the usual dinner time had become three o'clock in the afternoon. At the beginning of Queen Victoria's reign unpretentious folk like the Carlyles dined at six, more fashionable people at seven.

And what dinners they were! The author of *Host and Guest* tells us that 'in all grand dinners for ten persons in England, two soups, two fishes, and four *entrées* for the first course are considered indispensable; and two roasts, two removes, and half a dozen *entremets* for the second course. For a dinner of twenty, the *entrées* and the *entremets* would necessarily have to be doubled, being each increased to eight. . . .'

To the modern mind this is very puzzling, and bewilderment is increased when we consult the cookery books themselves and find recommended for a *first* course 'various soups, fish dressed many ways, boiled meats and stewed, tongue, ham, bacon, steaks, variously prepared, ragoûts and fricassées, meat pies raised, and in dishes, patties of meat, fish and fowl, stewed pigeons, puddings, boiled or baked, vegetables boiled and stewed'; and a second course which offers 'birds, and game of all sorts, shell-fish, cold and potted, collared and potted fish, pickled ditto, potted birds, spinach, preserved fruit tarts, omelettes, macaroni. . . .'

And these first two courses were followed by 'removes' and 'entrées', the former defined by Francatelli, whose famous *Cook's Guide* was still in use in the sixties, as 'large dishes placed at the top or bottom end of a dining-table, or served from the side-table; they mostly consist of roast, boiled, braised, or otherwise lightly dressed meats.' Entrées he defines as 'first course side dishes'.

Host and Guest from which we have already quoted, is more explicit. 'At dinners of any pretention,' he says:

the first course consists of soups and fish, removed by boiled poultry, ham, or tongue, roasts, stew, etc.; with vegetables, with a few made dishes as *ragoûts*, curries, hashes, cutlets, patties, *fricandeaux*, etc., in as great variety as the number of dishes permits. For the second course, roasted poultry or game at the top and bottom, with dressed vegetables, omelets, macaroni, jellies, creams, salads, preserved fruit, and all sorts of sweet things and pastry are employed, endeavouring to give an article of each sort, as a jelly and a cream. This is a more common arrangement than three courses, which are attended with so much additional trouble both to the guests and servants.

Whether the dinner be of two or three courses, it is managed nearly in the same way. Two dishes of fish dressed in different ways, if suitable, should occupy the top and bottom; and two soups, a white and a brown, or a mild and a high-seasoned, are both disposed on each side of the centre-piece: the fish-sauces are placed between the centre-piece and the dish of fish to which each is appropriate; and this with the decanted wines drunk during dinner, forms the first course. When there are rare French or Rhenish wines, they are placed in the original bottles, in ornamental wine vases, between the centre-piece and top and bottom dishes; or if four kinds, they are arranged round the plateau. If one bottle, it is placed in a vase in the centre.

The second course, at a purely English dinner, when there are three courses, consists of roasts and stews for the top and bottom; turkey or fowls, *fricandeaux*, or ham garnish, or tongue besides; with small laid-dishes at the corners, served in covered dishes as palates, curry, of any kind, *ragoûts* or *fricassé* of rabbits, stewed mushrooms, etc., etc.

The third course consists of game, confectionery, the more delicate vegetables dressed in the French way, puddings, creams, jellies, etc. . . .

When the third course is cleared away, cheese, butter, a fresh salad, or sliced cucumber, are usually handed round; and the finger-glasses precede the Dessert. . . .

The Dessert at an English table, may consist merely of two dishes of fine fruit, for the top and bottom; common or dried fruit, filberts, etc., for the corner or sides, and a cake in the middle with ice pails in hot weather. Liqueurs are handed round at this stage; and the wines usually drank (*sic*) are placed, decanted, on the table along with the dessert. The ice-pails and plates are removed as soon as the company finish their ice.

To the modern mind this is almost incomprehensible and matters are not made much clearer by studying an actual menu. The following, culled from a publication entitled *A New System of Domestic Cookery, by a Lady*, shows what was offered to guests at a fairly unpretentious dinner given by a middle class host:

Long Table Once Covered

Fruit Tart	One Turkey or Two Poults	Blancmange
	Mock Turtle Soup	
Harico		Sweetbreads larded
Mash Turnips	Jerusalem Artichokes	Stewed Spinach
	fricasseed	
Carrots thick round		
Cray fish	Savoy Cake	Dried Salmon in papers
	Macaroni Pudding	
Ham braised	Trifle	Chicken
	Fresh Pie	
Casserole of Rice		Pickled Crab
with giblets		
	Stewed Celery	
Sea Cale		Young Sprouts
	Apple Pie and Custard	
Fricandeau		Ox Rumps, and
		Spanish Onions
	Rich White Soup	
Jelly Form		Cheesecakes
	Fish	
	(Remove – Venison, or Loin of Veal)	

Light dawns when we realize that this is not the time-sequence of a meal but the plan of a table. In short, with the exception of the dishes which were substituted for others (the 'Removes') and the special dishes brought in separately (the 'Entrées') the food was all on the table at once. Even so the variety and quantity seem to us prodigious.

By the end of the sixties a new method was beginning to come into favour. It was known (somewhat improbably) as *diner à la Russe*, and a contemporary cook-book expresses some reservations about its advantages:

There have been endless discussions as to the relative merits of the two systems of serving; named, rather arbitrarily, the one *à la Française*, the other *à la Russe*. The first consists in setting the whole of a course on the table at once, taking each dish off to serve it[1]; in the second mode, the dishes are brought to table already cut up, which makes it difficult to present them otherwise than in fragments. . . .

Both systems have their advantages and disadvantages; the mode of serving *à la Russe* is undeniably simpler and more expeditious than that *à la Française*, the complications and slowness of which have been justly criticized; but in the former system, the necessity of cutting up all the dishes before the guests see them, puts an end to the possibilities of decoration which many cooks turned to so good account, and tends to destroy the tasteful and rich appearance which formerly characterized high-class cookery.[2]

Victorian cookery, up to about the middle of the century, was the last relic of the notion which had made mediaeval dining, on the grand scale, more like a theatrical pageant than anything we should recognize as a dinner-party. The great pies in the form of castles, the great cardboard dragons out of which tumbled a bewildering variety of fish: these had dwindled to elaborate table decorations, but the impulse was the same. One has only to look at the coloured plates in a contemporary cookery book such as Gouffé's, to realize that the presentation of a dinner was still thought of in terms of décor. In the recipe he gives for '*calf's head en tortue*', after elaborate directions for the actual cooking, he continues:

Make a bread border round a dish; place a bread *croustade* in the centre; put the pieces of bread round it; and pour over the ragoût, prepared with the tongue, cloves, &c; drain the brains, and put them on the top of the *croustade*.

Garnish round the *croustade* with the ears, sweetbreads, crayfish, gherkins, yolks of eggs etc. . . .

Put some crayfish, truffles, and cocks' combs, on five silver skewers; stick them in, as shown in the coloured Plate; glaze the truffles; and serve, with some Sauce *à la Tortue* in a boat.

For another recipe (for serving a fillet of beef) he recommends the cook to 'take a dish, and with some boiled rice, make a *socle*, or stand, on it, of the same length and breadth as the fillet, and three inches in height; brush it over with egg; and colour it in the oven. I may mention, at once, that this *socle* is in no wise part of the dish itself; it is not intended for eating, and is only introduced to raise the fillet, in order that the garnish may be seen to advantage.' And the garnish, once more, consisted of cocks' combs and truffles impaled on silver skewers.

The *socle* was 'not intended for eating'. One feels indeed that it was a vandalism to eat any of the dish. It ought to have been put under a glass shade like the stuffed humming birds and wax fruit which were such conspicuous ornaments of the Victorian drawing-room.

1 This was itself an innovation. The earlier method was to carve the dishes on the table. Even Royalty did this. King Louis XVIII being reputed particularly skilful.

2 Jules Gouffé, *The Royal Cookery Book*, 1868.

Even when such visual *tours-de-force* had been abandoned the dinners served in great houses continued to be both lengthy and elaborate, and in order to be convinced that such meals were served not only in France and England but all over Europe it is only necessary to study the menu of a banquet given by King Ludwig II of Bavaria in Munich in 1877. The occasion was a gathering of his pet Order of Chivalry, the Knights of St George. They were attired in robes of light blue silk with mantles of ermine and the fare was as follows:

> Turtle Soup
> Plovers' eggs – Caviare – Radishes
> St George's *Spiesse* (? a kind of mixed grill)
> Salmon, Sauce Hollandaise
> Turkey with new vegetables
> Sirloin of Beef with stuffed mushrooms
> Saucissons *à la* Richelieu, haricots verts
> Calves' ears with truffles
> River Crayfish, Herb Sauce
> *Mauwein*[1]
> Roast Snipe and Capons
> Asparagus with Melted Butter
> Pineapple au Riz
> Petit Fours
> Strawberry, Vanilla and Apricot Ices
>
> *Wines*
> Sherry
> Chateau Yquem
> Hermitage Moussec
> Champagne
> Forster Freundstück, Ausbruck, 1871
> Tokay
> Liqueurs

Dinner giving was necessarily an expensive business and required a large staff of servants. In the great houses of Belgravia there would probably be a regular steward or *maître d'hotel* as well as a French chef. In addition to these would be from a dozen to fifteen servants, exclusive of the butler and under butler, waiting at table. The cost of their keep, their liveries, their beer money, and their wages, would amount to from £1,600 to £2,000 a year. The gentlemen of moderate means had to make do with a much smaller number of servants, although the number employed would still seem very large by modern standards. So would the

1 Sir Harry Luke who discovered the menu in the museum at Herrenchiemsee and reproduces it in *The Tenth Muse* (1954) declares that *Mauwein* is a hock cup flavoured with sweet woodruff. Presumably it took the place of a sorbet.

dinner it was thought necessary to provide, for, says our author, 'it is within the power of every gentleman of fair means to give a good soup, a good fish, a couple of removes, and four *entrées* at the first course, and a couple of small roasts, a couple of removes, and a few *entremets* at the second course, and what can any reasonable man want in addition?' What indeed!

Writers of the period are loud in their denunciation of pretentious dinners given by people who could not really afford them; and even when they were given by people who could afford them they were accompanied by so much formality that they must often have been a weariness of the spirit as well as something of a strain on the flesh. 'Going in to dinner' was a ceremony in itself and was almost as much hedged round with protocol as a Coronation procession:

The host communicates to each gentleman the name of the lady he is to take in to dinner. If they are strangers to each other, the host introduces his friend to the lady. When the 'guests are met and the feast is set', the butler announces the latter to his master, who then offers his arm to the lady to be escorted by him. This should be either the oldest lady, the lady of the highest rank, or the greatest stranger; but in smart society precedence is no longer allowed for brides. The other guests follow arm-in-arm, and the hostess closes the procession, escorted by the gentleman who has been appointed to the honourable post, and who has been elected for one of the three reasons above-mentioned, as being the eldest or of highest rank, &c.[1]

We are not told what happened if the guests included a nonagenarian, a duke and a Chinese mandarin.

A certain Mr Walker 'formerly of Trinity College, Cambridge and afterwards a police magistrate' has some very sensible things to say about the formal set dinner of the mid-Victorian period:

The present system of dinner-giving I consider thoroughly tainted with barbarism and vulgarity, and far removed from real and refined enjoyment. As tables are now arranged, one is never in peace from an arm continually setting on or taking off a side dish, or reaching over to a wine cooler in the centre; then comes the more laborious changing of courses, with the leanings right and left, to admit a host of dishes, that are set out only to be taken off again, after being declined in succession by each of the guests, to whom they are handed round; yet this is the fashion and not to be departed from. With respect to wine, it is often offered when not wanted, and when wanted, is perhaps not to be had until long waited for. It is dreary to observe two persons, glass in hand, waiting the butler's leisure to be able to take wine together, and then, perchance, being helped in despair to what they did not ask for; and it is still more dreary to be one of the

1 Lady Colin Campbell, *Etiquette of Good Society*, 1911. It may seem surprising that such formality should have lasted until 1911, but the present author has been present at dinner parties in country houses where it was still observed in the early nineteen-twenties.

two yourself. How different when you can put your hand upon a decanter the moment you want it!

Englishmen were gradually becoming more civilized (that is to say more Frenchified) in their manner of serving wine. It is interesting to note that the custom of icing claret – it will be remembered that in the generation before, Keats had been in the habit of dusting his tongue with pepper the better to appreciate the coolness of iced Claret – was beginning to go out, for we are told that it was the custom in France 'to serve Claret with a tepid napkin round the Claret-jug or decanter into which the wine was poured or round the green glass bottle itself, if, as indeed it more frequently happened, the wine was not decanted. This gentle heat brings out advantageously the flavour and aroma of the wine.'

Englishmen were very far as yet from understanding the niceties of a succession of wines. At many tables it was the custom to serve Champagne throughout the meal and Claret and Port with the Dessert, which seems to us a very odd arrangement. Our author remarks however:

that a glass of Pomard, Nuits, or Chambertin, may be very well taken after the first mouthful of a good haunch of South Down or a *filet de boeuf à la poivrade* is swallowed. Neither should I object to a repetition of the dose (whatever Lord Brougham who contends for Claret after game may say to the contrary) after swallowing a slice of woodcock, partridge, or that excellent bird, so justly be-praised, the golden plover; but to reserve Burgundy for the *entremets sucrés* or dessert, is a piece of rampant snobbishness worthy or a *nouveau riche*.

. . . With good bins of Sherry, Madeira, Port, Claret, (white and red), Champagne, Hock and Burgundy, any gentleman is in a position to entertain his guests worthily. . . . At most London dinners in the season, Champagne, Sauterne, Barsac, Rhenish and Moselle wines are produced; but of the four latter wines scarcely more than a bottle of each is used, though three or four bottles of Champagne may be consumed, in a party of twelve.

Some of the prices of the sixties are of interest:

If gentlemen have personal friends or connections at Cadiz in whom they can confide to send them wine in the piece, they may lay in Amontillado, Montilla, Manzinilla at 10s. or 12s. a dozen less than they can obtain them at the wine merchants in England. Anything like a first rate Amontillado sold at English wine merchants at from 72s. to 84s. a dozen, while Manzinilla and Montilla range from 60s. to 70s.

Fabulous prices are given for old Ports, and East India Sherries and Madeiras, at the sales of well known *connoisseurs* in wine. Many East India Sherries are sold for nine and ten guineas a dozen, and much of the late Mr Justice Talford's Port went for eleven and twelve guineas a dozen. Though the wine was excellent, this was unquestionably a fancy price. There is no need to give so large a sum for an old and first-rate Port. Any man of ordinary acumen and intelligence, in addressing himself to a first-rate wine house in London may have excellent, if not first-rate, Port at about three to four guineas a dozen, and considerably cheaper if he buys it in the wood.

First-rate Claret has been rising in price during the last five or six years; but even in London, first-rate Clarets ought to be and are procurable at from four to five guineas a dozen, and the best sparkling Champagne at about the same price, or a shade lower. Sillery Champagne of the very highest quality is sold by wine merchants at six guineas a dozen. Burgundys of the highest quality are rare and difficult to find good; but excellent Beaune and Chablis can be obtained at two guineas a dozen in London, and considerably cheaper if imported direct.

A glass of Chablis, Barsac or Sauterne will be taken after the oysters, while a glass of Old Madeira or Sherry follows the soup. In the middle of the first course in France, they serve Champagne or sparkling Burgundy; and towards the end of the first course, the finer kinds of Claret white and red. With the roast comes Burgundy and Hermitage, and these wines, as well as Bordeaux, may be served with game. With the Dessert it is the custom in France to offer Malmsey and Malaga; but these wines are rarely produced in England though white and red Constantia and Frontignan are frequently produced.

In the last sixteen years the consumption of Champagne has doubled in England. In 1831, the quantity of French wine imported amounted, in round numbers, to 254,000 gallons, whereas in 1861 it amounted to 2,227,000 gallons.

Everybody in England, it seemed, was trying to ape the class two or three degrees above him in the social scale, and Thackeray, as might be expected, launched a regular broadside against 'Dinner-giving Snobs':

Suppose you, in the middle rank of life, accustomed to Mutton, roast on Tuesday, cold on Wednesday, hashed on Thursday, etc. with small means and a small establishment choose to waste the former and set the house topsy turvy by giving entertainments unnaturally costly – you come into the Dinner-giving Snobs Class at once. Suppose you get in cheap made dishes from the pastry cooks, and hire a couple of greengrocers, or carpet-beaters, to figure as footmen, dismissing honest Molly who waits on common days and bedizen your table (ordinarily ornamented with willow-patterned crockery) with tuppenny-ha'penny Birmingham plate. Suppose you pretend to be richer and grander than you ought to be – you are a dinner-giving Snob.

A man who entertains in this way – and – alas how few do not! – is like a fellow who would borrow his neighbour's coat to make a show in, or a lady who flaunts in the diamonds from next door – a humbug in a word, and amongst the Snobs he must be set down.

Poor Dinner-giving Snobs! You don't know what small thanks you get for all your pains and money! How we Dining-out Snobs sneer at your cookery and pooh-pooh your old Hock, and are incredulous about your 4s. 6d. Champagne, and know that the side-dishes of today are *réchauffés* from the dinner of yesterday, and mark how certain dishes are whisked off the table untasted, so that they may figure at the banquet tomorrow. Whenever, for my part, I see the head man particularly anxious to escamoter a *fricandeau* or a *blanc-mange* I always call out, and insist upon massacring it with a spoon.

Why, then, do we of the middle-classes persist in giving entertainment so costly, and beyond our means? This will be read by many mortals who are aware that they live on leg-of-mutton themselves, or worse than this, have what are called meat-teas, than which I cannot conceive a more odious custom; that ordinarily they are very sober in their way of life; that they like in reality that leg-of-mutton better than the condiments of that doubtful French artist who comes from the pastry-cooks, and presides over the mysterious stew-pans in the kitchen; why, then, on their company dinners should they flare up in the magnificent manner in which they universally do?

Everybody has the same dinner in London, the same soup, saddle of mutton, boiled fowls and tongue, *entrées*, Champagne and so forth. I own myself to being no better and no worse than my neighbours in this respect and rush after the confectioners' for sweets, etc.; hire sham butlers and attendants; have a fellow going round the table with still and dry Champagne, as if I knew his name, and it was my custom to drink those wines every day of my life. I am as bad as my neighbours.

And Thackeray adds, very pertinently:

If it be pleasant to dine with your friends, as all persons with good stomachs and kindly hearts will, I presume, allow it to be, it is better to dine twice than to dine once. It is impossible for men of small means to spend five-and-twenty or thirty shillings on each friend that sits down at their table. People dine for less. I myself have seen at my favourite Club, (the Senior United Services), His Grace the Duke of Wellington quite content with the joint, one-and-three, and half-pint of sherry wine, ninepence; and if His Grace, why not you and I?

The club, indeed, was the answer, so far as the middle class bachelor was concerned, but it was no longer the club as Dr Johnson would have understood it: simply a gathering of friends who met at regular intervals at one particular tavern. The nineteenth century club was something quite different. It had a house of its own, sometimes on a very grandiose scale, it was maintained by annual subscription and admitted no one but its members within its portals. Many such clubs grew up in London during the second quarter of the century. The author of *The Food of London*[1] makes the interesting suggestion that:

the battle of Waterloo was in one sense the cause of the present club system. With the cessation of war and so many soldiers 'out of work', the officers, accustomed to mess together when on duty, and appreciating the advantages of economy (the military and naval officers are anything but wealthy as a class), established a Club, mainly in the view of making their slender incomes carry them on as comfortably as might be. Hence originated the United Service, the Junior United Service, The Navy, The Guards, and the Army and Navy Clubs – the great success of the first named having acted as a great incentive to the others. The dignitaries of the Church, the Clergy and University Professors,

1 George Dodd, *The Food of London*, 1854.

observing how well the military and naval members were served, and wishing to share the advantages, established the United University and the Oxford and Cambridge Clubs. Then arose the Athenaeum, for the Judges, Barristers, Physicians, Authors, Philosophers, Artists; The Travellers, open to those who had 'seen the world', by penetrating a certain number of miles beyond the limits of England; The Oriental chiefly for all Indian Officers; The Carlton and the Conservative, for politicians of a certain hue; the Reform for politicians of opposite stamp, and others of lesser celebrity. They are now nearly forty in number.

Some of the clubs, especially those in Pall Mall, were erected on a most magnificent scale; the food was in general excellent. The celebrated Soyer was the chef at the Reform, presiding over a suite of rooms which measured 110 by 40 feet, comprising a kitchen, cold meat larder, sauce larder, pastry room, a butler's pantry, plate closet, a boucherie, a game larder, a vegetable kitchen, with all the impedimenta of stoves, spits, hot plates, ice drawers and the rest. But the point of the club was not to indulge in the higher reaches of gastronomy, their object was to serve good meals at a reasonable price. The average cost of a dinner at the Athenaeum for example in the early Victorian period was no more than 2s. 9¾d. and it was possible to dine at the Junior United Services for 2s. 3d. exclusive of wine. Moralists approved of clubs on the ground that they had added in abolishing the once fashionable vice of drunkenness.

The rising young barrister or literary man found the club an immense advantage. Thackeray looked back to the days when those who had not a half guinea at command

used to dive into dark streets in the vicinage of Soho or Covent Garden, and get a meagre meal at shilling taverns – or Tom, the clerk, issued out from Law Chambers in Pump Court and brought back your dinner between two plates from a neighbouring ham-and-beef shop. Either repast was strictly honourable, and one can find no earthly fault with a poor gentleman for eating a poor meal. But that solitary meal in Chambers was indeed a dismal refection. I think with anything but regret of those lonely feasts on beef and cabbage and how there was no resource for the long evenings but those long books, over which you have been pouring all day, or the tavern with its deuced expenses, or the theatre with its vicious attractions. A young bachelor's life was a clumsy piece of wretchedness then – mis-managed and ill-economized.

A great advance in civilization was made, and the honesty as well as economy of young men of the middle classes immensely promoted, when the ancient tavern system was overthrown, and those houses of meeting instituted where a man, without sacrificing his dignity, could dine for a couple of shillings. I remember in the days of my youth a very moderate dinner at a reputable coffee house cost a man half a guinea; when you were obliged to order a pint of wine for the good of the house; when the waiter got a shilling for his attendance; and when young gentlemen were no richer than they are now, and had to pay thrice

as much as those at present need to disperse to the maintenance of their station . . .
that is why we ought to be thankful for Clubs.

It was estimated that all the clubs of London, taken together, provided
between twenty and thirty thousand dinners each during the course of a
year, and this multiplied by the number of clubs made a very substantial
contribution to the feeding of the upper classes, or at least of the male
portion of the upper classes.

The 'male portion of the upper classes' (which included what the French
would call *la grande bourgeoisie*) was well catered for. 'But how', asks a
writer of the early years of our period, 'could those commercial and
working men who take but few meals at their own homes procure their
breakfast and dinner and tea and into what society are they thrown!' and he
proceeds to answer his own question by telling us that there were about two
hundred places in London 'which can fittingly come under the denomina-
tion of eating houses, occupying a place between the hotels on the one
hand and the coffee rooms on the other. At all these places joints of meat
are devoured every day.' Meat indeed there seems to have been in abun-
dance. The English were still among the great meat eaters of the world,
and we hear of 'Williams's boiled beef shop in the Old Bailey' and of innumerable chop houses where 'roast beef, boiled beef, roast haunch of
mutton, boiled pork, roast veal and ham, pigeon pie and rump steak
pudding' were part of the daily service.

At the 'alamode beef-houses' the visitor could ask for a 'sixpenny' or even
a 'fourpenny plate'. Readers of Dickens will remember that David Copper-
field, while he was lodging with the Micawbers, had considerable experience of looking for cheap meals in the middle of the day. Sometimes he
contented himself with stale pastry or a slice of currant pudding, but, he
adds:

when I dined regularly and handsomely, I had a saveloy and a penny-loaf, or a
threepenny plate of red beef from a cook's shop; or a plate of bread and cheese
and a glass of beer from a miserable old public house . . . called The Lion or the
Lion and something else that I have forgotten. Once I remember carrying my
own bread (which I had brought from home in the morning) under my arm,
wrapped in a piece of paper, like a book, and going to a famous alamode beef-
house near Drury Lane, and ordering a 'small plate' of that delicacy to eat
with it.

From this catalogue of dining opportunities which, no doubt, reflects
Dickens' own experience, there is only one serious omission. It was
possible for a poor man to visit one of the soup-houses where he was
served with 'a basin of prime soup, potatoes and a slice of bread' for
twopence. A less penurious individual could buy a steak at a butcher's,
carry it into a public house and have it grilled on the spot for a charge

of one penny. It was also customary to take cold meat to coffee shops, and to eat it there with the bread and coffee provided. But some of these establishments had already opened dining-rooms where cold ham and even chops and steaks could be obtained. It is interesting that this is spoken of as a novelty in the forties, and that one of the witnesses examined before the committees set up to investigate the eating habits of the metropolis declared that 'the custom had its origin in the request, as a matter of favour, on the part of some of the gentlemen who took coffee at his house, that he would furnish them with the means of partaking of a chop or steak without going to a tavern.' The bulk of his customers were what we should now call 'black-coated workers' who had neither the leisure nor the means for long and strong potations in the middle of the day.

Some reformers thought that the improvements which had taken place in public houses were by no means all to the good. The pot-house had given place to the gin-palace, decorated with magnificent crystal mirrors. Even the personnel of the establishments had been transformed for, as George Dodd tells us:

the old Boniface with his red nose and his white apron, has made way for the smart damsels who prepare their toilettes to shine at the bar. The comfortable landlady is less seen than formerly, esconced behind and amongst her rich store of cordials of compounds and liqueurs; she too, must pass under the hands of the milliner before making her daily appearance in public. Even the pot-boy is not the pot-boy of other days; there is a dash of something about him which might almost be called gentility; his apron is cleaner than were the aprons of pot-boys twenty years ago and the tray filled with quarts and pints of dinner-beer, carried out to the houses of the customers, seems to have undergone some change, for it is less frequently seen than 'in days of yore'.

There were in the middle of the nineteenth century, an enormous number of public-houses in London, it being estimated that the licensed victuallers numbered 4,500, the beer-sellers some 2,000, which meant that one house in every forty-five was a public house and served 350 of the inhabitants of the city.

The desolating glories of the gin-palace are among the most painful sights in London. If the gaudiest display of plate-glass, polished mahogany, and gilding were associated with anything that really contributed to the comfort of the people, there might be points to admire in the artistic arrangement in some of these places; but degraded wretchedness brings more money to the gin-palace than working-class respectability; and the drinkers, at every visit, rivet the chain that already binds them to the thriftless and impoverished part of the community.

An innovation of the early Victorian period was the coffee shop (not of course to be confused with the teashop of the late nineteenth century).

There had long been old-fashioned coaching inns, commercial dining-rooms in the city, tap houses and the taverns of the Fleet Street district as well as the humble cooks' shop, but the coffee shop was quite different. It was in origin a breakfast and tea house for the working man but by degrees it extended its range of business and managed to provide simple dinners to such as were willing to take coffee instead of beer. In the evening the coffee shop was used as a reading room, providing a good fire and a supply of newspapers and magazines, the only cost of admission being a few pence for a cup of coffee.

Between eating houses and dining-rooms there was a difference, if only a slight difference, of class; workmen in their white and brown aprons and paper caps took their meal at an eating house, but the city clerk with his black coat and silk hat patronized the dining-room which was very little more expensive. There was a supply of hot dishes from twelve noon to six in the evening, and of course most of the houses were to be found in the neighbourhood of Cheapside. Further east the coffee houses were more like taverns and they were frequented by merchants, dealing for the most part in foreign commodities as is indicated by the very names of the establishments: 'The Jamaica', the 'North and South American', the 'Levant' and the 'Baltic'.

In view of the public demand, and the support of the growing Temperance Movement', it is astonishing that, at first, so little is heard of tea. It is true that elegant ladies might refresh themselves, after the exhaustion of shopping in Bond Street, by stopping at Gunter's or some similar high-class establishment. Often they had ices brought out to them in their carriages. If they entered in order to eat confectionery, they frequently had a glass of port or sherry rather in the manner of the French *goûter*. The triumphant advance of tea really dates from the successful attempt to grow tea in India and Ceylon in every increasing quantity. This provided an article at once cheaper in price and apparently more acceptable to the average English palate than China tea had ever been. The way was open for the establishment of the teashop as we know it.

As with so many other national institutions, the teashop has no authenticated date and place of origin. It was not invented, it evolved. This is curiously illustrated by the very names of two of the great teashop 'chains' of London – The Express Dairy Co., which derived from the old Nell Gwynne milk shop in the Strand, and the Aerated Bread Company ('ABC'), which was a bakery business long before the day when, somewhere in the late 1870s, the manager of the shop at London Bridge started making cups of tea for his regular customers.

One of the other big teashop businesses, Messrs Lyons, did not evolve in quite the same way, but when in 1866 Joseph Lyons decided to give up music for business and the firm of J. Lyons & Co. Ltd was established, few

L

could have foreseen the final ramifications of that vast enterprise. The first Lyons teashop was opened in London in 1894, and a further stage in this new era of popular catering was begun.

In the provinces, too, the late nineteenth century saw the rise of the teashop in most of the industrial and business centres. Its new mode of catering was just in time to meet the demand, not only of male clerical workers, but of the increasing army of women who were beginning to take their place in the life of the city. If there had been no teashops it is hard to see where the pioneer typist could have gone for a meal. She would certainly not have ventured into a tavern, and the chop house was beyond her means. The convenience and cheapness of the teashops made them a permanent part of English social life.

So much was this so, that the old-fashioned confectioner's establishment became something of a rarity. Certainly the type of shop described (no longer ago than 1903) by George R. Sims would, today, take some finding. 'Port and sherry decanted and labelled', he says, 'are to be seen in most confectioners' shops where they serve soup, jelly in glasses, and sandwiches, and occasionally – very occasionally – hot meat patties. In some the wine licence is taken advantage of to keep a bottle of champagne on an instrument which allows it to be drawn off through a tap a glass at a time.' Equally curious is the dairy described by Sims in his *Living London* where one could drink curds and whey, accompanied by small spongy currant cakes.

In the eighties there was a real revolution in the dining habits of the English upper classes. They began to save themselves from all the complications of dinner-giving at home by entertaining their friends in restaurants. At the beginning of our period, of course, this would not have been possible: the restaurants simply did not exist, and no respectable woman would have dreamed of taking her meals in public.

After the disasters of Sedan and the Commune it was the French refugees who, in 1871, swarmed into London and found that the kind of café and restaurant to which they had been accustomed was not to be found in the English capital. The only exception seemed to be the Café Royal in Regent Street founded by the enterprising M. Nicol. At first it was a very small establishment indeed with stuffed pheasants, fruit and gilt-topped bottles in its window. Its fortune was made by the French immigrants and in the next thirty years it expanded into gorgeousness and took its place among the great eating-houses of the world.

For English people there was, at first, something a little raffish and daringly Continental in frequenting such places. For Continental they were. Pagani's in Great Portland Street began as a resort for foreign musicians; Gatti's and Romano's in the Strand had a similar origin but began to be frequented by English journalists and 'members of the lighter stage'. The

Cavour, in Leicester Square, was another Bohemian rendezvous with its long bar decorated with many-coloured glasses, its broad divan running along the wall with little tables beside it. Kettners' was a maze of private dining-rooms to which no respectable man would have taken his wife.

There were, however, other establishments on a grander scale and these were increasingly patronized as the century drew to its close. People of the utmost respectability began by dining out on Sundays, as this practice not only enabled them to escape from the inevitable cold meat but 'allowed the servants to go to church'. Colonel Newnham-Davis, in his admirable *Dinners and Diners*, first published in 1899, speaks of people 'who, as a rule, ring the changes for their Sunday dinner from the Savoy to the Carlton, from Prince's to the Berkeley'. Such people in the nineties had a wide choice, for a whole series of restaurant palaces had arisen each decorated in its own grandiose style. The Carlton and the Savoy were followed by the Ritz. Claridges' was rebuilt into a towering red-brick structure with granite columns and the porte-cochère laid with india-rubber to deaden the noise of the horses' hooves. Newnham-Davis describes the 'dignified room' where one dined:

The windows are draped with deep red curtains and purple portières; the carpet carries on the scheme of quiet reds, and the chairs have morocco backs of vermilion, with the arms of the hotel stamped on them in gold. The white plaster ceiling is supported by great arches, the bases of which and the walls of which are panelled with darkish oak, in which patterns of olive wood are set. The quiet-footed waiters in evening clothes, with the arms of the hotel as a badge on the lapels of their coats, are in keeping with the room.[1]

Not only the waiters were in evening clothes. The guests also were expected to dress for dinner at all those establishments already mentioned as well as at the St James's Restaurant in Piccadilly, the Cecil in the Strand, and in any of the three great hotels which had sprung up in the newly pierced Northumberland Avenue. If a man, for any reason, was not in evening clothes he could still dine in these establishments, but in the grill room, not in the restaurant.

Odd as it seems today, the station hotels at the principal railway termini attracted a similar smart clientèle and were planned and furnished on the same splendid scale. People who, in Newnham-Davis's phrase 'had faced the journey to Marylebone more than once on the Sabbath', found a lounge which was 'all faience, and marble and Oriental rugs, and great palms and easy chairs', and a banqueting hall in which 'the walls are of Norwegian marble, a marble of light greens and yellows and pinks; its ceiling is of cream and gold; the twelve marble columns that support the roof are white in colour, thickly veined with pink and grey; and over the

1 Lieut.-Col. Newnham-Davis, *Dinner and Diners*, 1899.

grill, which is at one end, is a long frieze depicting a number of beautiful ladies who are apparently meant for the Seasons. . . .'

The early Victorian merely dreamed that he dwelt in marble halls; now, if he had lived long enough, he could at least dine in them. Yet he might have felt, quite rightly, that all these splendid establishments of the end of the century marked the decay of the sentiment of 'Home, sweet Home'. Indeed, English life in the late nineties had become Continental to a degree which would have seemed impossible fifty years earlier. For the upper classes, at least, there was very little difference between London and Paris.

Relaxations and Dissipations

A French commentator[1] remarks, with tongue in cheek, that although the English, in the Victorian Age, took a very serious view of life, they were, none the less, human beings, and therefore in need of relaxations. It was the English Sunday in particular which impressed – and depressed – the foreign visitor, for, as we are told:

London in the sixties and early seventies was the saddest and most gloomy capital in Europe. In the morning Church Bells clanged over empty streets. An expression of misery might be read on the faces of the few hurrying pedestrians. A curious silence pervaded the thoroughfares. At the hours for repairing to Church or Chapel, sad-faced men and women and demure little hypocrites of boys and girls in stiff Sunday best, made dutiful marches. After Church came the awful mid-day meal of roast beef, Yorkshire pudding and apple tart. The afternoon was usually devoted to sleep.

The proletariat, as a rule, remained in bed until the public houses opened. Crowds of saddened creatures suffering yet from the effect of Saturday night's carousals clustered round the doors of the gin-palaces.

The upper classes, of course, had the 'social round' to keep them busy if not exactly happy. During the Season, if the weather was fine, it was customary to go to Hyde Park and either ride or drive or watch others doing so. Many returned after tea and, by a curious convention, while the fashionable venue in the morning was the stretch between Knightsbridge and Hyde Park Corner, in the afternoon it shifted to that part of the Park which lies north of the Achilles statue, the drive parallel with Park Lane. Meanwhile many ladies were going through the complicated ritual of 'leaving cards', and, after six-thirty, as Mrs Peel tells us, 'women drove from house to house to find each crowded with women and elderly men who drank tea, iced coffee, or cup, or ate sandwiches, cakes, strawberries and cream, and ices, listened to professional musicians, and gossiped.'

The professional musicians were also to be heard at after-dinner parties,

1 Jacques Chastenet. *La Vie quotidienne en Angleterre, 1837–1851*, 1961.

for a favourite social event of the period was the *conversazione*. Thackeray has left us a lively account of one such function:

Amidst the crowd and the scuffle, and the perpetual buzz and chatter, and the flare of the wax candles and an intolerable smell of musk – what the poor Snobs who write fashionable romances call 'the gleam of gems, the odour of perfumes, the blaze of countless lamps' – a scrubby-looking, yellow-faced foreigner, with cleaned gloves is warbling inaudibly in the corner, to the accompaniment of another. 'The Great Cacafogo', Mrs Botibol whispers as she passes you by. 'A great creature, Thumpenstrumpss, is at the instrument.' . . .

To hear this Cacafogo and Thumpenstrumpss, a hundred people are gathered together – a bevy of dowagers, stout or scraggy; a faint sprinkling of misses; six moody-looking lords, perfectly meek and solemn; wonderful foreign Counts, with bushy whiskers and yellow faces, with a great deal of dubious jewellery, young dandies with slim waists and open necks, and self-satisfied simpers, and flowers in their buttons; the old stiff, stout, bald-headed *conversazione roués* whom you meet everywhere – who never miss a night of this delicious enjoyment; the three latest lions of the season – Higgs, the traveller, Biggs the novelist, and Toffey, who has come out so on the sugar question; Captain Flash, who is invited on account of his pretty wife; and Lord Ogleby, who goes wherever she goes. . . . Who are the owners of all those showey scarfs and white neck cloths? – ask little Tom Prig, who is there in all his glory, knows everybody, has a story about everyone; and, as he trips home to his lodgings in Jermyn Street with his gibus hat and his little glazed pumps, thinks he is the fashionablest young fellow in town, and that he really has passed a night of exquisite enjoyment.

George du Maurier in his drawings for *Punch* is equally satirical, particularly of those who used the musical evening as a means of ascending a step or two of the social ladder. The anonymous author of *Party-Giving on Every Scale* tells us that:

Professors of music and singing – men of undoubted ability, but who, like many others, have their way to make in the world and do not find it ready made for them – are sometimes glad to give their services gratis at the houses of ladies possessing a large and fashionable circle of acquaintances, on the consideration of being presented to the most influential ladies present or those ladies who are likely to require professional services at their own parties. . . .[1]

Du Maurier's Mrs Ponsonby de Tomkyns is clever enough to take advantage of this situation:

Mrs Ponsonby de Tomkyns (*sotto voce to her husband*) 'Ponsonby!' – 'Yes, my Love?' – '*Who* is that, singing so divinely?' – 'Signor Jenkini, my Love, the famous new Tenor.' – 'Signor Jenkini, is it? Then get yourself introduced to Signor Jenkini as soon as he's done his song, and secure him for Monday fortnight.' – 'But, my Love, Signor Jenkini charges forty guineas!' – 'Tell Signor Jenkini that it's to meet the Duchess of Stilton, and he won't charge anything at

1 Anon. *Party-Giving on Every Scale*, 1882.

all!' – 'But, my Love, the Duchess of Stilton will never come to see the likes of us!' – 'She'll come fast enough to hear Signor Jenkini. Do as I tell you!' (*Ponsonby did as she told him, and everything happened as she had anticipated. The Duchess came, and a good many smart people besides; and the Signor sang for nothing but to the immortal honour and glory of the House of Tomkyns.*)[1]

The ordinary course of social life in London Society must have been pleasant enough to share in and even agreeable to watch. A foreign resident, who was 'for some eighteen months a secretary of legation' rises to lyric heights in his appreciation:

London society is far the most perfect thing of the kind in the world, and it must be a dull man who would fail to extract amusement and pleasure from it. . . . Its chief good is in what it offers him to look at – the carriages flashing back and forth at the dinner-hour, looking like caskets or Christmas-boxes with the most wonderful lining and furniture (the drapery and lace almost floating out of the windows), the balls and parties, the acres of fair-armed British maidens through which he may wander as in a wilderness, the odours of the midnight gardens, the breath of the dawn, and the first flush of sunrise over Hyde Park as the drowsy cabman wheels homeward and to bed.[2]

The same young American diplomat is, however, very definite on one point, the advantage of being a 'dancing man'. 'In London,' he says:

in order to 'get on' one must be great or famous, or one must dance. Unless a man is a very decided catch and an object to the 'mammas', dancing is about his only utility. The average London man of society thinks dancing a very slow amusement. He is either athletic and prefers hunting and yachting, or he is dissolute, and simple pleasures pall upon his jaded appetite. As a rule, too, the important young men do not dance. The greater a man is, the more he is careful to abstain from anything which will make him entertaining. His dullness is always in proportion to his distinction. . . . To be sure, all young people dance. How would 'golden youth' be possible if there were no ballrooms? But when they get towards five-and-twenty, those who can afford not to dance desert the balls for the concert-saloons. Young noblemen and eldest sons will spend a few moments at the parties, and as a great favour to the hostess, will walk through a quadrille with the prettiest girl in the room. But how can one who has at hand the *cancan* and the casinos find amusement in anything so puerile as the waltz? Who cares to talk to humdrum cousins when one may drink bad champagne with painted women in a gilt café near the Haymarket?

The temptation was even greater for those who had not been invited to dance or dinner party for, as our author points out, there was nothing for the solitary clubman to do after dinner but to seek 'the society of the ladies who frequent the Argyll and the Alhambra'.

1 *Punch*, 1879.
2 E. S. Nadal. *Impressions of London Social Life*, 1875.

There is plenty of contemporary evidence that men of the highest society frequented the dancing saloons. Albert Smith described the *male* part of the clientèle of the old Adelaide Gallery:

Let us point out to you the persons who pass in this droll Kaleidoscope of London life. That good-tempered young man leaning against the railing, and talking to a small silver-grey bonnet, is an Earl. He is making an engagement for the next dance. . . . By his side are two unmitigated Gents[1] in white coats, and hats out of the perpendicular, short sticks, and flaring cravats, who think they are 'doing the fast'. . . . The two young men, lounging around, arm in arm, are in the Guards. They are nodding to a good-looking fellow with long spiral mustachios and jet black eyes, in the reserved seats above, next to a very florid, merry-faced gentleman, whose blood is as nearly royal as may well be,[2] and voice the same. . . . Anon, a tribe of young *littérateurs* making the visit on the strength of the 'orders' of the journals with which they are connected. Next, a group of shop-boys, who would like to smoke if it were allowed; a few men-about-the-City from Mark Lane, Lothbury, and Throgmorton Street; some provincial visitors, one or two university men, out on the loose; and then a crowd of those faces you are so familiar with, in the London world, but whose names and families you never know.[3]

There was a curious democracy in London life at this period. Certainly in our own egalitarian days it would be difficult to find a place of entertainment containing such a cross-section of society.

The English upper classes seem to have lost in the nineteenth century the taste for music which had characterized them in the eighteenth, but they still went to the opera to see and be seen. Society women remained seated in their boxes, but during the intervals they received male visitors to chatter for a few moments over the rival merits of Grisi and Jenny Lind. The swells who had no visits to make stood in a body in the wide space in front of the orchestra and swept the boxes with their opera glasses.

As in Paris, privileged persons were allowed to go behind the scenes. Albert Smith describes the picture presented:

the gorgeous costumes of the opera just concluded, a mass of colours relieved by the simple black of half-a-dozen young aristocrats from the stalls, who are lavishing well-worn compliments in French of various merit. The stage is filling – fair girls in fleecy clouds of gauze, trip on by twos and threes, striking out their well-turned limbs and pointing their pliant feet, that no mischance amid the mysteries of dress may interfere with their flexible movements in the approaching *ballet*. . . . The little 'Vanity Fair' is at its busiest, when a lane is suddenly formed, and into the heart of the crowd glides the Pet of the Ballet. A graceful gyration or two, more a matter of habit than of business, and the little creature stands, with a gracious smile, to receive the incense every hand is bringing. . . . A

1 i.e. *not* gentlemen; but the 'white coats' are surprising.
2 Obviously a Royal Highness of some sort; could it have been the Duke of Cambridge?
3 Albert Smith. *Gavarni in London*, 1849.

Relaxations and Dissipations

Honoré Daumier, *Drama* (c. 1858)

Edgar Degas, *The Ballet* (1872); a performance of Meyerbeer's *Robert le Diable*

Opposite top: A scene on Boulogne pier, *c.* 1862

Opposite centre: Cremorne Gardens, 'The Chinese Platform', *c.* 1858.
These were among the most celebrated pleasure-gardens in London

Opposite bottom: The Cyder Cellars, *c.* 1850, an early example of the
London Music Hall

Melodrama poster, Chanfran as 'Rube', *c.* 1872   Hermann the Lion Tame
c. 1860

The Siamese Twins

Opposite: Adolf Menzel, *The Théâtre Gymnase* (1856); the Paris theatre which, more than any other, fostered the beginnings of domestic drama

Right: Fiddling clowns, *c.* 1870

P. T. Barnum with General and Mrs Tom Thumb

Prince Alfred, Duke of
Edinburgh, as Bacchus in
amateur theatricals at
Buckingham Palace, 1854

German students, c. 1860, showing the German passion for uniforms

Skating in Vienna, 1887; photograph by Oscar van Zel

Constantin Guys, *Children playing horse and carriage*

Duke, not a young one, salutes her, with the bow that has become as proverbial as a certain other Duke's touch of the hat. *Danseuses* know the value of Dukes – none better; and nothing can be sweeter than the answering look. But His Grace's attentions are merely courtesies, and he is as calm as an ice-lake. But look there. That young Marquis is in the Guards, and he is in love with her; and observe how restless his eye is. He sees a new bracelet of emerald on her arm, and he does not see his own last present; and although he is a Marquis, and a guardsman, and moreover a member of Parliament, who ought, at this moment, to be in his place, supporting the Religious Education Bill (on which he spoke very well the night before the Derby), he is as plebeianly jealous as any shopman out for a Sunday with his little milliner. And here comes another of her admirers, a Hebrew Croesus, with a bow not so fine as the Duke's, but with a waistcoat far finer than his – and he presents a *bouquet*, fastened into a jewelled band. And there comes . . . the writer of a leading journal – see how she smiles at *him*, though he brings neither a bouquet nor a fine waistcoat.

The theatrical ladies of the period were well aware of the virtues of publicity.

Opera was presented at Her Majesty's Theatre in the Haymarket, and the only other official theatres were Covent Garden and Drury Lane. However, from 1843 onwards, all theatres were allowed to produce any plays they wished, subject of course, to the censorship of the Lord Chamberlain. It would be absurd to pretend that the first half of Victoria's reign was one of the great periods of English theatrical history. The pieces presented were, for the most part, crude melodramas which the public nonetheless delighted in.

The cockney of the early Victorian period was an assiduous theatre-goer. The main houses, in addition to those already mentioned, were the Haymarket, the Adelphi, the Lyceum, Sadler's Wells, the Princess's, the Queen's, the Olympic, the Strand, the Coburg, the Royal Pavilion and the Garrick; and, writing in the year of the Queen's Jubilee, Sir Walter Besant makes the interesting remark:

These theatres were not open all the year round, but it was reckoned that 20,000 people went every night to the theatre. There are now thirty theatres at least open nearly all the year round. I doubt if there are many more than 20,000 at all of them together on an average in one night. Yet London has doubled, and the visitors to London have been multiplied by ten. It is by the visitors that the theatres are kept up. The people of London have in great measure lost their taste for the theatres, because they have gone to live in the suburbs.[1]

Before the great migration of the fifties almost everybody who worked in the City, lived in the City; and, in the East End this remained true for another century. And the East Enders were great patrons of the theatres, many of which were cramped and dirty to a degree which a later generation

1 Sir Walter Besant, *The Graphic*, Jubilee Number, 1887.

Opposite: A private dance, 1880

would have found intolerable. Blanchard Jerrold describes one such place which he visited with Gustave Doré when they were preparing their great book on London. The lowest kind of theatre was known as the 'penny gaff', and Jerrold says:

> The true penny gaff is the place where juvenile Poverty meets juvenile Crime. We elbowed our way into one, that was the foulest, dingiest place of public entertainment I can conceive: and I have seen, I think, the worst, in many places. The narrow passages were blocked by sharp-eyed young thieves, who could tell the policeman at a glance, through the thin disguise of private clothes. More than one young gentleman speculated as to whether he was wanted; and was relieved when the sergeant passed him. A platform with bedaubed proscenium, was the stage; and the boxes were as dirty as the stalls of a common stable. . . . The house was thronged; and as we entered, a man with a cloth reaching well over his shoulders, was just venturing upon the tightrope. The sea of upturned faces was almost the saddest sight I can remember. . . . Every human countenance was haggard, scarred with the desperate battle of life, defaced, degraded, or utterly brutalized. The stage, too, was crowded with an extraordinary company. The seal of poverty was on all those wondering heads; and of vice, upon most of them. We are changing all this, however, in the East, as it has been changed within the memory of middle-aged men, in the West.[1]

Jerrold was writing in the early seventies and the improvement he noted was due to the rise of the music hall, which, in the last quarter of the nineteenth century, transformed itself from a dingy dungeon into a glittering palace.

One of the pioneers of the old music hall was John Rhodes, who instituted impromptu concerts at an old hostelry called the Unicorn in Fountain Court, off the Strand. Here the coalheavers had been accustomed to assemble, and it was on their account that the place came to be known as 'The Coal Hole'. Rhodes provided hot suppers of such proletarian delicacies as stewed eels, tripe and onions, cowheel, and sausage and mash at very cheap rates, and the fame of his sing-songs soon spread far and wide. Edmund Kean, as well as other theatrical celebrities of the time, was frequently to be seen at The Coal Hole.

Thackeray describes a visit to the Cave of Harmony where he had not been for some time:

> Grigg and I went through the Piazza and down the steps of that well remembered place of conviviality. Grigg knew everybody; wagged his head in at the bar, and called for two glasses of his particular mixture; nodded to the singers; winked at one friend – put his little stick against his nose as a token of recognition of another; and calling the waiter by his Christian name, poked him playfully with the end of his cane, and asked him whether he, Grigg, should have a lobster kidney, or a mashed oyster and scalloped 'taters, or a poached rabbit, for supper.

1 G. Doré and B. Jerrold. *London – A Pilgrimage*, 1872.

The room was full of young rakish-looking lads, with a dubious sprinkling of middle-aged youth, and stalwart red-faced fellows from the country, with whiskey-noggins before them, and bent upon seeing life. A grand piano had been introduced into the apartment, which did not exist in the old days; otherwise, all was of yore.

A rival to The Coal Hole and the Cave of Harmony was the Cyder Cellars in Maiden Lane, and it was here that W. C. Evans, a former lessee of Covent Garden Theatre, had the ambitious notion of engaging professionals to entertain the company. The success of these enterprises encouraged him to move to larger premises, and he found in a handsome mansion in Covent Garden Piazaa (the site of which was later to be occupied by the National Sporting Club) a house suited to his purpose. It had already served as a family hotel 'with stabling for 100 noblemen and horses' and was famous for its lavish repasts. Evans converted what had been the dining-room into a concert hall with stage and supper tables.

Evans might be considered the grandfather of the music hall. In 1855 his 'Cave of Harmony' was enlarged by his successor 'Paddy' Green who built a new concert hall on the site of the garden at the rear. The new hall could accommodate 800 persons who consumed chops, steak, devilled bones and welsh rarebits washed down by copious draughts of ale and stout and not a little brandy and water, while listening to some of the best vocalists of the day. It is curious to note that ladies were not admitted except to one reserved box by the side of the stage. Perhaps that was the reason for the comparative propriety of the proceedings, and, certainly, when 'ladies' were admitted in the seventies, the place suffered a rapid decline.

The title of 'Father of the Halls' is usually given to Charles Morton, a Pimlico tavern-keeper, who in 1848 inaugurated A Musical Saturday Night at the Canterbury Arms, on the south side of Westminster Bridge. Patrons paid nothing for the entertainment, Morton's sole profits being derived from the sale of drinks and suppers, but his success was so great (it is perhaps hardly surprising when we learn that Sims Reeves was one of his early attractions) that he enlarged his premises to accommodate no less than 1,500 persons.

Not content with this, the 'people's caterer', as Morton was called, moved over the river, and on the site of an old inn at the junction of Oxford Street and Tottenham Court Road, he built the Oxford Music Hall. As in his former establishment, the patrons sat at little tables where drinks were served and hot suppers could be obtained till one o'clock in what had originally been a portion of the old inn. In this perhaps we may see the beginning of the separation between the two kinds of 'entertainment'. In later music halls even the little tables were abolished. The 'New Oxford', opened to the public in 1893, was a regular playhouse.

Writers today tend to look at the old Music Hall through a mist of nostalgia. Even those old enough to have known it in Edwardian days, describe the vast palaces and well-conducted establishments of that period. An anonymous journalist writing on the 'alls of the seventies and eighties paints a very different picture. He tells us that the Pavilion (not of course the modern Pavilion but an earlier building on the same site), the Trocadero which had arisen on the ruins of the Argyll Rooms, the Oxford in Oxford Street and Westons in Holborn, were small, hot, ill-ventilated and stuffy, and, he says:

The moral atmosphere was as warm as the physical. . . . No woman of the period with which I am dealing, with any regard for her reputation, would think of entering one of these places for entertainment. She would run the inevitable risk of being affronted by the Patrons of the Hall, and being outraged by words and gestures by the performers on the stage. Phryne swarmed in the auditorium – poor soul! – and by the bars lounged or swaggered the shameless males . . . who lived by the exploitation of female beauty.

Having once got his customer more or less comfortably seated, or propped up close to a bar, inside his ''all', the main object of the proprietor was to induce him to drink as much as possible of very bad wine and spirits at positively fancy prices. Phryne, always hovering near, exhibited a nice solicitude in forwarding the proprietor's views in this direction. The waiters, during the frequent 'waits' made a descent on the stalls, and, forcing their legs through the exiguous spaces, contributed largely to our discomfort . . . originally the ''all' was merely an annex to a big public house. The thing commenced in 'Harmonic Clubs', 'Free-and-Easy', and the like, and many of the customers and traditions of the 'Free-and-Easy' persisted for a long time under the mode and condition of things. Thus, the programme was, as yet, an unknown document, and the singers were introduced by a vigorous person who sat on an elevated arm-chair with his back to the stage, and his eye moving over the House. To this day I can never quite make out to what class of society the individuals belonged who sat round the Chairman's table. They must have had money, for cigars and brandy-and-soda, and even that Champagne which was innocent of grape, were consumed at their expense. An indifferent honest crowd, no doubt. Sharks, exploiters, peanut-markers, sporting touts, reinforced from time to time by a contingent of monied 'mugs'.

At the 'Mogul' in Drury Lane – afterwards known as the 'Middlesex' – presided nightly the King, Emperor, Titulary chief, or Chairman. This was a man named Fox. His face, in crimson by potations long and deep, was large, and beamed with good nature. His nose was immense and pendulous – more a proboscis than a mere nose. But the boys in the gallery – a rough lot they were – took old Fox very seriously indeed. It was quite amazing to witness the way in which, by merely rising and calling upon some delinquent by name, he could quell an incipient riot among 'the gods'. Thieves and their Trulls, the scourings of Drury Lane tributaries, and enormous denizens of the turnings off the 'Dials' – they were quelled by the menace of his eye, and trembled at the deep bass of his commanding voice. . . .

Leybourne was still singing 'Champagne Charlie is my Name' when I heard him, and an amusing sight was nightly afforded of various clerks from Lincoln's Inn, and shop boys from Islington, and young men-about-town on twenty-five shillings a week, waving their mugs of beer or 'goes' of whiskey and madly joining in the exhilarating chorus as though Champagne was their daily beverage. But it was not to join in his Bacchanalian choruses that the greater part of the audience crowded to hear Leybourne's songs. The 'star comique' was ever provided with offal for the pigs in the front. And it was when the orchestra began on the opening bar ditties like 'Oh, Why did She Leave her Jerimia?' that necks were craned and ears set. For the pornographic part of the show was now 'on'. The words of the song itself would not offend save by reason of their inanity. But between the verses the singer introduced long monologues known to musical bards as something 'spoken'. It was in these 'spoken' interpolations that Leybourne let himself 'go'. He cheerily set out to discover how far a pornographic artist could proceed with a music hall audience. Sometimes he played with suggestion and innuendo. But properly encouraged and liberally stimulated, he would spurt filth from his mouth as a juggler emits flames from the same orifice. The more reckless he became the more delighted grew his audience, that was Leybourne as I remember him. And Leybourne was typical of the Music Hall as it then was.

Other Music Hall artists there were, who, however disinclined they might feel in the matter, were obliged to follow in the wake of the 'lion comique'. Arthur Lloyd was a genuine humorist, and had a peculiarly velvet quality of voice which was conspicuous by its absence in the throats of his contemporaries. . . . 'The Great Vance' was another of the Music Hall favourites. This wonderfully over-rated person belonged to the Leybourne school of thought, and illustrated the swell of the period as accurately as was possible by a man whose aspirates were scarcely on a level with his aspirations. 'The Great MacDermott' came a little later than the trio I have named . . . MacDermott had been a sailor in the Royal Navy. . . . In the Fo'castle there was a constant demand for the very class of song which was finding so much favour at the hands of the groundlings when this songster took to the stage. And as a follower of Leybourne, the sailor-man turned comedian made his first efforts. He was minded if he could to 'go-one-better' than the creator of 'Champagne Charlie'. But that wonderful impersonator had already sounded the depths. MacDermott, however, soon asserted his claim to second place with such compositions as 'Moses and Ayron sat on a Rock'. These essays in an equivocal genre brought the singer quickly to the front. Yet it was not as an illustrator of pornographic minstrelsy that MacDermott was to make his 'hit'. When that wave of patriotism which its detractors called 'jingoism' swept the country, MacDermott was to the fore as the Laureate and Bard of the patriots. . . .

One of the female performers in the Music Hall of this time was Bessie Bellwood, famous not only for the sauciness of her songs but for the quickness of her repartee. Her speciality was depicting women of the coster class – which indeed was her own. She was immensely popular and thousands turned out to light the streets through which her funeral procession passed. Our anonymous journalist tells us that her occupation before she went on the stage was that of skinning rabbits in the East End, and he goes on to make the intriguing, but frustrating remark, that: 'Notwithstanding the obscurity of her origin and the mediocrity of her attainments, she was the chosen domestic companion of a Duke and of a Marquess!'

Albert Chevalier also made a speciality of coster songs but they were of a different quality altogether, being without any of the old roughness and indecency. Chevalier was indeed the herald of a new kind of music hall. 'The old music hall of the Great Vances and the Bessie Bellwoods was passing away. The new order of the Fragsons and the Margaret Coopers was imminent.'

It is as well to be reminded of the degree to which London has been cleaned-up since the days of which our author was writing. He paints a distressing picture of the condition of Leicester Square in the nineties:

The paling that surrounded the Gardens in the centre of the Square had been broken down. It became the receptacle of the least sanitary parts of the rubbish of the neighbourhood. And as the rubbish-heaps increased, augmented by contributions of dead dog and dead cat, the gamins of the place found it had become more and more desirable as a rallying-point and a play-ground. . . . Leicester Square was then the most disreputable spot on earth to be found in the centre of any capital in Europe. Here on the sunniest summer days might be found promenading some of the most villainous adventurers of the capitals of Europe. They cloaked themselves like Brigands, glared at the passing shop-girls with wicked black eyes, twirled their fierce moustaches, and rolled cigarettes with a diligence which they gave to no other innocent pursuit. They were the off-scourings of Europe. The swindlers, gamblers, or political rogues, the *souteneurs*, the craven shirkers of conscription, the European riff-raff, that chooses London as its favourite dumping-ground, were all to be found promenading in Leicester Square. John Leach has fixed the type in the pages of *Punch*. . . .

Among the filth and squalor of the un-reformed Square, the high edifice of the Alhambra rose, giving the absent touch of the Orient, to a locality sheltering many swarthy sons of the East. And there was something oriental in the entertainment, the chief feature of which was ballet. In the seventies, and before the coming of the Empire and kindred palaces, every man-about-town dropped in at the Alhambra at least once during the week. He was sure to find himself among friends. And in case that did not happen, he had offered to him the easy opportunity of picking one up. . . .

Certain of the habitués had an admission behind the scenes to what was known as the 'canteen', enjoying the privilege, which strangely enough, seems to appeal mostly to young and old age, of drinking Champagne made of gooseberries in the company of ballet girls in gauze skirts and no bodices to speak of. It has always struck me as strange that men accustomed to luxurious surroundings in their homes and clubs can extract any pleasure in becoming temporary participants of an existence, the dominant note of which is squalor, in which all the senses are disagreeably assaulted, the inevitable consequence of which is a poignant sense of personal degradation! The 'canteen' is, happily, a thing of the past.

Where London had its Caves of Harmony, Paris had its *cafés chantants*. Such establishments were unknown before the beginning of the Second Empire, but between 1852 and 1870 they sprang up everywhere in the French capital. One of the earliest was the *Café des Aveugles*, in the Palais Royal, with its orchestra of blind musicians. In an endeavour to protect the official theatres the law forbade actors to appear in costume in the unauthorized establishments and, even when the law was repealed, the practice continued. For one thing, it saved the management money.

Generally, the entertainment offered was not of a very high order, but some of the *cafés chantants* became famous, through a popular singer or a personality that imposed itself on the crowd. At the Bataclan, for example (situated in what was then the Boulevard du Prince Eugène and is now called the Boulevard Voltaire), a certain Darcier drew the public by songs, rather spoken than sung, which already expressed that revolt and bitterness of the proletariat which was shortly to express itself in the excesses of the Commune. His partner was Emma Valladon, known professionally as Thérésa. She had sung without much success, at the Alcazar Lyrique and then at the Eldorado. It was here that, by a sudden inspiration, she began to sing her sentimental songs with an accent of parody. They were an immediate success and by 1864 she had become one of the 'queens of Paris'.

Some of the *cafés chantants* of the Second Empire have survived, transformed, into our own time. There is still an Eldorado, a Bataclan and a Folies-Marigny and (most famous of all) a Folies-Bergère. Even the reformed music hall, both in England and France, had something raffish about it and it long remained a place where ladies in the proper sense did not feel at home. Nonetheless some of them visited it in an endeavour to 'see life' or for the purpose of writing about it. Mrs Peel tells us that, thinking it her duty as a journalist to have paid *one* visit to the Empire Promenade, she was at last allowed to hurry through it with her husband on one side and a stalwart cousin on the other. Mrs Humphrey Ward was even more daring when she said she wished – for the purposes of her writing – to visit the Bal Tabarin in Paris. A male friend agreed to accompany her, but only on condition that the visit took place in the middle of the day – when there was nobody there.

In England the young man-about-town indeed had no desire that the ladies of his family and acquaintance should accompany him to the music hall, for he sought there the company of 'ladies' of another kind: either the prostitutes who frequented the 'promenade' or those who actually appeared on the boards, the 'ladies of the lighter stage', as they were called.

Towards the end of the century it was the custom to take these women out to supper and the favourite resort was Romano's in the Strand. This had originally been a very humble establishment, and it was the well-known journalist Nathaniel Gubbins who dropping in there one night with Richard D'Oyly Carte and Alfred Cellier and liking the atmosphere of the place and the personality and quaint English of Romano's, publicized it and made it a success. And when Colonel Newnham-Davis, that pioneer among guides to gastronomy, wished to select a restaurant at which to entertain Miss Dainty, the choice of Romano's was inevitable; in fact it was chosen by Miss Dainty herself who demanded to be given her favourite table next to the door but sheltered by a glass screen from the draught. The good Colonel gives a lively description of the meal that followed:

When the handsome lady arrived – only ten minutes late – she swept like a whirlwind through the hall – past the flower-stall, over which Cleopatra presides, where I intended to ask her to pause and choose what flowers she would – in a dress which was a dream of blue, the constellation of diamonds on it, and as she settled down in her seat at the table, not quite certain whether to keep on the blue velvet and ermine cloak, or let it drop, I was told the first instalment of her news at express speed.

The dinner they ate is of interest, it consisted of *hors-d'oeuvre, Crème Pink'Un, truite, côtelettes de mouton, petits pois, pommes, perdreau, salade, artichauts, glace, champagne, café* and *liqueurs*. Even more interesting is the price of such a repast in the late nineties: £2 4s. Romano as was his custom visited their table to see that everything had gone well. He was

a dapper little Italian with faultless dress-clothes, with a small, carefully tended moustache, a full head of black hair, turning grey at the temples, and talking English, with a free admixture of Italian, and scraps of French. . . . Miss Dainty did not ask for the deep-red carnation that was in 'the Roman's' buttonhole; but before he had passed on she was pinning it into her dress, and when I ventured a very mild remark I was told that if I had not been mean enough to let her pass the flower-stall without offering her a buttonhole she would not have had to accept one from anybody else – a retort which was scarcely fair.

I asked Miss Dainty if she knew who the pretty lady dining with a good-looking grey haired man at a table at the end of the room was. She did know and gave me a full account of the lady's stage career, and . . . we ran over the professions of the various diners who occupied the triple line of little tables running down the room. The two men dining by themselves were powers in the theatrical world . . . there were as well a well-known theatrical lawyer talking business with a secretary to a successful manager; a dramatic author, who was proposing plays to a colonial manager; a lady with golden hair and a permanent colour to whom a young, small Judaic youth was whispering with great earnestness; a well-known sporting lord, dining by himself; a music-hall agent laying down the laws of contracts to a journalist; two quiet ladies in sealskin coats; and many others, nearly all connected with the great army of stageland.

Little restaurants were often provided with *cabinets particuliers*.

Not so very long ago, one of London's best-known supper houses was privately in the market, and a most suave and diplomatic member of the board was perpetually on the premises to show prospective purchasers over. And one Saturday afternoon there turned up, with an agent's order to view, a stern, cold, middle-aged lady, with eyes as bright as a magician's, a severe air, and decided views about how a possible vegetarian and highbrow restaurant should be conducted.

She sniffed disparagingly at the kitchen and complained at the lack of light on the staircase, but when they came to the little *cabinets particuliers* on the first floor she stared in amazement.

'Gracious,' cried she, 'who in the name of goodness patronizes these pokey little holes?'

'Madam,' replied the pastmaster in diplomacy, 'the *jeunesse dorée* and the ladies of the lighter stage. It is customary, before an hereditary peer weds the lady of his choice, to make a will, and sign over all his property to her; these are – er – the little offices at which are transacted and completed the delicate negotiations.'[1]

In the seventies and eighties, as Ralph Nevill tells us:

dashing young subalterns, instead of spending week-ends in the country, came up to town, went to a play or to a music-hall on Saturday night, lay in bed late on Sunday, and would then drive some fair damsel, if possible a light of the burlesque stage, down to the 'Star and Garter' at Richmond in a hansom. The hostelry in question, which has now [1923] ceased to exist, was a favourite resort of couples on the Sabbath. A number of these, after that now extinct meal 'a champagne lunch', would stroll out into the grounds where itinerant photographers did a brisk trade in taking likenesses on glass which, in a funny little frame edged with gold, were delivered before the evening return to town. A dinner at the Café Royal or Bristol would end the day; there was no dancing and no music, but plenty of fun.[2]

One can't help wondering if it was entirely wise for the dashing young subalterns to have their picture taken with the young woman who was their fancy for the moment. The cost of the original photograph must often have been many times exceeded by the cost of buying it back.

Both England and France have lost the pleasure gardens which were such a marked feature of life in the capitals of both in the late eighteenth and nineteenth centuries. The original impulse seems to have come from England with its Ranelagh and Vauxhall and it is interesting to note that when the French took up the idea they called one of their earliest pleasure gardens Vauxhall.

The most famous Parisian pleasure gardens of the Second Empire, as they had been under Louis Philippe, were the Bal Mabille, near the

1 Lieut.-Col. Newnham Davis, *op. cit.*
2 R. Nevill. *The World of Fashion*, 1923.

M

Champs Elysées, and the Bal Bullier in the Latin Quarter. Just before the beginning of our period, in 1847 to be exact, the Bal Mabille was transformed, for the expenditure of half a million francs, into a most attractive rendezvous. The garden was enlarged and surrounded by a garland of gilded vine leaves the stems of which blossomed into magnificent candelabra with 5,000 gas jets. The ballroom was adorned with mirrors and panels of red silk damask. To keep up the tone of the establishment the price of admission was fixed at two francs.

The clientèle was composed, for the most part, of actresses and 'lorettes' (i.e. rather inferior women of the town) and their cavaliers. There was not much dancing but (says a contemporary *Guide dans les Théâtres*, published in 1855) one picked up acquaintances, made assignations and organized pleasure parties and 'journeys which usually ended at Bade, Spa or Hambourg.' The dancing celebrities included Clara Fontaine, Rose Pompon and Céleste Mogador, and women like Cora Pearl did not disdain to show themselves at the Bal. We hear also of Finette, now remembered because she is represented in one of Whistler's finest etchings.

The Bal Bullier had formerly been known by the more poetical title of *La Closerie des Lilas*. It was more intimate, more familiar, less stiff than the Bal Mabille. Bullier himself was clever enough to attract not only the students of the Latin Quarter and their 'grisettes', not only the 'calicot' (the rather contemptuous name given to the young shop assistant or clerk) and his 'lorette',[1] but also the boulevardier, the 'grande demi-mondaine' who wanted a breath of low life, and the tourist. Tourists were always present, but in 1855 and 1867 (the Exhibition years) there were many more of them.

These various classes had special parts of the garden assigned to them, partly out of snobbery and partly because the proprietor wished to minimize the risk of a clash between the students and the 'calicots'. Although the latter were by no means rich they were better off than the students and dressed with more style, if not with more taste. The same was true of their women. It was on Sundays especially that they frequented the Bal Bullier and it was then that there was most danger of trouble with the students.

Another famous dancing place was situated in the Rue Cadet. It consisted of a large oblong dancing-floor with an alley on either side where women wishing to sell their favours walked – a kind of Empire Promenade in fact. The establishment opened early in 1859 with dancing on Mondays, Wednesdays, Fridays and Saturdays and concerts on the remaining three days of the week. Some of the best artists in Paris had been brought in to decorate the place. Other famous *bals* were the Prado and in Montparnasse,

---

1 Lorette was a general name given to the women of the town under Louis Philippe and the early years of the Second Empire, because so many such women lived in the district round Notre Dame de Lorette.

the Bal Constant also known as the Mille Colonnes. Dancing was in the open in summer, in a ballroom in winter. At first the bal was known as the haunt of rowdies, but Constant managed to suppress them and even to cater for two different clientèles, on different days. 'Lorettes' and 'grisettes' and their young men on one day and workmen's families, wives and daughters included, on another. The establishment was at the height of its prosperity in 1868 and 1869, and this was partly due to the free drinks and suppers which the proprietor was astute enough to offer to any journalist who would give him a puff. At these places and many others, one could find gaiety and animation and 'life'.

London still had many pleasure-gardens, indeed, in the middle of the century some two hundred open-air places of entertainment in, or within easy reach of the metropolis. Most of these were frequented by a somewhat lower class than had patronized Vauxhall and Ranelagh in their great days. One of the most popular was Cremorne in Chelsea. It was here that Whistler and his friends foregathered in the fifties and where he painted the canvas of *The Falling Rocket* which led Ruskin to accuse him of flinging a pot of paint in the face of the public. We have a vivid picture of the place from the pen of Hippolyte Taine:

Towards eleven that night we went to Cremorne Gardens a sort of *bal Mabille* where the day's madness was carried on far into the night. A crush and much shoving at the entrance . . . inside, especially at crossings in the walks, the press of people was dreadful, but it was possible to get a breath of air in the darker corners. All the men well or at least neatly dressed; the women were prostitutes but of a higher rank than of those in the Strand; light-coloured shawls over white gauze or tulle dresses, red *mantelets*, new hats. Some of their dresses may have cost as much as twelve pounds. But the faces are rather faded and sometimes, in the crowd, they utter shocking screams, shrill as a screech-owl. . . .

We sat down near three young women at a secluded table and ordered them sherry and beer. They drank moderately. Our bookish English and their racey speech collided in a grotesque manner. One of them was very gay and wild: I have never seen such overflowing animal spirits. Another, modest, quite pretty, rather subdued, was a milliner by trade, entirely dependent on herself. She has a friend who spends his Sundays with her. I looked at her carefully; it was clear she had the makings of an amiable and respectable girl. What had been the turning point?

Impossible to say how many of these women there are in London. Some say 50,000. There are houses full of them from cellar to attic. We escorted our three to the gate and paid their cab fares. Our own cab drove us home by way of streets, crescents and squares, which I did not recognize . . . from time to time, we saw beneath the dull light of a gas-jet, a belated street-woman, hungry and still hoping for a customer; or a pauper in rags, his feet tied up in more rags. As we drove I thought of the Haymarket at night, with its strolling, loitering women; of the Argyle Rooms, a kind of lust-casino which I had visited the previous evening. The spectacle of debauchery in this country leaves one with an impression of nothing but degradation and misery. Nothing brilliant, bold and smart, as in France. In the Argyle Rooms, when a gentleman wants to dance, an usher distinguished by a plaque, and wearing a white tie, fetches a woman for him; they often dance without exchanging one word. These poor girls are often beautiful, several of them look very gentle and decent; they often dance very correctly, smiling a little and never gesticulate; they are *décolletées*, but when dancing, keep their short capes on.

As for the men, by their appearance they are prosperous tradesmen ... middle class industrialists, or their sons, or their managers who visit the Rooms for relaxation from their work with figures, coal or other work. What they need is vulgar display, coloured glass lights, women in full evening, bold, loud dresses, white shawls embroidered with red flowers and exotic birds. They are well provided with money; a bottle of champagne costs twelve shillings. The evening will cost them six pounds. The tragic thing is that the man and woman both drink, they can do nothing until they are drunk!

Such were the relaxations and dissipations of London and Paris, and those of the other capital cities of Europe were not very different, nor those of the settled part of America. There was, however, one form of entertainment which Americans could claim as exclusively their own for it had no parallel in any other country. This was the showboat. In the Eastern States there was as much interest in the theatre as there was in Europe, and European actors were by no means averse to playing on the other side of the Atlantic. Men as eminent in their profession as Forrest, Booth and Macready played in New York and Philadelphia and had even ventured as far west as the Mississippi. But there were entire regions in what was then Frontier country which could only be reached by dirt tracks or paths through the wilderness, and for people who lived in isolated settlements there was little hope of entertainment of any kind, still less for the concerts and plays which many of the recent immigrants must have remembered with regret.

The great rivers provided the best means of communication. By them it was possible to penetrate through the wildest country, and the Mississippi and its tributaries formed one immense highway from Pittsburgh to New Orleans. The showboat arose as a kind of logical necessity.

No doubt the first entertainments on boats were spontaneous affairs provided by the crews of the river vessels themselves and with instruments of a most primitive kind. But when they tied up at a landing for the night they found that the local inhabitants were only too ready to welcome them ashore, as a break in the hard monotony of their lives. Perhaps they would be willing to pay for entertainment of a better sort.

The first professional actors to 'work the river' were Noah Ludlow and his eleven associates, but while these used it as a highway they mostly played ashore, at St Louis, Natchez and New Orleans where theatres already existed. Their cultural standard was high, for they offered *Catherine and Petruccio* (Garrick's version of *The Taming of the Shrew*), Kotzebue's *The Stranger* and 'by special request of the community', *Hamlet*. But all this was of no use to the smaller places on the river. It was in answer to their demand that the first deliberately planned showboat was launched at Pittsburgh in 1831, just before the beginning of our period.

The plan, the historian of the showboat tells us, 'was to drift with the current down the Ohio and the Mississippi, stopping for a one-night performance at each river landing where an audience seemed likely, and in late winter to sell or junk the boat at New Orleans . . . return to Pittsburgh by steamer, build another boat and repeat the trip next year.'[1]

The pioneer was a remarkable man named William Chapman, and his enterprise was so successful that he adopted it as a permanent way of life. By 1836 he was able to substitute for his drifting flatboat a small steamboat 'fitted up very comfortably after the manner of a theatre', and this had the enormous advantage of enabling him not only to keep better time and to avoid some at least of the hazards of the river, but to give performances on the return journey, thus doubling the profits.

The Chapman boat was a family affair and took care to provide 'family entertainment'. The owners of some of the rival showboats which soon began to swarm on the river were not so particular and helped to give the whole business a bad name. Even Chapman was sometimes met at a landing by a posse of angry locals determined to preserve their small community from contagion. But there could be no moral objection to the kind of entertainment offered by Chapman, nor even, in the *northern* reaches of the river, to the 'nigger' show put on by the rival showboat *Banjo*, one of the earliest examples of the black-faced semi-circle of comedians and singers which was soon to be familiar all over the world.

Some of the proprietors offered instead of drama and minstrel shows, a complete circus, the most ambitious of these being the *Floating Circus Palace*, built in Cincinnati in 1851. The boat was almost two hundred feet long and thirty-five wide, and contained, beside the big arena capable of containing forty trained horses at one time, a Dress Circle fitted with a thousand armchairs, a Family Circle with 1,500 cushioned settees and another gallery with seating for 900, with a special section for negroes. The whole was lighted by gas, and the steam calliope which announced its arrival could be heard five or six miles away.

The audiences were sometimes pretty rough, especially in Arkansas and many of the men 'came on board with a pistol in one pocket, a whiskey flask in the other, and long bowie knives sticking from their boots'. But every member of the showboat company had arms and knew how to use them, and the ushers were two professional pugilists from New York, who saw to it that order was maintained. The *Floating Circus Palace*

1 P. Graham, *Showboats. The History of an American Institution*, 1951.

continued to operate until 1862 when it was taken over by the Confederate Government as a hospital ship.

After the Civil War the showboat business slowly revived, chiefly through the enterprise of Augustus Byron French who launched his first boat *The New Sensation* in 1878 and who dominated the river until the end of the century. At first he merely floated with the current, but in 1885 he acquired a towboat (or rather a pushboat, for the main craft was propelled from behind) with the advantages already described. His enterprise, like Chapman's, was a family affair and he conscientiously tried to keep up the standard of entertainment. Once, finding, at some little place in Missouri, 'or maybe it was Arkansas', that the audience consisted entirely of men, French went before the curtain and said: 'Men, there is not a woman in the audience. Not a wife, mother, daughter, or sweetheart. This is not a show for men only. If you thought it was, you never made a bigger mistake in your life. My wife is a member of our troupe, and I respect her as much as any of you respect your wife. Now go, and as you pass out, get your money at the ticket office.'

This courageous and high-minded stand paid off. The audience melted sheepishly away and not one of them asked for his money back. Later that evening, when the company had gone to bed, the men returned with their wives and French opened up and gave them a show. The incident was much talked of and the reputation of *The New Sensation* was established for the whole length of the river.

What French offered was 'straight vaudeville': the only drama ever staged on one of his boats being *Uncle Tom's Cabin*, and that of course, could not be played in the Southern States. Otherwise, his entertainments were welcome everywhere, and his success, with a whole succession of boats, continued until his death in 1902.

Some of the twentieth-century showboats were more ambitious than anything that had been seen on the river before. They were indeed 'flamboyant giants', Markle's *Grand Floating Palace* advertising itself as representing 'More Capital, Brains and Energy Than All Other Shows of its kind; Largest Showboat in the World; $60,000 Invested'. The entertainment consisted of sensational 'specialty' acts spaced with music, performing dogs and, in 1902, the second year of its existence, musical comedy and moving pictures. *Absit omen!* It was the movies that were to put the showboats out of business. They had indeed already entered a long decline, as those who had put their money into them were beginning to find out just before the outbreak of the First World War. Some struggled on into the twenties and there was even a revival in 1928, but this time it was with tongue-in-cheek, a revival *pour rire*. A few showboats are still to be found at St Louis where they provide a tourist attraction as a quaint relic of the past.

What distinguished the pleasure-seekers of the mid-nineteenth century, in all countries, but especially in England, from those of any previous age was their enthusiasm for leaving their homes altogether and going to the seaside, and even further afield. One of the reasons why pious people in the middle of the nineteenth century were confirmed in their belief that the end of the World could not much longer be delayed was the extraordinary increase in travel. Had it not been clearly stated in the Scripture that one of the signs of the approaching Day of Judgment would be much going to and fro in the world and walking up and down therein, and was not this only too obvious in the fifties and sixties? In former times people had only travelled when they had to, except of course in the case of pilgrimages and these, even if we admit that Chaucer's Canterbury pilgrims got a lot of pleasure out of their journey, were supposed to be inspired by religious duty. Indeed, the state of the roads at any period between the collapse of the Roman administration and the last quarter of the eighteenth century was not such as to invite travel. When we consider that in the 1750s the lumbering stage coach took four and a half days to cover the distance between London and Manchester this will occasion no surprise.

Between them Thomas Telford the architect-engineer and John Macadam who invented the method of pressing into the dirt-tracks of his day thin layers of broken stone, created a real revolution, and by 1825 the speed of travel had probably reached the maximum possible before the invention of railways. Lighter and more efficient coaches and an elaborate system of horse-relays were able to make journeys of two hundred miles in about twenty hours.

The stage coaches, however, carried very few people, six inside and about ten on top, and although they brought new life to the villages and inns on their route the actual displacement of passengers – the number of man-miles travelled – was extremely small. And the heyday of fast coaching was very short. As Gilbert Sheldon remarks, drawing an apt parallel between road-transport and shipping, 'the history of the fast coach offers many analogies to that of the clipper-ship; both had been brought to the highest peak of perfection at the very moment when they were superseded. Before clipper-ship and stage coach alike, straining their utmost, urged on to and achieving almost incredible feats of speed, looms the menace of steam. . . . In 1830 the Liverpool and Manchester railway was opened.'[1]

By the beginning of our period a network of railways covered England and was rapidly spreading to every corner of Europe. There were those, like Ruskin, who thought that the railway had ruined travel. It destroyed what he called 'the power of deliberate survey of the countries through which the journey lay' and he looked back with regret to

1 G. Sheldon. *From Trackway to Turnpike*, 1928.

the happiness of the evening hours, when from the top of the last hill he had surmounted, the traveller beheld the quiet village where he was to rest . . . or, from the long-hoped-for turn in the dusty perspective of the causeway, saw, for the first time, the towers of some famed city, faint in the rays of sunset – hours of peaceful and thoughtful pleasure, for which the rush of the arrival in the railway station is perhaps not always, or to all men, an equivalent.

That was all very well, but Ruskin's father was a prosperous sherry merchant able to afford a private vehicle. It was the railways that made large scale travel possible and the middle classes of England were the first to avail themselves of the new facilities. The railways were convenient and they were cheap. Indeed, it was possible to go to Brighton and back for three shillings and sixpence and cheap prices brought many of the seaside resorts within reach even of the day tripper. One of the problems of Brighton and Bournemouth was no longer to attract custom but to keep out those who, by lowering the tone, might frighten away the more aristocratic clients. Bournemouth, says a contemporary guide book, 'is not provided with amusements of a popular character with the masses – by which we mean dancing saloons and such like means of entertainment. Its attractions are innumerable but of a natural and healthful character, and suited to the class of patrons who desire recreation and restored mental and physical energy. In catering for these its exemption from the ravages of the lower-class tripper is assured.' Still, even Bournemouth had 'a number of detached villas each marked by distinct and peculiar architectural features . . . apparting (*sic*) accommodation of varying extent, so as to be suited to the convenience of either large or small families, and adapted, some for extended, others for confined establishments.'[1]

Every age has its own affectations in phraseology; where the early Victorians talked about 'confined establishments', we speak of 'lower income brackets'. The meaning is the same and the plain fact is that, as the nineteenth century progressed, the English seaside resorts catered more and more for the lower middle classes.

Margate got off to a flying start because it was accessible to Londoners by boat. It was so near to London that it was possible for the family to be deposited in a boarding-house for a week or a fortnight and for Paterfamilias to come down on the Saturday or Sunday steamer. The Fathers' Boat was a fruitful source of jokes, innuendos and even of music hall songs in the fifties and sixties. The Great Vance was delighting audiences in 1868 with his song:

> Come listen to my ditty; I'm a merchant in the City;
>   I've got a wife, the best in life; she's forty, fat and fair;
>   And though I love her dearly, it happened very queerly;

1 *Visitors' Guide to Bournemouth*, 1842.

The Back of the Picture

Street Arabs in Stepney, 1888

Italian woman delousing children

Salvation Army shelter, 1892

Brothel in the Upper Tenderloin District of San Francisco, c. 1885

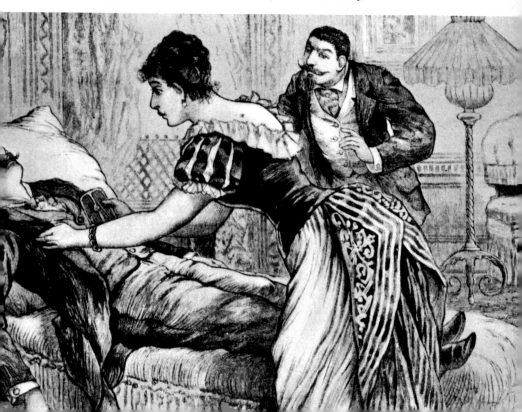

The Brothel in the Rue des Moulins, where Toulouse-Lautrec lived and painted; photographed by Lautrec's friend Gauzi

Opposite top: Copenhagen brothel, *c.* 1910

Opposite bottom: Courtesan's bedroom, a somewhat idealized version, *c.* 1900

Iron-founders at Varieux, France

Necktie workshop in a New York tenement, 1890; photograph by the reforming journalist Jacob A. Riis

'Bandit's Roost', New York; photograph by Jacob A. Riis

Paris Ignoré — « Fradin » - Rez-de-Chaussée - Pour 0 fr. 20, Soupe et droit de passer la nuit

Top: Night refuge, Paris, 1905

Bottom: Soup kitchen for the poor in Czechoslovakia

I sent her down to Margate, as she wanted change of air . . .
On Saturday according, the boat I soon was boarding
    And with a lot of husbands got, a jolly set were we.
Imagine my surprise, then, I chance to turn my eyes, when
    I saw a lovely damsel who was looking straight at me.
We got into conversation, I stood a cold collation;
    We soon got near to Margate pier; the time went quickly by.
Around her taper waist, then, my arm I just had placed when
    I heard a voice that brought me to my senses instantly.
Spoken: 'Oh, look, Ma! There's Father. Isn't it kind of him to bring
    your dressmaker with him on board?'
My feelings won't bear painting, my wife with rage was fainting,
    I'll draw a veil upon a scene so painfully severe.
Be careful I entreat you; your wives may come to meet you;
    Then take your arm away when you're in sight of Margate pier.

Careful mothers of families which were, or desired to be, *comme il faut* were in the habit, before deciding on their holidays, of consulting *The Queen*, which ran a special section of 'Notes and Queries' for their benefit. Some of the enquiries and answers make very entertaining reading, as when we learn that 'the western end of St Leonard's is called the most bracing' or that the 'season at Teignmouth lasts from June to September', or that 'Whitby is dressy, and there is a promenade and a band'. The editor is sometimes very stern with his correspondents: 'We never admit such enquiries as yours'; and even in the following there is a distinct hint of a rap on the knuckles: 'Mabel. Malvern is a summer resort, but we fear it would not be lively enough for you. Buxton or Matlock might do better.' However, Mabel's desires cannot have been very extravagant for we learn from a subsequent paragraph that 'There are no amusements in Buxton, but a fairly good band plays twice a day in the Pavilion.'

The really fashionable of course had no need to make these enquiries. They knew already where to go to, and if they consulted *The Queen* it was but to see their names in another column, headed, with a calm assurance of superiority now vanished from the world, 'The Upper Ten Thousand at Home and Abroad'. From this we too may learn that Brighton, and East-bourne and Folkestone were extremely fashionable places, Brighton especially:

The Sussex Fortnight is always rather a gay time in Brighton. Many make it their headquarters for Goodwood, and, after the racing there is over, stop on for the Brighton and Lewes events. The Pier, which has lately been almost deserted, is crowded again, the favourite time being from twelve to two o'clock, when the band plays. . . . This week the boards are occupied by *The Lights of London* played by Mr Wilson Barrett's company. At the Aquarium the Thuringian band gave several performances.

But Eastbourne was very little behind in gaiety:

The church parade on Sundays is a special feature here, and the, for the most part, well-dressed crowd, is as dense and almost as characteristic as similar gatherings on the Green, at Brighton, during the winter months. Good taste, however, happily predominates, though a few attract passing attention and un-enviable notoriety by their *outré* appearance and exaggerated style. . . . Recent arrivals include H.H. Princess d'Aremberg, H.H. the Princess de Taxis, the Duchess of Buccleugh, etc.

The travel column in *The Queen* did not confine itself to English resorts; its advice ranged from Cassel to Guernsey, from Coblentz to Colwyn Bay, from Scarborough to Ostend and Marienbad. But a note of warning was given concerning French bathing resorts, for 'in France, ladies who wish to avoid publicity have to rise very early, both sexes being accustomed to bathe *en costume* in view of the loungers on the beach.'

In England 'mixed bathing' was long considered improper and separate parts of the beach (or separate times of day) were set apart for men and women. In the middle fifties *Punch* carried several cartoons satirizing the caddish behaviour of young men in boats who persisted in rowing too near the ladies' bathing place. They certainly did not get much for their pains, for the bathing machines were provided with umbrella hoods over the steps leading down into the water, and as the fair bathers were clad in a voluminous robe which was tied round their necks and descended to their heels there was little to be seen of them when out of the water and even less when they were in. All that anyone ever saw of a woman bather was her head, with her hair floating behind her.

By the middle of the seventies however the female bathing costume had become more sophisticated. It consisted of a knee-length dress very little simpler than an ordinary dress of the period but with slightly shorter sleeves and, beneath it, trousers reaching to mid-calf, elaborately trimmed with lace. The strange thing is that people had become so accustomed to seeing women with narrow waists that corsets were considered necessary even in the water. Special 'rustless' corsets were advertised for this purpose; but, of course, many of the smart bathing costumes were never intended to be immersed in the water at all.

The strange thing is that men, in their separate enclosure, bathed naked, and that they continued to do so as late as the eighties, is shown by the following contemporary remark that 'the foreign custom, which puts men into bathing-costumes as well as women, has its advantages. If only this one of allowing the rescuer of a fair swimmer to carry his lovely burden on to the beach in sight of an applauding crowd, which cannot well be done arrayed as Englishmen are at present when they bathe.'[1] This must be one

1 E.C. Grenville Murray. *Side-Lights on English Society*, 1881.

of the most extraordinary reasons for wearing clothes ever put forward.

The English were certainly the pioneers of tourism. Even in the eighteenth century they were already travelling for travelling's sake, and Voltaire had noticed

> Le véritable Anglais, voyageant sans dessein,
> Achetant cher de modernes antiques,
> Et méprisant les saints et leur reliques.

At one period the Englishmen who went abroad were almost all of the highest classes, so that to many a foreigner Albion seemed to be peopled exclusively by 'milords'. In the eighteenth century young men of good family were sent abroad on the 'Grand Tour' as part of their education and they returned with Italian pictures and statuary and also (as many an Englishman feared) with some deplorable Continental vices. They travelled in their own carriages with their own servants and, of course, at considerable expense. Even the crowd which flocked to Paris in 1814 after the Abdication of Napoleon belonged, very largely, to the same class. The ordinary citizen, however prosperous, never thought of leaving his own country, and it was not until the beginning of Victoria's reign that the middle classes contemplated the adventure of going abroad.

It is one of the ironies of history that the impulse came from a zealous Baptist teetotaller named Thomas Cook. His object in arranging a special excursion from Leicester to Loughborough in 1841, at reduced prices, was to enable those who thought like him to attend a Temperance Rally. This was so successful that he began to arrange Sunday School Treats, and, by 1845, he was receiving from the Midland Railway Company a percentage on the tickets sold.

He crossed the Rubicon – or rather, the Channel – in 1855 when he offered, for the very moderate sum of thirty-one shillings, a trip from Leicester to Calais; and, in the following year, he advertised 'a grand circular tour on the Continent', taking in Antwerp, Brussels, the field of Waterloo, Cologne, the Rhine, Mainz, Frankfurt, Heidelberg, Baden-Baden, Strasburg and Paris. These efforts of a convinced teetotaller must have had the effect of introducing many Englishmen to the delights of the Continental apéritif; but that Mr Cook continued to have a social conscience is shown by the fact that in 1861 he issued nearly 2,000 tickets to Paris to enable sympathizers to take part in a working-men's demonstration.

These activities did not meet with universal approval. The average middle-class Englishman was, however, in little danger of being corrupted by Continental habits; indeed he tended to return from his 'Cook's Tour' more insular than ever and firmly convinced that all Frenchmen were immoral and all Italians lacking in hygiene. Also, he was very suspicious of Continental food, which he thought 'greasy' and over-flavoured with garlic.

As a mid-Victorian medical man remarks: 'In almost all country places out of England it is impossible to avoid the greasy dishes which are apparently preferred by all except our own countrymen; and a frequent consequence is rancid indigestion, with nauseous taste in the mouth, and flatulence or diarrhoea. A few drops of vinegar or lemon juice and a little cayenne pepper on the plate are the readiest correctives.'[1]

The good doctor was very strong on cayenne pepper which he seems to have regarded as a panacea for all ills, sea-sickness, for instance, during the horrors of the Channel Crossing. 'Should the stomach feel empty,' he says, 'and still more if any retching occurs, take bottled porter and biscuit spread with a little butter and cayenne pepper – which last article, by the way, amply repays the space it will occupy in a traveller's pocket throughout a journey, so useful is it on all occasions.'

Other authorities recommended the British tourist to roll cayenne pepper into a little bread pellet and swallow it if he felt any qualms about the food set before him at some Continental *table d'hôte*. It is amusing to note that even Baedecker – who, after all was a German – describes risotto as 'a kind of rice pudding, rich, to be avoided'.

But the real horror was garlic. 'Another article of cuisine that offends the bowels of unused Britons is garlic. Not uncommonly in southern climes an egg with the shell on is the only procurable animal food without garlic in it. Flatulence and looseness are the frequent results.' Chambers also maintains that only in Spain was tolerable bread to be procured, and he recommended the English traveller to take with him a supply of ship's biscuits.

It must be admitted that the majority of middle class travellers remained incurably insular and, when on the Continent, made no secret of their contempt for all things foreign. Thackeray grows positively savage when he comes to describe the conduct of the average Englishman abroad:

That brutal, ignorant, peevish bully of an Englishman is showing himself in every city of Europe. One of the dullest creatures under heaven, he goes trampling Europe under foot, shouldering his way into galleries and cathedrals and bustling into palaces with his buckram uniform. At church or theatre, gala or picture-gallery, *his* face never varies. A thousand delightful sights pass before his bloodshot eyes and don't affect him. Countless buoyant scenes of life and manner are shown him, but never move him. He goes to church, and calls the practices there degrading and superstitious; as if *his* altar was the only one that was acceptable. He goes to picture-galleries, and is more ignorant of art than a French shoe-black. Art, nature pass, and there is no dot of admiration in his stupid eyes; nothing moves him, except when a very great man comes his way, and then the rigid, proud, self-confident, inflexible British snob can be as humble as a flunkey and as subtle as a harlequin.

1 T.K. Chambers. *A Manual of Diet in Health and Disease*, 1876.

The more enterprising English holiday-makers were already finding their way in increasing numbers to Ostend, Trouville, Deauville, Arcachion, Biarritz, Aix-les-Bains, Homburg, Carlsbad, Cannes and Monte Carlo. Some of these places were spas and the pretence of health-seeking was still kept up. Waters were religiously drunk and 'cures' taken by those who did their best to dissipate the good effects on the spot before returning to London or Paris to dissipate them still further.

After the Franco–Prussian War, the German spas, such as Bad Ems and Homburg, declined in popularity. The French would not visit them, and those English who continued to do so found the gambling rooms closed and the gay cosmopolitan crowd no longer in evidence. Instead there were, in the words of a contemporary, 'a good many people who positively require the waters for purposes of health, and whose Bath-chairs are not an enhancing feature in the gardens of the Kursaals'.

The Pyrenees became fashionable during the Second Empire and their popularity continued until the end of the century and perhaps a little beyond. The Pyrenean valleys were charming, and the adventurous could push beyond the shrine where Bernadette saw the Madonna in her blue mantle to Gavarnie with its astonishing cirque of precipitous cliffs niched on the horizon line by the Brèche de Roland and garnished by the second highest water-fall in Europe. Those who wish for more can still hire sure-footed mountain ponies and give themselves the thrill of entering Spain on horseback.

In the sixties Cauterets and Luchon were gay places, but later they were completely eclipsed by the glories of Biarritz, whose popularity was originally due almost entirely to the Prince of Wales. The same prince did much for the popularity of Baden-Baden. It was his habit to stay at Homburg, but to go to Baden-Baden for the races. The social gossip of the period gives quite formidable lists of the nobility and gentry in residence at Homburg, although it is comforting to the patriotic to learn that 'the Duchess of Wechlenburg-Strelitz prefers Westgate-on-Sea'.

Trouville, with its famous *planches* was still fashionable, although the ultra-modish had already begun to rebel against its inevitable mixture of international *haut ton* and French bourgeoisie, and to move across the river to the spot where Deauville was rising among its sandbanks. Cheap transport was playing havoc with the resorts of the aristocracy even in the eighties. Two Sundays of racing, we learn, were spoilt by the influx of the wrong public. '*Avec ces baigneurs du Havre et les voyageurs des trains de plaisir on n'était plus chez soi. En revanche, celles du mardi, du jeudi et du samedi ont été charmantes. Jamais peut-être on n'avait vu moins de monde, mais chacun se connaissait.*' One can only hope that the restaurateurs were equally well satisfied.

When there was no racing there was the *tir aux pigeons*, a sport now condemned by the Royal Society for the Prevention of Cruelty to Animals but still practised by the cruel and barbarous Latins. Those who still lived at Trouville but found it common made a point of never going to the Casino, but of amusing themselves at very exclusive private parties. At Deauville one did not need to be so careful, although accommodation was still a little primitive, the demand for food and service exceeding the supply. But – '*il y'a la terrasse, la fameuse terrasse on l'on mange sous la tente . . . ce qui est très gentil, c'est le soir venu, de voir toutes les petites tables s'éclairer avec des lampes à abat-jour rose. Au loin le soleil se couche à la horizon avec des reflets d'or, une bonne brise arrive du mer,*' etc.

And at 'five o'clock' one could wear wonderful clothes on the wooden promenade; such clothes as those described by a frenzied gossip-writer in what was then a mondaine paper, *La Vie Parisienne:* '*une robe très drôle: fond vert foncé sur lequel se détachent des figures dites Kate Greenaway.*' Charming! It is interesting to note that there was already '*un petit bar Americain*' where it was possible to drink a '*gin coack-tail*'.

From Deauville it was the fashion in 1884 to pass to Dieppe, but the place was beginning to be a trifle dull even then, and the really fashionable hurried back to Paris as soon as they could to prepare for the real holiday of the year at Nice, or Cannes, or Monte Carlo, or, for those who had quieter tastes, at Bordighera or Villefranche.

Nowadays we tend to take our winters more strenuously or further afield, we ski at St Moritz or take a cruise to Jamaica. The modern age likes extremes. In cold weather it goes to colder places, and prefers its Mediterranean in the summer when the heat can be baking. Those who are still unsatisfied can have the skin burned off their backs at Rimini. But in the eighties an equable temperature, neither too hot nor too cold, was the desideratum, and people went to the *Côte d'Azur* to escape the fogs of London or the chills of Paris.

The Riviera was then out of the reach of trippers, and, besides, trippers were unable to afford winter holidays; so that, for a brief period, the aristocracy and its hangers on, the adventurers, the cocottes and all the shady but resplendent people who haunt towns of pleasure, had the whole coast to themselves. Not that they formed one amicable brotherhood by any means. There were wheels within wheels, circles within circles and a social ladder the complication of whose rungs would have made a modern head whirl. For the 'Smart set' at least from 1900 onwards has been too mixed itself to be as shy of mixing as the generation that preceded it. That generation, the generation we are considering in the present chapter, saw to it that something of the exclusiveness of its capital cities was transported with it to its new and temporary home by the Mediterranean.

The Club de la Mediterranée, organized by the now forgotten dandy, the Vicomte Vigier, was one of those institutions the membership of which was stamped with a certain social cachet. There were others whose object was similar although the purely gambling clubs were in general lax enough. Anyone who had money to lose was welcome. In the ordinary gambling rooms the *petits chevaux* was still played, for the French government, with that Latin logic incomprehensible to the northern mind, had not yet decided that the little horses were immoral, but that a very similar game, played with a rubber ball and a polished wooden bowl, was somehow unexceptionable. The real reason, the cynic might suspect, was that the *petits chevaux* took too long to run round their course, and that other games meant a quicker turnover for the Casino authorities.

Many gamblers lived in Nice, and took a daily conveyance to Monte Carlo. Some of them were compelled to walk back. Nice was a very pleasant place and the Promenade des Anglais crowded with people who knew one another, at least by sight. The carnival was still a more or less elegant affair, although the wise and delicately nurtured took care to return to their hotels before the horseplay started.

A comic opera company playing three times a week – with interminable intervals in the French fashion – was all that even the large *villes de plaisir* could expect. The entertainments offered were by modern standards extremely proper, not to say high-brow. Coquelin the elder would travel down from Paris, or Mlle Reichenberg and others of the Comédie Française, or perhaps the great Sarah herself. Colonne was still alive to conduct the concerts which still bear his name, and his orchestra of sixty discoursed sweet music.

Some of the farces presented may have been risky enough, but the costumes, even in the lighter theatres, were very proper. Nudity was not yet permitted on the stage. Ladies spent a considerable portion of their time in driving, on the safe eminence of a victoria seat. Gentlemen raised their hats with a flourish and conversed with their friends from the sidewalk. Love affairs were discreetly conducted even among the most dashing or the most notorious, and the *divorcée* was still frowned upon and excluded from good society. The general atmosphere was one of elegant flirtation. But not, alas! for all. Some of the English people to be found in the smaller watering places abroad were permanent residents and an interesting social note is provided by E. C. Grenville-Murray, who describes, with considerable sympathy, one such person:

She is the daughter of somebody under a cloud. Her father or perhaps her brother has gone to the dogs. She finds it pleasanter not to live in England. She has no taste for purposeless travelling, and soon establishes herself in some quiet watering-place such as Fécamp, Tréport, or St Valéry. She has sense enough to conquer her first impulse towards utter seclusion, and to select a place not *too* lonely; possibly she will go so far as to select Dieppe; but not Boulogne, which has too bad a name. . . . Coming without introduction and alone with her mother

to a new place . . . her acquaintance is now among the ephemeral passers by. . . .
She sits and works at some piece of tapestry, as the French ladies do at the local
assembly-rooms, while the band plays of an afternoon; she attends Sunday
services at the British Consulate; she is always superlatively neat in dress.

Several visiting Englishmen are interested in their fair compatriot, 'with
her beauty and with her air of melancholy, which she tries in vain to throw
off'; but when malicious tongues get busy, they leave for home without
saying good-bye. She and her mother are converted to Catholicism and
cultivate the local curé. By his good offices the girl finally marries a stout
and rather elderly Frenchman who agrees to take her without a *dot*.
What a novel this sad little story would make – and the situation must
often have occurred in real life.

It was the restless English who 'discovered' Switzerland. To the
eighteenth century traveller mountains were 'horrid' excrescences on an
otherwise smiling landscape. They were more a nuisance than a beauty. A
contemporary remarks that 'if one considers the Alps from the point of
view of their prodigious height, of their eternal snows and of the inconvenience and badness of the roads to be found there, then there are not
many delights to be looked for.'[1]

The Romantic Movement reversed this attitude. The hills of Westmore-
land and Cumberland were made respectable by Wordsworth, and in a
later generation the Alps were raised by Ruskin into monuments of moral
grandeur. Leslie Stephen declared in 1871 that 'when long ago the Alps
cast their spell upon me, it was woven, in a great degree by the eloquence of
Modern Painters. I hoped to share in Ruskin's ecstasies in a reverent worship of Mont Blanc and the Matterhorn.'

In 1857 the Alpine Club was founded in London, and appealed particularly to intellectuals. John Tyndall made an unsuccessful assault on the
Matterhorn in 1861, and between 1860 and 1865 Edward Whymper tried
five times in vain. He succeeded in the latter year but several of his
companions were lost during the descent.

Such enterprises were for the strong and well, but soon Switzerland
began to attract the weak and ailing, for it had been discovered that
consumptives benefited from the mountain air. Robert Louis Stevenson
was at Davos for the cure in the early eighties, and by this time the little
Alpine village had become quite a fashionable resort. The anonymous
author of *Davos Platz*, published in 1878, describes the scene:

The pines bend beneath their white burden but no snow cloud dims the
dazzling heights. There is no moisture in the air to deaden the rays of the powerful
sun and so, crowding balcony and terrace, are groups of people with parasols
and sunshades and broad garden hats of every form and description, working,

1 *Quoted by* H.K.Cook. *Over the Hills and Far Away*, 1947.

sketching, reading, smoking, drinking coffee or gaily chatting together as though it were July instead of January. Somewhat less lazy indeed than the denizens of the balconies are the groups of ladies and gentlemen who saunter along the broad highways or corso. Here the follower of fashion can exhibit her train with more satisfaction than in the Champs Elysées sweeping the dry crisp snow unsoiled by mud or dust.[1]

The last remark, which must surely be the most extraordinary reason ever given for going to Switzerland in the winter, reminds us that, in the late seventies even day dresses, to the disgust of Ruskin, had long trains.

The practical Swiss used toboggans to travel over the icy roads and the visitors were not slow to perceive that tobogganning could be turned into a sport. Even the invalid Stevenson tried it and was thrilled by the 'wooden steed . . . speeding like the wind'. Tobogganning soon spread from Davos to St Moritz, where it became in a short time highly expert. The first regular race was run in 1883, the Grand National Toboggan Race was inaugurated two years later and the famous Cresta Run established shortly afterwards.

It is surprising that skiing took so long to make its way. Skis were a Norwegian invention. In a clumsy form they had long been used by the peasants for getting about the country and, about 1860 they began to be employed for sport. It is an odd fact that they were completely unknown in Switzerland until they were imported by an Englishman who had learned to ski in Norway. Even so, the sport took a long time to catch on, and it is interesting to note that the pioneer Sir Henry Lunn had, as late as 1902, the greatest difficulty in persuading the proprietor of the hotel at Adelboden to open in the winter. The modern prodigious expansion of winter sports lies outside the scope of the present volume.

---

1 Anon. *Davos Platz*, 1878.

N

8 The Girl of the Period and the New Woman

The revolt against the oppressiveness of Victorian conventions took, so far as women were concerned, two forms: the serious and the frivolous. The former was represented by a remarkable regiment of high-minded ladies the latter by the 'Girl of the Period'. In any generation young women can be relied upon to scandalize their elders by their 'bold' behaviour. It is the same in every age and it is amusing to find an old Regency buck like Captain Gronow – who must in his youth have hobnobbed with Beau Brummell and Harriet Wilson – lamenting that the girl of the sixties did not conduct herself so well as the girls he had known in his youth:

I do not mean to say that there are not now, as there always have been in every state of society, beautiful and amiable women, combining good sense and high principle; but there are too many who seem to have taken for their ideal a something between the dashing London horse-breaker and some Parisian *artiste dramatique* of a third-rate theatre; the object of whose ambition is to be mistaken for a *femme du demi-monde*, to be insulted when they walk out with their petticoats girt up to their knees, showing (to do them justice) remarkably pretty feet and legs, and to wearing wide-awake hats over painted cheeks and brows, and walk with that indescribable, jaunty 'devil-may-care' look which is considered 'the right thing' nowadays – to make sporting bets – to address men as Jack, Tom, or Harry – to ride ahead in the Park – to call the paterfamilias 'governor', and the lady-mother 'the old party' – to talk of the young men who 'spoon' them, and discuss with them the merits of 'Skittles' and her horses, or the last scandalous story fabricated in the bay window at White's, the very faintest allusion to which would have made their mother's hair stand on end with dismay and horror – this is to be pleasant and 'fast', and amusing. The young lady who is weak enough to blush if addressed rather too familiarly, and so unwise as to ignore the existence of *les dames aux Camélias*, is called 'slow', and distanced altogether; in the London steeplechase after husbands she is 'nowhere' – an outsider – a female muff. The girl of the year 1862 who is not 'fast' is generally dull and *blasée*, pleased with nothing, and possesses neither the wisdom of age nor the *naïveté* of youth.

It was Mrs Lynn Linton, the well-known woman journalist, who invented the phrase 'the Girl of the Period', and her opinions about her were very similar to those of Captain Gronow. In a series of articles contributed to the *Saturday Review* in 1867 she made known her findings, nearly all of them derogatory. She was certainly a little hard to please for she seems to dislike equally the 'Husband Hunter' and the 'Old Maid'. But her particular indignation is reserved for girls who are 'fast'.

Announcing that she disliked the word because 'it is an Americanism and extremely vulgar, as are all Americanisms', she nevertheless makes great play with it:

A fast young woman has an inordinate love of gaiety, a bold determined manner, a total absence of respect towards her elders,[1] and sometimes even towards her parents; a flippant style of conversation and a glaring and sometimes immodest dress. She is not in the least sentimental, she does not read Scott or Byron[2] or Moore or even Lord Lytton. In the country she is a daring rider; in town she plays billiards. Her conversation is full of slang – so repulsive in a feminine mouth. We actually know of a young lady of fifteen who talks about being 'squisshy'! and of a gentleman having 'D.Ts'.[3]

All this might seem harmless enough, but Mrs Lynn Linton has other charges to bring:

The Girl of the Period is a creature who dyes her hair and paints her face. [She] envies the queens of the demi-monde more than she abhors them. . . . It cannot be too plainly told to the modern English girl that the net result of her present manner of life is to assimilate her as nearly as possible to a class of women we must not call by their proper – or improper names. If we must have only one kind of thing let us have it genuine, and the queens of St John's Wood in their unblushing honesty, rather than their imitators and make-believes in Bayswater and Belgravia.

Clever journalists have always found that the 'Modern Girl' was good for a hard-hitting article, or even a series of articles such as Mrs Lynn Linton contributed to the *Saturday Review*. Nearly all young women want to get married; it is merely a question of the tactics to be adopted. Our authoress thought the girls of the sixties were going the wrong way about it, and she issues the solemn warning: 'All men whose opinion is worth having prefer the simple and genuine girl of the past with her tender little ways and bashful modesties. . . .' What Mrs Lynn Linton does not say is how to bring these desirable qualities to men's notice.

> Full many a flower is born to blush unseen
> And waste its sweetness on the desert air,

1 *That*'s where the shoe pinches!
2 It is amusing to note that it was possible – in 1867 – to lament the decay of Lord Byron's influence on morals!
3 Mrs Lynn Linton in the *Saturday Review*, 1867.

an idea extremely repugnant to any normal girl; and in order to escape this terrible fate (particularly terrible in a period when the old maid was so much despised) young women indulged in the deplorable practice of flirting. The word – or the thing – seem to have been particularly prevalent round about the 1880s. The contemporary author of *Side-Lights on English Society*[1] devotes a large part of his book to flirts, explaining their mode of operation and listing all possible varieties of the species: 'the flirt who has plain sisters', the regimental flirt 'on Home Service' and 'on Foreign Service', the tourist flirt, the seaside flirt and even the ecclesiastical flirt.

The last named must seem rather a mysterious figure to the modern mind; but the Linnaeus of Flirting explains that he is referring to the daughters of bishops and deans who in his opinion are seldom 'lovers of books, pedagogic ways, or academical or ecclesiastical architecture'. Rather do they cast their eyes at military officers whose 'startling clothes when out of uniform, their moustaches and eyeglasses, nay, the odour of the choice cigars they smoke – have a tantalizing effect upon their senses'. Such frivolous comments sometimes cast a more vivid light upon the manners of an epoch than any number of solemn tomes.

The seaside was – it goes without saying – a happy hunting ground for flirts:

A ride upon the sands, even on the backs of ill-saddled donkeys, may easily be turned into an imaginary ride for life. A shrimping excursion, besides offering chances for a display of neat ankles, brings about solitary wanderings, two by two, among the rocks. A sail in a small boat in rough weather affords opportunities for the exhibition of nerve and nautical knowledge combined; while a fishing-party by torch-light leads to so many nice things in the way of huddlings together under one tarpaulin, little screams when the boat rocks, delighted exclamations and joint action when the fish is speared or netted, that the mere mention of it will set any acute girl blushing.

If the 'acute girl' is invited for a cruise on a yacht, she finds herself in an even more fortunate position. For there is

no horrid billiard-room to take up the time of the interesting man; no need to run away from cigar-smoke in the exhilarating fresh air. Frequent meals, and gay; frequent nips of liqueurs, or mulled wines, to keep the cold out, and prescribed as indispensable to health; and then the privilege of appearing to lose one's balance, and needing the prop of a stalwart arm. No visible impropriety either if the proprietor of the stalwart arm does hug a little in conveying the fair and unsteady one to a seat. Add to this that Etiquette, which would be shocked at seeing Miss Jill and Mr Jack walking up and down an hotel corridor for an hour at midnight, can look on unmoved at a moonlight promenade on the deck of a yacht, even when it extends pretty far into the small hours.

1 E.C.Grenville-Murray.

But why should such subterfuge be necessary. A growing number of women were beginning to think that the Adam's Rib theory of women's origin had been over-exploited in a patriarchal society. Was it not all part of a conspiracy to keep women down and to deny her her natural rights?

The revolt took various forms, one of them a protest against the way in which women were constrained to dress in the middle of the nineteenth century. 'Advanced' women soon began to realize that they could never compete with men in the work of the world so long as they were clad in the voluminous and hampering clothes of the mid-nineteenth century. Emancipation inevitably meant emancipation in dress. It is not surprising that the first impulse of dress reform came from America where reforming zeal found many outlets from anti-slavery agitation to 'Temperance'.

Amelia Jenks, shortly after her marriage to Henry Dexter Bloomer, ran a 'Temperance' journal called *The Lily*, but in the very year in which our survey starts she became interested in dress reform and by 1851 she had evolved a 'light, attractive and elegant style' which she proposed to substitute for 'the cumbrous, ugly, and inconvenient one to which women were condemned by the tyranny of fashion'. Mrs Bloomer was not alone in thinking that it was unworthy of the American Woman to be forever 'bowing to mere convention or rigid adherence to the feminine fashions adopted at profligate courts in Europe. . . . Daughters of the Republic should snap their fingers at the sneers of the Press.'

There was nothing in the least erotic in the proposed new dress. The skirt was to reach half-way between the knee and the ankle – and as recently as the eighteen-thirties it had not been very much longer than this. Nor were the legs to be exposed for, under the skirt, 'there should be trousers, cut moderately full and gathered in above the footwear'. The entire outfit (for which a paper pattern was supplied) was as follows:

The walking-dress consists of a figured silk bodice, purple and white in colour, with muslin wristlets, and a skirt ending six inches below the knees; trousers of the same material as the bodice, just covering the tops of the gaiters, and gathered in with a pretty two-inch ruffle; boots of black prunella, with elastic sides, and a straw hat or bonnet, with four-and-a-half inch brim, lined with coloured silk and set off with ribbon and tassels.

All this sounds feminine enough, but it was the trousers that caused all the excitement. For trousers were not only an article of clothing; they were a symbol of male domination, and the proposal that women should adopt them (almost entirely concealed by the skirt as they were) was seen as a threat to the whole structure of society. Indeed when a certain Miss Johnson, a zealous Bloomerite, appeared in the streets of Providence, Rhode Island, in the new costume, she was promptly arrested, and fined twenty dollars by the local magistrate on the ground that her garments 'resembled male attire'.

The ballad-mongers joined in the outcry:

> Listen, females all,
>   No matter what your trade is,
> Old Nick is in the girls,
>   The Devil's in the ladies!
> Married men may weep,
>   And tumble in the ditches,
> Since women are resolved
>   To wear the shirt and breeches . . .
>
> Female apparel now
>   Is gone to pot, I vow, sirs,
> And ladies will be fined
>   Who *don't* wear coats and trousers;
> Blacker boots and hats,
>   And shirts with handsome stitches –
> Oh, dear! what shall we do
>   When women wear the breeches?

That Mrs Bloomer had certain qualms herself is shown by her remark in the pages of *The Lily*: 'We trust that our lady readers will not be shocked at our "masculine" appearance, or that their gentlemen friends will not mistake us as belonging to their own sex'.

However in public she put on a bolder face and we have the authority of a Boston editorial for believing that

vulgar winks and jeers have no effect upon her. Should she by chance encounter low-minded persons who express uncomplimentary opinions, she neither drops her head in shame and pouts her lips, nor turns upon her heel with a cold look of contempt. Instead, she just walks past them, her countenance indicative of purity and happiness, and her thoughts filled with the goodness and wisdom of an all-wise Providence.

Mrs Bloomer, indeed, received a good deal of support in the American Press. The *Washington Telegram* looked 'forward with pleasure to the day on which every well-dressed lady, here and elsewhere, will adopt this sensible costume', and a reporter in Nashville, Tennessee, was moved to lyric heights when

our city was honoured by the presence among us of three of Alabama's fairest daughters, each magnificently attired in full Bloomer costume. As may be imagined they created quite a sensation. In fact, we never saw our town so stirred. It was perhaps Miss Julia Mortimer who attracted most attention. Her dress consisted of a scarlet bodice and costly barège skirt, above white cambric pantalettes, tipped with lace and fastened at the ankles with coloured ribands. The charms of Miss Alice Gray, who wore a rich purple bodice, with pink satin skirt and trousers, were also exhibited with considerable effect. The third member of the trio, Miss Dora de Kalb, adopted a green scarf, crimson bodice, and white satin skirt and 'continuations', and her swelling bosom was adorned with a diamond breastpin. This young lady's modesty of demeanour, coupled with her intelligent expression will always win her a host of admirers wherever she appears.

One cannot help thinking that so brilliant a fashion commentator was wasting his time in Nashville, Tennessee.

Yet it was all in vain. Wearers of the Bloomer costume might be as ravishing as the trio of 'Alabama's fairest daughters', or as high-minded as the wife and daughters of 'Mr Burleigh, the poet' who attended the anti-slavery convention at Syracuse, or as sensible and energetic as Mrs Bloomer herself – the women of America refused to be converted. And, in the autumn of 1851, Mrs Bloomer, disgusted with the lack of response in her own country, crossed the Atlantic with 'a bevy of trained representatives' to undertake the conquest of England.

Immediately on their arrival they set to work and on Wednesday, 11 September, strollers in the West End of London rubbed their eyes in astonishment when 'two ladies, in jackets and short petticoats, dark silk trousers, with cashmere footwear and bonnets, appeared in Piccadilly and St James's Square. . . . During the course of their walk they distributed handbills among the passers-by, addressed to the "Mothers, Wives and Daughters of England".'

On the following Sunday a complete batch of Bloomers appeared in St James's Park, but they met with such a hostile reception and with threats to duck them in the lake that they beat a hasty retreat to a carriage which was fortunately waiting for them in Waterloo Place. They tried again at the Great Exhibition, but again had to take refuge in a cab from 'the taunts and protests directed against them'. The reporter can scarcely conceal his astonishment that 'two of the party were members of a hitherto respectable family residing in Islington'.

The reaction in Ireland and Scotland (for the Bloomer evangelists spread their message far afield) was no more favourable. An Edinburgh paper referred to 'so-called ladies' and added: 'From enquiries on the subject, we learn that the ladies have come from America. We trust it will not be long before they return there.'

When Mrs Dexter, Mrs Bloomer's chief lieutenant, gave a lecture in the City Hall, Glasgow, there was nearly a riot. 'It was with some difficulty that Madam got off the platform and left by a side door. Had she not done so, she would probably have experienced a noisy demonstration from a group waiting for her at the front entrance.'

However, Mrs Bloomer got her own back on the Scots for she enquired very pertinently in a letter to the *Daily News* 'why the British public is so horrified at the idea of a woman dressing in trousers, seeing that they have for many years tolerated a number of men from the North of the

Tweed wearing petticoats and shockingly short petticoats, too'. We may well imagine that after this blasphemy against the sacred kilt, it was unlikely that Bloomerism would make much headway in Scotland.

The redoubtable pioneer turned her attention to London and a 'Bloomer Committee' was formed, 'to put things right in the metropolis'. A meeting was announced at the Royal Soho Theatre (presumably the Royalty Theatre in Dean Street) at which, it was promised, 'the ladies of the Committee will themselves appear in full Bloomer costume'. The theatre was crowded and when the curtain was rung up, 'twenty young ladies, all clad in the new costume, took their seats in a semicircle. The gentlemen [!] among the audience received them with ironical cheers and laughter. This caused some of the ladies (who were obviously of a timid disposition) to retire into the wings, to recover their composure.' However we learn from another contemporary account that 'the lecture was well received; and it was not until she began to discuss feminine suffrage that interruptions occurred'. Undeterred the lecturer declared that 'if Queen Victoria understood the real advantages of the Bloomer costume, it would undoubtedly be adopted by the Royal Family and Maids of Honour at Buckingham Palace'; and at the conclusion of the meeting 'three cheers were given for Mrs Bloomer and a young lady sang the National Anthem'. An attempt to promote a Bloomer Ball was less successful. A hall was hired near Hanover Square and tickets sold for fifteen shillings. Alas! only a few ladies ventured to appear in the new costume and *Punch* made fun of the occasion in a parody of *Locksley Hall*:

> Oh! my Bloomers, chicken-hearted! Oh! my Bloomers, what a fall!
> Oh! the dreary, dreary aspect of the barren Bloomer Ball!
> Tis as well, perhaps the ladies should avoid the London dirt
> By a higher range of clothing and a somewhat shorter skirt.
> But it cannot be expected we shall ever see the day
> When, in gentlemanly trousers, they'll be figuring away.
> As the husband, shall the wife be, he will have to wear a gown
> If he does not quickly make her put her Bloomer short-coats down.
>
> Tis the Ball! but oh! how dreary! – men and women don't combine;
> For, the latter to the former, are as one to ninety-nine . . .
> And at night along the pavement, near the corner of the Square,
> At each new alighting Bloomer, stood a noisy crowd to stare;
> But the crowd was disappointed, seeing what it witnessed then;
> Scarcely half-a-dozen Bloomers, nearly seven hundred men.

Still the Bloomerites refused to be discouraged. Meetings were held all over London, and Bloomerism became the topic of the day. The song writers got busy, and music titles were issued bearing such legends as the *Bloomer Polka*, the *Bloomer Waltz* and the *Bloomer Quadrille*. An enter-

Emancipated Woman

Georges Sand, *c.* 1870, a stout pioneer of female emancipation

George Cruikshank, *The Bloomers in Hyde Park*, 1852

Ladies' Dress Reform Meeting, Boston, 1874

Work girls in a factory in the Austrian Empire, 1897

Telegraph girls, 1871

Sea-battery, Normandy,
1893

Learning to Ride, *c.* 1890; photograph by Alice Austen

Isadora Duncan and her pupils, exponents of the neo-Classical movement in dancing

Alice Austen and two of her friends dressed as their brothers, 1891; a photograph by Alice Austen

Suffragette sandwich-women, 1914

Alumnae parade at Vassar College, 1903

prising publican put his barmaids into bloomers (for this was the word now given to the garments themselves), there was a debate on 'Bloomerism versus Tights' at the Coal Hole Tavern, and the Adelphi Theatre put on a 'screaming farce' entitled *Bloomerism, or the Follies of the Day*.

But Bloomerism failed to establish itself with the people who mattered and the *Morning Chronicle*, commenting on the Bloomer Ball, contrasted the men who attended with the women. 'The peerage was well represented, and also the House of Commons. The clubs, too, must have been practically emptied, for one lit upon faces familiar in the upper circles, belonging to Guards officers, dandies, authors, artists, actors, barristers and the like . . . As to the ladies, we may as well say at once that they did not compose the *élite*.' They were in fact the ladies from the Argyll Rooms and similar establishments and, said another contemporary account, 'by identifying it with the doubtful associations attached to the *débardeur* of a Carnival Ball in Paris, the Bloomer Ball in London has sealed the fate of the Bloomer costume for our modest and well-bred British womanhood'. It was not until the nineties that 'well-bred British womanhood' adopted bloomers for the new sport of bicycling, and Mrs Bloomer had her revenge at last. And when Mrs Bloomer, in the words of an obituary, 'passed into Paradise on Sunday, 30 December 1894', *Punch* felt constrained to make an *amende honorable* for all the ridicule it had poured on her head forty years before:

> So Mrs Bloomer's gone! but let her name
> Once more appear in Mr Punch's pages.
> Twas long ago, almost the Middle Ages
> That Leech's pencil advertised her fame!
>
> Her costume was unlovely – let it fade
> Forever from the ken of human vision!
> Though nowadays 'twould scarce provoke derision,
> If worn by pretty girls, and tailor-made.
>
> For by the lady-cyclist, as she plies
> Her pedal, neatly clad in knickerbockers,
> See Mrs Bloomer, first of Grundy-shockers,
> Now vindicated in Dame Fashion's eyes!

The bicycle was indeed a great emancipator, especially in its improved form. So long as it was the 'penny-farthing', with one very large wheel and one small one, it could not be ridden by woman at all. *Punch* referred to cycling in 1883 as an essentially manly sport: 'Women can't do *that*, you know, not even with divided skirts.' But by 1890 the bicycle, although it was still clumsy and primitive, with solid tyres and no gears, began to find riders everywhere. It suddenly became a fashionable craze especially in France where it was taken up by no less a person than the Prince de

Opposite: Vacuum Cleaner, *c.* 1910; the lady appears to be working her own machine.

Sagan, the acknowledged *arbiter elegantiarum* of Paris. A society for the cultivation of the new sport, was formed under the chairmanship of the Duc d'Uzès, and no less than three magazines founded to promote public interest. The French 'fashionables' met principally in the Bois, between the Porte Dauphine and the Porte Maillot, so that this particular avenue became known as l'Allée des Vélos. In London the favourite place and time for cycling was Battersea Park on Sunday morning. The bicycles were taken to the Park by servants. The ladies and gentlemen drove down in their carriages, rode the bicycles round and round the Park, handed them back to the servants and drove home to lunch.

The gravest fears were expressed that the new invention would have a deplorable effect on morals. If your daughter had a bicycle, how could you possibly oversee her movements? How could you prevent her from going off on expeditions with young men! The chaperon suddenly found herself left behind in a quite literal sense. And, apart from that altogether, would not the practice of bicycling lead to an undesirable muscular development of the female form?

A writer of the period with perhaps unconscious humour tries to re-assure his readers:

The ideal of English womanhood as represented in the sketches of George du Maurier is a faithful generalization from actual life, historically accurate in all its essential details. Even the lofty stature since the bicycle began to develop certain muscles and parts of the human frame, is now seen to be no figment of the artist's imagination. The feminine forms which, towering majestically above the thrones of wheelwork, look down upon the dwarfed passenger or equestrian, are today perceived to have been presented on no exaggerated scale in the pages of *Punch*. English women have always had a beauty and a durability of attractive-ness unique throughout the world. It is only of late years that to these qualities, consequent on improvements in their physical regimen, the maids and matrons of Britain have added a certain Junonian majesty of proportion.[1]

The fear that women were about to take over *all* the activities hitherto reserved for the male finds expression in the work entitled *Side-Lights on English Society*, from which we have already quoted:

The ambition of the modern woman is to show herself everywhere. She is no longer content with the drawing-room, the ballroom, and theatre; she must reign in the open air; and sports have been invented – croquet, skating, and lawn tennis – in which she can mix with men and dwarf them . . . picnics have become the rage; water-parties and walking-tours exhibit woman's taste in fancy costumes, and her powers of hand and foot, for she does not disdain to pull an oar, and will back herself for a 'discretion' to walk long distances. She has invaded the hunting-field and the shooting-covert; she has climbed on to the box-seat of

1 T. H. Escott, *Social Transformations of the Victorian Age*, 1897.

four-in-hands; and reforming our religion according to her own views of the aesthetic, she has given us Ritualism. The club remained, until lately, as a last refuge to man; but mixed clubs like the Orleans and the Lotos have already been started, and, before long, woman will have forced open the doors of the other houses. This will be the crowning triumph at which she has been aiming for years, and when she has achieved it, man's subjection will be complete. Then we shall see floating over White's and the Marlborough the emblems of female supremacy – a cambric handkerchief scented with opoponax.[1]

The author dedicates his little book to Queen Victoria, with the remark that 'a survey of the condition of the English people leaves one much to be thankful for, especially the fact that its best expression is modelled on the pure example of your Majesty's life'.

Queen Victoria was known to disapprove of the 'New Woman', but this did not halt her triumphant advance. She was in revolt not only against the stifling social conventions of Victorian life but against the stuffiness of its decor. It is therefore no accident that many of the most ardent Feminists were also Aesthetes.

The Aesthetic Movement was a peculiarly English thing: it had no equivalent on the Continent of Europe or in America, although *Art Nouveau* at the end of the century might be considered its child. It was one of the strangest things that have ever happened in English social history. It might indeed be called the Pre-Raphaelite movement emerging into public consciousness, not as a mere doctrine of how to paint, but as a gospel of how to live. It was not merely an interest in art on the part of fashionable people but art spilling over into fashionable life.

The original Pre-Raphaelite Brotherhood had been dispersed in 1854 but Rossetti still remained, and his disciple was Burne-Jones. At Oxford, Burne-Jones had shared rooms with William Morris who hated the industrialism of the Victorian Age and all its machine-made goods and who was determined to reform the entire system of interior decoration by a return to the crafts. Finding that he could not have the objects of everyday life made to his satisfaction he decided to make them himself, from chairs to stained-glass windows. The firm of Morris, Marshall, Faulkner and Co. was founded in 1862, but its influence was at first confined to a small circle; and it was not until 1869 that Morris received his first commission for non-ecclesiastical interior decoration. Meanwhile Whistler, full of the Japanese enthusiasm he had brought from Paris, had also met Rossetti in the early sixties and it was probably he who was responsible for their mutual passion for 'blue china'.

All this might have been without much effect on the general public but for a young man named Arthur Lasenby Liberty employed in the 'Oriental Warehouse' of Messrs Farmer and Rogers in Regent Street. In 1875 he

1 E.C. Grenville-Murray, *op. cit.*

opened his own shop, also in Regent Street, where it has remained ever since. It can surely be no accident that it was in the same year that *Punch* had its first cartoon of an Aesthetic room with fans mounted on a screen. In the following year the craze for blue china is satirized and there is a picture of an Aesthetic piano painted all over with sunflowers. In 1878 Oscar Wilde came down from Oxford. His fame had already spread beyond the limits of the university, but his actual apostleship was henceforth to be much more effective. He had an even greater genius for publicity than his rival, Whistler, and it was not long before the word Aesthetic was in everybody's mouth.

Indeed the seal of social success had already been set on the Movement by the opening, in 1877, of the Grosvenor Gallery. The moving spirits were a wealthy banker, Sir Coutts Lindsay, and a brilliant young journalist, Comyns Carr. The furnishings and appointments of the gallery were luxurious and it was conveniently situated in the heart of Mayfair. A restaurant was provided underneath the room where the pictures were shown. The Prince and Princess of Wales were present at the inaugural banquet, and the exhibition was the event of the Season. The Philistines might mock at the 'greenery-yallery, Grosvenor Gallery, foot-in-the-grave young man', but they could not stop the spread of the Aesthetic fever.

Nonetheless they did their best, and in the early eighties the battle between Aesthetic and Philistine was raging fiercely, with *Punch* firmly on the side of the Philistines. Jokes about young men contemplating lilies in lieu of luncheon occur in 1880, with references to 'Passionate Brompton', the inhabitants of which were in the habit of asking one another such questions as 'Are you intense?' or discoursing upon High Art with 'a certain hungry look of ineffable yearning towards the Infinite'. The master of the revels was George Du Maurier. He drew picture after picture of the Aesthetic interior with its Oriental vases, its Chinese screens, its Japanese fans and the inevitable sunflower; and he invented a whole series of Aesthetic characters, who became as real to the readers of *Punch* as Sam Weller and Mr Pickwick. They reappeared week by week and developed their eccentricities. There was Mrs Cimabue Brown (supposed to have been founded on Mrs Comyns Carr), there was Mrs Lyon Hunter (later refined to Mrs Leo Hunter); there was Prigsby the critic, Maundle the painter, and Jellaby Postlethwaite, the poet. They lived in a world of dados, of artistic wallpapers (it was a shock to *Punch* that wallpaper *could* be 'artistic'), of brass fenders, of Japanese fans and bunches of lilies in blue pots. They thought the paintings of Burne-Jones 'quite too utter'. In one cartoon Du Maurier shows a newly married couple examining a 'six-mark tea-Pot'. The 'Aesthetic Bridegroom' says: 'It is quite consummate, is it not?' and the 'Intense Bride' replies: 'It is indeed! Oh, Algernon, let us live up to it.'

Du Maurier's Aesthetes may seem too good to be true, but there is plenty of contemporary evidence for their existence in real life. A centre of the cult was the house at 84 Gower Street of Mr and Mrs George Robinson, noted art collectors and the author of *Mid-Victorian Memories* assures us:

I have often seen at the Robinsons a youth (whose name was neither Postle-thwaite nor Maundle, though it might well have been either) carrying throughout a whole evening in melancholy silence, a tall white lily, with whose droop he was evidently doing his best to bring his own figure into imitation. At the same house, a young woman, dressed, as it seemed to me, in nothing but an old-fashioned bathing gown and an amber necklace, whom I was asked to take to the supper-room, returned, to my enquiry of what I could get for her, the lugu-briously toned answer 'I seldom eat'. And these three words were all I could win from her then or thereafter.[1]

And Mrs H. R. Haweis had this advice to give to those young women who wished to cultivate *The Art of Beauty*:

Morris, Burne-Jones and others, have made certain types of face and figure once literally hated, actually the fashion. Red hair – once, to say a woman had red hair was social assassination – is the rage. A pallid face with a protruding upper lip is highly esteemed. Green eyes, a squint, square eyebrows, whitey-brown complexions are not left out in the cold. In fact, the pink-cheeked dolls are nowhere; they are said to have 'no character' – and a pretty little hand is occasion-ally voted characterless too. Now is the time for plain women. Only dress in the pre-Raphaelite style and you will be astonished to find that so far from being an 'ugly duck' you are a full-fledged swan.[2]

The Aesthetic man and the Aesthetic woman did indeed exist. They were to be seen in all the drawing-rooms with pretentions to culture and they could be recognized at once by their peculiar costume, which soon crystallized into almost a uniform. For men it consisted of knee-breeches, loose-flowing tie and a velvet jacket: in fact a polite modification of the French artist costume of the Romantic Period. Women also went back to the eighteen-thirties for their balloon sleeves but, in their own minds their dress was Mediaeval-cum-Renaissance. The Aesthetic lady wore no corsets, a loose robe embroidered with large sunflowers (this obsession with the sunflower being characteristic of the whole Movement), and flat shoes and she often wore her hair in a kind of frizz brushed forward over the eyes. It was an attempt to imitate the vague, no-period costume of the ladies in Burne-Jones's pictures and on the right kind of figure might have looked well enough. But there went with it an affected manner of walking, a slouch and a droop, an affected manner of talking (*Punch* was firmly convinced that no Aesthete could pronounce the latter 'r') and a fearful

1 R.E.Francillon, *Mid-Victorian Memories*, 1913.
2 Mrs H.R.Haweis, *The Art of Beauty*, 1878.

affectation of judgment and taste. The word 'precious' was adopted from Ruskin and used out of its context on all occasions.

We hear of an Aesthete (clad, of course, in the regulation knee-breeches) declining to take the prettiest girl in the room down to supper because 'I really couldn't go down to suppah with a young lady who wears mauve twimmings on her skirt and magenta wibbons in her hair'.

Ridicule of the Aesthetes spread to the theatre when, in 1861, Gilbert and Sullivan brought out *Patience*, with the hero, Bunthorne, in knicker-bockers, loose shirt and flowing tie and with the catchy song:

If you're anxious for to shine in the high aesthetic line, as a man of culture rare,
You must get up all the germs of the transcendental terms, and plant them everywhere.
You must lie upon the daisies and discourse in novel phrases of your compli-cated state of mind,
The meaning doesn't matter if it's only idle chatter of a transcendental kind.
    And everyone will say,
    As you walk your mystic way
If this young man expresses himself in terms too deep for *me*,
Why, what a very singularly deep young man this deep young man must be! . . .

Then a sentimental passion of a vegetable fashion must excite your languid spleen,
An attachment *à la* Plato for a bashful young potato, or a not-too-French French bean.
Though the Philistines may jostle, you will rank as an apostle in the high aesthetic band,
If you walk down Piccadilly with a poppy or a lily in your mediaeval hand.
    And everyone will say,
    As you walk your flowery way
If he's content with a vegetable love which would certainly not suit *me*,
Why, what a particularly pure young man this pure young man must be!

It was generally accepted among the Philistines that the male Aesthete was a poor, weedy creature lacking the normal masculine impulses; but everybody was compelled to admit that the female Aesthete could possess both brains and brawn:

    A daughter of the gods, divinely tall
    And most divinely fair . . .

The Aesthetic Movement had a Greek side as well as an Oriental side. Influenced by what has been unkindly called the 'five o'clock tea Antiquity' of Leighton, Albert Moore and Alma-Tadema, Aesthetic ladies, while they might plaster their walls with Japanese fans, aspired to look like Ancient Greeks. The ordinary fashionable clothes of the early eighties were extremely hampering and tight-fitting, and all dress reformers were agreed that 'draperies' would be an improvement.

One of the pioneers of the 'back to Athens' movement was a certain Mrs Pfeiffer who habitally wore 'Greek' dress, and appeared on a lecture platform 'dressed in a really beautiful costume, consisting of a Greek chiton of fawn-coloured Indian cachemere over a bodice and divided skirt of terra-cotta ottoman, with antique gold ornaments and belt. . . . A dress should be devised which would find favour in masculine eyes. We venture to think that the costume worn by Mrs Pfeiffer answers to this description.'[1]

Willing to help more hidebound ladies Mrs Pfeiffer issued a series of 'instructions' which were reported in *The Queen*.[2] They turned out to be much less revolutionary than might be supposed for, of course, the whole point of Greek drapery was that it was hung on the naked body. Aesthetic ladies wore an 'underdress', and it is hard to see how this differed in essentials from the ordinary fashionable dress on the day. The difference was in the drapery that went over it and Mrs Pfeiffer, after giving a whole page of elaborate instructions for managing it, concludes, rather gloomily, that 'some measure of taste and a knowledge of the hang of classical draperies are necessary to the due arrangement'.

This is easy to believe; and perhaps it is not surprising that some of the weaker sisters had the whole thing sewn on to the underdress and let it go at that. It must have been a comfort to them to learn from a trade catalogue that 'Messrs Liberty and Co. have made it their special study to reproduce – with due regard to the requirements of Modern times – the beautiful Soft-clinging Draperies so much esteemed in Ancient Greece'.

Still, all the dress reformers did not stop at Greek draperies; Lady Harberton at least was made of sterner stuff. She founded the National Dress Society, later transformed by the change of a single letter into the *Rational* Dress Society; and early in 1887 she held a meeting in Westminster Town Hall to launch the new campaign. Mrs Oscar Wilde was in the chair with, we may be sure, the full approval of her husband. Had he not himself called for a 'joyous and notable dress for men'?

Lady Harberton was the principal speaker and must certainly have commanded the attention of the audience for not only was she clad in 'Tarbush trousers of black satin merveilleuse with a sash round the hips,[3]

1 *The Pictorial World*, 1887.

2 *The Queen*, 1880.

3 'Round the hips'; thus conforming – unconsciously – to the prevailing mode of the eighties.

and a black velvet jacket trimmed with jet passementerie, caught together at the waist with a buckle over a full waistcoat of white satin and lace', but she emphasized the points of her discourse by cracking a riding whip.

In spite of this she said some very sensible things. She pointed out that

the dress of ladies is at present supposed to show the age and condition of the wearer whether married or unmarried. The older a woman gets, the more unnecessary things it is considered proper for her to pile on her unfortunate person. Her very bonnet is heavier; her mantle and dress of heavier and richer material; her skirts are longer and her *improver*[1] larger. She must have more hair on her head, no matter how it gets there.[2]

Lady Harberton estimated that the average weight of a grandmother's costume among the richer classes was not less than 15 lb. 'Women', she declared:

have an equal right with men to use the limbs that God gave them. . . . Petticoats are exhausting, unhealthy, dirty, and dangerous. The trouser is not only more comfortable, healthy and clean, but also more decent, as less liable to derangement. The modern idea of decency, which exposes the whole of the upper part of a woman's body for the mere sake of display when she is in full dress, but shrouds her legs in layer upon layer of material, is a very strange one, and it is time that it were altered; women should combine to do this and show that 'union is strength'.

If the news of this meeting reached America the ageing Mrs Bloomer may well have permitted herself a smile.

Different as their reformed costumes were – Greek chiton or Turkish trousers – the ladies on the platform were alike in this, that they wore no corsets. To discard the corset is, quite naturally, the hall-mark of the emancipated woman. Tight-laced epochs are – tight-laced. Freedom from physical constriction and freedom or behaviour go together, although the opponents of tight-lacing in the eighties did not put *that* forward as one of their arguments. Rather they relied upon the argument from health which was, indeed, valid enough. Mrs Haweis had protested against

a machine that, pretending to be a servant is, in fact, a tyrant – that, aspiring to embrace, hugs like a bear – crushing in the ribs, injuring the lungs and heart, the stomach, and many other internal organs. . . . In deforming the waist, almost all the vital organs are affected by the pressure, and the ribs pushed out of their proper place. . . . And the face betrays the condition of the inside. Who can forgive the unhealthy cheek and red nose induced by such a practice. Who can forget the disease which has come or is coming? What sensible man or woman can pity the fool who faints, perhaps in the midst of a dance or conversation, from

1 i.e. her bustle.
2 *The Pictorial World*, 1887.

the unbearable pressure on the heart, caused by stays and girdle – or, if they pity, do not also blush for her?

These sensible ideas met with an astonishing amount of opposition, especially from men. There was a spate of letters to the Press protesting against the abandonment of corsets: 'Those who have never tried tight-lacing are prejudiced against it . . . the most extreme lacing can be employed without injury to health. . . . Surely no one would argue against these necessary articles of dress merely on the ground of inconvenience to the wearer.' And so on and so on. One can only conclude that with a certain number of men, tight-lacing was (and still is) a form of fetishism.

Nevertheless, had they only known it, men were fighting a losing battle. The first college for women had been established by F. D. Maurice as long ago as the beginning of our period. Now, such institutions were taken for granted. In the world of work women were advancing everywhere, slowly but surely. In 1870 they were admitted to the Post Office as telegraphists, but when it was proposed that they should be recruited as clerks for the Savings Bank Department, the Controller said that he felt 'in common with the entire staff, the grievous dangers, moral and official, which are likely to follow the adoption of so extraordinary a course'. As for the Vote, that was still far in the future. Even so enlightened a statesman as Gladstone opposed the mere suggestion of women's suffrage on the ground that 'it would trespass upon their delicacy, their purity, their refinement, the elevation of their whole nature'.

In the conditions of the time, indeed, the Vote would have made very little difference. During the seventies a Woman's Suffrage Bill was brought in every year (except 1874) and every year defeated; but even if it had been passed the only beneficiaries would have been propertied women, and propertied women were either widows, or elderly spinsters. Spinsters whose parents were still alive had no legal possessions of their own, nor, of course, had wives.

Political freedom without economic freedom is a delusion, and the first nail in the coffin of the patriarchal system did not seem at the time to have any political significance. It was the Married Women's Property Act which became law in 1862. This, combined with the new facilities for divorce (for before 1856 a divorce could only be obtained by promoting, at considerable expense, a private Act of Parliament) was ultimately to transform the position of women in England; and although divorce still carried a social stigma, it did make it possible to bring an intolerable marriage to an end.

And there was something else which, although never mentioned in respectable society, did seem to promise an end to the age-long servitude of women and to the compulsion under which they laboured to produce

O

children regardless of the economic position of the family and of their own health.

Part of the mental climate of optimism in the second half of the nineteenth century was due to the conviction that the gloomy predictions of Malthus had been falsified by events. His doctrine, that population tends to increase in geometrical ratio while subsistence only increases in arithmetical ratio, had seemed to show that the problem of poverty was insoluble. Up to 1870 indeed there seemed no escape from this conclusion. The population-explosion (to use the phrase which has become current in our own day) was only kept within bounds by the high rate of infant mortality. In 1850 this rate for the upper classes was ten per cent, for the middle classes fifteen per cent, and for the lower classes reached the appalling figures of thirty per cent. Yet, although by the time of the Queen's Diamond Jubilee in 1897, the population had increased by about seven millions, there was no denying that the condition of the poorer classes in England had, in fact, improved. The rate of increase was slowing down, due, perhaps, in a contemporary phrase, to the 'disinclination, reflected from French and American precedent, of Englishwomen indefinitely to fulfil the functions of maternity'. In less mealy-mouthed language, Englishwomen were beginning to practise birth-control, with consequences unrealized at the time and not yet fully apparent three-quarters of a century later.

Hail Columbia!

When people use the word 'Victorianism', they are referring to a certain climate of opinion, conventions and morals which was certainly not confined to the small group of islands over which Queen Victoria ruled, nor even to her 'Dominions beyond the Seas'. On the other side of the Atlantic lay a vast territory which had thrown off the British yoke some two generations before Victoria came to the throne, and in this territory Victorianism was to be found in an even more acute form. Much has been written of the astonishing prudery of English life in the middle of the nineteenth century, but English prudery fades into insignificance when compared with the prudery of America at the same period.

The reasons for this are not far to seek. What we call Victorianism represents the triumph of middle class morality due to the emerging power of those who had always represented the Puritan strain in the English character. But in England their influence was contained and modified by that of other classes, particularly that of the old landed gentry who, for the most part, and in spite of the influence of the Evangelicals upon some of their members, had never been Puritans and had no intention of becoming so.

In America this counter-weight was lacking. The Founding Fathers of New England had been Puritans to a man and although other elements had entered into the composition of the American character and although the dream of a theocracy based on that established by Calvin at Geneva in the sixteenth century had had to be abandoned, they still dictated the tone of American life. America in fact, while it had given up much of the old theology had kept the old morality intact – at least in theory.

'It is impossible', says Eric John Dingwall, 'to understand the development of mode₁ America if we fail to grasp the significance of the failure of the Puritan experiment. . . . The early ideals were still taught and repeated parrot fashion, but they had lost their substance, for the living force had gone out of them. The faith which acted as a sustaining and revivifying agent had melted away.'[1] To parody a famous phrase of Gibbon, prudery might be described as the ghost of Puritanism, standing bareheaded beside the grave thereof.

And prudery was much more careful of the *forms* than Puritanism itself had been. The old Puritans had not hesitated, in their sermons, to call a spade a spade and a whore a whore. But soon propriety of language began to seem more important even than propriety of behaviour, and the most innocent and ordinary terms fell under the ban. We have already referred to the word-prudery of Victorian England. The Americans went even further and Thomas Gratton, in a book published in 1859,[2] gives some strange examples. A cock was called a rooster, 'a certain fowl' or a 'hen's husband'. Even 'bull' seemed too unequivocally male and the phrase 'gentleman cow' was used instead, even when reciting Longfellow's *Wreck of the Hesperus* where the offending word occurred.

These absurdities did not pass without protest. In 1873, A. M. Gow in *Good Morals and Gentle Manners for Schools and Families* (a rather ominous title one would have thought) had the good sense to ridicule the refinement of a lady who spoke of the 'limbs' of a table in order to avoid the use of the all too stimulating word legs. He tells the story of a young woman who had been injured in a railway accident. She was taken to hospital where the doctor in charge asked what was the matter. She replied that one of her 'limbs' was broken. Even when asked to be more specific she could not be persuaded to use the word leg. The doctor, out of patience, cried 'Which is it – the limb you thread a needle with?' 'No, sir,' she replied, 'it's the limb I wear a garter on.'

American prudery at this period was proverbial, but some of its manifestations have probably been exaggerated. It was John Van Buren, son of Martin Van Buren, President of the Unites States, who informed an English visitor that it was the custom to drape the legs of pianos in case they should give the gentlemen 'ideas'. This witticism, solemnly recorded, gave rise to the legend. But apart from this the symptoms of prurience masquerading as morality were plain enough.

One of the main activities of women reformers was to persecute the editors of newspapers and magazines in order to make them conform to the ladies' own notions of propriety. A deputation of five matrons from Chicago waited on the famous Charles Dana of *The Sun* to demand that he should denounce the Spanish dancer Carmencita who was enjoying considerable success. 'Carmencita's red and yellow gowns,' says Thomas Beer, 'covered her legs entirely and her shoulders were hidden in sleeves. It is plain that she wore corsets and nothing lewd is recorded of her performances in public, while in private she seems to have been an estimable,

1 E. J. Dingwall, *The American Woman*, 1956.
2 T. C. Gratton, *Civilized America*, London, 1859.

stupid creature.'[1] The protesting ladies had never seen Carmencita dance and knew nothing whatever of her private life. Dana advised them to go back to Chicago and suppress 'the Slide', a notorious night-house of which the ladies had never heard but which was well-known to every man-about-town in the city.

The editors of the highly respectable magazines, *Harper's*, *The Century* and *Lippincott's* received shoals of abusive and even threatening letters from female fanatics who objected to the very mention of liquor, 'including beer and claret', in the short stories appearing in their pages, who insisted that virtue should always be rewarded and vice never be unpunished, and that words like 'breasts', 'belly', 'damn', 'vomit' and 'rape' must never sully the printed page.

The old Puritan contempt for the body took the form of a horror of nudity which can only be described as pathological. In the Cruger mansion on Fourteenth Street the classical statues were provided with little aprons lest the guests at a ball should blush to learn the facts of human anatomy. This feeling no doubt was shared by the middle-classes in England, but there the aristocrats' tradition of importing classical statues and exhibiting them in their country mansions made the opinions of their social inferiors of less account. In America there was no such tradition and no such check. The notorious Anthony Comstock had declared that 'nude paintings and statues are the decoration of infamous resorts, and the law-abiding American will never admit them to the sacred confines of the home', and many of his fellow citizens agreed with him.

Even towards the end of the nineteenth century the people of Boston refused the work which the great American sculptor Augustus Saint-Gaudens had made for the façade of the public library on the ground that it included the figures of two naked children. Earlier, when Mrs Trollope visited an exhibition organized by the Pennsylvania Academy of Fine Arts, she found a screen in front of the room containing antique statues. A female attendant told her that she could enter, as all ladies could, 'when there be no gentlemen watching them'.[2]

It is astonishing that ladies were let in at all, for they were supposed to know nothing of the physical side of sex until they were married and even then to take no pleasure in it, but merely to submit themselves as victims to the 'animal passions' of their husbands. As in England at the same period this resulted in frustrations and tensions which went far to explain the neurotic frigidity of wives and the sad fact that so many husbands sought their sexual satisfactions elsewhere. This attitude led to some curious and unfortunate results; on the one hand to the growth of prostitution and on the other to the glorification, indeed the deification of

1 T.Beer. *The Mauve Decade*, 1926.
2 F.E.Trollope, *Domestic Manners of the Americans*, 1839.

the American woman as wife and mother. Foreign visitors were already, before the beginning of our period, noticing and recording the beginnings of a matriarchal society. Francis Lieber[1] remarked on the contempt with which husbands were treated by their wives and the latter's lack of gratitude for any services rendered. Such services were simply regarded as the right of the superior sex. Alfred Bunn,[2] writing in the fifties, speaks of women's rudeness to men, especially when travelling. Anthony Trollope[3] makes similar observations, remarking that American women had 'no perception of that return which chivalry demands of them'. French observers like A. d'Almbert[4] and the Comte de Soissons[5] a generation later were even more shocked by female tyranny, no different from the kind of influence that Frenchwomen exercised over their husbands. American women treated their menfolk as little boys, and the American man responded by throwing himself into business, divorcing himself from all cultural activities and finding whatever sexual pleasure he managed to obtain outside the home.

⊏It is small wonder that serious-minded people began to be gravely concerned with the condition of American morals. Unfortunately 'morals' meant, as it did in Victorian England, sexual morals. Corruption in politics and business seemed much less important, indeed to be justified by the 'Gospel of Wealth', unrestricted laissez-faire and that system of professional politics which has been described as 'two-party spoilsmanship'. That period of American history which lies between the time of reconstruction after the Civil War and the 'Progressive' period of the twentieth century is often called the 'Gilded Age'. Other equally expressive names are the 'Brown Decade', the 'Mauve Decade' and the 'Great Barbecue'. Any of these 'is sufficient to suggest the kind of impression these years have made in retrospect: a tasteless time, surely; a time of pale and pretentious shades and shapes, false fronts and other artificialities. Beneath the surface? Corruption; a time when representatives of business and government joined hands to supervise the plunder of the public pocketbook.'[6]

The political corruption of New York had long been notorious, and that bribery was the natural, and indeed, the only way of dealing with a police officer was taken for granted, but he was not the main beneficiary of the system. Thomas Beer speaks of 'Irish patrolmen who bullied contribution from bawds and gamblers, or took it from wretched immigrants in lawful

1 F. Lieber, *The Stranger in America*, 1835.
2 A. Bunn, *Old England and New England*, 1853.
3 A. Trollope, *North America*, 1862.
4 A. d'Almbert, *Flanerie parisienne aux Etats-Unis*, 1856.
5 S. C. de Soissons, *A Parisian in America*, 1896.
6 R. H. Walker, *The Poet and the Gilded Age*, 1963.

business who assumed humbly that the Yankee police were like all police. The hog's share of this income passed upwards from official glove to glove and vanished in a political haze over Tammany Hall.' The presiding figure in this was a taciturn, bearded man with long arms, known as Boss Croker, who had been in virtual control of New York for a generation, with the enthusiastic support of the Catholic Irish.

Ironically enough the man who challenged Croker was himself an Irishman and a devout Catholic, a prosecuting attorney named Goff, and when in 1894 the Senate appointed a commission to examine the morals of New York City, he proved himself an investigator of energy and integrity. There was a tremendous scandal, seized upon eagerly by the Republic Party and by all those Protestants who were convinced that the Catholic Church was indeed the Whore of Babylon. As a result brothels and gambling establishments were closed and Theodore Roosevelt was appointed to clean up the police.

A new era seemed to have dawned but, unfortunately, it didn't last. The corrupt politicians simply took cover or went abroad until the storm had blown over. 'And then, in the summer of 1895 the steamers brought home groomed, plump men from Paris in time to chaffer for paving contracts and the repairs of municipal buildings. Familiar faces showed once more in the saloons along Fourteenth Street or on the steps of Tammany Hall. The "boys" were back.'

What impressed many visitors to New York in the late nineteenth century was the rage for gambling. There was gambling even in the trains which brought the commuter to the great city (one train from Philadelphia even carried a special Club car) and once there the fun became fast and furious. It was notorious that at lunch time office clerks all over the town skimped their mid-day meal to steal into a pool room to bet on a horse race taking place in, perhaps, New Orleans or even farther away, or to hang over a stock ticker. Those who had leisure in the afternoons went to billiard-rooms or pool rooms, and in clubs in the evening gambling was universal. And it was reckoned that if many husbands spent most of the night playing poker their wives had already spent most of the afternoon in playing bridge. Many of the transactions on the Stock-Exchange were pure speculation and all over New York there were branch offices of the recognized brokers and the bucket-shops of the unrecognized.

'But these methods' says the lively author of *The Real New York*:

are by common consent, called business. The word gambling is reserved for more definite and material games, in which at least the trick wheel, the brace box, the loaded dice and the marked cards are real while the technique of the artist is beyond dispute. These games range from craps to Canfield's. If you come properly introduced you can play in the dingy, smelly room of a rear tenement,

1 T. Beer, *ibid*.

where the Ethiopian runs his policy shop and the coloured sportsmen 'ply the gigs', losing their money but never their faith in dreams . . . or you can, if properly introduced, revel in roulette or anything else while you loll in the sumptuous fauteuils of Mr Phil Daly. The Dean of the gambling faculty is Richard Canfield, Esquire, who receives select guests in a fortified castle on East 44th Street. You can tell it by the beautiful marble pillars. You may be able to get a card of introduction from some gentleman at your club and if you once pass the strong door you will find a home where ingenious sleight of hand is not the only art well cultivated, for the furnishings are impeccable and the pictures and objects of vertu show masterly connaissance.

Gambler Canfield is now chiefly remembered as having been painted by Whistler but in the early 1900s he was a figure of national importance. He was accused by the District Attorney of New York of having won nearly half a million dollars from the inebriated son of a multi-millionaire, but from this tussle Canfield emerged triumphant with his gains still intact.

When the redoubtable Boss Croker was the ruler of Tammany Hall he tried to close down the pool-rooms, but so many of the voters in New York were themselves gamblers that the politicians in general thought it wiser to let them alone. Even women took a hand in the game. 'The other day', says Rupert Hughes:

a smart dress making establishment was raided, and while the women were having hysterics of indignation and denying with tears that they were interested in horse flesh, the telephone bell rang. A policeman answered and a far-away voice began to tell racing returns. There are at least twenty pool rooms for women all over town and many of the men's places have women's rooms.

There is big money in the telephone pool room exchange and one man has a dozen operators at work. Regular clients simply register their bets by 'phone and get their returns, if any, by cheque. These places have no players, and the office door calls it a 'News Exchange'. They say that one of the men in Broad Street often handles over 10,000 dollars on one race . . . there are men in town who run from twenty-five to a hundred pool rooms each and the profits sometimes run to a hundred thousand dollars in a single day. Brooklyn and all the other towns about are sprinkled the same way. These big men have big lawyers, and fight the police with technicalities. Peter De Lacy is one of the chief of these, and owns several places; one of them in Park Road was open for ten years, and sometimes you see 300 men in it at once. The man known as 'The Allen' was raided one hundred and thirteen times, but the police courts have never convicted him.

The most ingenious devices were employed to defeat the vigilance of the authorities. Some of the pool rooms even pretended to be places of worship and when the police knocked at the door the roulette wheels, faro boxes and race bulletins vanished instantly and the company burst into song, singing favourite hymns like 'Shall we Gather at the River?' or 'Bringing in the Sheaves'. Some of the pool rooms ran discreet brothels as a side line.[1]

1 R. Hughes, *The Real New York*, 1905.

Hail Columbia !

The Statue of Liberty under construction in Paris

Wedding at West Union, Carter County, Nebraska, 1886

Tourists at the Niagara Falls, c. 1885

The Cocroft Family, 1886; photograph by Alice Austen

Men's ready-to-wear clothing establishment in Chicago, 1878

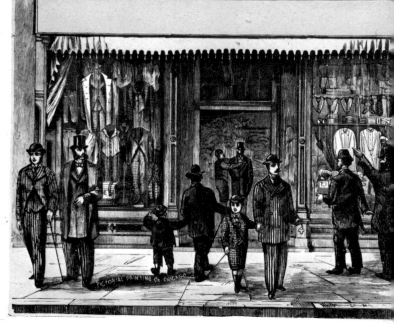

First trip on the 'El' (New York's Elevated Railroad), 1867

HOPE IS A
GOOD·BREAKFAST
BVT·A·BAD·SVPPER

A
LIFE·RETIRED
IS
WELL·INSPIRED

PLAIN·LIVING
AND
HIGH·THINKING

The corner seat, *c.* 1900

Opposite top: Country sports in Newhaven, Connecticut,
c. 1888; photographed by H. L. Dakin in one of the first action
photographs ever taken

Opposite bottom: American ladies cycling, *c.* 1880

Dinner given by Harrison G. Fiske; Byron's photograph of eminent bankers with vine-leaves in their hair

Playing faro in the Orient Saloon, Bisbee, Arizona

Consuela, Duchess of Marlborough and Lord Ivor Spencer-Churchill
by Giovanni Boldini, 1906

William S. Hart, one of the first
stars of the 'Western'

Left: Buffalo Bill

Henry Ford and Barney Oldfield in
Ford's Racer

All this the moralists seem to have happily ignored, content to concentrate their attention on sex in all its manifestations, even if these included art and literature. Puritanism had, as always, produced its inevitable crop of pornography, but unfortunately Puritans have never been able to decide exactly what it meant by the word 'obscene' (they are in the same difficulty today) and this confusion brought into prominence and power the kind of reformer whose activities do more harm than good.

No understanding of the climate of American opinion in the last quarter of the nineteenth century is possible without considering the career of Anthony Comstock. This extraordinary person (but, unfortunately, not extraordinary enough for he found many followers) was born in the village of New Canaan, Connecticut. He had little education, being till the end of his life unable to write or spell correctly, but he made up for this deficiency by his boundless self-confidence and his zeal for promoting 'purity'.

It is true that censorship enactments were already in force in America when Comstock came on the scene. A generation had passed since Alexis de Tocqueville could praise America because although 'attempts have been made by some governments to protect the morality of natives by prohibiting licentious books, in the United States no one is punished for this sort of work'. Massachusetts prohibited 'obscene literature' in 1842, and in the same year Congress forbade the importation of 'indecent' pictures into the United States. An act of 1865, slightly modified in 1872, prohibited the mailing of objectionable books and pictures thus erecting the Post Office into an instrument of literary and artistic censorship. But, says Ernest Sutherland Bates[1] sarcastically 'there was one saving grace in all these laws: it never occurred to anyone, apparently, that they should be enforced'.

It was Comstock who changed all that. He had already, in his capacity as a private smut hound, secured several convictions when, in 1872, he was recruited by the Young Men's Christian Association of New York City to carry on the good work in an official capacity. He at once showed his mettle by securing the arrest of two remarkable sisters, Victoria Claflin Woodhull and Tennessee Claflin, joint editors of *Woodhull and Claflin's Weekly*. This was an astute move on Comstock's part for the two women were widely (and, to some extent, rightly) regarded as exponents of 'free love'.

The Claflin sisters were set up in a stockbroking business in New York with the aid (rather surprisingly) of Commodore Vanderbilt. They ran it (again rather surprisingly) with success, but it only absorbed a fraction of their energies. In addition to editing the *Weekly*, Victoria, in particular,

1 E.S.Bates, *This Land of Liberty*, 1930.

was much seen – and heard – on public platforms, and she certainly made no secret of her opinions. 'Yes,' she shouted back to a heckler at one of her 'Social Freedom' meetings, 'Yes! I am a free lover! I have an inalienable, constitutional and natural right to love whom I may, to love as long and as short a period as I can, to change that love every day if I please!' One of the charges against her was that she was still on friendly terms with her divorced husband, Dr Woodhull, as Bates says 'in itself a sufficient sign of immorality'. As a leading feminist she had been nominated by the Equal Rights Party in May 1872 for President of the United States.

In the 2 November issue of the *Weekly* she 'spilt the beans' about the liaison between the famous minister of Plymouth Church, Henry Ward Beecher and Elizabeth Tilton, patting him on the back at the same time by remarking that 'the healthy vigor of public opinion for the last quarter of a century has been augmented and strengthened from the physical amativeness of Henry Ward Beecher'.

Beecher's relatives and friends were divided in their reactions. His sister, the ardent feminist Isabella Beecher Hooker, disapproved of his conduct, as his brother the Reverend Thomas Beecher did of his advanced opinions. Another brother, the Reverent William H. Beecher defended him, as did Harriet Beecher Stowe, the famous author of *Uncle Tom's Cabin*. Some thought that the *Weekly*'s attack on Beecher was to force him to come into the open as an exponent of free love. Others surmised that Comstock had been paid by Beecher's friends to defend him. 'The anarchist–spiritualist–free love world was in a dither.'[1]

The obvious response to the *Weekly*'s allegations would seem to be a libel action; Comstock chose to have the Claflin Sisters arrested on a charge of obscenity. There was a nation-wide furore. Half America was outraged – on one side or the other. Half was convulsed with merriment at this 'sensational comedy of free love', and the comedy turned to farce with the intervention of an eccentric millionaire named George Francis Train. In a paper called the *Train Ligue*, specially founded for the purpose, he demanded the suppression of the Bible Publishing Company for printing 'disgusting slanders on Lot, Abraham, Solomon and David'. When nothing happened, he published certain sections of the Old Testament himself under sensational headings. Comstock at last rose to the worm dangled before him. . . . 'Train was arrested and taken to the Tombs, from which he issued blithe statements to the press announcing that on his release he would found a Commune with himself as dictator and that his first act would be to hang all members of Congress. This engaging promise prejudiced a good many of the community in his favor'.[2] Meanwhile the Claflin Sisters were brought to trial – and the case dismissed.

1 S.Betzion, *Marriage, Morals and Sex in America*, 1953.
2 Bates, *op. cit.*

Comstock was bitterly disappointed but the affair had given him wide publicity. He was sent by his organization to Washington to promote the passing of a Federal law against obscenity. It is amusing to note that he was deeply shocked by the décolletage of the Congressmen's wives but entirely indifferent to a degree of political corruption among Congressmen which led to some of them being sentenced to imprisonment. 'Morals' for Comstock meant sexual morals and he succeeded in inducing Congress to pass what has been described as 'one of the most vicious and absurd measures that ever came before that august body'. It was a hopelessly muddled measure, confounding in one condemnation indecent books and pictures, the practice of abortion, and the dissemination of contraceptives. It was passed by Congress after a discussion lasting ten minutes!

It was a triumph for Comstock who, in 1873, was appointed 'Special Agent of the United States Post Office' to enforce the statute he had promoted. He travelled tirelessly up and down the country, arresting offenders and promoting societies for the suppression of vice. Disguised as a poor man he made a practice of appealing to the charity of abortionists and then had them arrested when they agreed to perform an operation on his imaginary wife. He boasted that he had caused the suicide of fifteen persons and among these was Ida Craddock whose only crime was that she had written *The Wedding Night*, a book praised by several clergy but pronounced obscene by a jury which was not even given the opportunity of reading it.

Comstock's last triumph was to induce the Police Commissioner in New York to suppress a production of *Mrs Warren's Profession* by 'the Irish smut-dealer George Bernard Shaw'. But his influence extended long beyond his death at the age of seventy-one and is not extinct even today.

It would be impossible to discuss manners and morals at this period without taking note of the large part played by religion in American life. The thirties, forties and fifties formed, says Carl Russell Fish:

distinctly and increasingly a religious period. It was not merely that the interest in religion itself was stronger than in the preceding generation but that the union between religion and morality was so strong that they became practically indistinguishable, and that almost every subject was invested with the religious qualities of certainty and enthusiasm. Every orator had to prove that his position was endorsed by the Constitution and the Bible.[1]

Religion took many forms, and the grouping of sects was conditioned to a large extent by the facts of American history. It was natural that the Quakers should be strong in Pennsylvania; in New England the Congregationalists (the descendants of the seventeenth century Independents) were the most powerful body; Providence, Rhode Island was (and always

1 C.R.Fish, *The Rise of the Common Man, 1830–1850*, 1927.

had been) Baptist; the Methodists were less localized. They were divided from the Baptists only by minor points of theology but at one with them in their emotional 'conversions' and their insistence on the strictest morals; and it was these two denominations which principally evangelized the West. Methodists and Presbyterians who both seemed to have forgotten that John Wesley had spent his life fighting the Calvinist doctrine of Predestination, had made an agreement that migrating New Englanders should be received in Presbyterian churches, and in many districts the two sects found it possible to work together.

The most powerful religious bodies in New York were the Episcopalian and the Dutch Reformed. The former was indistinguishable in organization and ritual from the Church of England and was beginning to be affected by those movements in the Anglican Church which can be summed up in the word Puseyism. In Pennsylvania such German sects as the Mennonites were settled in separate communities, preserving their own language. Their strict principles made it difficult for them to exist elsewhere. The same may be said of the Adventists. Their founder William Miller had confidently predicted the Second Coming of Christ for 1843, but the sect continued to attract recruits even after this disappointment and at the beginning of our period had communities stretching from Maine to Wisconsin. They kept Saturday, instead of Sunday, as a Day of Rest and this made it difficult for them to work with those who did not share their views.

The Biblical injunction 'Come out from among them and be ye separate, saith the Lord' was interpreted literally by the Mormons. The Mormon Church, with a new Bible in the Book of Mormon, had been founded by William Smith in 1830. America was tolerant of sectarianism but to many Mormonism appeared to be not so much a variety of Protestantism as a new religion. The Mormons were driven by their unpopularity from New York to Ohio, on to Missouri and then to Illinois. William Smith was actually killed by a mob. Fortunately, in Brigham Young the Mormons found their Moses to lead them to the Promised Land. This they found, in 1848, in the Valley of the Great Salt Lakes and two years later the community was firmly established. Polygamy, which to most people is the distinguishing trait of Mormon practice, was instituted in 1844 and abolished in 1890.

Unitarianism, although regarded by many as non-Christian, exercised a remarkable influence on intellectual and cultural life. The Unitarians were small in number, mostly scattered along the coast of New England, but in an age of great preachers William Ellery Channing stood out both for his eloquence and the sweet reasonableness of his doctrine. It has been claimed that he was more influential than any other single person in uniting religious fervour with an enthusiasm for social reform. Perhaps the most eminent Unitarian of all was Ralph Waldo Emerson whose fame spread rapidly throughout the English-speaking world and whose mysticism, shaking itself free even from Unitarian bonds, made a wide appeal to some of the finest minds and noblest characters of his time.

Catholicism at first made slow headway in the United States. It is true that in Baltimore, in New Orleans and to some extent in St Louis, it had long been the creed of the leading families, but Catholics were not numerous until the arrival of the Irish, fleeing from the Famine. Many of them arrived in a state of utter destitution, they were herded together in the vilest slums of American cities and were willing to work for starvation wages. Catholicism inevitably became associated in the public mind with the lowest stratum of society.

In these circumstances it is not surprising that there was considerable prejudice against Catholicism in general and Irish Catholics in particular. In many towns they suffered ostracism. Dion Boucicault, the popular Irish actor and playwright, remarks, in a letter written in the 1870s, 'I have heard a great deal too much of humiliating slights put upon Irish ladies at balls, and there are rules against us at one of the best clubs in town'. We hear of an Irish woman teacher whose rooms were searched for 'a nun's veil or penitential emblems' because, as her name was Kelly, she was presumed to be secretly a Catholic. But Boucicault was fair enough to remark that 'in society a bitter prejudice has been stirred up by the unseemly conduct of some Irish political blacklegs and, I should judge, by the constant immigration of humble people from Ireland'.

The prejudices were not all on one side. Some of the Irish priests were tolerant and enlightened men: some were not. Thomas Beer quotes a description of one of the latter kind supplied by an unnamed American-Irishman who was young in the 1880s:

Father Dan was a sour old prude, an educated peasant from South Ireland who had been a priest there before he came to the United States. He hated a Protestant and he despised Protestant education. Once he found me playing with some of my Nordic crowd on our street and told me: 'Remember, Owen, that you'll never see any of those lads in another world unless you should offend God and be sent to hell.'

In spite of the climate of Puritanism (Catholic as well as Protestant) it was in America that divorce first began to be tolerated in respectable society. As late as the end of the 1860s a *divorcée* was a pariah, however innocent she might have been. In *The Social Ladder* we read of

one woman of excellent family [who] married a man equally well known in New York's social organization. She bore his two children before he wearied of her. She had been an exemplary wife and mother. Immediately following the birth of her second child, her husband departed for Chicago, the Reno of that generation, and from what was then the Far West summoned her to join him. She was still

ill. Her baby was ailing. She refused, as he hoped she would. A few months later, notice was served open her that he had divorced her. From that day on she was regarded as an outcast, a fallen woman, by all her former associates. Society ignored her entirely. She was utterly guiltless. She had been deeply wronged by her rascally husband. That did not extenuate her offence. She was a divorced woman and, hence, socially dead.[1]

By the mid-seventies all this had been changed and a decade later we find hostesses complaining of the complications of seating the guests at dinner parties when ex-husbands and wives were present. By the end of the century a respectable dowager was boasting of being the only woman in Newport who, for thirty years, had had the same cook and the same husband.

Up to the end of the 1860s it might be said that the old New York families formed an exclusive aristocracy, visiting one another, inter-marrying among themselves, and rarely appearing in public. When they did so it was in the Assembly, or the Society of Patriarchs. They were highly cultivated, patronizing the Opera and promoting museums. Their dignified leaders were such people as Mrs Maturin Livingston, Mrs Alexander Hamilton, Mrs Archibald Gracie King and Mrs John Jacob Astor. But there were already signs of a certain opening of doors. Archibald Gracie King was the first man in New York Society to give a ball, not under his own roof, but in a public restaurant. He took over the great mirror-lined hall at Delmonico's, then at the corner of Fourteenth Street and Fifth Avenue. It is amusing to note that the invitations were distributed by Isaac Brown, sexton of Trinity Church and the social messenger of the day. The recipients were amazed, but accepted and the King ball started a fashion.

The usual social entertainment was a much simpler affair. It consisted of an 'At Home' on Saturday evening, with parlour games and dancing, the hostess herself distributing salad and punch, cake and candy. Waltzing was now permitted, although it was still looked at askance by the more puritan and old-fashioned families, who were equally shocked when the eminently respectable Union Club in Fifth Avenue installed a billiard table, and when dashing young men like Colonel de Lancey Lane, William Jay and Roosevelt Roosevelt startled the city by driving four-in-hand coaches.

It was even more startled to see young ladies of impeccable connections driving pony phaetons, for the girls of good families were rigidly guarded. They were chaperoned everywhere by their mothers, and their fathers also were expected to accompany them to a ball or the opera. Perhaps girls had slightly more freedom than their contemporaries in London or Paris, but there were certain parts of New York where it was unthinkable that they

1 Mrs J. K. van Rensselaer, *The Social Ladder*, 1924.

should venture alone. A debutante of the period relates that she used to accompany her father from their house on East Nineteenth Street on his way to business 'down town'. Canal Street was the social deadline and, when they reached it, the daughter turned back, as she could never have returned through the business district unescorted.

Dining at home was a most formal affair, the whole family assembling in evening dress at 6.30. Mrs Rensselaer writes:

The marshalling of the clan in the drawing-room, as though for an inspection by its heads, always preceded the evening meal. The dining table of that day was completely covered with a white cloth and many of its appointments now of china were then of heavy silver. The soup was brought in in a silver tureen. Four silver vegetable dishes were always upon the table, with a cruet stand and immense salt cellars, also of silver. Grace was asked before we began the evening meal, at the conclusion of which we returned to the parlour, where we chatted with visitors, coquetted, played and sang, while our elders gathered about the whist table.

It was in the period of expansion following the Civil War that the exclusiveness of the old New York families began to be threatened. In the 1870s there were still, in New York, many families that had lived there for two hundred years or more. Some of them were the lineal descendants of those who had come to Nieuw Amsterdam in the seventeenth century, not as immigrants, but as envoys of the Netherlands government. In the third quarter of the nineteenth they still regarded themselves as an aristocracy, and bore proudly such names as Lubbertse, De Peyster, De Peyster Spratt, Lockermans, Boaertus, Hardenbroeck Phillipse, Kierstede and Van de Boorgh Beekman. Among the most powerful of the families that held great estates in the province were the Van Rensselaers and the Schuylers, and a descendent of the former could still write proudly, as late as 1924, of

men of no social distinction [who] have become prominent in Society by marrying women of breeding. The Vanderbilts, the Astors, the Belmonts and other present leaders have attained their station largely through the infusion of aristocratic blood into their line through marriage with the old families. . . . Readers come to regard those persons most frequently featured by the press as belonging to 'old Knickerbocker families'. In nine cases out of ten their judgment is wrong. Prominent today in published accounts of New York social events are the Vanderbilts, the Astors, the Morgans, the Davidsons, the Belmonts, the Lamonts, the Vanderlips, the Villards, the Goulds. Only one of these families has enjoyed a social recognition in New York as far back as Civil War times. This was the Astors. Not a single one of the names cited above runs back in the annals of Society to the Revolutionary era. The first John Jacob Astor, born in Walldorf, Germany, came to New York in 1783 as a piano merchant.

One of the most influential figures of the day was Ward McAllister, *arbiter elegantiarum* of New York Society, who has been compared with Beau Brummell, and whose appearance suggested a more handsome Napoleon III. His father, Matthew Hall McAllister had been a prominent officer in the Georgia Hussars, the crack regiment of the South. He entertained on a lavish scale, including in his parties all the wits and beauties of the period, and he was the happy possessor of cellars full of excellent wine. The son inherited this civilized interest and Frederick Townsend Martin paints a charming picture of him 'as he sat back in his chair holding up his glass of Madeira so that the light filtered through the wine and turned it into liquid gold . . . and McAllister would tell us how many times it had crossed the ocean before it had been mellowed into perfection'.[1]

He retained all his life the charming and courtly manners of the South. He was much in Society, had a positive genius for organizing parties and soon became indispensable. It was he who was responsible for the now universally accepted phrase 'The Four Hundred'. In 1892, Mrs William Astor, who has been described as 'the last supreme leader the New York social system was to know', decided to give a ball. It was found that her ballroom could accommodate four hundred people and no more. As her friends and acquaintances numbered far more than this Ward McAllister was called in to scrutinize the lists and decide to whom invitations should be issued. He did this not only with efficiency but with delight, and as he made no secret of the matter, it came to the notice of the newspapers and the phrase passed into common parlance as the equivalent of *crème de la crème*.

One of the most extravagant entertainments hitherto known in the annals of New York Society was given by Mrs Bradley-Martin on 10 February 1897, in the grand ballroom of the new completed Waldorf-Astoria. The great room was transformed into a replica of a hall in the Palace of Versailles. Mrs Martin (rather oddly, since Versailles was not built in the sixteenth century) appeared as Mary, Queen of Scots. She wore (again with a nice sense of historical accuracy) clusters of diamond grapes made for Louis XIV and a splendid ruby necklace which had belonged to Marie Antoinette. To add to the chronological confusion August Belmont, one of the chief guests, wore a suit of gold-inlaid armour 'valued at ten thousand dollars, and Mr Martin, in a handsome brocade suit assumed the character of Louis XV'.

The hosts, with curious naïvety, had imagined that this entertainment would make them popular. They had purposely delayed sending out the invitations so that the guests would be compelled to obtain their costumes in New York instead of importing them from abroad. This was their

1 F. T. Martin, *Things I remember*, 1913.

notion of helping things along in a period of economic stagnation, but the public reaction was hostile and special police (under the control of Theodore Roosevelt, then Police Commissioner) had to be posted outside the Waldorf-Astoria to protect the guests as they arrived. The newspapers denounced the Bradley-Martins, the City Fathers raised their taxes, and there was such a storm of obloquy that they left America altogether and settled in England. But this did not prevent equally extravagant entertainments being given by others.

These were usually long and elaborate, beginning with a formal dinner party, followed by a dance, supper at midnight and an early breakfast. It was in the 'favors' given at the cotillion that the display of wealth was most apparent. A contemporary account relates that:

at the cotillion given by Mrs George Jay Gould in 1910, to announce the engagement of her daughter Marjorie to Anthony V. Drexel, Jr, the favours reached a climax of costliness. They were all the work of a noted jeweller. During one figure of the cotillion, which was led by Phoenix Ingraham, jewelled and enamelled pins, charms and rings were given to the women and scarf pins and scarf holders to the men. There were also other souvenirs of gold and precious stones.

Among those who thought that all this was much too formal and elaborate was the well-known hostess, Mrs Stuyvesant Fish. She provided simple dinners which lasted no more than fifty minutes, she mingled distinguished people from all walks of life with her 'Society' guests, introduced private theatricals and replaced the orchestra with a jazz band. This, if she had only known it, was the beginning of the end. It was the blast of the saxophone which brought the walls of Jericho tumbling down.

The climate of New York was anything but agreeable in the summer months. Even Italian imigrants found the humid heat oppressive and no one who could afford to leave it stayed in the city after the first days of June. Indeed there were many miles of residential streets with doors and windows boarded up. It was the women chiefly who went away, for most New York business men allowed themselves no more than a fortnight's holiday in the year. They joined their wives and families at weekends. New York in summer was described as a big bachelor apartment house and the loneliness of grass-widowers was thought to have a distinct influence on the mounting rate of divorce. In the words of Rupert Hughes from whom we have already quoted:

While Father Knickerbocker's wife may have deserted him and may be spending her days in a bathing suit and her nights on a moonlit piazza overlooking the ocean, there is usually a faithful stenographer who dresses quite as well, whom the stranger in town thinks to be Mrs Knickerbocker when they are seen together dining on some roof and sitting out some roof-garden entertainment. But the facts all come out in the wash.

Fortunately, although the science of refrigeration was still in its infancy, there were few reasonably prosperous families in New York which did not boast an ice-box replenished by regular deliveries. Charitable organizations gave it away in the poorer quarters, and this was one of their most useful services, for summer was nothing less than an inferno in the New York slums. Thousands of people spent the night on the roofs of apartment houses or lying on the pavements in the streets. On the worst nights the authorities allowed them to sleep in the parks. The Fire Department regularly turned its hoses on the streets to the delight of the slum children. And there was always Coney Island for those who could afford the very small fare required to get there. Here was all the fun of the fair with ingenious devices, roundabouts, scenic railways and side shows of every kind.

Richer and more fastidious people sought their relaxations elsewhere. There were country clubs, with golf courses and all amenities, in Westchester County. There were the inland towns of New Jersey: Englewood, Lakewood, Summit, Nuttly, and Lake Hopatcong. There was Staten Island to the south and further south still the long beaches of the New Jersey coast. And of course there was Long Island which, even if it did have a Coney Island in its territory, also found room for many expensive and aristocratic dwellings. But it was Rhode Island which contained the most fashionable of all resorts. It was (once again) Ward McAllister who was responsible for the rise of Newport as a summer resort. Rhode Island, purchased from the Indians in the mid-seventeenth century, was invaded early in the nineteenth by a few families from South Carolina and these were shortly followed by others from New York and Boston. Cottages and villas were erected and life was a placid and leisurely affair until Ward McAllister purchased Bayside Farm and began to mount a series of spectacular entertainments.

'Within a year after his arrival,' says Mrs John King Van Rensselaer:

picnics were no longer simple picnics. They had become *fêtes champêtres* at which one drank iced champagne and was served with viands more usually encountered at banquet tables. There were costume picnics and picnics on the beach. There were picnics held in the interior of the island and picnics on the yachts that . . . had begun to anchor in the harbour. When he had exhausted all the possibilities of picnics as sensation makers, Mr McAllister turned for diversion to affairs held at his farm. He introduced the summer colony to the cotillion dinner. The meal was usually served in the garden of his estate by the light of delicately tinted lanterns and shaded candles. After dinner the guests strolled about the garden and eventually went to the barn where Mr McAllister had had a hardwood dancing floor laid. Decorations of corn-stalks, sheaves of wheat and other rural symbols adorned the barn and there, to the music of a specially imported orchestra, the awakened and stimulated Society danced half the night away.

Other fashionable New Yorkers followed their leader to Newport. Among them were Mrs James W. Otis, Mrs James Wadsworth, Mrs Archibald Gracie King, Mrs J. Carson Brevoort, the George Tiffanys and the Henry Van Rensselaers. They emulated Mr McAllister in the extravagance of their entertainments. The arrival of Mrs August Belmont, whose father Commodore Matthew O. Perry, was a native of Newport, and whose husband was one of the richest men of his day, eliminated from social enterprises the last hint of rural flavour. She came prepared to make of the colony a centre for fashion. She succeeded and thereby abolished the old charm and tranquility of the resort . . . Mrs Belmont's wealth and energy enabled her to outdo even Mr McAllister. She became the recognized leader of the Society of her time.

From the McAllister picnics, Society turned to pageants; from his comparatively simple cotillion affairs, to enormous entertainments in which opera stars, actors, jugglers, magicians, and even entire circuses took part. Dinners became vaudeville shows; dances, sometimes closely approximating pagan festivals. The bizarre was glorified; the eccentric exalted by these easily bored folk. The money spent by members of this circle grew in amount with each year. In the early years of this century a certain leading family was said to have spent five thousand dollars a month on entertainment over and above the cost of the food and the wages of the servants.

In a word, money had, by 1900, almost completely broken down the exclusiveness of Newport Society.

Mrs Stuyvesant Fish, as in New York for a time, exercised a certain supremacy over the social life of Newport. Through her endeavour, Society was checked in its rapid slide down a gilded chute into crassness and vulgarity. She had great organizing ability, brains and taste. With the assistance of Harry Lehr, she contrived many original and charming entertainments in which wit and intellect occupied at least an equal place with extravagance. Her régime, while never absolute, marked the expiring flutter of the old dignified caste that had founded, and for many years had directed, the affairs of Newport.

So much for the upper crust but for the vast majority of the inhabitants of New York the pleasures of Newport and similar resorts were forever out of reach. By the end of the nineteenth century the population was already overhauling that of London and if the surrounding conurbation had been included it was probably already larger. It was the most cosmopolitan city in the world. There were more Englishmen than there were in a town like Nottingham and more Frenchmen than in a town like Dieppe. There were more Italians than in Florence and Venice put together and more Russians than the entire population of Kiev. New York was the largest Irish city in the world with the Irish population nearly three times as large as that of either Dublin or Belfast. The Germans amounted to two-thirds the population of Berlin or nearly as much as Hamburg and Munich put together. There were whole districts where hardly a sign was in English; the names and inscriptions were in Italian, German, Russian or French. There was China Town where many of the inhabitants did not speak any language but their own, and of course, a ghetto. As a contemporary account tells us:

Judea in New York has many faces. It has its millionaires living in palatial homes; it has its masters of music, drama, and all the arts; it has its gilded youth . . . it has its lower middle class that takes life serenely and comfortably; its music halls, its theatres, its decent fare. But in its lowest stages it furnishes New York with its most repulsive elements. The slums of the Yankees, the English, the Irish, the Italians, the Germans are at their worst more vicious, more shiftless, more helplessly and hopelessly bad than lowest Jewry. It is actually the higher average of intelligence and energy that makes the Ghettites hardest to forgive. The others are lazy and worthless and ugly because they are the sifted chaff of their races. These might all be so much better and live so much more wisely and cheerfully.

But they cling to the brawl and stench of the Ghetto, with its horrible streets and its more horrible tenements, so high and so crowded that in one square mile there are 250,000 souls – if souls they are. In rooms where the sun never reaches, and where the dust is never disturbed, men, women and children sleep, eat and perform all the necessary and unbeautiful functions of life. Shame is a different thing here from elsewhere; self-respect and respect for others are exotics that perish soon. In these places are sweat-shops too numerous for the law to reach. It is not only in the shops and low roofed lofts that they sew. The home also is a shop.

The sewing-machines whir all day and half the night, and the dancing needles stab the numb hearts into a brutish doggedness. Father, mother, the sons, the daughters and the little children turn and baste and work the button holes and stitch and hem hour after hour, winter and summer, cold season or hot. In the corner, perhaps, squats an old, old man. His eyes are weak and his trembling fingers drive the needle often into his own flesh, but still he sews. He is wracked with a consumptive cough, but still he sews. . . . At night he sleeps with coat and trousers for coverlets. At early light he is sewing again; and the endless seam goes on, interrupted only by the spasms of coughing, coughing, coughing.

At the sewing machine nearby, in the dark corner in the dim light, sits one of his daughters. She is of the age when spring stirs in the blood and the heart quickens with desire, when every woman is, or should be, a Juliet. But her heart is squeezed back in her bent and stunted breast. Her feet tread the dance of the eternal tread-mill; her hands caress the rough cheviot of a cheap sweat-shop coat; her eyes follow the line of it as the seams run forever under the eager needle. She hardly pauses to brush her neglected hair from her eyes; she cannot stop to sigh – and what should she sigh for . . . she knows nothing of joy; fatigue, pain, fever – these are life, she also coughs often and hard. Her old father's disease has caught her. She will not live to his age. In one thing at least she is blessed.

It is the same picture that Tom Hood had painted nearly a hundred years before in *The Song of the Shirt*.

In the negro quarters, and in much of the old 'East Side' there was a similar appalling poverty, and a forgotten versifier was moved to protest:

> In a great, Christian city, died friendless, of hunger!
> Starved to death, where there's many a bright banquet hall!
> In a city of hospitals, died in a prison!
> Homeless in a land that boasts free homes for all!
> In a city of millionaires, died without money![1]

The fortunate in America were probably as unaware of the poverty around them as their counterparts in Europe. The pursuit of wealth and luxury continued, and although old-fashioned people might lament that

the present generation will never know the charm and tranquility which was manifest whenever people like Mrs Schermerborn, Mrs William Astor, Mrs John Jacob Astor, Mrs Belmont and Mrs Paran Stevens entertained their friends . . . from the shores of the Pacific, from the banks of the Mononghahela, and from the great plains of the west and middle west came millionaires with their wives and children who were destined to change the old order into something entirely new.[2]

A rich newcomer, especially if he had beautiful daughters, found little difficulty in conquering New York Society. And then, in the charming words of the author already quoted, 'Venus Victrix, dowered with loveliness and dollars, set forth to conquer England.'

Miss Minnie Stevens, 'the Belle of Newport', became the wife of Lord Paget's son, Miss Beckwith married the eldest son of Lord Leigh, the beautiful Miss Mary Lester became Lady Curzon, and Miss Endicott of Boston the second wife of Joseph Chamberlain. Miss Consuelo Vanderbilt became Duchess of Marlborough, Miss May Goelet Duchess of Roxburghe, and there were two American Duchesses of Manchester.

Nor was it only the British aristocracy that was willing to trade coronets for dollars. Miss Schautz became Duchesse de Chaulne and Mrs Livermore Baronne de la Sellière. A French sociologist has listed for us some of the more spectacular transactions: Duc de Choiseul and Miss Forbes ($1,000,000), Marquis de Choiseul and Miss Clara Coudert ($250,000), Comte Guy de Rohan Chabot and Mrs Hayward ($200,000), Duc Jean-Élie Octave Decazes and Miss Isabel Singer ($2,000,000), Duc Charles Maurice de Talleyrand-Perigord and Miss Adela Simpson ($7,000,000).[3]

Before the Civil War this American export was almost unknown, but it

1 L.B.Cake, *Devil's Tea Table and Other Poems*, 1898.
2 F.T.Martin, *op. cit.*
3 Henri Bellamy, Mariages d'argent à la Belle Epoque, *Le Crapouillot*, April 1961.

became more and more frequent in the last quarter of the century. Already, in 1881, *Punch's Almanack* shows a group of 'New York Millionairesses' studying 'not Murray and Baedecker – oh dear no! – but Burke and Debrett'. Even those who were not millionairesses but had a sufficiency of the world's goods joined in this gold rush in reverse and all Europe was subject to the impact of 'Momma and the Girls'. Perhaps Thomas Beer is a little jaundiced in his picture of them in spring, flooding 'New York's marmored hotels, waving steamer tickets from table to table and threatening to meet each other in London. And autumn saw them home again, radiant in fresh frocks and hats rejected by the prostitutes of Paris as too gaudy for their use.' But they certainly startled the capitals of Europe with their loud and raucous voices (which Richard Harding Davis likened to the voice of an Indian squaw) and their uninhibited manners.

Many voices, however, were raised in defence of the American Girl who, said the *New York Herald*, was 'better dressed, better mannered, more lovable, and lovelier than any maiden of Europe'. For the nineties saw the beginning of that glorification of American womanhood which has gone on from that day to this.

Certainly in the upper ranges of society the American Girl swept all before her. Miss Jerome of New York made a sensational marriage with Lord Randolph Churchill and set the pattern, as it were, for similar alliances.

Such marriages excited in some members of the French aristocracy a curious mixture of envy and spitefulness, and when another Singer heiress – Miss Winarella Singer – became Princesse de Polignac and issued invitations for a buffet supper, 'at little tables', Count Robert de Montes-quiou replied: 'It will, I know, be charming, your supper at little sewing machines.' The Count (who is thought to have been the original both of Huysman's Des Esseintes and Proust's Baron Charles) had the reputation of a wit, but this can hardly be considered one of his happier efforts.

Perhaps the Franco–American alliance which excited the greatest in-terest of all was the marriage of Anna Gould of New York and Count Boniface de Castellane. It was a cynical transaction. Miss Gould was extremely plain but she brought her exquisite husband a dowry of fifteen million dollars. The Count considered that, having given her one of the most aristocratic names in France, he had discharged his part of the bargain. Her part was to provide the funds for his extravagances.

These were on a truly regal scale. For a private party he would have a stage erected at the Tir Aux Pigeons in the Bois and would hire for the evening the entire corps de ballet of the Opéra with an orchestra of two hundred musicians. He invited three thousand guests and two hundred and fifty of these were summoned beforehand to an 'intimate' but lavish dinner. Eighty thousand Venetian lamps were hung in the surrounding trees and sixty footmen in scarlet liveries were hired to attend to the guests and to 'group themselves on the grass' in artistic patches of colour. 'Bellair, the well-known upholsterer, had undertaken to supply the fifteen kilometres of carpet which would prevent any guests from experiencing the discomfort of the evening dew.'

In his *Confessions* Boni de Castellane relates how, with his uncle, the Prince de Sagan, he visited the President of the Municipal Council in order to arrange for the hiring of the Tir aux Pigeons. That worthy official was staggered by the proposals laid before him and ventured to enquire of his two elegant visitors what was the object of the projected fête.

'Sir,' said the Prince de Sagan, adjusting his eyeglass, 'this fête is given simply for our amusement – simply for our amusement.'

The amusement was not shared by the Count's father-in-law, Jay Gould, over in America, especially when he heard of all the other ways which had been devised for spending his money. For Boni was building a pink marble palace in the Avenue du Bois. It had a staircase as grand as that at the Opéra, an immense ballroom and a private theatre with seating for five hundred. The salons were hung with authentic Gobelin tapestries and fitted with priceless pieces of eighteenth-century furniture. The whole house was lighted with thousands of candles ('Electric light is for servants') in crystal chandeliers. When the Count and his wife received their guests fifty musicians played Royalist airs. One can only guess what the daughter of the American Republic thought about it all.

In addition to his town house Boni had two chateaux, and at one of these he entertained the King of Portugal, hiring for the occasion six hundred lackeys. Also, he had a house at Deauville, and a large yacht with a crew of a hundred.[1] Even the Gould millions began to feel the strain, and, after twelve years of married life, Anna had had enough. She had no difficulty in obtaining evidence against her husband, who had hardly pretended to be faithful to her. 'To Boni', says George Painter:

it seemed unthinkable that the American heiress to whom he had given his noble name, and whose wealth he was squandering with such exquisite taste, should not repay him with eternal gratitude and overlook his infidelities with prettier women. But his ugly little wife was about to put her foot down before the last of her fortune disappeared. 'You can't divorce him,' their friends exclaimed in horror; but 'I don't see why not,' she replied, adding in her still imperfect accent . . . '*je le hé, je le hé.*' On 26 January 1906 she left Boni without warning, taking their two sons, and on 11 April she divorced him. Soon it was clear to everyone that Miss Anna Gould was determined not only to save her money but to gain a still better title by marrying Boni's cousin Hélie de Talleyrand-Perigord, Prince de Sagan, who was nineteen years her senior. On 2 January 1908,

1 The number of Boni de Castellane's servants seems incredible. The figures are taken from Cornelia Otis Skinner's well-documented study *Elegant Wits and Grand Horizontals*, 1963.

at the funeral of their relative Charles de Talleyrand-Perigord, the furious Boni clubbed Cousin Hélie with his walking stick as they emerged from the church.[1]

It was small satisfaction. Boni was ruined and for the rest of his life eked out a living by buying and selling antiques on commission. Proust's opinion of the Prince de Sagan was that 'Gould for him spells principally Gold.' Certainly his wife still had plenty of money. As Canning might have said: 'The New World was called into existence to redress the (bank) balance of the Old.'

The attitude of the Puritan American middle classes to these events was curiously ambivalent. They were flattered and pleased with the success of these Daughters of America, but they continued to regard Europe as a sink of corruption from which all good Americans ought to be protected. Even expatriate Americans felt this to some extent and if there is mild exaggeration in the humorous remark that all the novels of Henry James were merely elaborate variations on the theme of 'The Innocents Abroad', the gibe was not without its grain of truth. Most Americans felt themselves to be morally superior to the inhabitants of the Old World and to those recent immigrants, who had not yet become completely 'Americanized', that is to all those who did not pay at least lip-service to the ideals of the Pilgrim Fathers.

Much of the effort expended in reforming the world was, no doubt, high-minded enough, but it sometimes took strange forms. As we have seen much of the impulse came from women, for no country in the world in the nineteenth century produced such a formidable crop of female crusaders, even if they were not all crusading for the same things. But most of them could meet, they found, on the 'Temperance' platform, and combine in the attack on the Demon Drink.

In the second half of the century the campaign had already been going on for a long time and although the passing of the Eighteenth Amendment to the American Constitution did not take place until 1917 and was not put into operation until 1920 (both dates being outside the period of the present survey) the movement had already had sufficient repercussions on American life to need treatment in some detail.

There had, in fact, been various prohibition 'waves' from the foundation of the American Temperance Society in 1826. In 1851 the first state-wide prohibition law was enacted in Maine, and four years later twelve more states had followed suit. There was a setback during the Civil War, but shortly afterwards – in 1869 – the Prohibition Party was founded to secure national prohibition by political action. There was a second 'wave' in 1880 and a third in 1907; and during the whole of this period a large part of American political and social life was conditioned and overshadowed by the struggle between the 'drys' and the 'wets'.

1 G.D.Painter, Marcel Proust, vol. 2, 1965.

Approaching Storms

The Field of Gettysburg, 1863

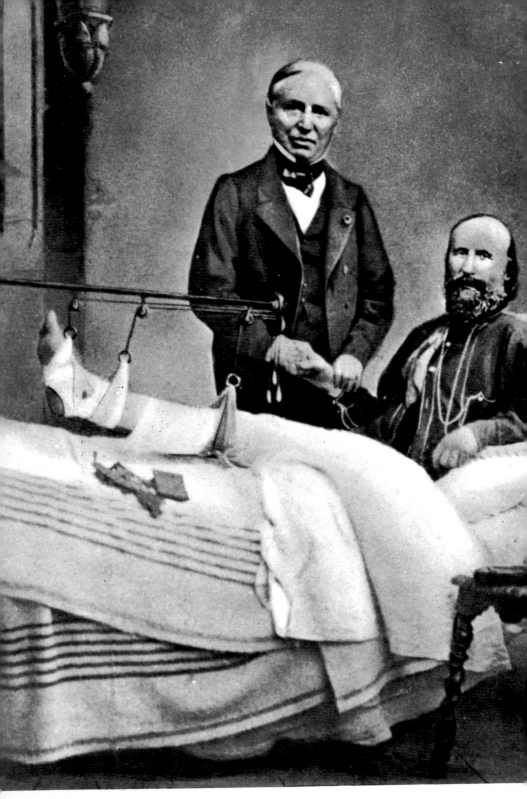

Garibaldi and his physician after the battle of Aspromonte (1862), in which he was wounded

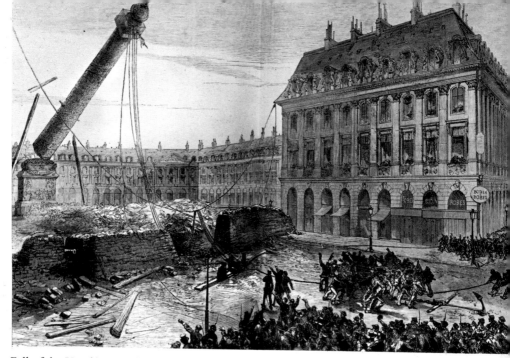

Fall of the Vendôme Column, during the Paris Commune of 1871

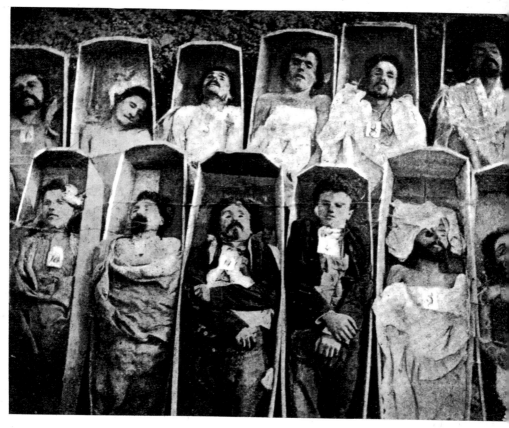

Bodies of executed Communards, 1871

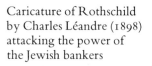

Caricature of Rothschild
by Charles Léandre (1898)
attacking the power of
the Jewish bankers

Crash on the Berlin Bourse, 1873

Opposite: Edouard Manet, *The Execution of Emperor Maximilian in Mexico*, 1867

Crown-Prince Rudolf and his wife

Crown-Prince Rudolf on his death bed

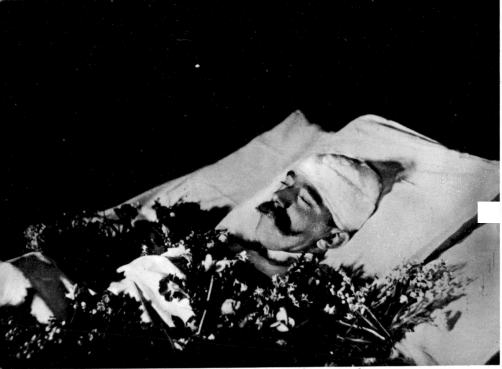

Arnold Böcklin, *War*, 1896

In this struggle there were many cross-currents and shifting alliances. The 'dry' campaign appealed to reformers and progressives, who called upon the new science of eugenics to help them in their fight for better health and better social conditions. It appealed to women who resented the time and money spent by their menfolk in the saloons. It appealed to Protestant prejudices against the wine-drinking immigrants from Catholic countries. The prohibitionists had no doubt whatever that God (or at least, the Protestant God) was on their side.

Their prejudices were reinforced by the undoubted connection in many cities between the saloon and corrupt politicians; and this was especially true in New York where the Irish had obtained a dominating position in the running of the city. Not without reason New York was regarded as the cesspool of iniquity, but, in the view of the farming communities all cities were tarred with the same brush. Some social commentators have seen the whole struggle as a fight between town and country. As Walter Lippmann remarked in 1927 (when prohibition was in force and the Eighteenth Amendment had not yet been repealed by the Twenty-first): 'The evil which the old-fashioned preachers ascribe to the Pope, to Babylon, to atheists, and to the devil, is simply the new urban civilization, with its scientific and economic and mass power.' And he prophesied that the repeal of the Eighteenth Amendment, which he foresaw, 'would mean the emergence of the cities as the dominant force in America, dominant politically and socially as they are already dominant economically'.[1]

Among the rural communities of the Middle West there was an 'agricultural myth' which, as Andrew Sinclair tells us, held that 'farmers were the only true democrats. They were the representatives of the best in the American tradition. The cities held the idle rich and the owners of mortgages and the dregs of Europe. When William Jennings Bryan denounced the East as "the enemy's country", he voiced a rural prejudice older than the Declaration of Independence.'[2]

But the rural communities were fighting a losing battle, and when Bryan was defeated by McKinley in 1896, it was, in fact, already lost. In 1860 only one in five Americans lived in cities; by 1900 it was twice as many. Twenty years later the city dwellers were in a majority. The old mirage of the frontiersman and the cowboy of the Wild West still excited nostalgia, but the average American in the new century was a very different kind of person. America in fact had become a great industrial nation and was soon to be the greatest in the world. No longer did she need to learn from Europe; Europe was beginning to learn from her. The Old World was beginning to understand that progress meant Americanization, but, paradoxically enough it was not this kind of Americanization which was to

1 W. Lippmann. *Men of Destiny*, 1927.
2 A. Sinclair, *Prohibition*, 1962.

Opposite: May-Day demonstrations in Dresden, 1890

make most impact on Europe. It was American music and dance rhythms, in a word – Jazz!

It would be impossible in the present work to attempt an account of all the controversies to which the existence of jazz has provoked, or even to try to define what jazz is. Indeed we are told that 'the reason why jazz cannot be defined is the fact that it is a language . . . a distinctive rhythmic-melodic-tonal idiom – as is, say, Japanese *gaga-ku* or Balinese gong music. And a language . . . cannot be defined.'[1] Attempts have been made to distinguish between jazz and ragtime, but it is admitted that they had a common origin. Perhaps it is permissible to say that ragtime is jazz that has not yet realized its possibilities.

Nineteenth-century composers (Schumann, for example) had made occasional use of syncopation, but the essence of ragtime was the *continuous* 'use of irregular syncopations, the melody and harmony often both being syncopated, sometimes against one another, polyrhythmically'. How did this come about and who started it?

The answer is, of course, the American negro. 'Jazz is the negro's art and . . . almost all the great jazz musicians are negroes.'[2] Yet the negro alone did not produce it. It was essentially a marriage between the primitive music they brought with them from Africa as slaves, and the hymns and folk-tunes of the American South. These tunes were sufficiently simple in themselves to encourage improvised variations, and the borrowings made it possible to transform 'an almost motionless folklore into an art capable of all kinds of evolution'.

The American negro took over the perfected instruments of the whites in preference to the primitive instruments of his ancestors and the crude ones he had been able to make for himself on the plantations. But he used them to different effect, playing the piano percussively and plucking rather than scraping the strings of the bass viol. Drums played an important part in establishing the beat, and this was purposely, or perhaps instinctively, monotonous and unaccented, thereby facilitating the improvising of rhythms.

To many, especially those whose ear had been trained by listening to the classics, the new music was extremely distasteful. One of the leading American critics condemned it as 'a meaningless stirabout, a commotion without repose, an epilepsy simulating muscular action', and added 'better than bad music is no music, and to let our beloved art subside finally under the clangor of subway gangs and automobile horns, dead but not dishonoured.' However, many people, especially the young found it strangely stimulating and exciting.

1 W. Hobson. *American Jazz Music*, 1940.
2 A. Hodeir. *Jazz: its Evolution and Essence*, 1956.

Even when jazz music seemed to be sad, it imparted, in W. Hobson's words, 'a spirited propulsive buoyancy, what might be called a momentum built up with the stress and accent suspensions'. Everybody wanted to dance, and it was suggested that 'its extreme propulsive effectiveness as dance music' was due to the fact that it provided 'the kind of rhythm most similar to the rhythm of the human body, which in motion is a momentum of "accent" and "stress" suspensions from or towards positions of balanced rest'.

It was in vain that the respectable *Times-Picayune* of New Orleans disclaimed responsibility for jazz although it was well known that it had taken its rise among the negro musicians who played in the cabarets, brothels and gambling hells in the old Storyville district of that city. Jazz tunes, said the editorial, were

manifestations of a low streak in man's tastes that has not yet some aid in civilization's work . . . jazz music is the indecent story syncopated and counter-pointed. . . . On certain natures, sound loud and meaningless has an exciting, almost an intoxicating effect, like crude colours and strong perfumes, the sight of flesh or the sadic pleasure in blood. To such as these the jazz music is a delight and . . . gives a sensual delight more intense and different from the languour of a Viennese waltz.[1]

In these well-intentioned remarks the writer displayed his complete ignorance of the history of dancing. It is a strange fact that no civilized person seems to be able to invent a dance. All he can do is to take some peasant dance (which in its origins is usually a fertility dance and therefore essentially 'indecent') and make it just sufficiently decent to be used on the dance floors of civilized society. The waltz itself when it first appeared had the same sort of impact as jazz a century later. It was denounced as corrupting, and even Byron (of all people) wrote a satire on its alleged indecency.

Then, when it had been accepted, it gradually became 'languorous' and boring and something new had to be found. It is possible to watch the search for something more stimulating moving eastward across Europe to lands where there was still a peasantry capable of uninhibited enjoyment. Poland provided the polka and Hungary the mazurka. And then when the peasantry of Europe was exhausted, there was nothing for it but to turn to the negro. Jazz arrived at the exactly propitious moment in time.

Efforts were made to stay its progress. We hear from the *Musical Leader* that 'the General Federation of Woman's Clubs has taken up the fight against jazz . . . the services of the *Ladies' Home Journal* have been enlisted . . . that form of music seems doomed'. But the *Musical Leader* was mistaken. Jazz continued its triumphant progress. From New Orleans

1 *Times-Picayune*, New Orleans, 1918.

it spread to Chicago and then to New York. From there it set out to conquer the world.

The Paradox of the Nineties

It is tempting to doubt that there would ever have been an English Decadence at all if a handful of English literary men, taking advantage of the new ease in communications, had not fallen into the habit of popping over to Paris, sitting on a café seat, sipping a glass of absinthe and, perhaps, buying a copy of *Les Fleurs du Mal* to read in the train on the way back.

Swinburne, of course, had been influenced by French writers a generation before, but *his* god had been Victor Hugo. Baudelaire was more heady stuff, and he had scarcely been dead for a decade when George Moore, the pioneer of this *nouvelle vague*, discovered him. Even the title of the book Moore brought out in 1878 is cribbed from the Master. He called it *Flowers of Passion*. In it he speaks of 'strange sins without a name',[1] and among the verses included is a poem entitled:

> *A Sapphic Dream*
> Perfumes that make the burdened senses swoon
> And weaken will, large snakes who oscillate
> Like lovely girls, immense exotic flowers,
> And cats who purr through silk-enfestooned bowers
> Where white-limbed women sleep in sumptuous state.
>
> My soul e'er yearns, in such a dream as this is,
> Visions of perfume, moonlight and the blisses
> Of sexless love, and strange unreachèd kisses.

It is a catalogue of Baudelairean properties: perfumes, exotic flowers, oscillating snakes, cats and 'white-limbed women'. Even the 'unreachèd kisses' seems an unconscious echo of Baudelaire's wry joke about making love to a giantess, and, of course, the whole poem is merely a pale, pale copy

---

1 It is odd how this notion persists. There are no 'sins without a name'; they have all been expertly classified and labelled for a very long time. The Greeks are said to have had thirty different words for homosexual practices alone.

of *Les Femmes Damnées*. Yet we must agree with Hoxie Neale Fairchild who, while laughing at Moore's 'infantile diabolism', makes the justified and not altogether unkind remark that 'historically . . . the rubbish is of interest; but to dwell upon it would be unfair to a man who reveals his maturer merits and defects only in his prose.'[1]

George Moore, indeed, seems never to have tried verse again, but there were others to take up the torch, and chief among these was Arthur Symons who made himself the apostle of the Decadence. According to him the new movement 'has all the qualities that we find in the Greek, the Latin decadence: an intense self-consciousness, an over-subtilizing upon refinement, a spiritual and moral perversity'.[2] This is a mere echo of Rémy de Gourmont and Huysmans.

That Symons had been profoundly affected by Huysmans' strange novel *A Rebours* needs no stressing. Indeed, it could hardly have been otherwise. *A Rebours*, says Mario Praz, 'is the pivot upon which the whole psychology of the Decadent Movement turns; in it all the phenomena of this state of mind are illustrated down to the minutest detail, in the instance of its chief character, des Esseintes. . . . All the prose marks of the Decadence, from Lorrain to Gourmont, Wilde and D'Annunzio, are contained in embryo in *A Rebours*.'[3]

Symons was determined to meet some of the French writers whose works so much intrigued him, and, in 1890, he made a trip to Paris in the company of Havelock Ellis. The two young men attended one of Mallarmé's 'Tuesdays' in the little apartment in the Rue de Rome and Huysmans was introduced. While in Paris the two Englishmen saw much of him. They visited him in his government office, went with him to a café to drink vermouth and even, in Havelock Ellis's own words, 'spent an evening with him in the apartment of his friend and Gourmont's, Madame Courière, a tall and gracious person . . . she was Gourmont's "Sixtine" and also perhaps the original of Madame Chantelouve in *Là-bas*, which had just then been published.'[4]

This was indeed to find oneself in the very Temple of Decadence, and, on his return to London, Symons set about the work of spreading the French gospel with more enthusiasm than ever. Sometimes it is difficult to be sure when Symons is translating from the French and when he is writing a poem of his own. Baudelaire's

> Une nuit que j'étais près d'une affreuse Juive . . .
> Je me pris à songer près de ce corps vendu . . .

1 H. N. Fairchild, *Religious Trends in English Poetry*, Vol. V. *1880–1920*, 1962.
2 A. Symons, *The Decadent Movement in Literature*, 1893.
3 M. Praz, *The Romantic Agony*, Tr. from the Italian by Angus Davidson, 1933.
4 H. Ellis, *From Rousseau to Proust*, 1936.

becomes

> As I lay on the stranger's bed
> And clasped the stranger woman I had hired . . .

But with Baudelaire the reader feels that the flames of Hell are near enough to scorch. The Englishman seems to be just playing at vice; and when he writes

> I would die exquisitely, of the bliss
> Of one intense, intolerable kiss

we just don't believe a word of it. Sometimes the image evoked is merely ludicrous:

> Your kisses, and the way you curl,
> Delicious and distracting girl,
> Into one's arms, and round about,
> Inextricably in and out . . .

What on earth is happening? Was the poet making love to a contortionist?

The following has a greater air of reality, but had Symon really seen what he describes or is it merely a memory of a drawing by Forain or Caran d'Ache?

> The feverish room and that white bed,
> The tumbled skirts upon a chair,
> The novel flung half-open, where
> Hat, hair-pins, puffs, and paints are spread . . .
>
> And you, half dressed and half awake,
> Your slant eyes strangely watching me,
> And I, who watch you drowsily,
> With eyes that, having slept not, ache;
>
> This (need one dread? nay, dare one hope?)
> Will rise, a ghost of memory, if
> Ever again my handkerchief
> Is scented with White Heliotrope.

A man who has run through the whole gamut of possible and 'impossible sins' is, naturally exhausted and feels that life has nothing more to offer:

> I have outlived my life, and linger on,
> Knowing myself the ghost of one that was.
> Come kindly death, and let my flesh, being grass,
> Nourish some beast's sad life when I am gone.
> What joy is left in all I look upon?
> I cannot sin, it wearies me. Alas!

Symons himself 'lingered on' for nearly forty years, but some of his fellow Decadents were not so fortunate. Lionel Johnson died at thirty-five, Ernest Dowson at thirty-three, Hubert Crackenthorpe at thirty-one, Aubrey Beardsley at twenty-six.

Of these the most talented were undoubtedly Beardsley and Dowson, the one as a book illustrator, the other as a poet. For Dowson was a true poet although a minor one; and if he takes up the same themes as Arthur Symons, he manages to convey, much more convincingly, a real *frisson*, as in his typically named *Impenitentia Ultima*:

> Before my light goes out for ever if God should give me a choice of graces,
> I would not reck of length of days, nor crave for things to be;
> But cry: 'One day of the great lost days, one face of all the faces.
> Grant me to see and touch once more and nothing more to see . . .
>
> 'But once before the sand is run and the silver thread is broken,
> Give me a grace and cast aside the veil of dolorous years,
> Grant me one hour of all mine hours, and let me see for a token
> Her pure and pitiful eyes shine out, and bathe her feet with tears . . .
>
> 'Before the ruining waters fall and my life be carried under,
> And Thine anger cleave me through as a child cuts down a flower,
> I will praise Thee, Lord, in Hell, while my limbs are racked asunder,
> For the last sad sight of her face and the little grace of an hour.'

The general public, never an avid buyer of slim volumes of verse by unknown poets, might have remained blissfully unaware of the very existence of the Decadent Movement, but for the impact of *The Yellow Book*, founded by Henry Harland and Aubrey Beardsley in 1892. Nothing like it, as Holbrook Jackson points out:

had been seen before. It was newness *in excelsis*: novelty naked and unashamed. People were puzzled and shocked and delighted, and yellow became the colour of the hour, the symbol of the time-spirit. It was associated with all that was bizarre and queer in art and life, with all that was outrageously modern. Richard Le Gallienne wrote a *prose fancy* on *The Boom in Yellow*, in which he pointed out many applications of the colour with that *fin de siècle* flippancy which was one of his characteristics, without, however, tracing the decorative use of yellow to Whistler, as he should have done.[1]

Whistler himself had nothing to do with *The Yellow Book* or with the Decadent Movement as such. His fight with Ruskin, his ridicule of the moral anecdote in painting, his exchange of witticisms with Oscar Wilde, his 'Ten O'Clock' lecture had no doubt prepared the ground for the

1 H. Jackson, *The Eighteen Nineties*, 1913.

Fin de Siècle

A poster by Henri de Toulouse-Lautrec, 1890

Gustave Moreau, *Salome* (1876); the painting in which many of the writers of the *fin de siècle*, from Huysmans to Wilde, found inspiration

Top: Jane Avril doing the splits, *c.* 1895

Bottom: The Moulin Rouge, 1895

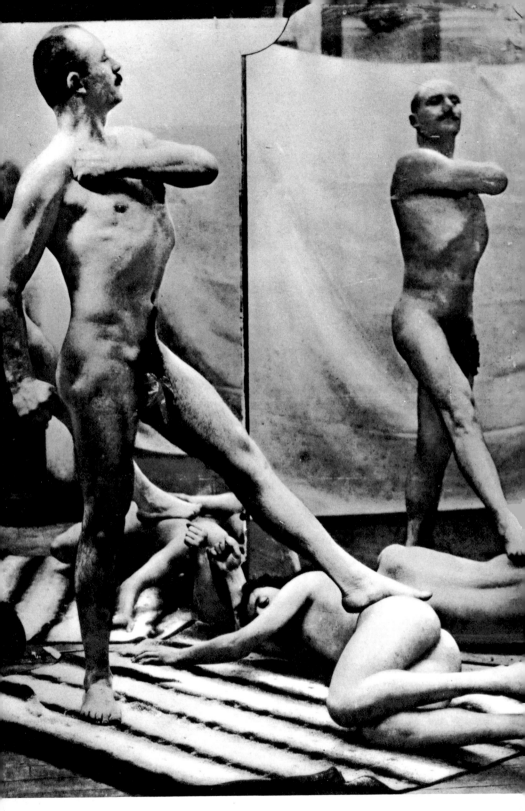

The Triumph of Man, an allegorical photograph

La Goulue of the Moulin Rouge

Can-Can dancer, *c.* 1895

Music-Hall figurante

Aija, 'Fille de Joie'

Liane de Pougy

La Belle Otéro

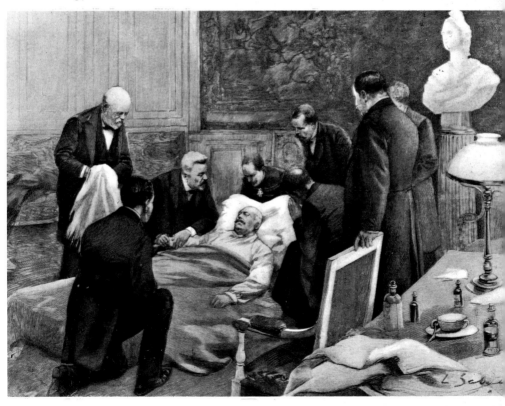

Deathbed of President Félix Faure (official version)

Opposite: Statue of Cléo de Mérode (1896) by J. A. J. Falguière. The public was scandalized not by the deformation of the body, but because it was nude

Aubrey Beardsley, *The Fat Woman*

doctrine of 'art for art's sake', but the morbid streak in all the men of the nineties owed nothing to him. Whistler was about as morbid as a colonel of cavalry. And although he admired Beardsley as an artist, in temperament the two men had nothing in common.

The sinister reputation of *The Yellow Book* (which it has retained to this day) was almost entirely due to Aubrey Beardsley. Certainly there was no hint of diabolism in the contributions to the first four numbers of such innocuous artists as Walter Crane, John Sargent, Wilson Steer, Charles Furse and Sir Frederick Leighton. Nor was there anything revolutionary or daring in the writings of Henry James, Richard Garnett, George Saintsbury, Edward Gosse or William Watson. It is true that there was a poem by Arthur Symons which some readers thought profane and a sprightly 'Defence of Cosmetics' by Max Beerbohm which the author felt constrained, in the second issue, to explain was only meant as a joke. It was Beardsley and Beardsley alone who shocked and startled; and when the editor Henry Harland was forced to choose between Beardsley and William Watson (who sent him an ultimatum to that effect) he chose to retain the blameless poet and to let the disturbing artist go. He actually withdrew No. 5 of *The Yellow Book* because it contained some of Beardsley's designs.

Arthur Symons left with Beardsley and in the following year started *The Savoy* which, although contributed to by Ernest Dowson, George Moore and Bernard Shaw, was really conceived as a vehicle for Beardsley, and so it remained. And it was Beardsley who summed up, in the public mind, all the tendencies of the Decadent Movement which contemporaries found both rather frightening and altogether ridiculous.

Punch which had done so much to laugh the Aesthetes out of court now proceeded to do the same for the Decadents. Its principal target was Beardsley and when he produced a poster for *A Comedy of Sighs* at the Avenue Theatre, *Punch* printed an amusing parody of Tennyson's *Lady Clara Vere de Vere*:

> Mr Aubrey Beer de Beers
>   You're getting quite a high renown;
> Your Comedy of Leers, you know,
>   Is posted all about the town:
> This sort of thing I cannot puff,
>   As Boston says, it makes me 'tired':
> Your Japanese-Rossetti girl,
>   Is not a thing to be desired . . .
>
> Aubrey, Aubrey Beer de Beers,
>   Are there no models at your gate,
> Live, shapely, passable and clean?
>   Or won't they do to 'decorate'?

225

O

> Then by all means bestrew your scenes
> With half the lotuses that blow
> Pothooks and fishing-lines and things
> But let the human woman go![1]

And it proceeded to provide instructions for any emulator of the Beardsley manner in a poem entitled *How it is Done*:

> Take a lot of black triangles
>   Some amorphous blobs of red;
> Just a sprinkle of queer spangles,
>   And ill-drawn Medusa's head;
> Some red locks in Gorgon tangles,
>   And a scarlet sunshade spread . . .
>
> Take an hour-glass waist, in section,
>   Shoulders hunched up camel-wise;
> Give a look of introspection
>   (Or a squint) to two black eyes;
> Or a glance of quaint dejection,
>   Or a glare of wild surprise;
> Slab and slob them all together
>   With a background of sheer sludge;
> (Like a slum in foggy weather),
>   And this blend of scrawl and smudge
> Vend as art . . .

Beardsley's most famous work is the illustrations for Wilde's *Salomé*, published in 1894. They are certainly brilliant as designs, but as illustrations they must be considered a failure; they do not even attempt to evoke the atmosphere of first century Judaea. Wilde did not like them; indeed, he did not like the work of Beardsley at all, and he never had much sympathy with the movement of the nineties which he had done so much to inspire. When the first number of *The Yellow Book* appeared he called it 'dull and loathsome; a great failure – I am so glad'. Perhaps he was conscious too that the illustrations to *Salomé* added an extra touch of Satanism to the book which did his reputation no good.

Yet Wilde could not escape being identified in the public mind with the *fin de siècle* movement. Had he not in the eighties made himself the apostle of 'art for art's sake'; had he not proclaimed with witty insolence that 'the first duty in life is to be as artificial as possible. What the second duty is no one has as yet discovered'? And from his undergraduate days onward he had set out to realize in his own life the dangerous doctrine of Walter Pater that:

1 *Punch*, 1894.

226

not the fruit of experience, but experience itself is the end. . . . While all melts under our feet, we may well catch at any exquisite passion, or any contribution to knowledge that seems by a lifted horizon to set the spirit free for a moment, or any stirring of the senses, strange dyes, strange colours and curious odours, or work of the artist's hands, or the face of one's friend. . . . What we have to do is to be for ever curiously testing new opinions and courting new impressions.[1]

Wilde was just as much influenced by French writers as lesser men like Arthur Symons and *A Rebours*, which was published in 1884, at the very time when he was most frequently in Paris, must have made an instant appeal to him. The strange character of the hero, Des Esseintes, founded as it was, at least in part, upon the living original of Count Robert de Montesquiou, must have seemed to Wilde the very incarnation of his own ideas. Huysmans' vivid and highly mannered style, with its archaisms, its accumulation of jewelled epithets, its heaping up of visual images, presented a kind of saint of aethetic sensibility burning (as Pater had recommended) with a hard gem-like flame. It is easy to see that without the example of *A Rebours*, *The Picture of Dorian Gray* would never have been written.

Wilde's first, and last, novel came out in 1891. None other of his works – we have his own testimony – gave him so much pleasure to write. For the two main characters in the book – Lord Henry Wotton whose theories prove so corrupting to his protegé and pupil Dorian Gray – are Wilde himself. The book is profoundly disturbing. It is not that there is anything indecent in it – there is nothing indecent in any of Wilde's writings – but the climate of sensibility into which it introduces the reader is certainly abnormal.

Wilde himself claimed that there was a 'terrible moral' in *Dorian Gray*, and, indeed, since its young hero comes to such a hideous end, it might seem to prove – if proof were needed – that 'art for art's sake' inevitably leads to 'sensation for sensation's sake', that the palate which demands condiments must go on to demand ever stronger and stronger condiments; and that he who seeks only the satisfaction of his own sensibility must end by finding '*le bonheur dans le crime*'.

The Picture of Dorian Gray is the first of Wilde's writings in which the theme of homosexuality, while never expressed, is clearly implied. For the most part the English Decadents were not homosexual. Their erotic experiences (when they existed otherwise than in their overheated imagination) were with women. Wilde himself married and begot two sons. It has been suggested[2] that it was Robert Ross, whom he met in 1886

1 W. Pater, *The Renaissance: Studies in Art and Poetry*, London 1873. It is significant that the passage quoted was omitted in the edition of 1877.
2 *In Oscar Wilde and the Black Douglas*, by The Marquess of Queensberry, in collaboration with Percy Colson, 1949.

when Ross was an undergraduate at Oxford, who first introduced him to homosexual practices. But there must have been rumours afloat soon after Wilde himself came down, for, as early as 1881, George du Maurier published in *Punch* a cartoon of 'Maundle' which is quite plainly a carica-ture of Wilde. He is depicted as saying to his hostess: 'How consummately lovely your son is, Mrs Brown. . . . Why not let him remain for ever content to *exist beautifully*?' The sinister implication is well concealed, but it is there all the same.

It is strange that, ten years later, in *Intentions* Wilde should make almost the same remark: 'There is something tragic about the enormous number of young men there are in England at the present moment who start life with perfect profiles, and end by adopting some useful profession.'

Dorian Gray and *Intentions* both appeared in 1891; a fateful year for Wilde, for in it he was to meet a beautiful youth who was to lead him on and on to the final catastrophe: 'Fate knocked at the door of 16 Tite Street, in the person of Lionel Johnson, old Wykehamist, poet, distin-guished Oxonian and homosexual, bringing with him Lord Alfred Douglas.'[1]

His association with 'Bosie', as Lord Alfred Douglas was called by his intimates, made it certain that Wilde's proclivities could no longer be concealed. It has been denied that they were lovers, but Bosie insisted on behaving as if they were. He even made Wilde enter the Savoy with him by the principal door – Wilde having previously tried to enter by a side-door – so that everyone would notice them and say: 'That's Oscar Wilde and his boy.' Certainly Bosie's arrogance, his extravagance and his hatred of his father, the Marquess of Queensberry, made Wilde's tragedy in-evitable.

The crash came at the culminating point of his career. The first night of *The Importance of Being Earnest* had been a triumph but a few days later he found Lord Queensberry's card, with its insulting inscription, at the Albemarle Club. His friends, his real friends, advised him to take no notice. Frank Harris told him to go abroad and take his wife with him. But Bosie was determined on a *cause célèbre*. Indifferent to the fate of Wilde, and even to the scandal attaching to his own name, his only wish was to humiliate his father, and if possible to have him imprisoned. Wilde allowed himself to be persuaded to bring an action for criminal libel against the Marquess of Queensberry.

The details of the trial have been exhaustively treated elsewhere. It is sufficient to note that Wilde's action failed and he was himself arrested on a criminal charge. At the first trial the jury could not agree and he was granted bail. All his friends urged him to escape – Frank Harris even had a

1 *Ibid.*

yacht waiting in the Thames to take him away – but he refused to go. At the second trial he was found guilty and sentenced to two years imprisonment with hard labour. When the newspaper placards announced the verdict, the prostitutes danced in the streets.

Strange as it may seem to the modern mind, so familiar with the idea of sexual inversion, to many of the late Victorians it seems to have been really unknown. They concluded that it was one of those 'new', 'nameless', and 'impossible' sins the Decadents were always talking about. Even those who had had a classical education, even those who had read about the 'favourites' of English kings, or had any acquaintance with eighteenth-century literature (had not Charles Churchill devoted a whole satire to the subject?) were as much puzzled as the ordinary, respectable middle-class father. Did such things really happen? And if so, what had happened to Wilde was no less than the Judgment of God. Here was a man at the summit of his success, with two plays running in London – the plays were kept on but the author's name was expunged from the hoardings – suddenly transformed into a convict. The moral-minded were deeply shocked; and the Philistines rubbed their hands to think that a career which had always been an insult to their stupidity had been brought to so ignominious an end.

Not only Wilde's career but the Decadence itself. Few of the Decadents had been among Wilde's personal friends and they continued to write their verses and to drink themselves to death. Some of them turned to Catholicism, as Wilde himself did on his death-bed. It is not for us to query the sincerity of their motives, but motives are never simple. As Holbrook Jackson remarks:

they wanted to experience the piquancy of being good after a debauch. They realized that a merited kiss was not half so sweet as a kiss of forgiveness, and this subtle voluptuousness eventually taught them that the road called decadence also led to Rome. The old romanticism began by being Catholic; Théophile Gautier strove to make it pagan, and succeeded for a time, but with Huysmans romanticism in the form of decadence reverted to Rome. In England, the artists who represented the renaissance of the nineties were either Catholics like Francis Thompson and Henry Harland or prospective converts to Rome, like Oscar Wilde, Aubrey Beardsley and Ernest Dowson. If Catholicism did not claim them some other form of mysticism did, and W. B. Yeats and George Russell (A.E.) became Theosophists. The one who persistently hardened himself against the mystical influences of his period, John Davidson, committed suicide.

But none of these was representative of the British public. We still speak of 'the naughty nineties' and the 'Beardsley Period' but that is because artists and writers have an unfair advantage in imposing their image on an epoch. To the men who actually lived in the nineties, even Wilde was only the central figure in a scandal, Beardsley an eccentric illustrator of rather dirty books, and of the mere existence of the Decadent poets he was almost entirely unaware.

Even in literature they hadn't the field to themselves, for we are apt to forget that the nineties saw also the rise of Henley, Stevenson, Kipling and Bernard Shaw. Henley, and Kipling, in particular, spoke for an England which did not regard itself as decadent in the very least. The decade indeed was the very heydey of Imperialism, and of that Jingoism which is today almost as remote from our sympathies as the posturing of the Decadents. It was in 1878, at the time of the Russo–Turkish War that the 'Great Macdermott', one of the music-hall idols of the day, took the town by storm, and added a new word to the English language, by singing:

> The 'Dogs of War' are loose, and the rugged Russian Bear,
> Full bent on blood and robbery, has crawled out of his lair . . .
> · He hunger'd for his victim, he's pleased when blood is shed,
> But let us hope his crimes may all recoil on his own head.

> We don't want to fight, but by Jingo if we do,
> We've got the ships, we've got the men,
> And got the money too.
> We've fought the bear before, and while we're Britons true,
> The Russians shall not have Constantinople.

It was Disraeli who brought back 'Peace with Honour' from the Congress of Berlin, which had, in fact, ensured that the Russian would not have Constantinople. It was Disraeli who, six years before, in 1872, had, in a speech at the Crystal Palace, committed the Conservative Party to the policy of Imperialism. In 1874 he became Prime Minister and in 1876 Queen Victoria became Empress of India.

Seeley's *Expansion of England* came out in 1883 and is said to have converted Lord Roseberry to Imperialism. Men of different loyalties and backgrounds were touched with the same excitement. There was not only glory in it, there was profit too. As the explorer Stanley had told the Manchester Chamber of Commerce, 'there are forty million people beyond the gateway of the Congo, and the cotton spinners of Manchester are waiting to clothe them'. And Joseph Chamberlain, who went to the Colonial Office in 1895, could proudly declare: 'I believe in this race, the greatest governing race the world has ever seen; in this Anglo-Saxon race, so proud, so tenacious, self-confident and determined, this race which neither climate nor change can degenerate, which will infallibly be the predominant force of future history and universal civilization.'

In 1887 came the Queen's Jubilee, with homage from the ends of the earth, and a reminder to the general public how much of the world map had been painted red. Ten years later the Diamond Jubilee reinforced the same lesson. Was it not plain that the British were the greatest people on earth?

Britain had not been engaged in any major war since the Crimea. Even that had been fought far away, and further still were the frontier fights and colonial campaigns against the Zulus or the hill-tribes of the North-West Frontier of India. Many young Englishmen were beginning to feel that they were missing 'all the fun', but they could share vicariously in the triumphs of *The Soldiers of the Queen*:

> It's the Soldiers of the Queen, my lads,
> Who've been, my lads,
> Who've seen, my lads,
> In the fight for England's glory, lads,
> Of its world-wide glory let us sing;
> And when we say we've always won,
> And when they ask us how it's done,
> We'll proudly point to every one
> Of England's Soldiers of the Queen!

Such sentiments were not confined to the man-in-the-street. Writers of talent, and even of genius, glorified the man of action who was willing and able to 'take up the white man's burden', and to thank whatever gods may be for his unconquerable soul. Henley and his 'young men' who wrote for the *National Observer*, thought of themselves, says H. N. Fairchild, 'as realists, full-blooded grapplers with actuality, and rugged participants, as individuals and as patriotic Englishmen, in the good struggle for existence'.[1] So did Stevenson and Kipling.

There was an element of what we have learned to call 'over-compensation' in all this, for as the same author points out, 'Kipling who wanted to see everything, had very bad eyesight, and he never fully recovered from childhood traumatic experiences; Henley was a one-legged arthritic cripple; Stevenson was a tubercular invalid.'

Their exaltation of violence is perhaps seen at its most disquieting in Henley's poem *The Sword*:

> Edged to annihilate
> Hilted with government . . .
> Scything and binding
> The full sheaves of sovranty . . .
> Clear singing, clean slicing;
> Sweet spoken, soft finishing;
> Making death beautiful . . .
> Arch-anarch, chief builder,
> Prince and evangelist,
> I am the Will of God:
> I am the Sword.

1 H. N. Fairchild, *Religious Trends in English Poetry*, 1962.

Kipling was not quite so blatant, but, as Fairchild remarks, he 'was probably the more dangerous of the two precisely because his imperialism was high-minded enough to conceal from himself and from his public its baser implications'.

For baser implications there were. The decade which produced *The Yellow Book* on the one hand and the poems of Henley and Kipling on the other also produced 'the boom in "Kaffirs", the Jameson Raid, the Boer War and the enthronement of the South African plutocrat in Park Lane'.[1] It also produced the Yellow Press, and we may allow Holbrook Jackson to sum up for us the paradox of the nineties:

> The eighteen-nineties were to no small extent the battleground of two types of culture – the one represented by *The Yellow Book*, the other by the Yellow Press. The one was unique, individual, a little weird, often exotic, demanding the right to *be* – in its own way even to waywardness; but this was really an abnormal minority, and in no way national. The other was broad, general, popular; it was the man-in-the-street awaiting a new medium of expression. In the great fight the latter won, *The Yellow Book*, with all its 'new' hopes and hectic aspirations, has passed away, and *The Daily Mail*, established two years later, flourishes. In a deeper sense, also, these two publications represent the two phases of the times. The characteristic excitability and hunger for sensation are exemplified in the one as much as the other, for what after all was the 'brilliance' of Vigo Street but the 'sensationalism' of Fleet Street seen from the cultured side? Both were the outcome of a society which had absorbed a bigger idea of life than it knew how to put into practice, and it is not surprising to those who look back upon the period to find that both tendencies, in so far as they were divorced from the social revolution of the nineties, were nihilistic, the one finding its Moscow at the Old Bailey, in 1895, the other in South Africa, in 1899.

For the South African War was by no means the walk-over that had been so confidently predicted. The Boer farmers gave a very good account of themselves, and their 'unsporting' but effective tactics were extremely troublesome to generals who were still thinking in terms of the Crimea. 'I suppose', said Balfour 'as usual, we shall muddle through', but there were some in England who were beginning to wonder if the 'effortless superiority' of the Anglo-Saxons was not going to be more and more questioned as the century drew to a close. There were other competitors in the field. Other nations were joining in the scramble for Africa, and when it became plain that the old Imperial regime in China was tottering to its fall, the British found, to their annoyance, that they could not just go in and take over as they had done in India. The *Globe* had remarked, earlier in the nineties, that China would never be 'safe' until it was under the protection of the British flag. But when the moment for action came and 'the Dowager Empress in a last desperate effort to rally her people against

1 H. Jackson, *op. cit.*

the "foreign devils", gave the West its opportunity, Britain was not allowed to act alone. A consortium of European powers appeared to assert, with Japanese aid, the white man's supremacy. And prominent in that group was Germany.'[1] The political picture of the twentieth century was already beginning to take shape.

1 G. Heard, *Morals since 1900*, 1950.

11 High Life's Last Fling

For our picture of an epoch we are more dependent than we care to admit on the incidence of artistic talent. To what social milieu does the most brilliant illustrator of the day, the man who makes himself the 'mirror of the passing show', belong? If we think of life in Paris in 1900 as a matter of driving in the Bois and dining at Maxim's it is because we see it through the eyes of Sem. If we think of life in London about the same period as a matter of the saloon bar and its sporting, rather raffish inhabitants it is because we see it through the eyes of Phil May.

The dominant flavour of an epoch is, to a large extent, determined for us by some man of talent – or even of genius – who has made us conscious of it, and such a man is usually a pictorial artist not in the realms of 'high art' but of illustration. Nonetheless, that epochs have a dominant flavour is certain and this is determined by people who are at any moment, the most in the public eye. It *is* true that if you wanted to catch London at its most characteristic at the beginning of the present century you would have looked in at the bar of the Cri'; and if you wanted to catch Paris at its most characteristic you would have taken a stroll in the bright spring sunshine in the Bois de Boulogne.

French society, like its counterpart in England, was subject to the same tyranny of the calendar. It was necessary, on pain of losing caste, to perform certain actions and to be at certain places at certain times of the year. The Season began after Easter and for this *tout le monde* had to be in Paris, where even the day was regulated. It was essential to be seen in the Bois de Boulogne about noon. One returned to the centre for luncheon. Then the women visited their dressmakers, attended the opening of art exhibitions or charity bazaars. The men retired to their clubs. Between five and seven o'clock was recognized as the time for polite adultery. Then, in full evening dress, one dined either in a private house, or a restaurant: and then, if a man was alone, he probably went on the round of cabarets and night-haunts known, significantly, as the 'Tour of the Grand Dukes'.

The Season ended with the Grand Prix and then the fashionable world dispersed to the northern seaside resorts: Deauville, Dinard, Trouville, Cabourg (the Balbec of Proust). Nobody then, or until much later (until the end of the 1920s in fact) thought of going to the Riviera *in summer*. It was possible however to go as far south as Biarritz, cooled by the Atlantic breezes.

With the first tints of autumn the seaside was abandoned in favour of country house parties; and in mid-December, 'everybody' returned to Paris for the Little Season. This was, in some ways, the liveliest part of the year, with the Opéra and the theatres in full swing, a time of innumerable dinner parties, private dances and masked balls. In the early spring one went to Monte Carlo or Cannes, until Easter when the cycle of fashionable servitude began again.

Everywhere the *monde* went the *demi-monde* went too and the latter occupied such an important position in France during this last heyday of High Life that any study of manners and morals must take it into account. In his penetrating book on the period Armand Lanoux remarks: 'Just as during the Second Empire, with less *brio* but even more widely spread there reigned over the kingdom of love a caste which was neither the aristocracy, nor the bourgeoisie, nor the people, nor the theatre, but which participated in all four: the *demi-monde*.'[1]

Its members occupied a middle rank between the aristocracy of the *demi-castors* (that is those Society women who, more or less openly broke the rules of marital fidelity, women artists and the like) and the prostitutes of the streets and brothels. The cocotte was a kept woman, usually the *maîtresse-en-titre* of a well-known man. Even if he were not well-known he had to be rich, for the lady expected a house of her own, a carriage (sometimes hired by the month), a mink coat, a string of pearls and 1,500 francs a month. Some of the *grandes cocottes*, of course, received very much more. The dress bills alone must have been considerable for it was taken for granted that such women must always be in the height of the fashion. The tune might be the same as that of the *femme du monde* but it was played in a major key: a perfume slightly more insistent, more frou-frou in the lace petticoats, the bust a trifle more emphatic, more feathers in the hat, more jewels on the corsage. Yet the differences were merely differences of emphasis, and the real *mondaines* did their best to compete. The witty Albert Flament notes, in his description of the Grand Prix of 1899: 'On the lawn, squadrons of cocottes adorned with all that little men with great names have cared to give them. So-called *femmes du monde* are still in a stand apart, but the manner in which they are got up witnesses

1 A. Lanoux, *Amours 1900*, 1961.

quite plainly that, with rare exceptions their desire is to resemble as closely as possible the ladies on the lawn.'

The fashionable race course was one of the most notable of the meeting places of *monde* and *demi-monde*. Another was the Bois. It was absolutely essential for every woman who was, or wanted to be, in the public eye, to ride or drive in the Bois de Boulogne every morning during the Paris Season. The favourite rendezvous was the Allée des Acacias. Scores of contemporaries have given verbal descriptions of the scene, and fortunately, there was also present the great pictorial artist who called himself Sem.[1] He has left us a series of albums full of drawings, pushed, it is true, to the point of caricature but, perhaps for that very reason, more truthful than truth.

He shows us the world of pleasure in the Bois, at Monte Carlo and Deauville; we watch King Edward VII and King Leopold II of the Belgians in their motor-cars; the Duc de Morny, Prince Ivan Troubetskoy, Prince Galitzine, Count Robert de Montesquiou and Boni de Castellane, the spendthrift husband of the rich American Anna Gould, Pierpont Morgan (his nose printed, cruelly, in red) four Barons Rothschild, Edmond, Henri, Alphonse and James, and the Aga Khan; Aristide Briand and Clemenceau, the actors Coquelin and Mounet-Sully, the writers Rostand, Willy, Colette and Henri Bernstein, the artists Forain and Caran d'Ache, Consuela, Duchess of Marlborough, and, of course, all the ladies of the theatre and the *demi-monde* most in view: Réjane and Cavalieri, *la belle Otéro* and Liane de Pougy, Eve Lavallière, Cléo de Mérode and Polaire.

Sem's pencil is at its most cruel whenever he caricatures Polaire. She did not pretend to be pretty and was even billed during her tour of the United States as 'the ugliest woman in the world'. What seems to have fascinated everybody was the smallness of her waist. It was an epoch of small waists but in Polaire's case the tight-lacing was so extreme that (as we can see in photographs) fashion had crossed the line which divides it from fetishism. There was, indeed, something perverse about her whole personality. Contemporary chroniclers compared her to Salome, or to a snake coiled upon itself. She regarded herself as the incarnation of Colette's Claudine; she made contact with the young writer not yet as famous as she was afterwards to become, and the two could be seen together almost any day between five and six, their arms enlaced, skating together at the Palais de Glace.

There is an extraordinary passage in *La Morale de Paris*[2] in which Paul Adam censures the *grandes cocottes* of the opening years of the twentieth century, not for their morals but for their looks:

When one is present at the races at Lonchamps or Auteuil, one is first stupefied,

1 His real name was Georges Gourset.
2 P. Adam. *La Morale de Paris*, c. 1906.

then revolted by the extreme ugliness of the most celebrated and sumptuous cocottes. Among the fifty or so who parade in the paddock, hardly ten are worth the half-louis which a student might offer the local tart. Old, coarse-featured, wearing strange wigs, with tired eyes and loose flesh under the maquillage, they frighten the naïf provincial who has run up from the country to see these admired beings. The pearls they wear, the expensive jewels which are the symbols of their prestige, do not persuade us otherwise. The inimitable Sem in his album, shows us the naked truth about them. They are figures out of a nightmare and one has to ask how any cultivated man could spend an hour in the company of such gorgons without disgust.

'The Courtisane', cries Adam, in an outburst of patriotic fervour, 'is the incarnation of the national ideal of beauty. Those whom fortune favours fail in their mission if the cocottes they admire are mediocre. They lead the foreigner to believe that the French have no taste. . . . Only Cléo de Mérode,' he concludes, 'Liane de Pougy, Cavalieri and one or two others are capable of incorporating our idea of the Muse.'

Although both were beautiful in their way there could be no greater contrast than between Caroline Otéro, known as *la belle Otéro* and Liane de Pougy. Caroline was greedy, unrefined and rather careless of her appearance. She came to life when dancing; her vitality was prodigious. She had come to Paris at the age of fourteen and was soon dancing at the Palais de Cristal, then at the Cirque d'Eté. She had kept at least the trappings of her religion, for Albert Flament, whose eye missed nothing, saw her clad in black emerging one afternoon from Notre Dame des Victoires. She had been lighting a candle to the Virgin for a special intention: success that evening in her semi-nude dance at the Folies-Bergère.

Where Otéro was all opulent flesh and passion Liane de Pougy was all delicacy and refinement. She had a thin face, a small mouth, a sensitive little nose. She was born in 1869, the daughter of a captain in a lancer regiment, and at the age of sixteen was married to a naval officer. He grew jealous, to such a degree that he fired at her two revolver shots, both hits. Fortunately the bullets did not wound her to the heart but only in the – posterior. After her divorce she was soon launched in the *demi-monde*, finding, as so many others had done, a useful springboard in the Folies-Bergère. It was a sign of her quality that she wrote to the Prince of Wales asking if he would deign to applaud her on her first appearance. He did.

She continued to appear on the stage, more perhaps as a *figurante* than an actress, but soon had an apartment in the fashionable Avenue Victor Hugo and a villa at Bordighera. Naturally she appeared in the Bois, and naturally also at Maxim's. Maxim's was the favourite rendezvous of all these ladies.

It began in 1895 when a certain Maxime Gaillard opened a modest café for coachmen in the Rue Royale. After seven years of only moderate success he sold it to a man named Benois who had the sense to keep the name of the establishment unchanged. Soon it attracted a fashionable clientèle, having become known as a place where *les clubmen* could take their *petites amies*; but this was not the only attraction. The management allowed in a number (the maximum was ten) of *cocottes* who had not yet found a permanent protector. The only requirement was that they should be fashionably, but not outrageously dressed, and should behave themselves. If one of the men dining alone wished to ask one of these ladies to his table, the invitation was passed, discreetly, through the maître d'hotel who was known as 'Hugo'.

Hugo was indeed a man of infinite discretion. He kept a little notebook[1] in which he listed the names of *cocottes* including some of the best known, like Emilienne d'Alençon. At the end of her description he put the letters R.A.F. – *rien à faire*. This meant that she was already launched. For those who were not he put the letter Y.M.C.A. This had nothing to do with the Young Men's Christian Association. It meant *Y a moyen de coucher avec*.

'Everybody,' except *l'épouse légitime*, went to Maxim's: Prince Galitzine, Prince Karageorgevitch and Prince George of Greece; and, of course, the Russian Grand Dukes Cyril, Boris, Michael, Nicolas, Dimitri and Vladimir, whom it was correct to address by their Christian names. French aristocrats like the Prince de Sagan and the Duc de Morny and rich industrialists like Michelin and Dubonnet; the stars of the stage, legitimate or otherwise: Sarah Bernhardt, Caruso, Chaliapine, Mayol and Harry Fragson (shot dead by his aged father for reasons which are still obscure) and Gaby Deslys, the mistress of ex-King Manoel of Portugal, whose price, according to Hugo, was a thousand francs for fifteen minutes; pioneers of aviation like Louis Blériot, Gordon Bennett and Santos Dumont; painters and illustrators like Boldini, Helleu, Forain, Sem and Caran d'Ache, and (rather surprisingly) Widor, the organist at St Sulpice.

It can be imagined that the members of this mixed clientèle did not always love one another. 'Mme Otéro', says Hugo

was dining one evening *chez* Maxim's,[2] entirely covered with jewels, necklaces, bracelets, rings on all fingers (including thumbs) a tiara and an aigrette. . . . She looked like a shrine . . . Mme Liane's table was still unoccupied. . . . Finally she appeared, in a perfectly fitting dress of black velvet without a single ornament. There was a moment of surprise which changed to stupor when Mme Liane stepped aside to reveal her maid. She was wearing her maid's cap but her dress had diamonds sewn all over it. . . . The Grand Duke Vladimir gazed at her open-mouthed. . . . Liane, escorted by M. le Comte de T—, sat down, to a burst of tumultuous applause. Mme Otéro, furious, rose to leave and as she passed Mme

1 Frequently drawn upon by Armand Lanoux in his admirable *Amours 1900*.

2 '*Chez Maxim's*' and not *chez Maxim* is the correct usage. Anglomania caused Maxime Gaillard to anglicize the name of his restaurant and it has been known as Maxim's ever since.

de Pougy's table could not refrain from a burst of terrible Spanish oaths. Liane, with the air of an angelic schoolgirl put out a delicate tongue.[1]

At the age of forty-one, as beautiful as ever, she became Princess Chika by her marriage to the nephew of Queen Nathalie of Serbia. On the death of the Prince in 1945, she entered the Third Order of St Dominic and retired to a convent in Lausanne. She died in 1950.

She was not the only cocotte of the period to turn to religion before the end; Eve Lavallière was a notable and edifying example. She was born at Toulon of Italian parents, but the family soon moved to Perpignan. The father, who was in the tailoring trade, was a man of violent temper. In a moment of jealous rage he mortally wounded his wife and then shot himself. The orphan daughter was placed in a convent where she was extremely unhappy. She worked for a while in a dress shop but she dreamed of a stage career and tried to join a touring company at Narbonne. Frustrated in the attempt, she ran away to Paris, and managed to get a job as a *figurante* in *La Belle Hélène*. The sudden death of one of the principals gave her her chance, and in a very short time she was a star at the Variétés. Unlike so many of her sisters Eve Lavallière, as she was called herself, really had talent. She excelled in the plays of Capus, but her most spectacular success was gained in a play entitled *Le Roi*, by Robert de Flers, Gaston de Caillavet and Emmanuel Arène (modern readers know it as a film with Maurice Chevalier as the Ruritanian King) produced at the Variétés in 1908. Eve Lavallière was the perfect incarnation of the left-wing politician's gay but tender wife who not only has an affair with the visiting monarch but falls in love with him. All the real monarchs who found themselves in Paris at this period wanted to see *Le Roi*; and King Edward VII (himself so like the King in the play) postponed his departure for two days in order to be present when Lavallière was playing. Alfonso XIII whom she had refused to receive in her dressing-room because his late arrival had spoiled one of her speeches, met her at Biarritz and covered her with compliments. King Manoel of Portugal was even more *épris* and sent her a pearl necklace. The wits of the day said that she was Eve to men and Lavallière to kings.

Was there already a certain ambivalence in calling herself Lavallière? For if the historical La Vallière was the mistress of Louis XIV, she had repented of her love for the King and finished her days in a convent. Eve Lavallière seems to have had a premonition that her life would follow the same course. She was a woman of extreme sensibility, given to bouts of black despair. In the middle of her triumph at the Variétés she tried to commit suicide by throwing herself in the Seine and was only prevented from doing so by a workman who happened to be passing.

1 Hugo. *Vingt ans maître d'hôtel chez Maxim's*, 1919.

It would be impossible to gather from the pious biography by Raymond Marcerou,[1] that she had anything to repent of. She seems indeed to have been faithful to one man, Fernand Samuel the director of the Variétés. (His real name was Louveau but he changed it to Samuel in order to further his career. This has been called the most subtle form of anti-semitism.) On his death she took up with a German diplomat named Von Lucius, who invested Lavallière's fortune in his own country. On the outbreak of war, he tried to get it out, and indeed succeeded, but the result was that Lavallière was suspected by the French police of being mixed up in a spy-ring, and she was forced to take refuge in London. It was here that she met the Abbé Chasteigner who was responsible for her conversion. She returned to France a changed woman. She gave up rouge and scent, ceased to have her hair dressed and even refrained from having a missing tooth replaced. She made several attempts to enter a convent, but was repulsed. She joined therefore the Third Order of St Francis and, as Sister Eve, went to Tunis as a medical missionary. She died in France in 1919 and was buried in the Franciscan habit.

Eugénie Buffet was another *grande cocotte* of the period who, if she didn't actually die in the odour of sanctity, ended her career as a kind of *Notre Dame de la Charité*, officially recognized for her support of good causes. She began life as a singer in the cafés chantants and bars of Marseilles and in her confessions[2] tells us that she was almost dying of starvation when she was taken up by a certain Comte Guillaume d'Oilliamson. He brought her to Paris. She was twenty at the time and the year was 1886. She tells us frankly what happened:

> The Comte, after a short stay in the Hôtel Continental, set me up in a furnished apartment in the Rue Richepanse, had me given lessons in deportment, acted as my chaperon, introduced me to the *grands couturiers*, modistes and manicurists, paid for my beauty treatments, took me to grand restaurants, accompanied me to the races and behind the scenes in the theatres, covered me with jewels. . . . I was soon launched and on a level with all those who, a few months earlier, would have laughed at my rags and my *gaucherie*. I found myself in the company of Prince Louis de Tarente, François de Noailles, Comte Serge de Morny, the Duc de Morny, Gabriel du Tillet, the Prince de Poix, the Comte de Clermont-Tonnerre, the Marquis de Pracomtal. The most distinguished and celebrated men paid court to me.

When she parted from her first count, she soon found another one, Comte Arnold de Contades (part of the interest of her confessions, published it is true nearly half a century later, is that she scorns dots and dashes and gives the full names of the people concerned), who set her up

1 R. Marcerou. *Du Théatre à Dieu. Eve Lavallière*, 1927.
2 Eugénie Buffet. *Ma Vie, mes Amours, mes Aventures*. Confidences recueillies par Maurice Hamel, 1930.

Theatre and Music

Camille Clifford, 'The Gibson Girl'

Puccini's *Girl of the Golden West* at the Metropolitan Opera, New York, in 1913, with Caruso, Amato and Destinn. Caruso is about to be hanged

Cavalieri, the famous beauty and opera singer   Melba as Manon Lescaut

The famous Joachim Quartet, after a painting by Lajos Bruck

Everett Shinn, *London Hippodrome* (1902)

Georges Seurat, Study for *Le Chahut*

Anna Held, an actress celebrated for her small waist

Design by Léon Bakst
for Ida Rubinstein's
costume in *St Sebastian*,
a ballet by D'Annunzio
and Debussy for
Diaghilev (1911)

Stanislavski's production of Chehov's *Uncle Vanya* at the Moscow Arts
Theatre in 1899

Opposite: Nijinsky

Wassily Kandinsky, *The Singer* (1902-03)

in her own house at 17 Rue de la Trémoille. She tried to continue her theatrical career, appearing at the Variétés and the Menus-Plaisirs, but without much success and her life was so typical of that of the kept woman of her time that it is worth describing in some detail. We cannot do better than to do so in her own words:

In the morning I was in the Bois, an accomplished horsewoman [how did she become so, one can't help wondering] in the afternoon I went driving in an English pony-cart, in the evening there were sumptuous dinners where aristocrats and people of the theatre mingled. I knew the intoxication of race-courses and casinos and of that *Jardin de Paris* where, late in the evening, all the pretty women of my time were to be seen . . . Emilienne d'Alençon, then the mistress of Duc Jacques d'Uzès, Lucie de Kern, that *bourgeoise de la galanterie*, Angéle de Varennes who had everything she needed and killed herself for love, Marie Delannoy the mistress of kings (for all the kings and emperors of the period had enjoyed her favours), Clémence de Pibrac . . . Liane de Pougy . . . la belle Otéro . . . Louise Hayman who spent her time quarrelling and being reconciled with Prince Karageorgevitch . . . Jeanne de Béthune who asked of Lesbos the joys she could not find elsewhere.

There follows a list of lesbians of the time, including the Marquise de Belboeuf, sister of the Duc de Morny who boasted: 'My brother and I have had all the prettiest women in Paris.' It is almost as if a juvenile Proust was taking notes in the wings.

The one professional beauty of the period who could claim, with justice, that she had never been a *cocotte*, was Cléo de Mérode. She was one of the earliest Beauty Queens having won, in 1896, a competition organized by *L'Illustration*. She danced at the Opéra, and Leopold II, King of the Belgians was so much taken with her that he offered her a house in Brussels and a villa at Ostend. She declined, but this did not prevent her name being linked with his, as he made no secret of his infatuation. She posed, for the head only, to the sculptor Falguière and the latter had the unfortunate idea of attaching the head (which everyone recognized) to the nude statue of a dancer. Both Cléo and the sculptor denied that the body was hers, but the boulevard strollers shook their heads and tapped their noses. They knew better. Even when she went on tour in America the same stories followed her. She denied them in vain.

Leopold was more successful with another stage performer who made no secret of being also a *grande cocotte*. She was the daughter of a concierge; her real name was Emilienne André, but she was soon launched on the stage as Emilienne d'Alençon. In 1889, at the age of nineteen, she was appearing at the Cirque d'Été in a conjuring act involving rabbits, and one night she found in her dressing-room a large basket of orchids. She thought them horrible, and wondered why the *monsieur* couldn't send roses like everybody else. Then she looked at the card: 'Duc d'Uzès'.

241

R

This was the son of the famous Duchesse d'Uzès, who had protected and financed General Boulanger. He carried Emilienne off to London and lodged her at the Savoy. The rabbits came too and occupied a cupboard in the apartment. Before the family managed to pack the young man off to Africa (where he died of fever) Emilienne had cost him two million francs. Her next conquest was Leopold II. Finally she married a jockey. She is now chiefly remembered for having invented the publicity stunt of having her diamonds stolen. The fact that it has been used so often since as to raise only a laugh should not detract from the glory of having thought of it first.

It was not necessary to be a cocotte in order to be involved in amorous adventure with the highest in the land. When Félix Faure, President of the French Republic, was found dead in the Elysée Palace on 16 February 1899, it was rumoured that he clasped in his hand a lock of the hair of Meg Steinheil, a well-known *femme galante*. She has been called the Pompadour of her epoch. Like the original Pompadour she was a *bourgeoisie* and, at an early age, had married a man considerably older than herself, the painter Adolphe Steinheil who turned out costume pieces in the style of Meissonier. He had a studio in the Impasse Ronsin off the Rue de Vaugirard. The couple had a daughter but soon decided to live separate lives, although under the same roof. Here Mme Steinheil established a salon which was frequented by *Tout-Paris*. She was an attractive, lively and intelligent woman. She sang well and accompanied herself on the piano. On the social side she was a kind of Madame de Verdurin as depicted by Proust.

Her visitors included some great names: the composers Gounod and Massenet, the painters Bonnat, Henner and Meissonier, the sculptor Bartholdi (who modelled the Statue of Liberty from a girl picked up in a Montmartre brothel), the writers Zola, Pierre Loti and François Coppée, official personages like the *Ministre de la Marine* and the Vice-President of the *Chambre des Députés*, the Grand Duke Vladimir and even (it was rumoured) the Prince of Wales.

In her memoirs[1] she described the *vaste chambre* in which she received her guests. It was decorated in the *style artiste* then fashionable, with furniture (real or imitation) of the period of Louis XIV and Louis XV, cabinets full of precious objects and the walls covered with tapestry. She boasts that she sometimes received 'hundreds' of guests. Steinheil was not a particularly successful painter and the question naturally arose: who paid for all this? The answer seems to be a certain iron-master named Borderel; but there were others.

In 1897 she accompanied her husband to Savoy where he wished to paint the alpine manoeuvres of the French army; and here she attracted the attention of Félix Faure who had recently become President of the Republic. Soon she was visiting the Elysée Palace every day and, it was said,

1 Mme Marguerite Steinheil. *Mes Memoires, c.* 1910.

frequently stayed the night. According to her own account she was helping the President to write his memoirs! Certainly he provided her with a key of the back door of the Elysée and an *agent* in plain clothes to follow her wherever she went.

What really happened on the night of 16 February 1899 has never been satisfactorily explained. Certainly the wood engraving which appeared in *L'Illustration*[1] showing the last moments of the President – he is in bed surrounded by doctors – bore little relation to reality. The *Président du Conseil* made a statement in the *Chambre des Députés* in which he said that he had been called to the Elysée at eight o'clock and had found the President half dressed and in the hands of the doctors, while a priest recited the prayers for the dying. He did not say that he was already dead. One of the deputies was indiscreet enough to ask: 'Did you know that Mme Steinheil visited the President that day at six o'clock?'

Mme Steinheil had indeed visited the Elysée. She arrived at 5.30 p.m. and the President, a man of fifty-nine, swallowed two aphrodisiac pills in anticipation of the pleasure he hoped to have with her. Unfortunately, Cardinal Richard, Archbishop of Paris, arrived at the same time and it was necessary for the President to receive him. The Cardinal noticed that Félix Faure seemed to be in a considerable state of excitement and disinclined to attend to what was said to him. Scarcely had the ecclesiastic retired than the Prince of Monaco was announced. He bore an important message from the Kaiser concerning the Dreyfus Affair but Félix Faure hardly listened to him and the Prince, realizing that the President had a lady visitor – he had seen her waiting in the office of the *chef de cabinet* Le Gall – made his excuses and left. Félix Faure swallowed two more pills.

At about a quarter to seven, Le Gall heard cries from the 'boudoir' of the President. The door was locked but he broke in and found Félix Faure dead and Mme Steinheil *toute nue*, in hysterics. A *chef de cabinet* should be ready for any emergency. Le Gall succeeded in calming the lady, got her somehow into some of her clothes[2] covered her with a fur coat and smuggled her out of the Elysée and into the cab which took her home. The President's body was put in a decent posture and then – and only then – the doctors and Mme Faure were summoned. When the photographer arrived next morning he found the President lying in state in full evening dress with his orders and medals. He was given a magnificent funeral.[3]

In spite of the rumours flying about, Meg Steinheil continued to lead her social life; and then – in May 1908 – there came another scandal: a

1 *L'Illustration*. February 1899, p. 120.

2 One of the complications of adultery at this period was that it was impossible to put the corset on again without the assistance of a maid.

3 This version of what happened is based on the account given by Paléologue in his *Journal de l'Affaire Dreyfus*.

double murder mystery which caused almost as much excitement in France as the Dreyfus Affair itself. Early in the morning of 31 May the police were summoned to the Impasse Ronsin to find two corpses, those of Adolphe Steinheil and of Mme Japy, mother of Meg Steinheil. They had both been strangled. Meg herself, so she said, had been terrorized and tied up by three men and a woman dressed in long, flowing black robes. No less a person than the *Chef de la Sûreté* was immediately on the scene, and this in itself caused some comment. It was as if the Chief of Scotland Yard should personally intervene on a Sunday morning in a murder that had just occurred in a back street in Chelsea. But even stranger things were to follow. There seemed something half-hearted in the efforts made by the authorities to track down the burglars who were supposed to have committed the crime, and the mystery would probably have been '*classé*' (that is, pigeonholed as insoluble) if Mme Steinheil had not herself intervened. Outraged that the general public made no secret of its opinion that she had herself strangled her husband and her mother, she called in the aid of the press. Unfortunately the stories she told were so inconsistent and her wild accusations against various persons so unconvincing that she was herself arrested and confined in the horrible old prison of St Lazare.

There she stayed for more than a year, and her trial, when it finally came on in November 1909, was the sensation of Paris. As the *dossier* contained 15,000 pages we shall not attempt to summarize it here. She was acquitted, retired to England, married the sixth Baron Abinger and died, a widow, at Hove, as recently as 1954.

The mystery remains unsolved, and none of the theories suggested is wholly convincing. Mme Steinheil herself professed to believe that the burglars, if burglars they were, were searching for some mysterious 'papers' which had been placed in her hands by Félix Faure. A certain Dr Locard[1] puts forward the following theory which, fantastic as it is, might seem to make some kind of sense. Mme Steinheil, faced with a number of urgent bills she could not meet, telephoned to one of her rich lovers and implored his help. He arrived, but a quarrel arose, the noise of which brought the husband, timid and complaisant as he was, to the scene. There was a struggle during which he was strangled accidentally by the visitor. Meg's mother, roused by the clamour, swallowed her dental plate and died of shock. After consultation the two survivors got in touch by telephone with a *très haut fonctionnaire* who hurried to the Impasse Ronsin and arranged the evidence of the pretended burglary with the connivance of the *Chef de la Sûreté*. But to make this possible the visitor must have been comeone who had at all costs to be preserved from scandal. Who was he? Doctor Locard calls him '*boyard, beaucamp mieux que boyard*' which would

[1] Quoted by Armand Lanoux in his *Amours 1900*. See also his *Le Roman vrai de la IIIe République*, Paris, 1957.

seem to imply that he was a Russian Grand Duke, perhaps the Grand Duke Vladimir, who was commonly reported to be one of Meg's lovers. Whatever the real solution the affair certainly sheds a lurid light on the manners and morals of the Third Republic.

It is not that High Life in England was very different. Indeed for many of the upper classes, from the King downwards, the Channel had ceased to exist. They were perfectly at home at Maxim's, or at Deauville, Biarritz or Monte Carlo. No longer did the London Season, with the rest of the year spent in rural pursuits, content the pleasure-seekers. *The Graphic*, commenting in 1908 upon 'the growth of cosmopolitanism throughout the world', remarked that 'the London Season is gradually being removed from the programmes as an "Unfashionable" item. . . . In June and July now thousands pour into London from the Provinces, the Colonies, the United States, and the Continent, but the tendency is for Mayfair to empty except when there are Court entertainments.'

In any case when the London Season was officially over, the 'German-Bath season' began and lasted until the middle of September. From the middle of September to the middle of December was the 'country house season' and then the fashionable crowd moved to the South of France and stayed there until the middle of May. The favourite resort was still Monte Carlo, which says the caricaturist Sem:

is still Paris, but a Paris transfigured, renewed by the splendid light which magnifies everything, makes men look younger and women more beautiful, as every winter[1] draws hither the rich visitor from every corner of the world to this delightful shore. For Monte Carlo is also London and New York, it is the High Life of the great capitals of the world, condensed during the Season on this splendid rock, in a fairytale of light and luxury.[2]

Certainly 'everybody' went to Monte Carlo, including ladies of the utmost respectability and high-mindedness such as Mrs C. S. Peel who reported that 'sooner or later all the world was to be seen in the Rooms, in the Square or on the Terrace, though there I never went because of the pigeon shooting. At Monte Carlo I saw for the first time Lady Randolph Churchill in the height of her dark, Southern beauty . . . Mrs Langtry, and a man whose face I have never forgotten. He was Mr Carson, now Lord Carson.'[3]

The Casino had long been in existence, but circumstances now combined to give it an international social significance it had hardly enjoyed before. Comfortable expresses were run from all the capitals of Europe. A particu-

---

1 That Monte Carlo and similar places on the Rivièra might be visited in summer never occurred to anyone until long after our period – until the late nineteen-twenties, in fact.

2 Sem, *Monte Carlo*, 1904.

3 Mrs C. S. Peel, *Life's Enchanted Cup*, 1933.

larly luxurious one was the St Petersburg–Vienna–Cannes Express which had card- and writing-saloons in addition to the dining car, where the cuisine was equal to that of a first-class restaurant. 'So very smart are some of the travellers', remarks a contemporary newspaper, 'that they insist on dressing for dinner.' Indeed, so wealthy and extravagant were the majority of the passengers brought from Russia to the Riviera that it became the dream of every ambitious *demi-mondaine* to be kept by a Grand Duke.

Biarritz, owing to the continued patronage of King Edward VII, was as fashionable as Monte Carlo, and there it was possible to combine the amenities of country house life with the pleasures of being abroad. *The Queen* reported in 1909 that 'In perfect weather the Biarritz and Bayonne Foxhounds met on Saturday in the grounds of the Hotel d'Angleterre. . . . Among the spectators and others looking on in automobiles and carriages were the Grand Duke Alexander and his family, Prince Alexander of Oldenburg, Princess Eugenie of Oldenburg, the Duke of Leuchtenbourg . . . Sir Malcolm and Lady Morris, Mrs Cavendish-Bentinck, Mrs J. Tyrwhitt Drake. . . .'

During the 'German-Bath Season' the same cosmopolitan crowd flocked to Wiesbaden, Ems and Marienbad, the last named being particularly favoured by Edward VII. The supposed object of his stay there was to take the 'cure', but as he firmly declined to drink the waters or to cut down on his diet, the benefits must have been more psychological than physical. It is true that, when abroad, he ate a Continental breakfast instead of his usual morning repast of haddock, poached eggs, bacon, chicken and wood-cock, but he continued to eat a five course luncheon, an elaborate tea with cakes and muffins and a seven course dinner. Besides this, as Virginia Cowles tells us, 'snacks consisting of lobster salad and cold chicken were often served at eleven in the morning to appease the King's hunger, and even after dinner a plate of sandwiches, and sometimes a quail or a cutlet, was sent up to the Royal apartments'.[1]

In this he was merely following the custom of the time for the Edwardians (the well-to-do Edwardians, that is) had prodigious appetites. But he was a real innovator in some ways, or perhaps it would be truer to say, a restorer of ancient glories. Queen Victoria had had 'Drawing Rooms' followed by tea. King Edward held a 'Court' in the evening, followed, as a contemporary tells us, by 'a luxurious buffet supper, accompanied by particularly good champagne served from tables set out with the Royal gold plate'.

We should probably find the formality of Edwardian life stifling, but it was less stuffy than life in Victoria's day if only in the fact that King Edward admitted to his entourage people who would never have penetrated

1 Virginia Cowles. *Edward VII and His Circle*, 1956.

to royal circles at an earlier date. He was alleged to have a particular liking for Jews and he was certainly very friendly with Sir Ernest Cassel and the Rothschilds. It is true that they paid their way in philanthropy and artistic patronage. 'A Foreign Resident' notes that:

apart from the fostering Hebrew, English art and music could scarcely live in the English capital. The encampments of the Israelitish army, from their City head-quarters near Swithin's Lane, extend due West first, then by way of Piccadilly, in a north-westerly direction, into the heart of Beds. and Bucks. Other invading armies bring havoc in their van and leave desolation in their rear. The invaders' line of march is marked by bounties distributed at every point. The nobility could today as ill dispense with the Jews as could the Monarchy itself.[1]

The only people who did not like it were the old-established country gentry who could no longer compete with the new rich. It was estimated that to entertain the King at a 'shooting luncheon' was considerably more expensive than a county ball used to be. The country gentleman of moderate means found himself quite out of it. In the words of the anonymous author of *Society in the New Reign*:

His mother may have been among the beauties at the Court of Queen Victoria and Prince Albert, but as for going to Court himself in the present reign, this modest territorialist, in the crowd of smart and moneyed Medes, Persians, Elamites, and Mesopotamians, New York dandies, Chicago belles and Hebrew money-brokers, would find himself in an *entourage* rather less intelligible to him than that thronging the presence-chamber of the Grand Lama.

A writer of the early years of the century was much concerned with this degeneration of the meaning of the word 'Society'. Its proper meaning, he said, was that of a 'more or less privileged class as opposed to the community at large', and he adds, sarcastically, that 'Society in this sense is usually accorded (and will always receive from me) the initial capital letter to which, as the Englishman's divinity, it is clearly entitled'.

A footnote offers an illuminating commentary both on the writer and his period:

The word 'Society' in its limited sense has further acquired of late years a secondary signification akin to the French phrase, *le monde où l'on s'amuse*. It means, not only an exclusive class of men and women who are popularly supposed to be 'in the swim', but also those people who devote their lives to gaiety and amusement, which are commonly supposed to be the distinctive pursuits of the leisured and wealthy. To describe this second class the word 'smart' has lately come into fashion; and even though it be responsible for that horrible phrase, 'The Smart Set', it serves its purpose fairly well. For instance, when a

1 'A Foreign Resident', *Society in the New Reign*, 1904.

lady novelist or Mayfair Savonarola denounces Society at large (an unprofitable occupation at best), the censure unreasonably includes, let us say, the Duke of Norfolk, who is certainly a member of Society, and no less certainly of blameless character. If, on the other hand, the preacher, or the novelist, were to qualify the objects of their invective by the word 'smart', then the withers of high or polite Society would be unwrung, and the Duke, to whom nobody could impute smartness, would escape unmerited condemnation.[1]

King Edward gave his patronage to many things that Queen Victoria would have frowned upon. He was, for instance, an enthusiastic patron of the lighter stage, particularly of the Gaiety. As Prince of Wales he was frequently to be seen in a box – and behind the scenes – of the old Gaiety Theatre in the Strand. Here the curtain fell for the last time on 4 July 1903, but by 26 October a new Gaiety had arisen at the Aldwych. To the astonishment of sober minded people the King and Queen Alexandra attended the opening night.

We should remind ourselves that there was nothing improper in the performances at the Gaiety. They had shed completely the vigour and vulgarity of the old music hall, and the scanty costumes which were later to become usual in revue were never seen. The women who took part in such pieces as *Our Miss Gibbs* simply wore the fashionable clothes of the day, and George Edwardes, the presiding genius, certainly spared no expense. Some of the hats worn by the chorus cost sixty guineas each.

But of course the chief attraction of the Gaiety was the presence of the Gaiety Girls themselves and the Gaiety stage door was, for many a young man about town, the gateway of romance. 'To know a Gaiety Girl', says W. MacQueen-Pope, 'to take her out to sup, that was a cachet about town. The girls adorned the restaurants to which they were taken. Some of the most beautiful always had their own table reserved and were treated like queens.'[2]

'The glamour of the footlights,' says the same writer, 'and the notoriety attaching to all things theatrical, appears to have completely overwhelmed our gilded youth, in whose eyes domestic beauty unadorned by art has grown less attractive than the variegated charms of the ballet and the chorus.'

So far, the situation was no different from that in Paris and other European capitals. But to the astonishment of foreign commentators, 'the *jeunesse dorée* of London, officers of the Guards, members of the most elegant and exclusive clubs like the Marlborough, and Whites,'[3] not

---

1 H. E. W. Stutfield, *The Sovranty of Society*, 1909. The Mayfair Savronarola was, of course, Father Bernard Vaughan, famous for his sermons on 'The Sins of Society'.

2 W. MacQueen-Pope, *Gaiety, Theatre of Enchantment*, 1949.

3 Raymond Reconby in *L'Illustration*, June 1909.

Before the War

Edvard Munch, *Anxiety* (1896)

Fashions at an art exhibition in Paris, 1907

Caricature by Bruno Paul of Prussian tourists in Bavaria; from *Simplicissimus*, 1899

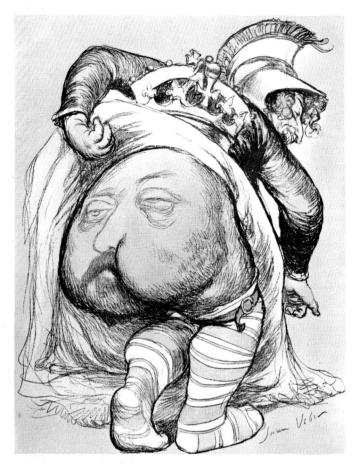

L'Impudique Albion, a caricature of Edward VII from *L'Assiette au Beurre*, 1903

Opposite: Henley Regatta, 1914

The King and Queen of Rumania travelling by modern transport, 1901

Opposite: The racecourse at Nice, *c.* 1911

Billings' horseback dinner at Sherry's, Fifth Avenue, 1903; photograph by Byron

Opposite: George Wesley Bellows, *The Stag at Sharkey's*

Gino Severini, *Dynamic Hieroglyph of the Bal Tabarin* (1912)

Archduke Franz
Ferdinand and his
family

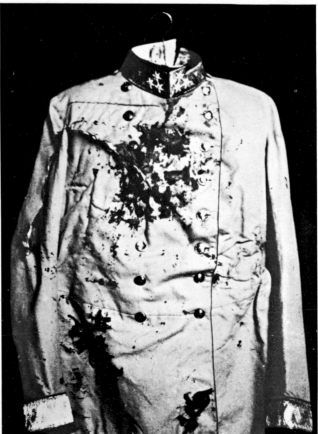

The blood-stained tunic
of Franz Ferdinand
after his assassination at
Sarajevo

content with taking the Gaiety Girls out to supper, began to marry them.

This was not altogether a novelty in England. Even in the eighteenth century Lavinia Fenton, who played Polly Peachum in the original production of *The Beggar's Opera*, had become Duchess of Bolton (although she had to wait about twenty years before her situation was 'regularized'). Elizabeth Farren became Countess of Derby. The process had continued during the nineteenth century, Harriot Mellon becoming Duchess of St Albans; Belle Bilton, Countess of Clancarty; and Connie Gilchrist, Countess of Orkney.

But now, in Edwardian times, the stream swelled to a torrent. Denise Orme, of *Our Miss Gibbs*, became Baroness Churston; Sylvia Storey, another Gaiety Girl, Countess Poulett; Olive May married Lord Victor Paget, heir presumptive to the Marquess of Anglesea. She died Countess of Drogheda. Camille Clifford, the original 'Gibson Girl', married the Honourable Lyndhurst Bruce.[1]

Reconby continues to record with surprise that 'even when the husbands were not lords they were at least millionaires. . . . Miss Hilda Harris gave her hand to Mr Drummond, the rich banker; Mary Fairbairn, May Kennedy and Christina Humphries became the wives of three extremely rich Americans, Smithson, Peter Kelly and Anderson; Miss Eva Hillesdon changed her common name for that of the Marquise de Florac.'

The Gaiety Girls were models of respectability, but it is remarkable that even the 'ladies' who frequented the Promenade at the Empire and who were frankly in search of clients, behaved with almost equal propriety, at least in public. Indeed, they knew that the slightest hint of uproarious behaviour would cause them to be excluded from what was not only a pleasant place to pass the evening in, but the best of all shop-windows. As W. MacQueen-Pope tells us:

the women of the Empire were the aristocrats of their 'profession'. And they looked it. Amazing creatures, amazingly dressed, of all races and speech, blondes, brunettes, redheads, they moved quietly to and fro, with a rather feline grace. . . . They were unmistakable, yet their manners were excellent. They never accosted a man, at the most he might feel the soft touch of a hand against his or the faint pressure of a silk-clad body if he stood by the rail watching the show.[2]

The Empire was famous all over the world and 'Empire builders' in another sense made it their first port of call when they found themselves back in London. They were sure to meet someone they knew. Indeed, the Empire was a kind of club, open to anyone with the price of a theatre ticket, properly dressed (for the Management 'reserved the right to refuse admission') and reasonably well behaved. On the whole the young men who

1 See also Cranston Metcalfe. *Peeresses of the Stage*, 1913.
2 W. MacQueen-Pope. *The Melodies Linger On*, 1950.

frequented the Empire Promenade *were* well behaved – except on Boat Race Night. Even on such an occasion there were limits, rigidly enforced by the manager Mr Hutchins, and his cohort of stalwart assistants. Hutchins in full evening dress and wearing white gloves would approach any roisterer who was getting too rowdy and touch him lightly on the shoulder. He was immediately ejected. He did not mind this in the least. Being 'chucked out of the Empire' was quite a feather in the young man's cap. Of course, he immediately sought re-admission and was puzzled when his money was refused at the box office. What he did not know was that Mr Hutchins had a small piece of white chalk concealed in the palm of his right hand, and when he touched the offender on the shoulder he left an almost imperceptible mark.

To the moralists the mere existence of the Empire Promenade was an offence and many campaigns were launched to have it closed down. The proper place of the 'Ladies' was the street and there they ought to be. Mrs Ormiston Chant began a regular war against the Empire and the management was sufficiently concerned to put up a kind of trelliswork screen between the Promenade and the stage. It is hard to see what purpose this served, but, in any case, the young men about town would have none of it. They demolished it and among the most active in this work of destruction was a young man called Winston Churchill. In the end, however, Mrs Ormiston Chant succeeded in having the Empire Promenade abolished and the women were driven on to the streets. One can only wonder who was better off.

Contemporary commentators, like H. E. M. Stutfield, were certain of one thing: that 'Society' had been transformed since the accession of King Edward VII. Not only had it been invaded by *nouveaux riches* of all kinds but even its older members had been caught up into a faster current. 'It is curious', he says:

how the craving for publicity has invaded all classes, including the highest: few even of our recognized social leaders now appear to be able to dispense with the notice of the Press. In former days such people maintained a sort of grandiose aloofness; their magnificence was accentuated by the halo of mystery that shrouded their daily doings from the public gaze, and anything that savoured of playing to the gallery was considered the height of bad form. Today they are smitten with the universal mania for notoriety.

Perhaps the Edwardian period was the last in which rich people could convince themselves that they gave pleasure to the general public by parading their good fortune. 'The main object of modern Society is to enable the well-to-do people to display themselves, their handsome clothes and other paraphernalia, to a world that is always lavish of its admiration of such things.' It certainly seems as if the majority of people in the middle and lower classes shared this view, for we are told that poor Lady Warwick, perorating on Socialist platforms, complained 'that the reporters devoted more space to her toque and her muff than to her oratory'.

Nevertheless there were some, even if they were not as grand as Lady Warwick, who were beginning to be shocked by the contrast between abject poverty and blatant riches: a contrast plain enough to anyone with eyes to see and hearts to feel. It was only necessary to emerge from the glittering portals of the Savoy Hotel and walk along the Embankment, any night, even in the depths of winter. R. D. Blumenfeld records in his diary:

I walked home along the Embankment this morning at two o'clock. . . . Every bench from Blackfriars to Westminster was filled with shivering people, all huddled up – men, women, and children. The Salvation Army people were giving away hot broth, but even this was merely a temporary palliative against the bitter night. At Charing Cross we encountered a man with his wife and two tiny children. They had come to town from Reading to look for work. . . . This unemployment question is really a great problem.[1]

Even those who were employed seemed, sometimes, little better off. The average wage for a working man in London in the period just before the First World War, was 'round about a pound a week'. This was the title of a book published in 1913, in which the author asked:

How does a working man's wife bring up a family on 20s. a week? Assuming that there are four children, and that it costs 4s. a week to feed a child, there would be but 4s. left on which to feed both parents. . . . If the calculation were to be made upon half the sum, would it be possible? The food of the children in that case would amount to 8s. To allow the same amount to each parent as to each child would not be an extravagance, and we should on that basis arrive at the sum of 12s. a week for the food of six people. That would leave 8s. for all other expenses. But rent alone may come to 6s. or 7s., and how could the woman on 20s. a week manage with 1s. or perhaps 2s., for coal, gas, insurance, clothes, cleaning materials and thrift?[2]

Seebohm Rowntree, that great pioneer of sociology, describes the case of a woman whose husband was earning seventeen shillings a week:

To make both ends meet with that sum for a large family of children was no easy matter. Each week . . . as soon as she received the 17s. she put aside the money required for rent, and then planned out exactly how she could spend the remainder to the best advantage. The family never had a joint of meat, but occasionally she managed to afford 6d. for a sheep's head or to buy 6d. worth of 'meat pieces'. At the birth of a child she employed a woman for a week to nurse her, to whom she gave 5s. and her board. As soon as she knew that a child was

1 R.D.B's 'Diary, 1901'.
2 Mrs Pember Reeves, *Round About a Pound a Week*, 1913.

coming she began saving odd coppers until the 5s. was collected, and so she was able to pay the woman before she left the house. During the time she was nursing her children she lived chiefly upon bread and tea. Who can wonder that some of her children died during their first year?[1]

Indeed, the children of the hard-working honest poor were fed on a diet of about half the cost of that provided for children in a workhouse. It is small wonder that the infant mortality was appalling. Seebohm Rowntree obtained the figures for York and found that while in the 'servant-keeping class' the number of children who died in their first year was ninety-four per thousand, in the poorest class it was 247 per thousand – that is, nearly one in four.

It was not only the children who suffered. Jack London in his angry book *The People of the Abyss* remarks:

The statistics of London tell a terrible tale. The population of London is one-seventh of the total population of the United Kingdom, and in London, year in and year out, one adult in every four dies on public charity, either in the work-house, the hospital, or the asylum. When the fact that the well-to-do do not end thus is taken into consideration, it becomes manifest that it is the fate of at least one in every three adult workers to die on public charity.[2]

Perhaps the most shocking thing about it was the complacency with which this state of affairs was accepted. When some poor old woman died of starvation in an East End attic the verdict of the coroner was 'self-neglect'. Noel Streatfeild describes a distribution of soup presided over by her mother in the early years of the century, and remarks that:

neither the tradesmen who provided the materials for the soup, nor those ladies who served it, appeared to think it wrong in a rich country that families could be in such want that they would queue with jugs for a pennyworth of soup. There was nothing wrong with the people of that date, they were just as kind hearted and easily moved as we are today, it was that the way they thought was different; poverty was something that happened – just as people were born cripples, you helped, but you did not expect to cure them – indeed there were many who supposed that it would be upsetting God's purpose if you did.[3]

There were those, however, who felt differently and by the end of our period the climate of opinion had certainly changed. Socialism was no longer a dirty word and this change was largely due to the small body of high-minded men and women who called themselves the Fabian Society.

It began – ironically enough – in a haunted house in Notting Hill Gate, where two young men, Edward Pease and Frank Podmore, were investiga-

1 E. Seebohm Rowntree. *Poverty*, 1901.
2 Jack London, *The People of the Abyss*, 1903.
3 Noel Streatfeild, *The Day Before Yesterday*, 1956.

ting a ghost. They were both interested in psychical research, but, as the ghost failed to put in an appearance, they fell to talking, during their long vigil, of other matters and found that they were equally interested in the theories of Henry George. *Progress and Poverty* had just been published in England and America, and seemed to many to offer a new gospel of hope.

A 'New Hope' group was started and began to meet in Pease's rooms every Friday, and it was from this group that the Fabian Society, so to speak, hived off. It discovered itself, says Professor Laski, 'to be an essentially socialist movement in the spring of 1884, though it is clear that its members lacked then, and for long years afterwards, the sense of being part of a great international movement guided by the same objectives'.[1] George Bernard Shaw was one of the earliest members, and was soon joined by Sidney Webb, Sydney Olivier and Annie Besant.

The year 1886 was a very alarming one for the Establishment.[2] Trade was bad, there was much unemployment, and riots in Trafalgar Square. John Burns and Hyndman, the founder of the Social Democratic Federation, were tried for sedition. They were acquitted, but it was plain that their activities had evoked little sympathy among the general public. The Fabians decided to operate by different methods. Their policy was one of education and infiltration. They published *Fabian Essays*, they organized public lectures, they got themselves elected to School Boards and Select Vestries. Shaw used his position as music critic for *The Star* to expound socialist doctrines; the Webbs (thought of henceforward in the plural, Sidney Webb having married Beatrice Potter in 1892) began their tireless accumulation of facts.

The Fabians in general accepted the historical analysis of Karl Marx but rejected his prophetic dogma, thereby earning the hatred of Engels and cutting themselves off from Continental Socialism. They rejected violent revolution as a method of bringing about desirable social change. In a word, they were very English and very upper middle class. Their patient tactics made little or no appeal to the working classes. Nonetheless, they played an important part in the creation of a Socialist Party in England, and in the return of no less than thirty Labour members in the General Election of 1906. What was more important, they convinced intelligent people that Socialists were not necessarily cranks or fanatics. If, in some sense, 'we are all Socialists now' – as Sir William Harcourt said – it is very largely their work.

It is, of course, only too true that, in *le monde ou l'on s'amuse*, people cared for none of these things. The social round continued, and the

1 Prof. H. J. Laski in *Ideas and Beliefs of the Victorians*, 1949.
2 It is a useful word, but of quite recent origin in this sense. For the early Fabians the Establishment could only have meant the Church of England.

revolution in taste and dress between 1910 and 1914 – the impact of the Russian Ballet – merely added a new piquancy to the life of pleasure. It was the same in Paris, London, Vienna, New York. For Society life was a continuous fête. The Comte de Fleury, the most fashionable social commentator of his day, describes the scene in the Champs-Elysées on any night of the Season:

In the motor cars, the coupés, one sees, enveloped in lace, tulle, light satins full of reflections, ladies of all ages, but chiefly in the summer of life, the full flowering of their youth, like roses garnishing the dinner table, and who also have their drops of water, the tears of their coronets and necklaces on the flesh of their shoulders and the curls of their hair.

There are *messieurs* in the depths of all the carriages. The open overcoat shows the black satin revers, the immaculate shirt-front, the piqué waistcoat. Their pumps shine. . . . It is dinner-time in summer, the heat of the day over. The heavens turn green and the last rays of the sun lend an orange tint to the sky which hangs like a velarium over the Bois de Boulogne. . . . *Ce qu'on aura bostonné, valsé ce primtemps; c'est incroyable.*

Surely so agreeable a social round will never come to an end! Surely a world so admirably arranged will go on for ever! And having exhausted the pleasures of Paris, it will be time to go off for 'the shooting'. But in 1914 the shooting was of a different kind.

The war that couldn't happen (and learned books had been written to prove that it was impossible) had actually broken out. At first it was regarded as the merest incident. The most popular slogan of the day 'Business as usual, during alterations to the map of Europe', summed up the prevailing mood. On the other side the Germans believed that they would be in 'Paris before the leaves fall'. The leaves fell five times before peace came, and with them the flower of European youth. A whole generation was wiped out, and the world could never be quite the same again.

Of course hope revived in the twenties, when people still dreamed of 'a Land fit for heroes to live in' and of having made 'a world safe for democracy'. It is no part of our purpose to show how these hopes were betrayed. It gradually dawned on the comfortable middle classes that the kind of life they had established for themselves between 1848 and 1914 had gone for ever. So far as they were concerned, the Age of Optimism had passed into history.

General

Adburgham, A., *A* Punch *History of Manners and Modes, 1841–1940*, 1961.
Benedict, R., *Patterns of Culture*, 1932.
Besant, Sir W., *London in the Nineteenth Century*, 1907.
Cabanès, A., *Moeurs intimes du Passé*, 1909–13.
Chastenet, J., *Le Siècle de Victoria*, 1947.
Cunningham, W., *Laissez Faire*, 1913.
Cunnington, C.W., *Feminine Attitudes in the Nineteenth Century*, 1935.
Cole, G.D.H. and Postgate, R., *The Common People*, 1938.
Escott, T.H., *Social Transformation of the Victorian Age*, 1897.
Flügel, J.C., *Man, Morals and Society*, 1945.
Graves, C.L., *Mr Punch's History of Modern England*, 1921.
Gretton, R.H., *The English Middle Class*, 1917.
Greville, C., *Memoirs*, 5 vols. 1880.
Guérard, A.L., *French Civilization in the Nineteenth Century*, 1914.
Halévy, E., *Histoire du Peuple Anglais au XIXe siècle*, 1902.
Houghton, W.E., *The Victorian Frame of Mind*, 1957.
Ideas and Beliefs of the Victorians, by various hands, 1949.
Lyall, A., *The Future of Taboo in these Islands*, 1936.
Nevill, Lady D., *Under Five Reigns*, 1910.
Nevill, R., *The World of Fashion, 1837–1922*, 1923.
Peel, Mrs C. S., *A Hundred Wonderful Years, 1820–1920*, 1926.
Quennell, P., *Victorian Panorama*, 1937.
Somervell, D.C., *English Thought in the Nineteenth Century*, 1929.
Trevelyan, G.M., *British History in the Nineteenth Century*, 1922.
Trevelyan, G.M., *Illustrated English Social History*, Vol. IV, 1952.
Uzanne, O., *La Française de Siècle*, 1886.
Veblen, T., *The Theory of the Leisure Class*, 1926.
Blackwoods Magazine
Le Crapouillot

Englishwoman's Domestic Magazine
Household Words
L'Illustration
Illustrated London News
Illustrierte Zeitung
Jugend
Ladies' Field
Methodist Times
The Nation
Pall Mall Gazette
Pictorial World
Punch
The Queen
Saturday Review
Simplicissimus
The Times
The Town
Working Man's Friend and Family Instructor

1   The Year of Revolutions

Ausubel, H., *In Hard Times*, 1960.
Blanc, L., *L'Organisation du Travail*, 1839.
Communist Manifesto, 1847.
Darimon, A., *A Travers une Révolution*, 1884.
Engels, F., *Conditions of the Working Classes in 1844*, 1892.
Fish, C.R., *The Rise of the Common Man, 1830–1850*, 1927.
Guedalla, P., *The Second Empire*, 1922.
Grummage, R.G., *History of the Chartist Movement*, 1894.
Hugo, V., *Souvenirs Personnels, 1848–1851*, 1952.
Marx, K., *Das Kapital*, 1883.
Orth, S.P., *Socialism and Democracy in Europe*, 1913.
Owen, R., *The Life of Robert Owen, Written by Himself*, 2 vols. 1857–8.
Proudhon, *What is Property?* 1840.
Unwin, Mrs Cobden, *The Hungry Forties*, 1904.
West, J., *History of the Chartist Movement*, 1947.
Woodham-Smith, C., *The Great Hunger*, 1962.

S

2 Mid-Victorian England

Anon, *The Habits of Good Society*, c. 1855.
Calverley, C.S., *Verses and Translations*, 3rd ed. 1865.
Chastenet, J., *La Vie quotidienne en Angleterre, 1837–1851*, 1961.
Christie, O.F., *The Transition from Aristocracy, 1832–1867*, 1927.
Cruikshank, R.J., *Charles Dickens and Early Victorian England*, 1949.
Cunnington, C.W., *The Perfect Lady*, 1948.
Dickens, C., *Oliver Twist*, 1838.
Dickens, C., *Hard Times*, 1854.
Dodds, J.W., *The Age of Paradox*, 1953.
Doyle, R., *Bird's Eye View of Society*, 1864.
Dunbar, J., *The Early Victorian Woman*, 1953.
Emerson, R.W., *English Traits*, 1856.
Francillon, R.E., *Mid-Victorian Memories*, 1913.
Franks, A.H., *Social Dance*, 1963.
Heasman, K., *Evangelicals in Action*, 1962.
Hunt, M.M., *The Natural History of Love*, 1959.
Ideas and Beliefs of the Victorians, 1949.
Kellett, R., *Religion and Life in the Early Victorian Age*, 1938.
Maigron, L., *Le Romantisme et les Moeurs*, 1910.
Nisbet, A., *Dickens and Ellen Ternan*, 1959.
Patmore, C., *The Angel in the House*, 1854.
Taine, H., *Notes on England*, 1872.
Thackeray, W.M., *The Book of Snobs*, 1843.
Wingfield-Stratford, E., *Those Earnest Victorians*, 1930.
Wingfield-Stratford, E., *The Making of a Gentleman*, 1938.
Young, G.M., (edit.) *Early Victorian England*, 2 vols. 1934.

3 Monde and Demi-Monde

Anon (J. O. Field), *Uncensored Recollections*, 1924.
Anon (J. O. Field), *More Uncensored Recollections*, 1926.
Adburgham, A., *A* Punch *History of Manners and Modes*, 1961.
Allen, M., *La Vie quotidienne sous le Second Empire*, 1948.
d'Alméras, H., *La Vie parisienne sous le Second Empire*, 1933.
d'Armiel, P., *Le Parc aux Biches*, 1931.
d'Artiste, P., *La Vie et le Monde du Boulevard*, 1930.
Arthur, Sir G., Bt., *A Septuagenarian's Scrap Book*, 1933.
Austin, A., *The Season*, 1861.

Bac, F., *Napoléon III Inconnu*, 1932.
Bac, F., *Intimités du Second Empire*, 1931–2.
Bac, F., *La Cour des Tuileries sous le Second Empire*, 1930.
de Beaumont-Vassy, Vicomte E., *Les Salons de Paris*, 1868.
de Beaumont-Vassy, Vicomte E., *Mémoires sécrets du dix-neuvième siècle*, 1874.
Beck, A.H., 'The House of Worth' in *Leader Magazine*, 28 June 1950.
Bellinger, M., *Confessions*, 1883.
Bellesart, A., *La Société française sous Napoléon III*, 1932.
Bingham, D.A., *Recollections of Paris*, 1896.
Bouchot, H., *Les Elégances du Second Empire*, 1898.
Boulenger, M., *Le Duc de Morny*, 1925.
Cardigan and Lancastre, Countess of, *My Recollections*, 1909.
Chambers, Major, *Recollections of West End Life*, 1858.
Chancellor, E.B., *The Pleasure Haunts of London*, 1925.
Cosmopolitan, A, *Random Recollections of Court and Society*, 1888.
Crouch, E.E., *Les Mémoires de Cora Pearl*, 1886.
Dansette, A., *Les Amours de Napoléon III*, 1938.
Daudet, A., *Trente Ans de Paris*, 1888.
Delvan, A., *Amours Second Empire*, 1958.
Delvan, A., *Les Plaisirs de Paris*, 1867.
Delph, C.A., *The Real Lady of the Camellias*, 1927.
Disher, M.W., *Winkles and Champagne*, 1938.
Ellis, S.M., *A Mid-Victorian Pepys*, 1923.
Falk, B., *The Naked Lady*, 1943.
Foucher, P., *Entre Cour et Jardin*, 1867.
Frichet, H., *Amours et Plaisirs de Paris*, 1932.
de Goncourt, E. and J., *Journal*, English ed. 1937.
Grenier, L., *Le Quartier Latin*, 1961.
Halévy, L., *Carnets*, Vol. I, 1935.
Hayward, W.S., *Mémoires d'une Biche anglaise*, 1864.
Harrison, M., *Rosa (Rosa Lewis of the Cavendish)*, 1962.
Holden, W.H., *The Pearl from Plymouth*, 1950.
Hollingshead, J., *My Lifetime*, 2 vols. 1895.
Houssaye, A., *Confessions*, 1891.
van Hutten, Baroness B., *The Courtesan*, 1938.
Jollivet, G., *Souvenirs de la vie de Plaisir sous le Second Empire*, 1927.
Ketton-Cremer, R.W., *Felbrigg, The Story of a House*, 1962
Kracauer, S., *Offenbach and the Paris of his Time*, 1937.
Kurtz, H., *The Empress Eugénie*, 1964.
de Lasio, P., *L'Amour à Paris sous le Second Empire*, 1896.
Loliée, F., *Femmes du Second Empire*, 1907.
Lonegan, W.F., *Forty Years of Paris*, 1907.

Loviot, C., *Alice Ozy*, 1910.
Masson, D., *Memories of London in the Forties*, 1908.
Metternich, Princess P., *My Years in Paris*, 1927.
Meyer, A., *Ce que mes yeux ont vu*, 1911.
Nevill, R., *The Man of Pleasure*, 1912.
Nevill, R., *The World of Fashion*, 1923.
Nicholson, R., *Autobiography of a Fast Man*, 1863.
Officer, An English, *Society Recollections*, 1907.
Officer, An English, *More Society Recollections*, 1908.
Pearl, C., *The Girl with the Swansdown Seat*, 1955.
Peat, A.B.N., *Gossip from Paris during the Second Empire*, 1903.
de Rochefort, H., *The Adventures of my Life*, 1896.
Rouffe, M., and Casevitz, T., *Hortense Schneider*, 1930.
Romi, *La Conquête du Nu*, 1957.
St Helier, Lady, *Memories of Fifty Years*, 1909.
Sala, G.A., *Twice Round the Clock*, 1859.
Saunders, E., *The Age of Worth*, 1954.
Schirokauer, A., *Païva, Queen of Love*, 1935.
Skinner, C.O., *Elegant Wits and Grand Horizontals*, 1939.
Smith, C., *Short History of St John's Wood*, 1942.
Stutfield, H.E.M., *The Sovranty of Society*, 1909.
Thouvenel, *Le Sécret de l'Empereur*, 1889.
Uzanne, O., *La Française du Siècle*, 1886.
van de Velde, M.S., *Random Recollections of Court and Society*, 1888.
Vaudoyer, J.L., *Alice Ozy*, 1930.
de Viel-Castel, Comte H., *Commérages*, 1930.
Vizetelly, E.A., *The Court of the Tuileries*, 1907.
Wheatley, H.B., *London, Past and Present*, 1891.
Wilhelm, J., *La Vie à Paris*, 1947.
Wyndham, H., *Society Sensations*, 1938.
Yriarte, C., *Les Célébrités de la Rue*, 1864.
Yriarte, C., *Portraits Parisiens*, 1865.
Zed, *Le Demi-Monde sous le Second Empire*, 1892.

4   Poverty and Prostitution

Acton, W., *Prostitution considered in its Moral, Social and Sanitary Aspects*, 1857.
Anon, *The Bitter Cry of Outcast London*, 1884.
Ausubel, *In Hard Times*, 1960.
Clephane, I., *Towards Sex Freedom*, 1935.
Dingwall, E.J., *The American Woman*, 1956.
Flexner, A., *Prostitution in Europe*, 1913.

Greenwood, J., *Seven Curses of London*, 1869.
Heasman, K., *Evangelicals in Action*, 1962.
Lippard, G., *The Quaker City*, 1844.
Lippard, G., *New York: its Upper Ten and Lower Million*, 1853.
McCabe, J.D. Jr., *The Secrets of the Great City*, 1868.
McCabe, J.D. Jr., *New York by Sunlight and Gaslight*, 1882.
Mayhew, H., *London Labour and the London Poor*, 4 vols, 1851–62.
Morley, J. (Lord Morley), *Recollections*, 1917.
Paterson, A., *Across the Bridges*, 1911.
Ritchie, J.E., *The Night Side of London*, 1957.
Ruskin, J., *Unto This Last*, ed. 1899.
Taine, H., *Notes on England*, Tr. by E. Hyams, 1957.
Unwin, Mrs J.C., *The Hungry Forties*, 1904.

5 Hymn Books and Chasubles

Besant, Sir W., 'Fifty Years Ago', in *The Graphic Jubilee Number*, 1887.
Fison, Mrs W., *Hints for the Earnest Student*, 1850.
Hare, A.J.C., *The Years with Mother*, 1952.
Heasman, K., *Evangelicals in Action*, 1962.
Home, C.S., *Nonconformity in the Nineteenth Century*, 1907.
Sherwood, M.M., *The Fairchild Family*, 1847.
Vidler, A.R., *The Church in an Age of Revolution*, 1961.
Watson, E.W., *The Church of England*, 1914.
Ward, W., *W.G. Ward and the Oxford Movement*, 1938.
Young, J.R., *Modern Scepticism*, 1865.

6 The Inner Man

Campbell, Lady C., *Etiquette of Good Society*, 1911.
Chambers, T.K., *A Manual of Diet in Health and Disease*, 1876.
Curtis-Bennett, Sir N., *The Food of the People*, 1949.
Dodd, G., *The Food of London*, 1856.
Drummond, Sir J.C., and Wilbraham, A., *The Englishman's Food*, 1939.
Francatelli, O.E., *The Modern Cook*, 1846.
Gouffé, J., *The Royal Cookery Book*, 1868.
Hackwood, F.W., *Good Cheer*, 1911.
Humphry, Mrs ('Madge' of 'Truth'), *Manners for Men*, 1897.
Kirwan, A.V., *Host and Guest*, 1864.
Lady, A. (Mrs Rundell), *A New System of Domestic Cookery*, n.d.
Luke, Sir H., *The Tenth Muse*, 1954.
Newnham-Davis, Lt.-Col. H., *Dinners and Diners*, 1899.

7 Relaxations and Dissipations

Anon, *Davos Platz*, 1878.
Anon, *Party-Giving on Every Scale*, 1882.
Anon, *Visitors' Guide to Bournemouth*, 1847.
Bertaut, J., *L'Opinion et les Moeurs*, 1931.
Booth, J.B., *Old Pink 'Un Days*, 1924.
Booth, J.B., *London Town*, 1929.
Booth, J.B., *Pink Parade*, 1933.
Booth, J.B., *The Days We Knew*, 1943.
Chambers, Major, *Recollections of West End Life*, 1858.
Chastenet, J., *La Vie quotidienne en Angleterre, 1837–57*, 1961.
Cook, H.K., *Over the Hills and Far Away*, 1947.
Disher, M.W., *Winkles and Champagne*, 1938.
Doré, G., and Jerrold, B., *London – A Pilgrimage*, 1872.
Fielding, B., *The Duchess of Jermyn Street*, 1964.
Graham, P., *Showboats: The History of an American Institution*, 1951
Grenville-Murray, E.C., *Side-Lights on English Society*, 1881.
Harrison, M., *Rosa (Rosa Lewis of the Cavendish)*, 1962.
Heckstall-Smith, A., *Sacred Cows*, 1955.
Leigh, P., *Manners and Customs of the English*, 1849.
Marsden, C., *The English at the Seaside*, 1947.
Nadal, E.S., *Impressions of English Social Life*, 1875.
Nevill, R., *Yesterday and Today*, 1922.
Nevill, R., *The World of Fashion*, 1923.
Newnham-Davis, Lt.-Col. N., *Dinners and Diners*, 1899.
Newnham-Davis, Lt.-Col. N., *The Gourmet's Guide to Europe*, 1903.
Peel, Mrs C.S., *Life's Enchanted Cup*, 1933.
Perugini, M.E., *Victorian Days and Ways*, 1932.
Ritchie, J.E., *Night Life of London*, 1853.
Sheldon, G., *From Trackway to Turnpike*, 1928.
Smith, A., *Gavarni in London*, 1849.
Wheatley, H.B., *London, Past and Present*, 1891.

8 The Girl of the Period and the New Woman

Anon, *London Society*, 1864.
Chambers, T.K., *A Manual of Diet in Health and Disease*, 1876.
Escott, T.H., *Social Transformation of the Victorian Age*, 1897.
Francillon, R.E., *Mid-Victorian Memories*, 1913.
Grenville-Murray, E.C., *Side Lights on English Society*, 1881.
Harper, C.G., *Revolted Woman*, 1896.

Haweis, H.R., *The Art of Beauty*, 1878.
Linton, E.L., *The Girl of the Period*, 1883.

9 Hail Columbia!

Adams, J.T., *A Searchlight on America*, 1930.
d'Almbert, A., *Flânerie parisienne aux États-Unis*, 1856.
Amory, C., *The Proper Bostonians*, 1947.
Beer, T., *The Mauve Decade*, 1926.
Bellamy, H., 'Mariages d'argent à la belle époque', in *Le Crapouillot*, April 1961.
Bristed, C.A., *The Upper Ten Thousand*, 1852.
Van Wyck Brooks, *America's Coming of Age*, 1915.
Brown, H.C., *In the Golden Nineties*, 1928.
Bryce, J., *The American Commonwealth*, 1888.
Bunn, A., *Old England and New England*, 1853.
Cake, L.B., *Devil's Tea Table and Other Poems*, 1898.
de Castellane, Count Boni, *Confessions*, 1924.
Dermigny, L., *U.S.A. Essai de Mythologie Américaine*, 1956.
Dingwall, E.J., *The American Woman*, 1956.
Ditzion, S., *Marriage, Morals and Sex in America*, 1953.
Fish, C.R., *The Rise of the Common Man, 1830–1850*, 1927.
Gow, A.M., *Good Morals and Gentle Manners for Schools and Families*, 1873.
Gratton, T.C., *Civilized America*, 1859.
Hobson, W., *American Jazz Music*, 1940.
Hodeir, A., *Jazz: its Evolution and Essence*, 1956.
Hughes, R., *The Real New York*, 1905.
Kinnaird, Lady E., *They married Well*, n.d.
Lieber, F., *The Stranger in America*, 1835.
Lippman, W., *Men of Destiny*, 1927.
Martin, F.T., *Things I Remember*, 1913.
Nevins, A., *American Social History*, 1923.
Pearson, H., *The Pilgrim Daughters*, n.d.
van Rensselaer, Mrs J.K., *The Social Ladder*, 1924.
Sinclair, A., *Prohibition*, 1962.
de Soissons, S.C., *A Parisian in America*, 1896.
Times-Picayune, New Orleans, 1918.
Trollope, A., *North America*, 1862.
Trollope, F.E., *Domestic Manners of the Americans*, 1837.
Walker, R.H., *The Poet and the Gilded Age*, 1963.
Washburn, C., *Come into my Parlor*, 1934.
Wester, D., *The Saga of American Society*, 1937.
Wilson, S.P., *Chicago by Gaslight*, 1895.

10   The Paradox of the Nineties

Bott, A., *Our Fathers*, 1931.
Bott, A. and Clephane, I., *Our Mothers*, 1932.
Burdett, O., *The Beardsley Period*, 1925.
Douglas, Lord A., *Oscar Wilde and Myself*, 1914.
Ellis, Havelock, *From Rousseau to Proust*, 1934.
Fairchild, H.N., *Religious Trends in English Poetry*, 1962.
Farmer, A J., *Le Mouvement esthétique et 'décadent' en Angleterre*, 1937.
Hichens, R., *The Green Carnation*, 1894.
Jackson, Holbrook, *The Eighteen Nineties*, 1913.
von Krafft-Ebing, Richard Freiberr, *Psychopathia Sexualis*, 1893.
Mallock, W.H., *The New Republic*, 1877.
Pater, W., *The Renaissance*, 1873.
Praz, M., *The Romantic Agony*, 1933.
Queensberry, Marquis of, and Colson, P., *Oscar Wilde and the Black Douglas*, 1949.
Sherard, R.M., *The Life of Oscar Wilde*, 1906.
Street, G.S., *The Autobiography of a Boy*, 1894.
Symonds, A., *The Decadent Movement in Literature*, 1893.
Symons, A., *A Study of Oscar Wilde*, 1930.
Wilde, O., *The Picture of Dorian Gray*, 1891.

11   High Life's Last Fling

Adam, P., *La Morale à Paris*, c. 1906.
Balfour, M., *The Kaiser and his Times*, 1964.
Benson, E.F., *As We Were*, 1934.
Bloch, I., *Sexual Life of Our Times*, 1908.
Blumenfeld, R.D., *R.D.B's Diary*, 1930.
Buffet, E., *Ma Vie, mes Amours, mes Aventures, Confidences recueillies par Maurice Hamel*, 1930.
Castelnau, J., *En remontant les Grands Boulevards*, n.d.
Cowles, V., *Edward VII and his Circle*, 1956.
Edes, M.E., and Frasier, D., *The Age of Extravagance*, 1955.
Foreign Resident, A, *Society in the New Reign*, 1904.
Heard, G., *Morals since 1900*, 1950.
'Hugo', *Vingt ans maître d'hôtel Chez Maxim's*, 1919.
Keppel, S., *Edwardian Daughter*, 1958.
Lanoux, A., *Amours 1900*, 1961.
Lanoux, A., *Le Roman vrai de la IIIe République*, 1957.

London, J., *The People of the Abyss*, 1903.
Magnus, Sir P., *King Edward the Seventh*, 1964.
Marcerou, R., *Du Théâtre à Dieu: Eve Lavallière*, 1927.
Metcalfe, C., *Peeresses of the Stage*, 1913.
Peel, C. S. Mrs, *Life's Enchanted Cup*, 1933.
Pope, W. MacQueen, *Gaiety, Theatre of Enchantment*, 1945.
Pope, W. MacQueen, *The Melodies Linger On*, 1950.
Reeves, Mrs P., *Round About a Pound a Week*, 1913.
Rowntree, E. Seebohm, *Poverty*, 1901.
Steinheil, M., *Mes Mémoires*, c. 1910.
Streatfeild, N., *The Day Before Yesterday*, 1956.
Stutfield, H. E. M., *The Sovranty of Society*, 1909.

ACKNOWLEDGMENT

The author acknowledges his indebtedness to authors and publishers for their permission to quote from the following books: *Napoléon III Inconnu* by Ferdinand Bac (Hachette, (1932); *The Social Ladder* by Mrs. J. R. Van Rensselaer (Henry Holt and Co, 1924); and *Notes on England* by Hippolyte Taine, translated by Edward Hyams (Thames and Hudson, 1957).

INDEX

Aerated Bread Company, 145
Albert, Prince Consort, 25, 31
Alençon, Emilienne d', 241–2
Alexander II, Czar, 63
Almack's, 108
Alma–Tadema, 191
Alméras, Henri d', 60
Andrews, Emily, 31
Angely, Countess Régnault
   de Saint-Jean d', 47
Angeville, Pauline d', 58
Aremberg, Prince d', 60
Aremberg, Princess d', 170
Armstrong, Eliza, 113
Arnold, Matthew, 125
Arnold, Thomas, 42–3
Astley's, 71, 72
Astor, Mrs John Jacob, 206
Astor, William, 105
Astor, Mrs William, 208
Asubel, Herman, 29
Aumale, Duc d', 48
Austin, Alfred, 69
Aylesbury, George, Marquis of, 45
Aylesford, Lady, 82–3
Aylesford, Lord, 82–3

Bac, Ferdinand, 52, 56, 59
Baedeker, 172
Baird, Abington, 80
Bal Bullier, 162
Bal Constant, 163
Barbès, 22, 24, 25
Barnardo, Dr, 86, 90
Barrett, Wilson, 169

Barton, William, 99
Barucci, Julia, 62
Baudelaire, Charles, 221, 223
Baudry, Paul, 60, 64
Beardsley, Aubrey, 224–6, 229
Beaufort, Duke of, 40
Beecher, Henry Ward, 202
Beecher-Stowe, Harriet, 202
Beer, Thomas, 196, 198, 205
Bell, Laura, 69
Bellanger, Auguste, 57
Bellanger, Marguerite, 56–7, 60
Bellwood, Bessie, 157
Belmont, August, 208, 211
Bennett, Reverend Mr, 125
Bentinck, Lord George, 44
Bernhardt, Sarah, 73, 175
Besant, Sir Walter, 122, 153
Bignell's Café, 98
Bismarck, 63
Blanc, Louis, 19, 24, 29
Blandford, Lord, 82, 83
Blanqui, Auguste, 21, 22, 24, 25
Blessington, Lady, 46
Bloomer, H. Dexter, 181
Bloomer, Mrs Amelia, 71, 181–5
Bonnard, Madame, 53
Booth, Bramwell, 112, 115
Booth, Mrs Bramwell, 115
Booth, General, 112, 164
Booth, J. B. ('Costs'), 78–9, 80
Boucicault, Dion, 205
Bradley-Martin, Mrs, 208–9
Brougham, Lord, 139
Broughton, Mrs, 113

266